SAFETY MANAGEMENT IN CONSTRUCTION

(Principles and Practice)

S.K. BHATTACHARAJEE
Consulting Engineer

KHANNA PUBLISHERS®
Investing in Learning®
Operational Office :
4575/15, Onkar House, Opp. Happy School,
Ground Floor, Daryaganj, New Delhi 110 002
Phones : 011-45033819 • *Mob.* 09811541460
email : contactus@khannapublishers.in

Published by :

Romesh Chander Khanna & Vineet Khanna
for **KHANNA PUBLISHERS**
2-B, Nath Market, Nai Sarak
Delhi- 110 006 (India)

Website : www.khannapublishers.in

Hologram & Description

To all readers of our books, from yourself if being defrauded by pirates to prevent, please make sure that there is an Hologram on the cover of our books with the below specifications. If you find any book without Hologram and Description, please mail us at **contactus@khannapublishers.in**

Thanking you

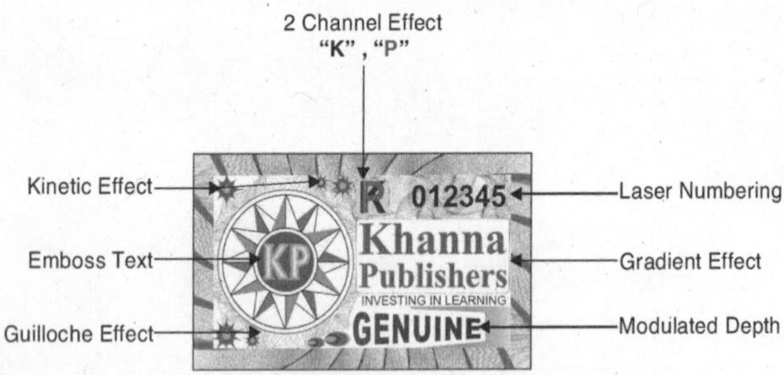

ISBN No. 978-81-7409-299-1

First Edition : 2011

Second Reprint : 2026

Price Rs. 459.00

To my parents
Late Purnendu Kumar Bhattacharjee
And
Late Rajlakshmi Bhattacharjee

Preface

Almost all major construction projects are undertaken now-a-days in a highly competitive environment with a rush to meet deadlines. The designs are also competitive to cut costs and sophisticated construction machinery is deployed to expedite the progress of work in order to meet the scheduled dates. Side by side, it so happens that the site activities are handled sometimes by sub-contractor's men not properly trained or qualified. When all these factors are compounded with negligence, complacency, construction errors or material deficiency, the project is likely to be prone to frequent safety hazards and accidents resulting in damage to life and property. To avoid such a situation, safety should be given due importance right from the planning and design stage to the construction field and even during the post-construction service period.

In the planning and design stage, future structural safety can be assured from a correct assessment of the external loads and safety factors, the environmental stresses, soil-foundation interactions and adequate proportioning of the structural elements as per standard engineering practice and relevant provisions of codes. The safety of the structures and the workmen during the construction period depends largely on taking adequate caution and safety measures to prevent accidents.

During the post-construction service period, structural safety is often compromised due to lack of maintenance, misuse and over-loading of the structure. Catastrophic failures may also occur during this period due to wrong assessment of wind/earthquake forces and corrosion effects. Natural calamities like flood or landslide also take a toll on the life of a structure very often. Continued noise creates an unsafe work environment. Foundation failures are also common due to shock and machine vibrations. The project schedule may also be seriously interrupted due to vehicular accidents during transportation or handling of materials.

This book brings to focus all the above safety aspects in construction projects and presents a broad outline of the management decisions needed to be taken in each stage to ensure human safety, structural safety and stability. In addition, special attention has been given in the text to safety problems faced during demolition or dismantling of structures. The text also contains a short discussion on the necessity of conducting safety audits and legal problems likely to be faced by builders due to safety hazards and accidents occurring at site. A brief introduction to forensic study has also been included in the text, which should be of interest to the readers.

Lastly, a separate chapter has been devoted to explain the fundamentals of the concept of reliability in statistical terms and its relation to the safety of a structural system at any point of time. Guidelines have also been given for augmenting the reliability of different types of structural systems.

Examples of safety hazards and case reports drawn from real-life experiences from a wide spectrum of construction projects like buildings, industrial structures, bridges and roads have been incorporated in the text with suggested safety measures.

It is hoped that the book will be useful to structural designers, field engineers and management personnel in charge of construction sites. The book is also expected to be a valuable companion to the students specializing in safety management and preparing for professional examinations.

The author thankfully acknowledges the materials and safety concepts drawn from various books and articles, a list of which is given at the end of the text and the readers, desiring to have more information on the subject are advised to read them.

South Subhasnagar **Sudhansu Kumar Bhattacharjee**
Kolkata-700065
July, 2010

Contents

CHAPTER 1

Concept of Systems Approach to Safety Management

1.1 INTRODUCTION

Construction work occupies a large part of economic activities in the housing sector, the industrial sector, the infrastructural sector and to a lesser degree in the agricultural sector also. Construction projects in all these sectors may be classified broadly in the following groups depending on the type of construction:

- Buildings: These vary from small residential buildings to large multistoried office buildings, housing complex, educational institutions, hospitals, recreation centers, factory sheds, warehouses. Under this category may be included the utility and service buildings also.
- Industrial structures: They include the supporting structures for heavy machinery, plants, equipments, material handling plants, oil and gas pipe lines etc.
- Tall structures: They include cooling towers, chimneys, transmission towers, silos and overhead water tanks.
- Liquid retaining structures
- Marine civil engineering structures
- Hydraulic structures: They include dams, barrages, canals etc.
- Sewage and industrial effluent treatment plants
- Special structures: They include off-shore platforms, nuclear plants etc.

Many of the above construction projects are complex, multi-disciplinary in nature and are executed in a highly competitive environment deploying modern technology and sophisticated equipments to bring down costs and also to ensure completion of the projects within the scheduled time-frame. Moreover in the construction industry the work environment changes all the time from one site to another. All these aspects coupled with the engagement of different types of sub-contractors with their practice of deploying ill-trained semi-skilled and unskilled persons in large numbers pose a serious impediment to a safe working practice, thus pushing the construction industry in the high-risk category. This is manifested in the high rate of accidents resulting in injuries and casualties of human beings with damage to property.

1.2 FREQUENCY OF ACCIDENTS AND SAFETY HAZARDS

From available data it is revealed that more than 10 million workers engaged in construction work receive injuries in the course of one year throughout the world. It is also a more or less established fact that the accident rate in construction is about 3 times the rate in the manufacturing sector and, approximately, one out of 6 workers engaged in the construction industry suffers injury at one time or other in a year. Some of the injuries, of course, are minor in nature and not so serious, though the victims are incapacitated for some time. But in many other cases the victims succumb to the injuries or are permanently disabled.

Records of fatal accidents reveal that about 70 to 80% of all fatalities at site are due to fall from a height or due to collapse of structures on them. Besides this, vehicular accidents, failure of erection cranes, electric shocks, fire, sudden collapse of shuttering during concreting etc. cause fatal injuries at many sites.

Finished projects are also vulnerable to safety hazards and damages in the post-construction service period due to faulty design, failure of foundations due to machinery vibration, failure of bridge foundations due to scour, environmental degradation and unforeseen natural calamities like earthquake, storm, flood, landslide etc. Safety is also compromised when there is lack or absence of maintenance for a prolonged period causing gradual deterioration of strength in the structural components due to fatigue, corrosion or exposure to harmful chemicals.

1.3 CAUSES OF STRUCTURAL FAILURES

Case studies indicate to the fact that major structural failures are caused by one or more of the following factors:

- Design errors
- Construction errors

- Material deficiency
- Lack of maintenance
- Misuse of finished structures
- Failure due to unforeseen external forces

1.3.1 Design Error

Design errors may occur from adaptation of designs not conforming to construction methods, lack of understanding of critical load combinations, selecting inadequate safety margins and lack of attention to functional requirements. Design errors may be committed either during performance of known tasks, such as standard design and detailing or, performing new tasks, not previously experienced by the designer. The designer's ignorance or oversight regarding fundamental structural behaviour is also responsible for many faulty designs. Design errors increase the probability of failure of a structure. As such, the designer should have a clear idea in building physics, likely behaviour of structural components under the influence of critical loads and the effectiveness of the materials specified.

1.3.2 Construction Error

Construction errors occur in many forms during the whole process of construction. Construction errors are also the source of many safety hazards during the maintenance period and many a times, during a rehabilitation process. Human errors in demolition work may trigger catastrophic failures and unintended collapse of the existing structure.

Construction errors generally originate from misinterpretation of drawings, working in contravention of details shown, sudden change in construction methods, lack of attention to safe working condition at site, building inadequate and risky temporary structures and platforms, flouting of standard safety norms, complacency on the part of the workmen, deployment of semi-skilled and unskilled persons on critical jobs, mishandling of cranes and equipments, flouting of electricity safety norms, poor workmanship because of lack of regular checking and supervision at site, misinterpretation of specifications and many other errors during construction.

1.3.3 Material Deficiencies

Material deficiencies originate from providing and using materials not conforming to specifications resulting in construction of defective and weak structures. Use of below-grade aggregates, fine sand in place of coarse sand, use of ordinary bolts in place of high tension bolts of same diameter, use of cement from very old stock are some of the examples of material deficiencies. Safety of the structures is affected seriously, when structures consisting of defective materials are exposed to extreme weather conditions, corrosion and face natural calamities. Many structural failures have roots in the use of defective materials when it is exposed to even mild tremors or a wind much below the design value.

1.3.4 Lack of Maintenance and Misuse of Finished Structures

Any safety hazard due to either or both of the above factors can be attributed to wrong handling or negligent use on the part of the users during the service period. It is the responsibility of the owner or the users to maintain a building structure, an installation or a bridge handed over to them after construction. But, it is common knowledge that, very often, wrong handling and overloading are done without thinking of the consequences. Using a bottom chord of an ordinary tubular truss for lifting loads are one of the many examples in this matter. Sometimes, owners neglect maintenance of important structures citing paucity of funds. They also sometimes remain complacent for a long period after completion of a project, neglecting any necessity of maintenance, thinking that the structure will remain intact and safe for all times to come.

Reliability is seldom assessed during the service period, except in the case of important structures. Environmental degradation, local damages, corrosion effects and fatigue failures are often ignored at initial stages, resulting in a serious multiplier effect in creating safety hazards at a later stage, involving enormous cost in rehabilitation and repairs or closure of the facility in many cases. Many structural failures have occurred due to complete absence of any maintenance and repair, even though the structure has performed well during the initial period of its service life.

1.3.5 Failure Due to Natural Calamities

Natural hazards like earthquake, storm, flood, landslide etc., are primary causes of many catastrophic structural failures with loss of human lives all over the world. The loss can at least be minimized, if not avoided altogether, if the intensity and harmful effects of these external forces are estimated in a rational way during the planning and design stage and structures are proportioned and designed accordingly. Every country has its own national codes of practices, which give excellent guidelines to the designer in this matter.

1.4 SYSTEMS APPROACH IN SAFETY MANAGEMENT

The brief enumeration regarding the causes of structural failures stated earlier, reveals that the safety of a structure along with human safety can be reasonably assured if proper attention is given to the safety problems right from the planning and design stage and is extended to the construction and even to the post-construction service period, when the structure is likely to be subjected to the aggressive forces of the environment and natural calamities. In view of the complexity of the problem of maintaining safety of a structure for such a long time under the action of different types and combinations of safety hazards, a systems approach is considered to be logical in safety management. The operation research, system analysis, reliability analysis and all decision-making processes are integral part of this system approach. In this matter the main thrust of safety management is directed to the following aspects:

(*a*) A quantitative approach to find out solutions to safety problems

(*b*) Development of deductive and inductive logical approach in the process of collection of relevant data from the problem area, formation of justifiable theories and mathematical models, application of theses models to the specific problems to get optimized solutions.

The methods adopted by this system of safety management consist of the following steps:

(*a*) Structuring a problem by collecting all relevant data from site and old records and identifying the objectives

(*b*) Construction of the design process or developing a mathematical model (for ill-structured problems) to eliminate or mitigate the safety hazards

(*c*) To find out optimized solutions by applying standard mathematical tools, following the provisions of codes and local safety regulations.

(*d*) Implementing the solution in the specific problem area.

(*e*) Monitoring and controlling all operations at site to achieve the desired objectives.

(*f*) To assess periodically during the service period the reliability of the structure and its components and connections and finding out solutions through an effective maintenance strategy and/or rehabilitation/repair/strengthening or replacement of components, as required.

In the systems approach, the management models may be either deterministic or probabilistic depending on whether the safety problem is well-defined or ill-structured. The models may be static or dynamic (*i.e.*, changing with time), depending on whether the constraints remain unchanged or change with time. For example, a simple repair strategy adopted at a particular time may have to be changed to a strategy of component replacement if a number of vital structural components are found to be seriously damaged beyond repair at a later date.

For complex problems involving a number of variables with various types of constraints, having either predictable or random nature of relationship between the variables, linear programmings are often done and computers are used now-a-days for evaluation of safety problems for important structures, to get optimum cost-effective solutions in the quickest time.

In very complex and ill-structured problems like building safety models against flood and scour damages, it becomes sometimes impossible to frame any deterministic mathematical solution covering all the basic parameters of the problem. Simulation techniques are usually applied in such cases along with help of existing knowledge-based expert systems available from recorded case reports.

After deriving a solution, it is applied with proper control (in the design process through peer review and at site through adequate on-site supervisions) adopting suitable methodology and systematic approach. Side by side, a system of continuous monitoring with regular feed-back should be developed. For this reason the systems approach is always dynamic. No ad-hoc decision-making should be entertained in safety management. In the systems approach there should be a definite objective or goal, which is to be achieved through a systematic approach in design considerations, material selection, implementation, control and feed-back for further scrutiny and improvement in quality.

The background fundamental principles and concepts necessary to develop a systems approach in safety management are discussed in the following chapters along with an introduction to the reliability of structures.

QUESTIONS

1. Explain how the stability of a structure may be compromised due to design errors.
2. In what circumstances serious errors may creep in a structural system during the construction period. What may be the likely adverse effect of such errors during the service life of the structure?

3. As it is not possible to eliminate fully the safety hazards due to natural calamities, what should be the rational approach in the design?
4. What is meant by systems approach? Explain how the principles of systems approach may be gainfully applied to ill-structured problems in safety management.
5. What are the ill effects of material deficiency and lack of maintenance on the serviceability of structures?

CHAPTER 2

Instability, Hazard Scenario and Limit States

2.1 INTRODUCTION

The design of a structure is an essentially decision-making process with the objective of arriving at a satisfactory solution to meet the following requirements:

- Safety
- Serviceability
- Functional requirements
- Economy

A structure is considered to be safe when it is stable against actions of external forces at all times during its design life. If a structure exhibits unwanted deformations, fracture or distortions under load or if it tends to collapse under certain loading conditions, the structure becomes a safety hazard to the users. Moreover, an unstable structure is not a reliable structure. A structure may be unstable due to:

- Static instability
- Geometric instability
- Structural instability

2.1.1 Static Instability

A condition of static instability creeps in a structure when the structure as a whole or any part of it undergoes a rigid body motion under the application of external loads. Examples of structural instability are:

(*a*) Tilting of buildings, constructed on unstable slopes or loose soil.

(*b*) Steel portals having joints forming hinge mechanisms, rotating under slight external disturbances.

(*c*) Damage to a structure caused by heaving of soil (in case of black cotton soil).

In all such cases, the structure shows signs of rigid body rotation and there is every chance of an eventual failure.

An unsafe condition due to any inherent static instability cannot be accepted. This can be avoided by proper site investigation and planning before the design is finalized. For example, to prevent tilting of a building due to unstable ground slope or heaving of soil or presence of loose compressible soil under the foundation, it is necessary to conduct a thorough soil investigation to assess in advance the soil condition and take adequate measures in the planning and design stage to prevent tilting of the structure. For this it is required that the structural arrangement, details, sizes and specifications of the structural components should be compatible with the anticipated behaviour of the structure under the soil condition and the expected external loads.

2.1.2 Geometric Instability

Structures are considered geometrically unstable when the equilibrium of forces under external loads is attained only after a deformation has occured to the original shape of the structure.

A geometrically unstable structure undergoes large unwanted deflections under external loads before they become stable. Bulging of timber shutters due to pressure of green concrete is an example of geometrical instability commonly encountered by a site engineer, if the design and supporting arrangement of the shutters are not given due attention beforehand. Collar-jointed pipe posts with a hinge joint in the middle can be in equilibrium under a horizontal disturbing force even after the alignment is disturbed. Though the structure may not collapse, geometrically unstable structures create problems in finishing work and have low aesthetic rating.

Geometrical instability in a structural system can be avoided by proper proportioning of the structural components and detailing correctly the joints. Geometrical instability can also be prevented by suitably introducing redundancy in the system. For example, the bulging of a timber shutter can be prevented either by suitably increasing its thickness or by providing additional supports, thus reducing the effective span and introducing continuity and redundancy in the support system. Similarly, to prevent geometrical deformation at collar joints in a vertical pipe-line, additional clamps may be provided at joint locations to prevent undue deformation of the pipe line at the collar-joint. A geometrical instability by way of unwanted deflection may occur in the fabrication or erection stage of a steel truss joint, if 20 mm diameter bolts are wrongly put in 24 mm diameter holes meant for 22 mm diameter bolts. This can be rectified easily by replacing the bolts by 22 mm diameter bolts.

2.1.3 Structural Instability

Under the influence of external loads, internal stresses are generated in the individual members of a structure, resulting in a certain amount of deflection or deformation from its original shape. So long as the quantum of the external loads remain within permissible limits and the line of action of the loads do not vary beyond a permissible limit, the deflections or deformations caused by such loads are also kept in check. However during the service life of a structure, it may so happen that the material used in the structure is degraded due to adverse environmental effects like corrosion, fatigue, wear and tear or there may be sudden overloading of the structure during a storm, earthquake, or due to inadvertent handling of the system during service period, sudden impact, failure of the supporting soil etc. In such cases the structure or a part of it may cross the limit of endurance exhibiting large deflection, buckling and an eventual failure and the system is then considered to be structurally unstable.

Instability in structures due to above are illustrated in Fig. 2.1.

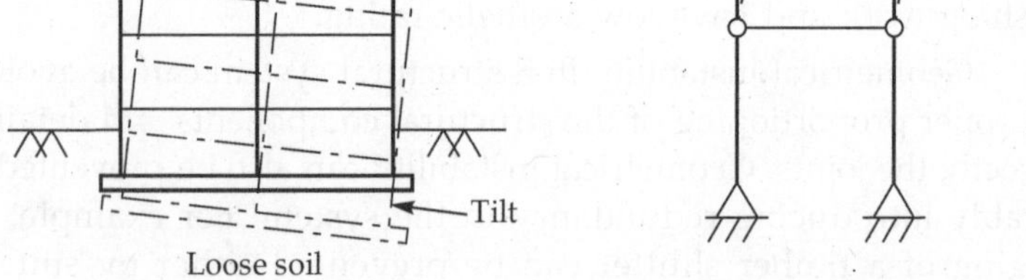

(*a*) Static instability (rigid body rotation due to differential settlement)

(*b*) Static instability (rigid body rotation due to too many hinges in the frame)

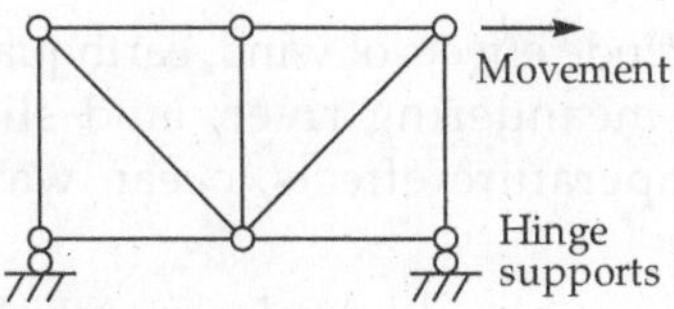

(*c*) Static instability
(rigid body translation even under minor horizontal disturbing force)

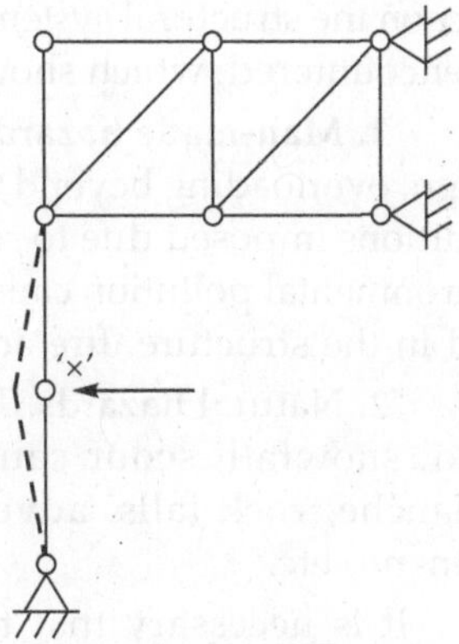

(*d*) Geometric instability
(Equilibrium of hinges '×' can be attained only after a finite displacement of the joint, causing change in geometry)

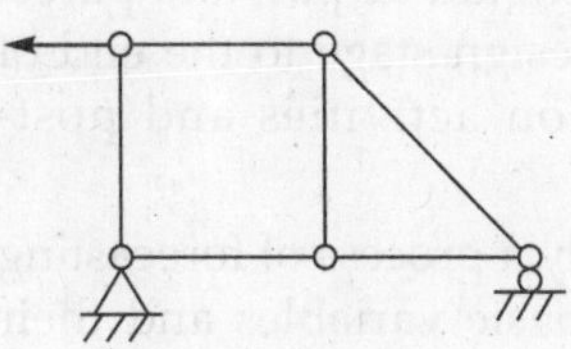

(*e*) Geometric instability
(One diagonal is missing)

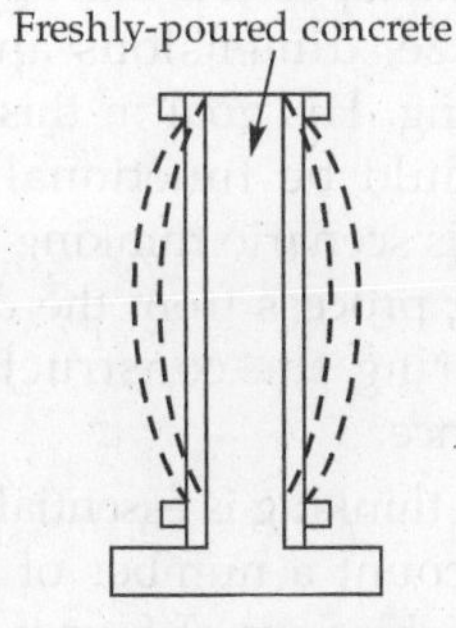

(*f*) Geometric instability
(Bulging of form work due to lack of adequate lateral supports)

(*g*) Structural instability
(Buckling of steel column when external load exceeds the critical value)

Fig. 2.1 Instability in structures.

2.2 HAZARD SCENARIO

While the static instability and geometrical instability of a structural system may be avoided by proper planning and designing, the case is not so for structural instability problems, as lot of hazardous situations may arise during the construction stage and also during the service life of the structure, that need to be assessed, visualized and estimated right at the planning and design stage. The term "Hazard Scenario" relates to this assessment and study of the interaction of the above uncertain complex hazardous factors and developing models to reflect the probabilities of their occurrence and effect on the structural system. In general, two broad classes of hazards are encountered, which should be taken into consideration.

1. Man-made hazards. These include errors and negligence in design, overloading beyond allowable limit, vehicular impact, fatigue conditions imposed due to repeated use beyond capacity, man-made environmental pollution causing serious deterioration in the materials used in the structure, fire accidents etc.

2. Natural hazards. These include effects of wind, earthquake, flood, snowfall, scour caused by meandering river, land slide, avalanche, rock falls, adverse temperature effects, ocean waves (Tsunami) etc.

It is necessary that the designer should apply his mind to identify the hazards likely to hit the structure during construction and also in its post-construction service life. He should try to develop and explore models that would reflect and quantify the effects of all likely future hazards to the extent possible and apply the results of the study in formulating the size, dimensions and specifications for the structure he is designing. His goal in this regard will be to design the structure that would be functional, safe for the users and economical as well. This scenario thinking should be part and parcel of the decision-making process from the design stage to the end of the service life, covering the construction activities and post-construction maintenance.

Hazard scenario thinking is essentially a process of forecasting reality, taking into account a number of basic variables and their interactions. These variables are of four types:

- **Variables in soil strata.** In the form of soil-foundation interaction
- **Environmental variables.** In the form of wind, earthquake, snowfall, environmental corrosion, temperature variation etc.
- **Structural variables.** In the form of geometry of the structure and material properties
- **Utilization variables.** In the form of live loads imposed on buildings, cranes, equipments etc. and moving loads on bridges. These are imposed on the structure at different times in different locations during and after construction.

The interactions of these different types of variables at different times in different intensities create a hazard scenario, which has profound influence on the behaviour of the structure and its safety.

A structure may experience a single hazard at any point of time like a storm or earthquake. The same structure may also be subjected to several hazards at a time like deterioration of material quality due to intense corrosion along with severe wind effects as observed very often in coastal areas. All such eventualities should be taken into consideration right in the design and planning stage.

Hazards can also be easily assessed if data are available of the behaviour and failures of similar structures built elsewhere. It has been seen that more than 50% of all structural failures occur during the construction stage due to errors and negligence and 25% to 30% of failures can be traced to errors in design or lack of prior understanding the likely behaviour of the structure under the influence of a given system of loads or ignoring a particular hazardous condition that may have a critical effect on the stability of the structure. The balance may be attributed to user's fault.

2.3 SAFETY MEASURES AGAINST HAZARDS

Adequate safety measures should be taken to counteract hazards to ensure the safety of a structure. The following guidelines may be followed in this regard as a general principle:

- Hazards should be eliminated or minimized at source.
- Hazards should be avoided if possible by modifying the structural arrangement.
- Hazards, if they are inevitable, should be covered by suitable warning systems and safety devices with frequent monitoring.
- Safety provisions should be provided in the structural design to minimize losses due to hazards to the extent possible under the constraints of economy.
- Accept hazards that cannot be counteracted. Accept low level damages by suitable modification of the structural system instead of incurring prohibitive costs by over-designing the structure.

In many cases, a balanced approach may have to be taken by suitably combining two or more safety measures, say by proper dimensioning of the structure, introducing adequate safety factors in design and ensuring at the same time quality control and supervision during construction, followed by a pre-planned maintenance strategy.

It is to be noted that a completely hazard-free structure cannot be built without incurring prohibitive costs. As such the probability of occurrence of extreme unforeseen hazardous situations has to be accepted during the whole life of the structure. But their intensity, duration and frequency should be studied and the structural system should be so designed as to keep the damages within an acceptable limit.

2.3.1 Evaluation of Hazard Scenarios

The evaluation of hazard scenarios leads to a number of design conditions, in which the external loads are found to interact with the structural variables and environmental variables (as stated earlier) in different ways at different times (during or after construction), producing a number of critical conditions. These critical conditions, which may eventually lead to lack of safety or an eventual structural failure, are known as "Limit States", which are to be visualized right in the planning and the design stage.

2.4 LIMIT STATES

In the whole process of designing a structure the primary objective of the designer is to arrive at a solution that gives safety and serviceability throughout its design life, as well as an overall economy in the cost of construction and maintenance. A design solution would be appropriate if it is ensured that there is an acceptable probability of the design life of the structure not being curtailed due to effect/s of hazardous conditions or "Limit States". This probability is chosen in such a way that a reasonable practical balance is obtained between the construction cost and the maintenance cost. Because a cost too low in construction may lead to a substandard structure needing continuous high level maintenance. On the other hand, an over-designed structure may need very little of maintenance, but its initial cost of construction may be prohibitive.

Limit states are therefore related not only to the stability of the structure, its conditions of serviceability, but also to its total life cycle cost and take into account all possible and probable modes of failures, that can be visualized through the process of evaluation of the hazard scenarios.

These limit states may be grouped into three main categories, namely:

1. Ultimate limit states: covering the failure modes or collapse of a structure due to hazardous conditions like overloading, wind, earthquake, deterioration of materials etc.

2. Serviceability limit states: covering problems of local damage due to large deflection, vibration of machinery and various

other conditions that may crop up affecting serviceability during the service life of the structure.

3. Other limit states: covering problems of fatigue, fire hazards, corrosion, accidental loading due to explosion, collision etc.

Limit state method of design

The design based on the limit state concept is done in the first stage for the most critical limit state (usually the limit state of collapse), considering the values of the characteristic loads, the characteristic strength of materials used and the partial safety factors as applicable to that particular limit state. The member sections obtained after this initial design exercise are then checked for other limit states and the sections and material specifications are modified, if necessary, to keep the probability of system failure or local damage within the acceptable limits.

2.5 CHARACTERISTIC LOAD

The characteristic load takes into account the normal variations in the load acting on a structure. Using statistical concepts, suppose *n* numbers of residential flats of same type have maximum live loads $q_1, q_2, q_3 \ldots q_n$ during their design lives. If *n* is sufficiently large (that is, observations are carried out on a large number of flats, with '*n*' being greater than 30), it may be assumed that these loads will be normally distributed about a mean value of say '*q*' with a standard deviation '*s*'. Then the characteristic load (Q_{ck}) may be expressed as:

$$Q_{ck} = q + z * s$$

where, z = coefficient corresponding to 95% probability of the load not exceeding the value of Q_{ck}.

However, such data as $q_1, q_2, q_3 \ldots q_n$ are not readily available to express all sorts of loads in statistical concept. Hence, for the purpose of structural design, it is assumed that the design loads adopted in the standard code of practices like IS: 875-(Part 1–4) for dead loads, imposed loads, wind load, earthquake loads and snow loads would have a 95% probability of not to be exceeded during the design life of the structure. Hence these values are taken the characteristic load values.

2.6 CHARACTERISTIC STRENGTH OF MATERIALS

As it is not possible to produce products like cement, steel etc. exactly of the same composition and standard, even with the help of the most modern manufacturing process, instruments and machinery, some variations creep into the quality of the products. The characteristic strength of materials takes into account the statistical variations in the resistance of the material against external loads. It is expressed as:

$$f_{ck} = f_m - z * s$$

where f_{ck} = characteristic strength

f_m = mean value

s = standard deviation

and z = coefficient corresponding to 5% of the test results falling below the value of characteristic strength

It may be noted that the above equation is written with a minus sign, as we are concerned with the minimum strength, whereas, in the equation for characteristic load the plus sign denotes the maximum load.

For steel materials, the characteristic strength corresponds to the yield stress, taken as 0.2% proof stress, which means the stress at which the slope of the stress-strain curve deviates from the initial tangent modulus by 0.2% strain.

2.7 PARTIAL SAFETY FACTORS

The characteristic values of loads and material, as stated above, cater for the normal variations in the imposed load and material strength. But, there are other uncertainties in the whole life of a structure that may cause variations in strength and resistance of a structure and theses variations may be of different magnitude at different point of time.

These variations are caused mainly by:

- Faults in construction due to bad workmanship like inadequate curing of concrete.
- Presence of impurities in construction material like excessive clay in sand or dirt/scales over steel material.
- Reduction in strength due to repeated reversible loading causing fatigue.
- Environmental corrosion affecting severely the steel reinforcement in RCC structures or steel members of steel structures.
- Neglect of secondary stresses caused by creep, shrinkage, loss in pre-stressed steel, thermal gradient across slabs.
- Errors in load assessment.

Additional safety factors called 'partial safety factors' are applied to the characteristic loads and characteristic strength of materials to cover uncertainties caused by the above factors. Different partial safety factors both for the loads and material strength are used to arrive at the design load and design resistance value, while calculating stresses. However, in general terms it can be said that,

Design load = (Characteristic load) **multiplied by** (partial safety factor for load)

Design strength = (Characteristic material strength) **divided by** (partial safety factor for material)

2.7.1 Partial Safety Factors (for design of reinforced concrete structures by Limit State Method)

As per I.S.: 456-2000.

LIMIT STATES & LOADS	*Partial safety factor for load*	*Partial safty factor for material*	
		steel	*concrete*
Limit state of collapse			
(*a*) DL + IL	1.5 × (DL + IL)	1/1.15 = 0.87	1/1.5 = 0.67
(*b*) DL + WL	1.5 × (DL + WL)	1/1.15 = 0.87	1/1.5 = 0.67
(*c*) DL + IL + WL	1.2 × (DL + IL + WL)	1/1.15 = 0.87	1/1.5 = 0.67
Limit state of serviceability (deflection)			
(*a*) DL + IL	1.0 × (DL + IL)	1.0	1.0
(*b*) DL + WL	1.0 × (DL + IL)	1.0	1.0
(*c*) DL + IL + WL	[1.0 × DL + 0.8 × (IL + WL)]	1.0	1.0
Limit state of serviceability (cracking)			
(*a*) as for deflection	as for deflection	1.0	1/1.3 = 0.77

While considering earthquake effects, Substitute EL for WL.

It may be noted here that the partial safety factor for concrete at limit state of collapse is 1.50, assuming that such concrete will be 'controlled' concrete.

In addition to partial safety factors, the characteristic strength of concrete (f_{ck}) and the characteristic tensile strength of steel (f_y) are further factored when designing for flexure and axial compression.

Flexure

Design strength of concrete in flexure

$$f_y = \frac{[0.67 f_{ck}]}{\gamma_m} = \frac{[0.67 f_{ck}]}{1.5} = 0.45\, f_{ck}$$

Design strength of steel in flexure $= \dfrac{f_y}{1.5} = 0.87\, f_y$.

Compression

Design strength of concrete in axial compression = $0.4\, f_{ck}$.

Design strength of steel reinforcements in axial compression = $0.67\, f_y$.

The above factors are applied in the design of reinforced concrete members in axial compression only, when the eccentricity of the applied axial load does not exceed 0.05 times the lateral dimension of the member.

Shear

Design strength of steel reinforcement in shear

$$= \frac{f_y}{1.15} = 0.87\, f_y$$

Torsion

The effect of torsion is taken care of in the design by introducing additional shear reinforcements as per provisions of the code.

The actual strength, characteristic strength and design strength of reinforced concrete structural members are shown in Figure 2.2.

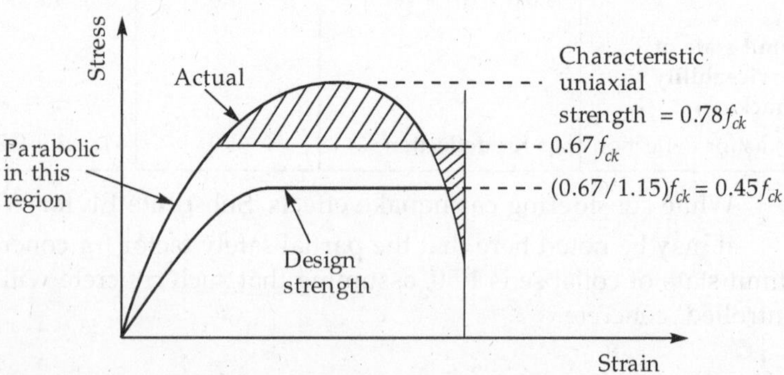

Fig. 2.2 Reinforced concrete stress-strain curve.

2.7.2 Partial Safety Factors (For design of steel structures by limit state method as per IS: 800-2007)

Limit states and loads	PARTIAL SAFETY FACTORS FOR LOAD
Limit state of collapse	
DL + LL + CL	1.5 DL + 1.5 Leading LL + 1.05 Accompanying LL
DL + LL + CL + WL/EL	1.2 DL + 1.2 Leading LL + 1.05 Accompanying LL + 0.6 WL/ER
DL + WL/EL	1.5 (or 0.9)* DL + 1.5 WL/EL
DL + ER	1.2 (or 0.9) * DL + 1.2 ER
DL + LL + AL	1.0 DL + 0.35 × (LL + Accompanying LL)
Limit state of serviceability	
DL + LL + CL	1.0 × (DL + LL + Accompanying LL)
DL + LL + CL + WL/EL	1.0 × DL + 0.8 × (LL + Accompanying LL + WL/EL)
DL + WL/EL	1.0 × (DL + WL/ EL)
DL + ER	not to be considered
DL + LL + AL	not to be considered

When actions of different live loads are to be simultaneously considered, the leading live load shall be the one causing higher load effects on the member.

*This value is to be considered when the DL contributes to the stability against overturning or the DL causes reduction in stresses due to other loads

DL = Dead load LL = Live load CL = Crane load
WL = Wind load EL = earthquake load ER= Erection load
AL = Accidental load

PARTIAL SAFETY FACTOR FOR STEEL MATERIAL (γm)

Design strength = Ultimate strength / γm.

	γm
1. For resistance governed by yielding	1.10
2. For resistance against buckling	1.10
3. For resistance governed by ultimate stress	1.25
4. For resistance of bolted connections	
(*a*) Friction type (shop and field bolts)	1.25
(*b*) Bearing type (shop and field bolts)	1.25
(*c*) Rivets (both shop and field rivets)	1.25
(*d*) Welds in shop fabrication	1.25

(*e*) Welds in site fabrication 1.50

2.8 WORKING STRESS METHOD OF DESIGN FOR REINFORCED CONCRETE STRUCTURES

The limit state method of design has now been adopted in India and widely used in the design of RCC framed buildings and various types of industrial structures following the provisions of IS: 456-2000. The limit state method is also being gradually extended and used in the design of other structures like liquid-retaining structures, tall RCC chimneys, water tanks and RCC bridges. However, machine foundations are still being designed conservatively using the working stress method. So also, the working stress method is used in design of pile foundations and marine structures.

In the working stress method, the loads given in the Indian Standard Code of Practice No: IS: 875 (part 1 to 4) are taken as design loads, *i.e.*, the partial safety factor for load in working stress method is 1.0. In this method, the concrete section and its reinforcements are so proportioned that the calculated stresses of concrete and steel are within their respective 'permissible allowable stresses', which are specified in IS 456:2000, Code of Practice for Plain and Reinforced concrete (Fourth revision) for direct compression, tension, flexure and shear. These permissible allowable stresses have been fixed by allowing adequate 'factor of safety' on the characteristic strength of concrete and the yield stress of reinforcement steel. For torsion, additional longitudinal reinforcements are provided for torsion moment and additional web reinforcements are provided for shear due to torsion.

In respect of liquid retaining structures like water tanks the permissible stresses are further lowered to ensure a crack-free structure. Reference may be made in this respect to IS: 3370 (Part 1 to 4): Code of practice for design of liquid retaining structures.

RCC road bridges are also still designed as per working stress method following the provisions and guidelines in Indian Roads Congress code nos: IRC: 5-2000, IRC: 6-2000, IRC: 78-1999, IRC: 83-2002. and IS: 24-2001. Latest revisions are to be followed for updated guidelines.

2.9 WORKING STRESS METHOD OF DESIGN FOR STEEL STRUCTURES

Almost all steel structures are still designed in this country by working stress method. The concept of limit state has recently been introduced in design of steel buildings and a revision of the code IS 800-1984 has been done. For steel railway and road bridges, silos, chimneys and other special structures, the working stress method is still widely used, though they are being replaced progressively by limit state methods of design.

In the working stress method of designing steel structures, the stresses in steel are calculated from design loads, which are same as the working loads given in IS 875-(Part 1 to 4) and the member sections are so proportioned that the calculated stresses are within the 'permissible allowable stresses', obtained by dividing the yield stress by a factor of safety. Usually the members are initially designed for the dead and imposed loads and then checked for wind and earthquake forces. Finally the structural components are checked against serviceability conditions and secondary stresses due to local buckling, crippling, deflection, lateral buckling and other factors due to thermal gradient, fire hazards, corrosion etc.

2.10 COMPARISON OF SAFETY FACTORS IN WORKING STRESS METHOD AND LIMIT STATE METHOD

The working stress method is not exactly applicable to a semi-plastic material like concrete. It is also not strictly applicable for slender columns whose deflections are not always proportional to the applied loads.

In steel structures designed by working stress method, the margin of safety, which is equal to (Excess strength)/(Required strength) is not uniform in tension, compression and bending. This is because, while purely tensile members can withstand stresses up to the ultimate tensile strength, for bending it is limited by local buckling and for compression and also limited by crippling and warping of the thinnest part of the structural member. Also, the working stress method does not make any distinction between the dead load, which is fairly constant and live load that may vary widely. The allowable permissible stresses in the working stress method for concrete and steel have been fixed allowing a uniform factor of safety to yield for all the above conditions of distresses.

On the other hand, the design based on the limit state method overcomes many of the disadvantages of the working stress method, as it is based on the 'partial safety factors', applied both to the characteristic loads and characteristic strength of materials and the values of the partial safety factors are varied for different limit states.

As a result, in the limit state method, there is more elastic stress range available at working loads.

However, even with the above shortcomings, the working stress method is still considered to be a very useful and simple method of designing both concrete and steel structures.

2.11 STABILITY OF FOUNDATIONS

The overall safety of any structure is closely related to the stability of its foundation system under all critical load combinations and external environmental influences. Keeping in view the above factors, the designer should proportion the foundation dimensions, material specification and specify the method of construction in such a way that the following conditions are satisfied:

- The foundation must be safe against **shear failure** of the soil underneath.
- The foundation must be safe against undue **settlement** causing damage to the structure with deficiency in its functioning.
- The foundation must be safe against **overturning** due to critical combinations of external loads.
- The foundation must be safe against **sliding**.
- The foundation must be safe against underground **erosion, scour** (in case of bridges and marine structures), **mine subsidence** and **adverse corrosive effects from the soil**.

The safety criteria against shear failure demands that the soil pressure under the foundation remains within the allowable bearing capacity of the soil, which depends on the foundation type and the soil characteristics.

When foundations are subjected to direct load and moments, the maximum soil pressure should be less than the allowable bearing capacity of soil and the foundation should preferably not be subjected to uplift on the tension side. In very special cases, building basements may have to be designed as floating rafts if they are to be rested on very weak soft soil having very low bearing capacity. When pile groups are subjected to direct load with moments, the maximum load in the pile should be less than the safe load carrying capacity of the pile.

In case of loose sand with high permeability and high water table, there is every chance of 'piping' or 'boiling' of sand due to heavy seepage of water during construction. The foundation can be safely constructed if the situation is visualized at the planning stage after proper soil investigations with introduction of sheet piles and/ or dewatering.

In case where deep open cuts are done to construct a foundation in soft clay, the bottom of the foundation may 'heave' and the sides tend to collapse simultaneously. Uncontrolled heaving of soil at foundation level may cause repeated side collapses, burying the newly-placed reinforcements and the whole construction process may be seriously interrupted. In such cases, the sheet piles should be driven well inside the soil so that the seepage path is longer and the velocity of seepage flow is well under control. In addition, well point system of dewatering may have to be adopted to save the foundation from complete submergence under water during construction. The stability of the foundation in such cases depends mostly on the correct assessment of the ground realities and measures taken to combat the disastrous effects.

When a structure is subjected to uplift, as in the case of transmission towers, the foundation should have adequate factor of safety against such uplift. In such cases, either the foundation is made heavy (incurring extra cost) or the soil surcharge above the foundation level should have adequate dead weight to provide the required factor of safety. For footings below water table, the submerged weight of earth is to be taken when assessing the soil surcharge over the footing. In special cases such additional surcharge loads are made of mass concrete blocks so that they are never excavated during the service period of the structure.

A foundation is also subjected to soil erosion, subsidence of soil underneath, scour, forces from river currents, flood and adverse corrosive reactions from soil. These are mainly site-specific problems and all these factors seldom act together at any particular place. However, there may be serious deterioration in the stability of the foundation even if only one or two of the above factors are active and are neglected in the design stage and in the service life of the structure. The condition is more acute in case of marine structures, bridge foundations and foundations for hydro-electric structures like dams and barrages, where proper inspection of the condition of the foundations cannot be done during the service period of the structure.

The stability of a foundation is also to be assured against critical combinations of superstructure loads with either wind or seismic forces, which are to be assessed from the guidelines given in the national codes.

The following are the general guidelines for factor of safety to be maintained in the design and proportioning of foundation elements:

1. Factor of safety against overturning

= [Stabilizing (restoring) moment]/[Overturning moment]

(*a*) For stability of a structure, as a whole

Restoring moment should not be less than:

[1.2 × overturning moment due to characteristic dead load] + [1.4 × (maximum overturning moment due to imposed loads)].

(*b*) For rigid retaining walls,

Factor of safety against overturning should be at least 1.5 for granular soil and 2.0 for cohesive soil

2. Factor of safety against soil pressure

Allowable bearing capacity of soil should be lesser of:

(*a*) [Net ultimate bearing capacity of soil, calculated as per IS: 6403-1981]/[factor of safety, usually 2.5 to 3.0 for soil and 6 to 8 for rock]

and

(*b*) Net soil pressure that can be imposed on the foundation base, without exceeding settlement limits prescribed in IS: 1904-1975.

3. Factor of safety against sliding

Factor of safety against sliding

= [Horizontal resistance]/[Horizontal force]

(*a*) For structure as a whole, FOS against sliding should not be less than 1.4.

While computing the factor of safety, only 0.9 times the characteristic dead load will have to be taken into account.

(*b*) For rigid retaining walls, FOS against sliding should be at least 1.5 for cohesion-less soil backfill and 2.0 for cohesive soil backfill.

4. Slip circle failure

(*a*) For rigid retaining walls, FOS should be at least 2.0 against slip circle failures.

5. Factor of safety against anchorage

(*a*) FOS, when anchorage is to be provided for overhang members (during construction or service period), should be such that static equilibrium would remain intact, even when the overturning moment is doubled.

6. Other conditions for stability of foundations in specific

cases

(*a*) For shallow foundations, the depth of foundations should be at least 50 cm below the natural ground level.

(*b*) For foundations in black cotton soil, the depth of foundation should be at least 3 to 3.5 metres below ground level to avoid movement due to shrinkage of soil and heaving

(*c*) For foundations in laterite soils, the foundation should be placed below the permanent water table, where the laterite formation is in a saturated condition.

(*d*) For foundations submerged in water, the buoyancy effect should be considered.

(*e*) In areas of landslip and mine subsidence, foundations should be designed considering the load and the soil characteristics and also considering the likely behaviour of the structure in such conditions.

(*f*) For foundations subjected to uplift (pull-out), a factor of safety of 2 to 2.5 should be adopted against the pull-out capacity of the footing.

(*g*) For raft foundations, the stability should be assessed from settlement considerations.

(*h*) For bridge foundations, the depth of foundation should not be less than 2.0 metres below the depth of maximum scour for pier and 1.2 metre for abutment. Besides this, the depth of the foundation should be adequate from consideration of bearing capacity, settlement and suitability of the bearing strata.

(*j*) All foundations should preferably be so proportioned that the soil pressure below the foundation remains as uniform as possible under all critical load combinations, to avoid undue differential settlement and loss of contact of the foundation with the soil underneath.

2.12 SAFETY PLAN

Before any design work is started a coordinated action plan should be prepared which covers usually the following aspects:

- Broad outline of the project, which gives an idea of the dimensions of the project
- Material specifications
- Brief design considerations giving the load combinations
- Control plan during construction

- Maintenance plan with instructions for the users.

Most of the items of the above list relate in fact to the safety and stability aspects of the project, though they are termed in different manners by the engineers. As for example, the broad outline and the basic dimensions of the project control the stability aspect. The material specifications cover the environmental variables and the related safety requirements. The design considerations, that contain the load combinations, are in fact a list of the safety hazards, which are likely to be encountered during the construction as well as during the post-construction service life of the project. The safety aspects during construction are taken into account in the control plan for construction in which the method of construction and the machinery to be deployed during the construction period are addressed. Lastly the maintenance plan reveals whether the structure is likely to be under-designed or over-designed, which has direct bearing on the safety aspects during the service life and the over-all life cycle cost of the project. As a result a control plan prepared as above can also be termed as the basic 'safety plan' for the project. In the following chapters all the above safety requirements will be discussed in more details.

QUESTIONS

1. How a structure may develop geometric deformation or excessive deflection leading to safety hazards?

2. How would you differentiate safety hazards posed by:

(*a*) Tilting of a building

(*b*) Bulging of concrete forms during concreting

(*c*) Wear and tear due to corrosion

3. What is meant by 'Hazard Scenario'? Differentiate between a man-made hazard and a natural hazard. Is it possible to eliminate all hazards or should the effect of some of them be minimized? In what circumstances hazards may have to be accepted?

4. Define the term 'characteristic load' and 'characteristic strength of materials'. Explain why partial safety factors are applied to the characteristic loads and characteristic strength of materials, while designing a structure by limit state method? What is the value of partial safety factors in the working stress method of design?

5. How the characteristic uni-axial strength of concrete is factored successively to arrive at the design strength of concrete in flexure?

6. Mention the values of the partial safety factors to be considered for design by limit state of collapse in the following cases:

(*a*) for controlled concrete material

(*b*) For steel material

(*c*) For Dead loads + Imposed loads for concrete structures

(*d*) For Dead Load + Imposed Load + Wind Load for concrete structures

7. What is meant by ultimate strength of steel material? How the design strength of steel is calculated from the ultimate strength in cases of buckling and yielding of steel members and for bolted connections for design by limit state method?

8. Explain the basic differences between the working stress method of design and the limit state method of design.

9. What are the conditions to be fulfilled to achieve stability in foundations against settlement, overturning and sliding?

10. Write explanatory notes on:

(*a*) Quality control to avoid safety hazards

(*b*) Effectiveness of pre-planned maintenance during service life of a structure to avoid safety hazards.

(*c*) Allowable bearing capacity of soil

(*d*) Margin of safety in working stress method of design

(*e*) Safety hazard due to boiling of sand in excavated pit

(*f*) Slip circle failure

(*g*) Stability of foundations submerged in water

(*h*) Stability of foundations in black cotton soil

(*i*) Factor of safety against pull-out forces on foundations.

CHAPTER 3

Safety Considerations in the Design of Steel Structures

3.1 INTRODUCTION

The response of any structural system to different types of loads is generally influenced by the material properties of the member components and the type of their end connections. While a structural system may comprise steel, concrete or composite sections, their end connections may be either pinned, semi-rigid, fully-rigid or a combination of them. While evaluating the behaviour of all such structural systems, the relevant properties that should be considered are the strength, stiffness and the deformation capacity (*i.e.*, the ductility of the material used).

3.2 RESPONSE OF STEEL MATERIAL UNDER LOAD

In view of above, the behaviour of steel structures in different stages of loading is different from that of reinforced concrete structures. This is due to the fact that steel material exhibits ductility *i.e.*, deformability of the material under load and capacity to absorb stresses during deformations without fracture. The stress-strain relationship of steel material is usually determined by uni-axial tension of test specimens and the test results are plotted as a stress-strain curve of the type shown in Figure 3.1.

There are four distinct points in the above stress-strain curve of a ductile material like steel, which is of interest to the designer. These are denoted by:

(*a*) Point '*a*': which is the limit of proportionality up to which the relation of stress and strain is linear and Hook's Law is valid. The slope of this straight line from origin to point '*a*' is the value of the Young's modulus for the particular steel material.

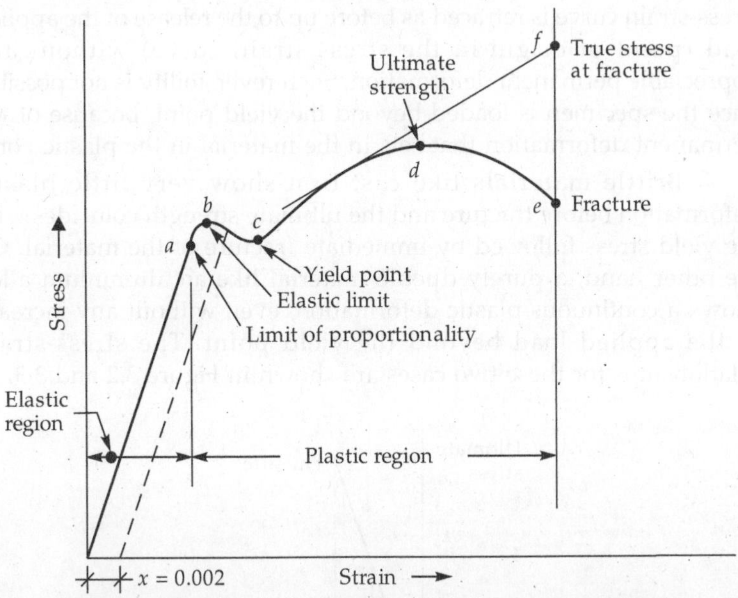

Fig. 3.1 Typical stress-strain curve of steel test specimen.

(*b*) Point '*b*': the yield point of the material, which denotes the elastic limit and the onset of the plastic behaviour of the material.

(*c*) Point '*c*': Some steel materials do not show a definite yield point at point '*b*' above. In such cases, the yield point is fixed at 0.002 strain *i.e.*, by drawing a straight line with slope equal to the Young's modulus (E) from a point $x = 0.002$ strain (*i.e.*, 0.2% elongation). The yield point either '*b*' or '*c*' fixes the yield stress of the steel material.

(*d*) Point '*d*': This point denotes the ultimate strength of the material. Beyond the yield point, with continued increase of loads, the specimen shows larger permanent deformation at a reduced modulus, due to plastic flow, until the ultimate strength is reached.

(*e*) Point '*e*': Beyond the point of ultimate strength, the cross-section of the test specimen decreases faster than the applied load drops off, until the specimen is fractured, which is denoted by point '*e*'. However, because of the rapid reduction of the cross-sectional area in this loading zone, the true stress at fracture is much higher than the ultimate stress, attained earlier at point '*d*'. As a result there is every possibility of a collapse of the structure if the actual stresses in a major load-bearing component exceed its ultimate stress.

Because of the elasticity of the material, if the applied load is reduced before the limit of proportionality (point '*a*') is reached, the stress-strain curve is retraced as before up to the release of the applied load (point of origin in the stress-strain curve) without any appreciable permanent deformation. Such reversibility is not possible once the specimen is loaded beyond the yield point, because of the permanent deformation that sets in the material in the plastic zone.

Brittle materials like cast iron show very little plastic deformation before fracture and the ultimate strength coincides with the yield stress followed by immediate fracture of the material. On the other hand, a purely ductile material like an aluminium alloy shows a continuous plastic deformation, even without any increase in the applied load beyond the yield point. The stress-strain relationships for these two cases are shown in Figure 3.2 and 3.3.

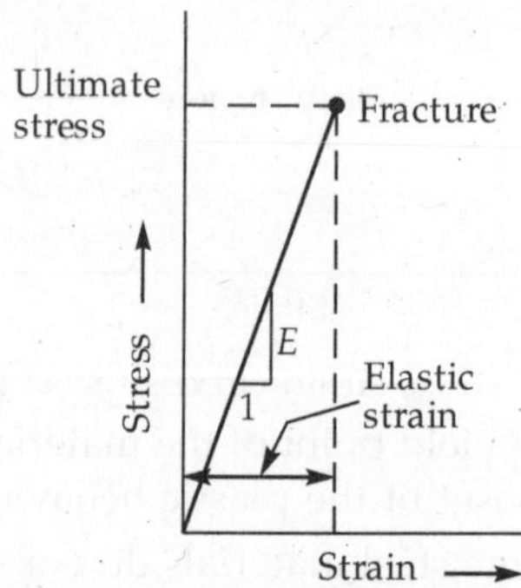

Fig. 3.2 Stress-strain curve for brittle material.

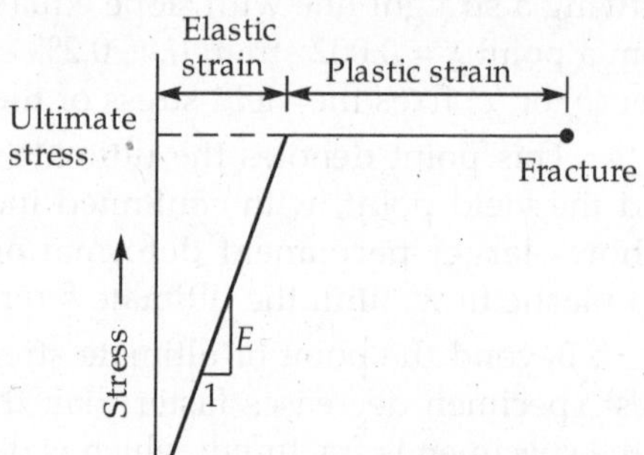

Fig. 3.3 Stress-strain curve for ductile material.

It may be noted that the stress-strain relationship of ordinary structural steel, as shown in Fig. 3.1 earlier, exhibits a behaviour in between that of a brittle material and a fully ductile material, because of work-hardening of the steel material prior to the development of fracture.

3.3 FATIGUE FAILURE OF STEEL

The ultimate strength of any steel material is obtained from tensile tests of specimens on single application of load, applied slowly and in small increments. However, experiments have shown that when a steel member is subjected to repeated reversible stress cycles to the order of one million or more cycles, the member fails by cracking at a stress much below the ultimate stress, though the response to higher loads are quite satisfactory at the initial stage of the loading process. Such a failure caused by decreased resistance of the material due to repeated alternating stresses is termed as fatigue failure Fig. 3.4).

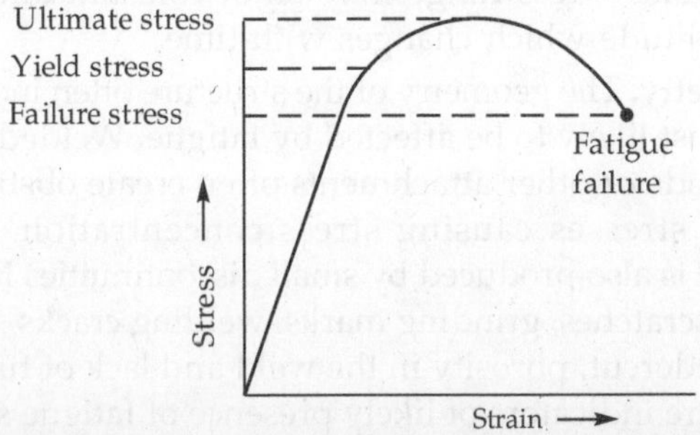

Fig. 3.4 Stress-strain relationship showing fatigue stress.

A fatigue failure is a distinct possibility in supporting structures for cyclic vibratory loads, in bridge girders and cranes, if not properly taken care of in the design process itself.

A most common example of fatigue failure is the snapping of a steel paper clip, when bent back and forth a number of times, until it snaps into two pieces.

The most widely reported case of fatigue failure is that of the crash of the Comet1 jet commercial airliners of British Overseas Airways Corporation which started its maiden commercial flights in the year 1952 and met a tragic end in 1954, when two of them mysteriously crashed while climbing to higher altitudes. On enquiry it was found that the reason of the crash was low-cycle metal fatigue. It was later experimentally confirmed that, with each and every flight the fuselage was pressurized and de-pressurized several times as the aircraft climbed and descended heights. This initiated formation of tiny micro-cracks at the window corners which coalesced later to form a critical crack length triggering a fatigue failure, which ripped the surface of the aircraft, followed by explosive decompression. Subsequently, the corners of the windows were rounded and the skin thickness was made four times that of Comet1 and multiple load paths for primary load-carrying members were adopted.

3.3.1 Factors Contributing to Fatigue in Steel Members and their Connections

Fatigue failures are reported worldwide in aircraft frames, ships, bridges, cranes, crane gantry girders, pressure vessels, vibrating machinery supports, transmission towers, masts, chimneys etc. Research work carried out at many countries reveals several factors that influence the fatigue life of steel structures.

Stress range. The fatigue stress depends on the value of the range of stress. Fatigue failure is imminent if the fluctuating stresses cause plastic deformations in the steel member or in parts of their connections. This stress range may be of constant amplitude or of variable amplitude which changes with time.

Geometry. The geometry of the structure often indicates clearly the region most likely to be affected by fatigue. Welded connections, bolt holes, studs or other attachments often create obstruction to the free flow of stresses causing stress concentration. Local stress concentration is also produced by small discontinuities like, corrosion pits, surface scratches, grinding marks, welding cracks, deposition of weld slag, undercut, porosity in the weld and lack of fusion in weld. These spots are indicators of likely presence of fatigue stresses. Plate distortion, lack of fit and misalignment of joints also contribute to fatigue stresses. Some of the possible effects in welded joints which may contribute to fatigue are shown in Fig. 3.5.

Material properties. Variations in chemical composition and metallurgical properties of materials, stress-strain behaviour and homogeneity are prime factors to varying degrees of fatigue in metals like steel and aluminium.

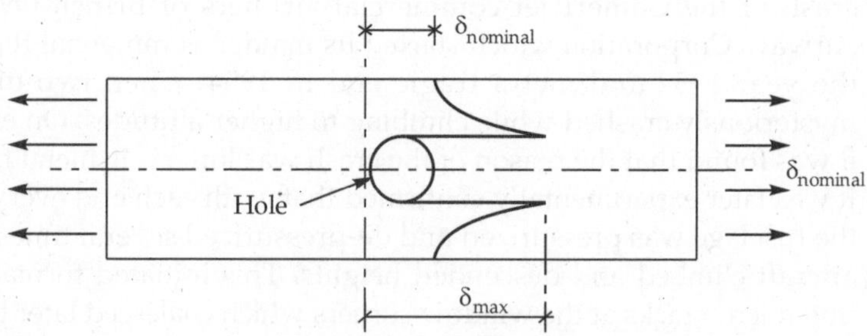

(*a*) Stress concentration

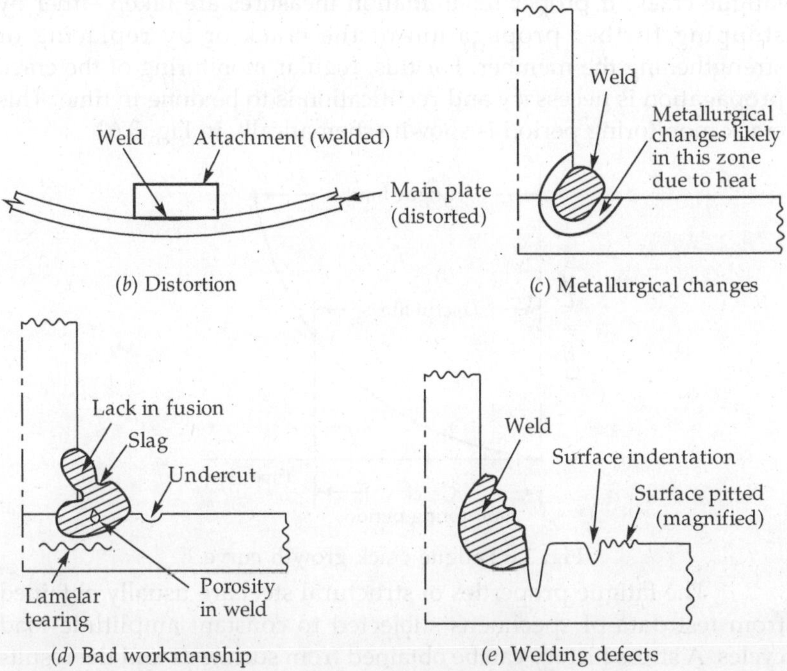

Fig. 3.5 Factors causing fatigue failure in welded joints and steel members.

Environment. Fatigue failures are accelerated in steel structures left unprotected in an environment subjected to high degrees of corrosion. As a result, fatigue failures are often reported in coastal areas and marine structures, where the applied loading produces a high mean stress.

A fatigue failure looks like a brittle fracture. Fatigue cracks are initiated in regions of high stress concentration and in parts affected by corrosion. Once such cracks are formed, they eventually extend through the member and gradually become large enough to cause failure of the component. As there is always a time gap between the formation of a fatigue crack and the failure of the member, the formation of a fatigue crack does not mean that the structural component is in imminent danger of a failure. Failure always occurs when the crack develops to a critical size reducing dangerously the effective load carrying capacity of the member and the time gap between the start of a fatigue crack and the eventual failure depend on the intensity of the reversible loads, shape and propagation of the crack and the geometry of the member. The useful life of a structure can be extended to a great extent even after the formation of the initial fatigue crack, if proper rehabilitation measures are taken either by stopping further propagation of the crack or by replacing or strengthening the member. For this, regular monitoring of the crack propagation is necessary and rectification is to be done in time. This crack monitoring period is shown schematically in Fig. 3.6.

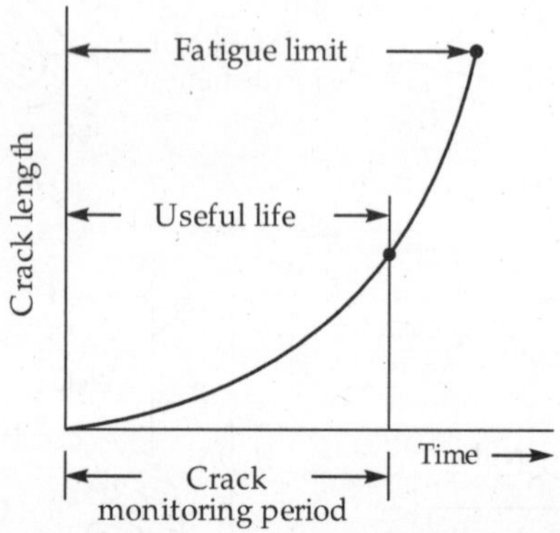

Fig. 3.6 Fatigue crack growth curve.

The fatigue properties of structural steel are usually obtained from test data of specimens subjected to constant amplitude load cycles. A stress history can be obtained from such tests and the results are usually illustrated by the following curves:

1. A curve showing a typical fatigue load cycle, the stress amplitude and the range of stress applied. This is shown in Fig. 3.7.

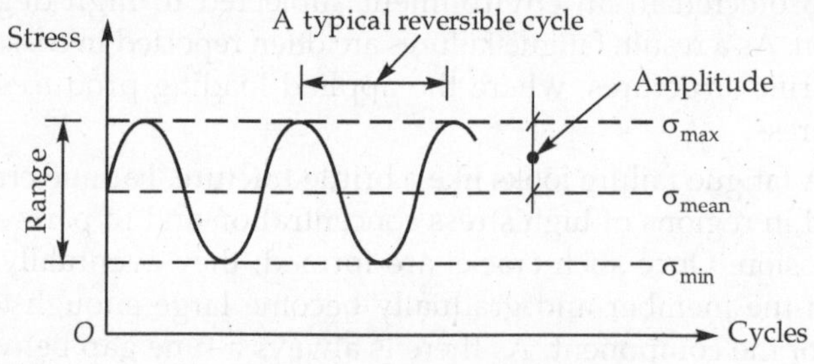

Fig. 3.7 Typical fatigue load cycles.

Here, the stress range = $\sigma_{max} - \sigma_{min}$

Mean stress = ½ × ($\sigma_{max} + \sigma_{min}$)

Stress amplitude = ½ × ($\sigma_{max} - \sigma_{min}$)

2. A curve showing the complete fatigue behaviour of the metal, known as the S-N curve (stress amplitude vrs. cycles to failure) at a particular mean stress (δ_{mean}) level. This is shown in Fig. 3.8 (*a*) and (*b*).

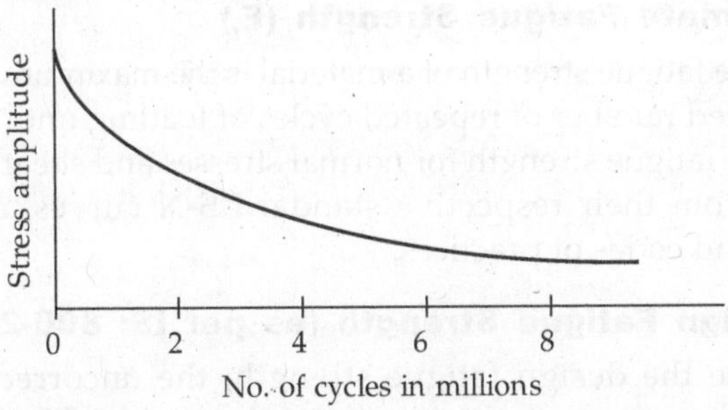

(*a*) Typical S-N curve at a particular mean stress

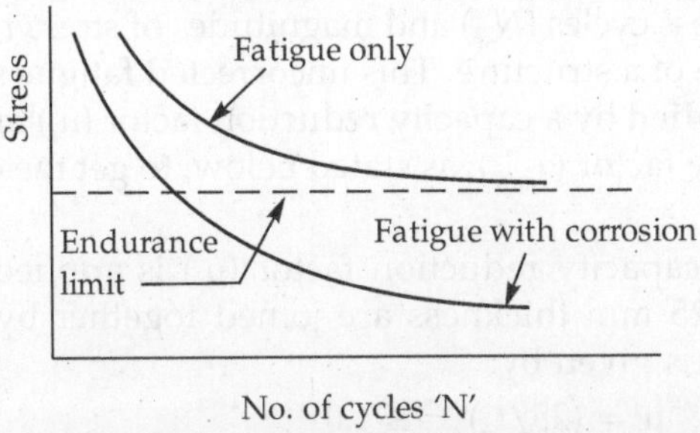

(*b*) S-N curve showing fatigue with or without corrosion

Fig. 3.8

From the curve, it is obvious that the fatigue life increases at lower stress levels and takes an almost infinite fatigue life at a particular stress level, where the curve approaches to be asymptotic to the horizontal line. The stress corresponding to this asymptote is called the **'endurance limit'** of the material. The endurance level therefore indicates the stress level that should be maintained in the design of the structural system if the designer wants to ensure that a failure is least likely to occur on repeated reversible loadings.

3.3.2 Fatigue Life

The fatigue life of any structural component indicates the number of reversible loading cycles that the component should endure before the onset of a fatigue failure. Experiments in fatigue loading show that a mean tensile stress reduces the fatigue life of steel members. Comparatively a mean compressive stress lengthens its fatigue life. Consequently, when any steel member is designed for fatigue resistance, attention should be given to verify whether the stress level in the tension zone is satisfactory from fatigue point of view.

3.3.3 Ultimate Fatigue Strength (F_f)

The ultimate fatigue strength of a material is the maximum stress range for a specified number of repeated cycles of loading until failure. The value of the fatigue strength for normal stresses and shear stresses are obtained from their respective standard S-N curves, available in literature and codes of practices.

3.3.4 Design Fatigue Strength (as per IS: 800-2007)

To calculate the design fatigue strength, the uncorrected fatigue strenght values are first obtained from the standard S-N curves for normal as well as shear stresses, corresponding to the relevant number of stress cycles (N_{sc}) and magnitudes of stress range expected during the life of a structure. This uncorrected fatigue strength value is then **multiplied** by a capacity reduction factor (μ_r) and **divided** by a partial safety factor ($\gamma_{m\,ft}$), as stated below, to get the design fatigue strength.

1. The capacity reduction factor (μ_r) is applied when plates greater than 25 mm thickness are joined together by fillet or butt welding. This is given by:

$$\mu_r = (25/t_p)^{0.25} \leq 1.0$$

where t_p = actual thickness in mm of the thicker material joined.

2. The partial safety factor for strength ($\gamma_{m\,ft}$) is applied as under:

For fail-safe condition, *i.e.*, when the structural system has redundant paths, providing alternative load paths,

$\gamma_{m\,ft}$ = 1.00 when there is access of inspection and maintenance

= 1.15 when access is poor.

For non-fail-safe condition, *i.e.*, when the structural system is of non-redundant nature,

$\gamma_{m\,ft}$ = 1.25 when there is access of inspection and maintenance

= 1.35 when access is poor.

Hence the design fatigue strength = $[\mu_r/\gamma_{m\,ft}]$ × (Fatigue strength for normal/shear stresses as obtained from *S-N* curves).

The design fatigue strength should not exceed the stresses allowable under elastic limits. However, as a general rule, it is assumed that when the actual normal and shear stresses are less than 0.40 to 0.55 times the ultimate tensile strength (f_y), the endurance limit will not be crossed and therefore no further assessment of fatigue is necessary. The partial safety factors, if judiciously determined in the design process, enable the designer to have more effective control over fatigue failures.

3.3.5 Measures to Control Fatigue Failure

As mentioned earlier, the safety and integrity of a structural system can be easily assured when the system is under a single application of static load only. Many structures however are subjected to various types of dynamic loads which act on the system **at random** and some of these dynamic loads may be of **cyclic nature**. Under the action of such loads there is every possibility of localized permanent damage in the material initiating small fatigue cracks. Initially these cracks may be formed due to various reasons like, imperfections in the homogeneity of the steel material, dislocations in connections, lack of weld penetration, porosity in the weld, wrong detailing etc. Fatigue failure is accelerated if the structure is exposed, in addition to dynamic loads, to adverse environmental corrosion, reducing the static load carrying capacity. Eventually, as the structure is subjected to more and more number of the load cycles, these small cracks develop into larger ones and in the long run a critical crack length is reached, when the member is likely to fail by brittle fracture even at some stress much lower than its usual static load carrying capacity. Such failures may be sudden if not detected at an early stage. However, instead of depending on site intervention during the service life of the structure, the problem of fatigue failure should be dealt with at the planning and the design stage itself. Suitable counter measures are therefore necessary while formulating the design strategy, selecting materials and carrying out the detailed engineering work. Several such measures are suggested here which may be of interest to the reader.

Design strategy

While formulating the design strategy for important structural members subjected to cyclic loads, two structural concepts have evolved over the years. One is a **"fail-safe" structure**, in which the primary load carrying members are duplicated, so that the structure survives even when one of them meets a fatigue failure. This principle is followed in the design of the main suspended cables of a suspension bridge by introducing more cables than what is necessary for strength purposes. This way, the stresses in the suspended cables are kept much below their endurance limit, keeping the factor of safety against permissible stresses as high as 5.0 to 6.0. Provision of redundancy in the structural system by way of providing additional load paths reduces fatigue stresses. Tension and compression diagonals in the panels of trussed girders provide such redundancy in the structural system and stresses in both the diagonals are reduced.

The other is a **"safe-life" structure**, which is designed to remain in use for a given period of time before any fatigue failure occurs. In this strategy, only selected components of the whole structure will be thoroughly investigated and designed for fatigue to ensure that no critical crack will appear any time before regular inspections. This is essentially a damage-tolerant design, which allows the development of sub-critical cracks which will not grow to critical length suddenly between two consecutive inspections. This principle is followed in the design of cranes, machine supports and vibratory platforms and other structures in situations where regular inspection can be done rather frequently.

Another common design strategy is to keep the mean stresses, both in tension and compression, below the endurance limit of the steel material so that under normal loading conditions, even with or without any corrosion effect, the structure may not have fatigue failure during the service life. This strategy however may lead to an over-designed structure. This is essentially a variant of the earlier principles.

The designer may apply suitable partial safety factors in the design to control effectively and accurately the safety of a structure under fatigue loads. In this respect, the partial safety factor for material resistance may be altered and adjusted to cover the uncertainties in fatigue conditions. These uncertainties are more pronounced in welded joints and stud connectors, as there is limited statistical data available regarding fatigue loadings and their effects on the material strength. To overcome this problem, the modern design concept includes the provision of a **'safety index'**, to cover numerically the uncertainties involved in fatigue assessment. In fact, the use of the safety index in every construction detail or in every structural member results in a consistent fatigue assessment and ensures a targeted reliability for any given problem situation.

Monitoring of structural details to control fatigue failure

In many cases it has been noticed that the structural drawings are flawed in many respects so that the connections become prone to fatigue failure. Sharp corners in gussets, notches and holes in the region of maximum stresses usually contribute to stress-concentration. Tension members with superfluous holes are easily affected by stress concentration. Return welds in tension bracings perpendicular to the direction of tension force accelerate fatigue failures through cracks in welds. Re-entrant cuts in gusset details may also add to stress concentration. All these defects can easily be removed if the structural details are thoroughly checked by qualified people.

Welded components are prone to fatigue cracks due to change in the properties of the connecting steel members. Moreover cracks generated in a welded connection may propagate to both the connecting members, damaging eventually both of them. While all the harmful effects of a welded connection cannot possibly be eliminated, the following measures may be taken while detailing welded structural components.

Eccentricity in a welded connection should be avoided. To avoid such eccentricity in the welds, fillet welds should be on both sides of the connecting members of same length and size.

Butt welds have better resistance against fatigue than fillet welds. Continuous welds are preferable to intermittent welds in this regard. When alternatives are available in the detailing of structural components these aspects should be kept in mind.

All welding work should be done following standard engineering practices and the details should comply with the relevant codes.

Additional protective paints should be used on structures in corrosion-prone areas.Regular inspection should be arranged at site and all reports about micro-cracks, their nature, location and progress should be recorded followed by suitable remedial measures to control further propagation of such cracks. Periodic in-service inspections of members and connections likely to be affected by fatigue stresses are recommended. Inaccessible connections should be avoided if they are prone to fatigue stresses.

Lastly, proper guidelines should be formulated for repair of cracks in structural components. Repair of fatigue cracks should never be done by welding, as they are likely to propagate more cracks or equally severe defects. Bolted splice plates should be provided in such cases. The remaining fatigue life may be assessed any time during the service life of a structure using fracture mechanics methods.

3.4 BUCKLING FAILURE OF STEEL MEMBERS

3.4.1 Lateral Buckling

A steel beam which has a narrow flange width compared to its unsupported length is likely to twist and buckle about the minor axis even before its load carrying capacity from strength consideration about the major axis is reached. This behaviour is termed as 'lateral buckling'. Lateral buckling creates an unstable condition which reduces the margin of safety, otherwise available from strength consideration. Moreover, if the ends are restrained against twisting, instability caused by lateral buckling may lead to 'warping' and rotation of one flange relative to the other flange about the minor axis of the beam section.

Due to lateral buckling the beam is deflected in the lateral direction in the form of a sine wave. In the plastic range, in the limit state, the lateral bending go on increasing even without any substantial increase in the major axis bending moment. That is, there may be a critical moment in the plastic range, when the safety of the beam is seriously compromised due to continued lateral bending without any increase in the applied load.

Lateral buckling depends on the slenderness ratio (l_{eff}/r_{min}) of the member. An increase in the value of the slenderness ratio brings about a decrease in the permissible stress values. On the other hand, a lower value of the slenderness ratio increases the permissible stresses and hence the lateral stability. This lateral stability can be effectively controlled by proving additional lateral supports to the compression flange, thus reducing the effective length of the member. In many cases it becomes necessary to control lateral buckling by suitably modifying the section so that the value of r_{min} is increased.

Lateral bending is more pronounced in steel beams subjected to horizontal loads or thrusts. Bending due to these external loads is usually accompanied by twisting of the beams, unless they are not restrained by lateral supports or bracings. The chances of lateral instability also increase considerably, if a beam section is so proportioned that the major axis bending moment is sufficient to cause a near-yield stress, leaving very little margin for resisting lateral buckling.

3.4.2 Buckling of Steel Compression Members due to Primary Buckling

For a steel compression member like a column or the compression member of a steel truss, there is a critical value of the axial load, beyond which the compression member will fail by buckling. This critical value of the applied load depends on two factors, namely:

- Least radius of gyration of the compression member
- Boundary conditions

For an axially loaded column, pinned at both ends, the critical load for buckling is given by the Euler's equation:

$$P_{cr} = n^2 \times \pi^2 \times E \times I/L^2, \text{ where, } n = 1, 2, 3 \text{ etc.}$$

Obviously, there are infinite numbers of critical buckling loads. But the designer is interested only in the value of the minimum critical load, which is obtained when $n = 1$.

i.e. $P_{cr} = (\pi^2 \times E \times I)/L^2$

For $n = 2$, $P_{cr} = 4 \times P_{cr}$ (min)

For $n = 3$, $P_{cr} = 9 \times P_{cr}$ (min)

These 3-buckling modes are shown in Fig. 3.9.

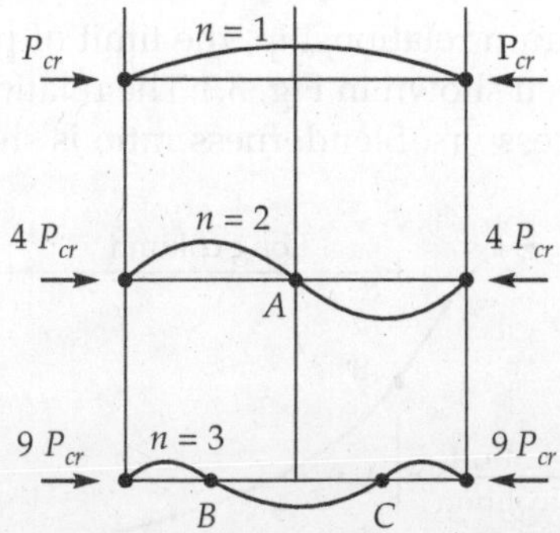

Fig. 3.9 Buckling modes of a column pinned at both ends.

The Euler's formula is applicable when the length of the compression member is large (more than 30 times the least lateral dimension). Accordingly, the critical slenderness ratio is that ratio, at which the Euler's column formula does not apply. This point, shown as "*B*" in Fig. 3.10, demarcates a long column from a short column.

A steel column may also buckle due to imperfections in the fabrication work, due to corrosion effects or due to mal-alignment of the loads. In all such cases safety of the column is affected, if not attended to in time.

From the buckling modes shown in the above figure, it may be noted that, if the column (pinned at both ends) is braced at the points of contra-flexure, the critical load for buckling increases significantly. That is, the column will carry higher loads without buckling if it is braced at inflexion points. Side by side, the lower is the slenderness ratio the higher is the chance for buckling.

Compression members may buckle at a substantially lower load, if the member is not straight, but is bent initially. In such cases, the column will be subjected to an additional moment due to eccentricity of the applied load., thereby lowering the critical buckling load.

3.4.3 Critical Buckling Stress

A compression member may ultimately fail, when the critical buckling stress exceeds the yield stress of the steel material. To be more exact, buckling failure starts when the limit of proportionality is arrived, followed closely by the yield point. The critical buckling stress for a column pinned at both ends,

$$\sigma_{cr} = \frac{P_{cr}}{A} = \frac{(\pi^2 \times E \times I)}{(L^2 \times A)} = \frac{(\pi^2 \times E)}{(l/r)^2}$$

The stress-strain relationship, the limit of proportionality and yield point have been shown in Fig. 3.1 The relationship between the critical buckling stress vrs. Slenderness ratio is shown in Fig. 3.10.

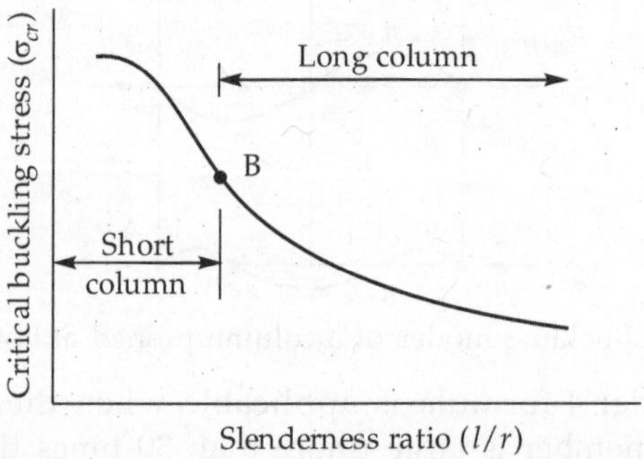

Fig. 3.10 Critical buckling stress vrs. slenderness ratio.

3.4.4 Failure of Thin Plates due to Buckling

A thin steel plate is a flat plate the thickness of which is much less than its lateral dimensions. When such plates are subjected to in-plane compressive loads, they buckle at critical stresses well below the elastic limit of the material. The buckled shape of a material (magnified) unsupported at sides and subjected to a compressive load is shown in Fig. 3.11.

If the plate is treated as a simply supported wide column, then from the theory of column buckling,

$$\sigma_{cr} = \frac{P_{cr}}{A} = \frac{(\pi^2 \times E \times I)}{(L^2 \times A)}$$

In this case, $A = bt \qquad I = I_y = \dfrac{bt^3}{12}$

Putting these values, $\sigma_{cr} = \dfrac{(\pi^2 \times E \times t^2)}{(12 \times L^2)}$

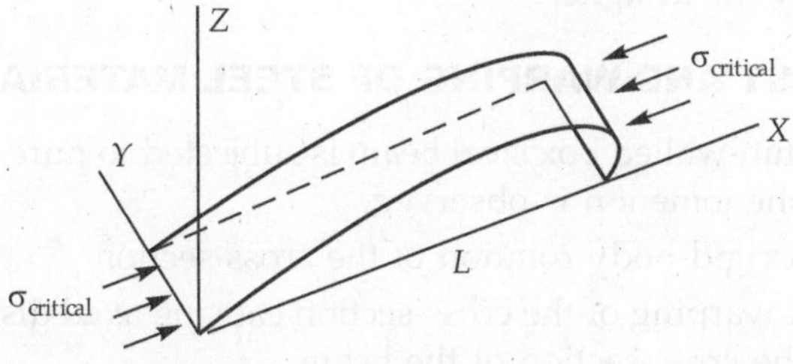

Fig. 3.11 Magnified buckled shape of a thin plate unsupported at ends.

This is the rough estimate of critical stress, if the poisson effect is ignored and is accurate enough for practical design purposes. Calculation of critical stress values for other boundary conditions and buckling modes are beyond the scope of this book. For this the reader is advised to consult specialized literature involving the theory of plates and shells.

3.4.5 Failure of Steel Plates due to Crippling (Secondary Buckling)

If a compression member consisting of thin-walled components (like columns fabricated by welding four plates along their edges) is not provided with lateral bracings and stiffeners, there may be distortion in the cross-section due to what is called "crippling" (Ref. Fig. 3.12). Crippling causes secondary (local) instability and is usually confined to localized areas. When the cross-section is distorted, the member loses its load-carrying capacity. However, so long as the edges of the column remain straight, the steel material in this region continues to carry the load, until yielding takes place leading to failure.

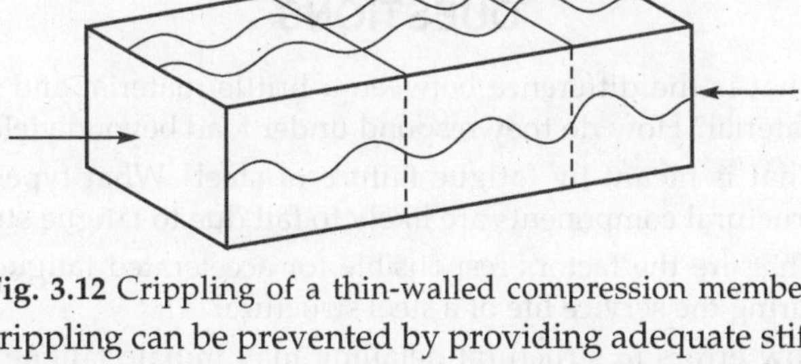

Fig. 3.12 Crippling of a thin-walled compression member.

Crippling can be prevented by providing adequate stiffeners at suitable intervals thus reducing the size of the panels, thereby increasing the resistance to local buckling. When stiffeners are welded, a clamped edge condition is imposed and the load-bearing capacity vis-avis local buckling is considerable enhanced. There are important guidelines in the codes for designing these stiffeners which should be consulted by the designer.

3.5 TWIST AND WARPING OF STEEL MATERIAL

If a thin-walled box steel beam is subjected to pure torsion, the following phenomenon is observed.

(*a*) A rigid-body rotation of the cross-section

(*b*) A warping of the cross-section causing axial displacements normal to the cross-section of the beam

The above rigid-body rotation and warping occurs simultaneously and the resulting shear strain is equal to the sum of shear strain due to pure torsion and shear strain due to accompanying warping. The twist and warping of the cross-section of a thin-walled box is shown in Fig. 3.13.

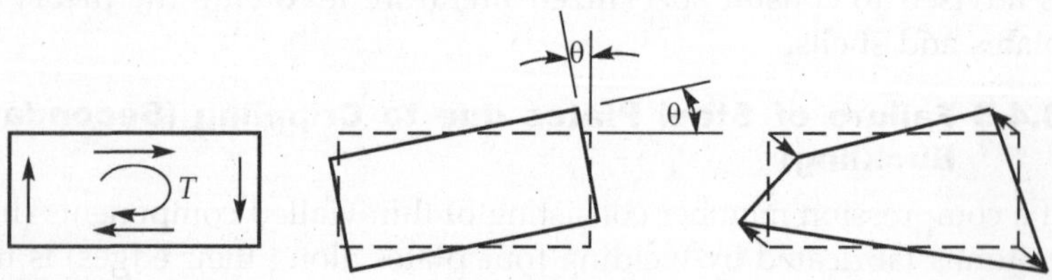

(*a*) Thin-walled box section in pure torsion (*b*) Rigid-body rotation due to twist (*c*) Axial displacement due to warping

Fig. 3.13 Effect of warping.

It is to be noted in this connection that, if the cross-section is square, there is only rigid-body rotation due to twist and there is no warping. Due to the same reason, a steel tube does not show signs of warping in pure torsion.

QUESTIONS

1. What is the difference between a brittle material and a ductile material? How do they respond under load beyond yield point?
2. What is meant by fatigue failure of steel? What types of steel structural components are likely to fail due to fatigue stresses?
3. What are the factors responsible for accelerated fatigue stresses during the service life of a steel structure?
4. How errors in structural detailing may initiate fatigue failure?

5. Suggest suitable counter measures to ensure safety of a structural system under fatigue loads.
6. Write short notes on the following:
   (*a*) Fatigue life of a steel structural member
   (*b*) Ultimate fatigue strength
   (*c*) Design fatigue strength
   (*d*) S-N curve for fatigue
7. Enumerate the circumstances when a steel structural member may fail due to buckling.
8. Write explanatory notes on:
   (*a*) Critical buckling stress
   (*b*) Primary buckling and secondary buckling (crippling)
   (*c*) Warping and twist in thin-walled steel box sections

CHAPTER 4

Safety Considerations in the Design of Concrete Structures

4.1 INTRODUCTION

Unlike steel which is treated as a homogenous material, reinforced concrete is a composite material comprising cement, coarse aggregates, fine aggregates and reinforcement rods. Concrete is stressed non-uniformly under the influence of external loads. When under compression, stresses concentrate around the stone aggregates as they are harder than the fine aggregates and have higher modulus of elasticity. Stresses also concentrate at pores and voids which are abundant in concrete. As a result stresses are never uniformly distributed in a concrete section even if the applied load is uniform. Non-uniform distribution of stress is more predominant in concrete produced from bad workmanship. Even in the same concrete mix, test results of concrete cubes show marked differences in strength because of non-uniform spread of the constituent particles and voids. In addition, there is always a certain degree of uncertainty in having the proper strength, as most of the concreting work is done at site under variable working conditions, environment and curing. All these factors make a difference between the construction with a homogenous material like steel which is produced under controlled condition at steel mills and a heterogeneous material like reinforced concrete produced under variable site conditions.

An axially loaded concrete test specimen fails due to lateral rupture of the concrete under the influence of longitudinal compressive stress and lateral tensile stress (secondary stress). (Ref: Fig. 4.1). Moreover, concrete, being a brittle material, fails without any warning in many cases if the reinforcements are inadequate or improperly placed and this type of sudden failures are accentuated if there is weakness in the concrete strength due to bad workmanship.

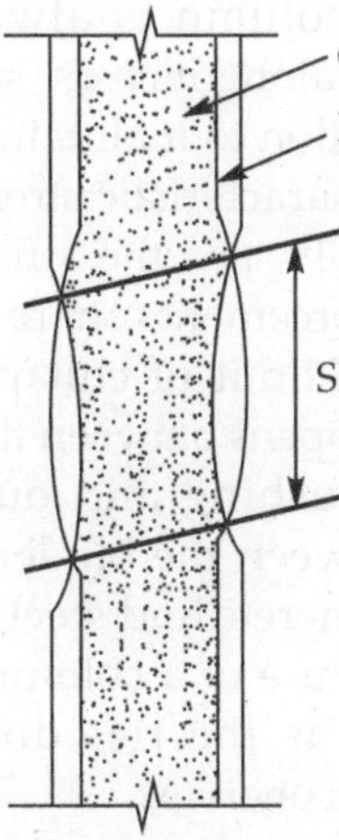

Fig. 4.1 Column failure due to axial compression.

Keeping in view the above facts, the values of the characteristic loads, characteristic strength and their partial safety factors as enumerated in chapter 2 have to be chosen to suit the different loading conditions at limit states of collapse and serviceability. These considerations should conform to the basic requirement that a structure should have an acceptable level of safety under service loads and a reasonable probability of survival with minimum of damages at different limit states. It may be noted in this connection that the partial safety factors for concrete at different limit states are based on the assumption that all concrete will be done in-situ and will be 'controlled' concrete.

4.2 BEHAVIOUR OF REINFORCED CONCRETE MEMBERS UNDER LOAD

4.2.1. Columns

Columns and struts are the most usual types of compression members in reinforced concrete structures. According to shape, a column or a strut may be square, round, rectangular, hexagonal or octagonal. Depending on the slenderness ratio they are classified as pedestals, short columns or long columns. As per geometry, a column may be single, braced together or continuous through a floor. According to end fixity, the ends of a column may be pinned or fixed at ends with different degrees of fixity or a column may even stand as a vertical cantilever. However, in spite of so many varieties, a column is essentially a compression member, with additional bending effects.

A reinforced concrete column is always provided with longitudinal reinforcement rods along its axis, supplemented by ties or spirals in the transverse direction to maintain its integrity. At low range of stresses (at about ½ × characteristic strength of concrete) the column behaves almost elastically, *i.e.*, the stresses and strains are proportional and the steel reinforcements share only a small part of the axial load. As the ultimate limit of collapse is approached a redistribution of load-sharing happens between the concrete and steel, when the concrete fails by crushing and outward buckling of longitudinal reinforcements between the binders. (Ref. 4.1). Failure in this case occurs when both concrete and steel attain their ultimate load-carrying capacities. The failure of a column provided with ties is also abrupt and complete, as the ties do not help much in containing the inner core of the concrete.

To allow for the small eccentricities in verticality and connections for cast-in-situ short, axially-loaded columns, the design load in the limit state is fixed in the codes by the following relation.

$$P = 0.4\, f_{ck} \times A_c + 0.67 f_y \times A_{sc}$$

where f_{ck} = characteristic compressive strength in concrete

A_c = Area of concrete

f_y = Characteristic tensile strength of reinforcement

A_{sc} = area of longitudinal reinforcements in the column

4.2.2 Buckling of Reinforced Concrete Compression Members

Using high-strength concrete and adopting improved methods of construction it is now possible to design columns of smaller sizes for any given load. This practice has led to the introduction of sleek columns in many cases whose cross-sectional areas are small compared to their lengths. Such a column tends to buckle about the minor axis. A buckled column poses serious safety hazard to the user and gives an ugly look to the external finishes, even if the column does not collapse completely. A column may buckle at a load much lower than its ultimate load-carrying capacity. The critical buckling load in such cases depends mainly on the slenderness ratio about its minor axis (l_{eff}/r_{min}), which again depends on the degree of end fixities and the minimum radius of gyration. In addition, most reinforced concrete columns are subjected to additional moments from end-fixities and also due to external horizontal forces. These forces together initiate in some cases an early buckling mode unless they are braced at suitable intervals. For architectural reasons columns are sometimes built double-storey high. To avoid buckling failure of such columns, they should either be braced or the size should be altered to avoid an early buckling failure. In general, it may be said that a column free to buckle side-ways is always weaker than a similar column braced against side-sway.

The Euler's formula given for axially-loaded steel columns earlier in chapter 3 is equally applicable for a reinforced concrete column. From the formula, it is evident that the critical stress due to buckling decreases with increase in the slenderness ratio and the failure modes depend on the end-fixities. That is, for the same cross-section and length, the critical load of buckling is four times high for a column having fixed ends than a column having hinged ends. For effective lengths for various other intermediate conditions of end fixities, the codes of practices give excellent guide-lines for compliance.

4.2.3 Axial Tension in Reinforced Concrete Members

Reinforced concrete is not suitable for use as a tension member, as its capacity to resist tension is quite low compared to its compressive strength. However, when the axial tensile force is quite low, a reinforced concrete member produces a stress considerably less than its allowable tensile strength in the elastic range. At this stage, both concrete and steel behave elastically and share the applied tensile force. With further increase in the load, a stage is reached when the concrete can no longer resist the tension and then the concrete cracks and the steel reinforcements resist the entire tensile force. At this stage the actual tensile stress in the concrete section is equal to the applied tension divided by the area of the steel reinforcement, the concrete no longer sharing any part of the load. If the load is further increased, a stage may reach when the tensile stress in steel will reach its ultimate tensile strength, when the steel will begin to yield and the whole concrete section will fail. Hence the maximum strength of a concrete member under axial tension is that which causes the steel to reach its yield point.

i.e., $$P_{\text{tensile}}\,(\text{max}) = f_y\,A_s$$

where f_y = characteristic strength of steel material

A_s = area of tensile steel.

This is the maximum useful strength of a tension member till the reinforcement rods start yielding. However, for reasons of adequate safety, the force transmitted to any tension member should not be allowed to exceed ½ × P_{tensile} (max). Even at this stress, the concrete would have micro-cracks, contributing nothing towards strength, but helping in providing cover to the reinforcements against corrosion or fire hazards.

Reinforced concrete circular tanks and containers are built in many projects both underground and over-ground to retain water or other fluids. In such cases tension develops due to hoop stresses in the circular walls. But for reasons of better serviceability, cracks are not allowed in these structures. In order to achieve this, the codes specify low values of permissible stresses in steel so that the corresponding stress in the surrounding concrete is kept sufficiently low so that the section remains crack-free.

4.2.4 Bending in Reinforced Concrete Members

Plane concrete beams are weak in flexure and fail in tension even at a very low load. Steel bars are therefore placed in the beam in the form of reinforcements as close as possible on the tension side leaving adequate cover for protection against corrosion and fire hazards.

At low loads, as long as the tensile stress in concrete is less than its modulus of rupture, the entire concrete section is effective in compression and there will be no crack on the tension side.

At normal service loads, though the steel bars take the tensile stress, cracks develop on the tension side of the concrete beam, as the tensile stress in the vicinity of the steel bars exceeds the maximum tensile strength of concrete. Though these cracks are very small hair-line cracks initially, these cracks gradually move upwards right up to the neutral axis of the beam section, as load is increased. Because of the presence of these hair-line cracks all reinforced concrete beams are designed as 'cracked' section, where the concrete above the neutral axis takes the bending compression and the steel reinforcements resisting the bending tension.

Subsequently when the loads are further increased substantially so that the beam section reaches the ultimate limit state of collapse, the beam yields and eventually failure occurs to the beam section. Such failure in a reinforced concrete beam may happen in any of the following modes.

- When the quantity of steel in the tension region is moderately low (*i.e.*, the section is 'under-reinforced'), the steel reaches its yield point first with widening of the hair-line cracks in concrete, resulting in a significant deflection (yielding) of the beam. The beam is then considered to be virtually on the point of collapse. The failure in such a way due to the yielding of steel reinforcement is gradual, preceded by visible signs of distress over a period of time. The user gets signals of the pending failure in such cases and can take safety precautions.

- If the quantity of steel is quite large, *i.e.*, if the beam section is over-reinforced, the concrete on the compression side crosses its crushing strength first, leaving the reinforcement steel rods under-stressed. As a result, the concrete in the compression region eventually gets crushed, before the onset of yielding of the steel reinforcements. The failure in such a case happens suddenly in an explosive manner, hardly giving any distress signal to the user.

As such, if the external loads fluctuate and if there are possibilities of over-loading during the service life, the beam should be designed as "under-reinforced', so that failure would occur only by the initial yielding of the steel, rather than by abrupt crushing of the concrete in the compression zone. Considering all these factors and all possible hazard scenarios, as mentioned in chapter 2, partial safety factors to the characteristic loads have been suggested in the codes of practices to avoid failure.

4.2.5 Diagonal Tension and Shear

The tension reinforcements in a concrete beam resist the flexural tension and the mode of bending failure is dependent on whether the beam is under-reinforced or over-reinforced. While the rods in the tension zone, if properly designed and detailed, can resist early compression failure of the beam, these rods cannot resist the shear when loads increase substantially so as to cross the shear-carrying capacity of the plain concrete. With increase in the external loads, shear stresses also increase proportionally all over the beam. This shear acts along with the local tensile stress and the combined effect of shear and flexural stresses cause local tensile stress diagonally. When this diagonal tension exceeds the modulus of rupture of concrete, diagonal cracks appear and the beam shows signs of distress. Shear reinforcement is provided to arrest the formation of these diagonal cracks.

Three distinct causes, based on the support conditions and type of loads are responsible for propagation of diagonal cracks at any particular section of the beam.

- Presence of large bending moment and large shear
- Presence of large bending moment and low shear

- Presence of low bending moment and large shear
- Presence of low bending moment and low shear

Figure 4.2 shows the regions of simply-supported and continuous beams where there is likelihood of diagonal cracks due to the above reasons.

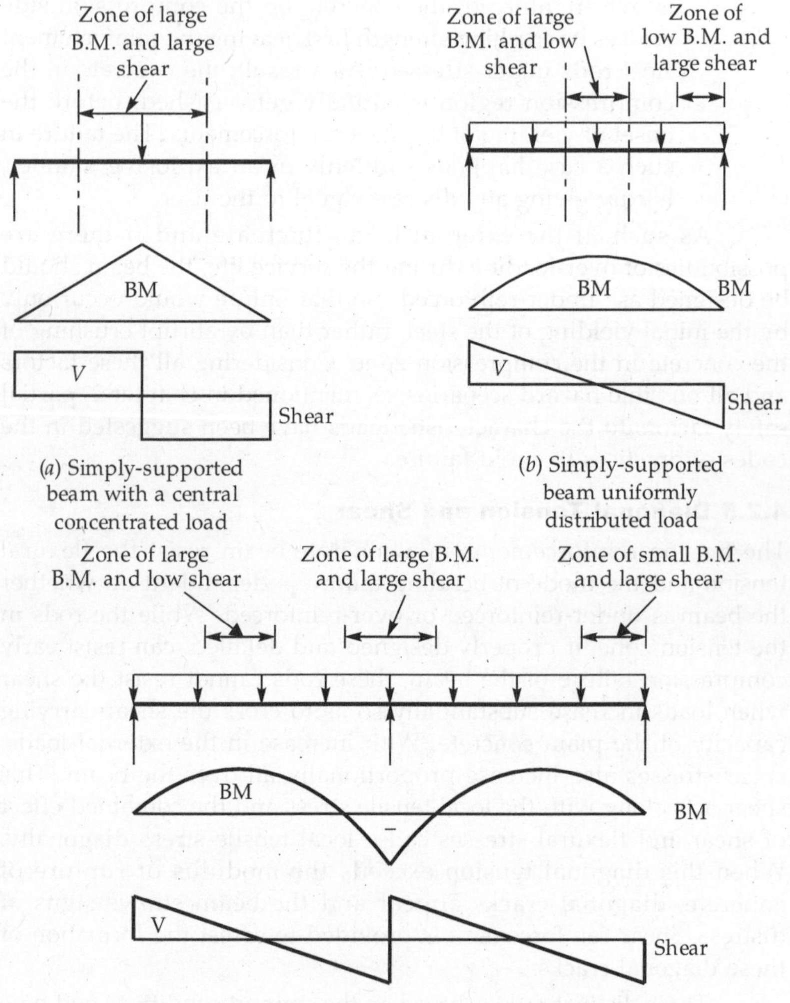

(*a*) Simply-supported beam with a central concentrated load

(*b*) Simply-supported beam uniformly distributed load

(*c*) Continuous beam with uniformly-distributed load

Fig. 4.2 Probable locations of diagonal cracks in beams.

4.2.6 Shape of Cracks

At locations where the flexural tension is small, but shear is high, diagonal cracks appear mostly due to high shear stresses and these cracks are usually inclined at about 45 degrees. These cracks are termed as web-shear cracks (Ref. Fig. 4.3).

At locations where both flexural tension and shear stresses are high, vertical flexural cracks appear first and these cracks eventually bend in a diagonal direction. These cracks are called flexure-shear cracks. (Ref. Fig. 4.4).

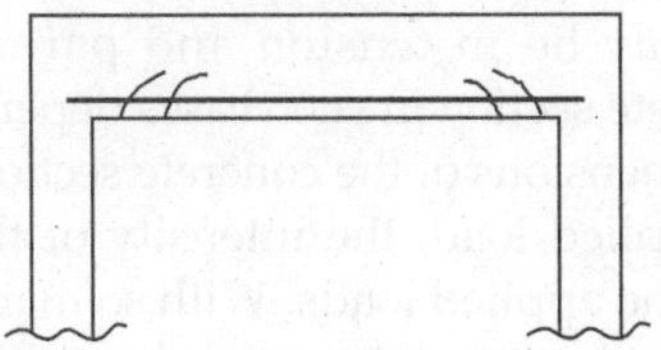

Fig. 4.3 Typical web shear cracks.

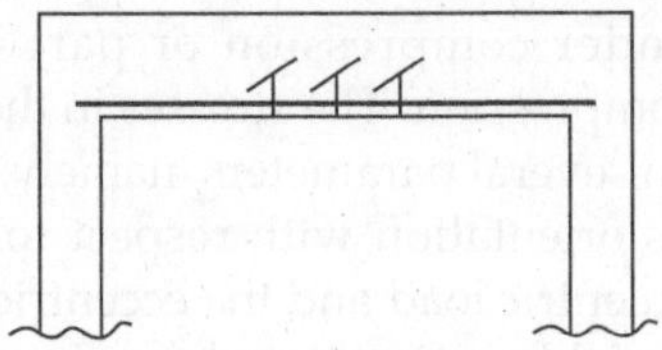

Fig. 4.4 Typical flexure shear cracks.

If there is inadequate shear reinforcement, the diagonal cracks, once formed, extend very quickly from the tension zone to the compression zone, crossing diagonally the entire beam. If such beams are overloaded due to some other reasons during its service life, the cracks widens further and split the beam and failure occurs. Shear failures are often of explosive nature and happens suddenly, if not attended in time. As shear failure cannot be predicted very accurately with precision because of its brittle nature and sudden occurrence, adequate safety margin on the high side should be provided while designing the beam for shear to prevent such types of failure.

4.2.7 Bond and Anchorage

Bond is the grip or frictional resistance between reinforcement rods and the surrounding concrete. Adequate bond is necessary for effective performance of a reinforced concrete beam as a composite section. Bond stress is inversely proportional to the sum of the perimeter of the bars. Hence the bond stress can be reduced by increasing the perimeter of the bars. This can be done by using greater number of smaller bars and using deformed bars which have greater grip with the concrete.

Bond failure may occur near supports where the shear force is high. Cracks and splitting of concrete are the results of bond failure. Because diagonal cracks due to shear failure are common at supports, shear and bond failures often occur simultaneously, if higher diameter rods are used without checking the bond stresses.

A local bond failure may occur at loads much lower than that the ultimate collapse load of the beam. This may widen the cracks causing a larger deflection of the beam. However, this will not lessen the ultimate carrying capacity, so long as the anchorages of the rods over the supports are intact. As such, to arrest bond failure, small diameter rods should be used with adequate cover and end anchorages as per guidelines given in the codes.

4.2.8 Compression with Bending

When reinforced concrete members are subjected to simultaneous bending and compression, the concrete section may be either fully under compression or part of it may be in tension and part in compression. The stresses in the concrete section in such cases depend on several parameters, namely, the dimensions of the concrete section, its orientation with respect to the applied load, the intensity of the eccentric load and the eccentricity of the applied loads. With so many variables, it is often difficult to find out in a straightforward way the stresses in the concrete and steel for sections under eccentric loads, particularly if there is biaxial bending. The design then involves a few intermediate trials before the sections and the reinforcements are finalized.

In the elastic range (*i.e.*, when extreme fibre concrete stresses are in the order of ½ × ultimate stress and the eccentricity of the applied load is very small), the resultant concrete stresses can be calculated by simply adding the axial compressive stress and the bending stress, considering the transformed un-cracked area of the concrete and steel. In this case it is assumed that the concrete section would fail in compression while the tension steel may be far from the yield point.

For large eccentricities, *i.e.*, when the applied moment is sufficiently large, tension cracks appear, making the concrete area in the tension zone ineffective. Failure is then initiated by the yielding of the steel with further propagation and lengthening of the cracks and a still further shift of the neutral axis towards the compression side. It is then followed by a secondary compression failure by crushing of the concrete.

In the above, the design considerations in respect of the probability of failure of concrete under simultaneous compression and bending have been discussed without going into the detailed calculations. The reader will find them in standard text books on reinforced concrete structures.

4.3 FATIGUE IN REINFORCED CONCRETE MEMBERS

Experiments have shown that when a reinforced concrete member is subjected to repeated compressions million times over, the strength of concrete decreases rapidly due to micro-cracking. The fatigue (endurance) limit depends on the number of loading cycles. Figure 4.5 shows a typical endurance curve for reinforced concrete.

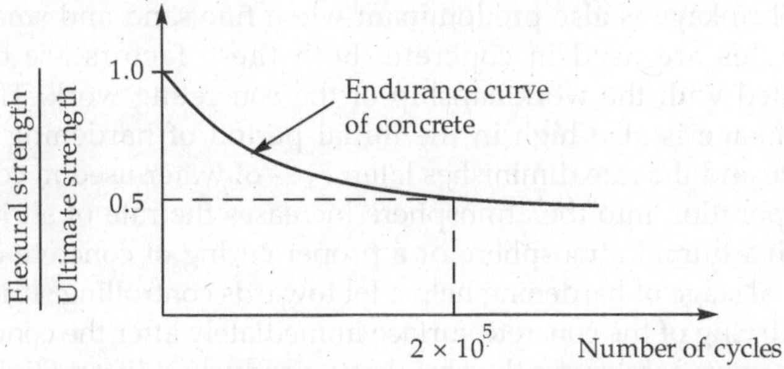

Fig. 4.5 Typical endurance curve for reinforced concrete.

From the above curve, it is to be noted that the ultimate strength of concrete is reduced by about 50%, when the number of reversible cycles approach a two million mark. The lowest value of the fatigue limit corresponds to the concrete stress when micro-cracks develop. The fatigue limit also depends on the cycle characteristic *i.e.*, the ratio of the maximum and the minimum stresses in a cycle. Reinforced concrete crane beams or reinforced concrete foundations subjected to dynamic machine loads need to be analyzed for fatigue.

4.4 CREEP

Though concrete is assumed to be an elastic material at low range of stress and it is assumed that the stress and strain are proportional, concrete actually behaves as an extremely rigid plastic material that is prone to progressive plastic deformation under sustained loading. This property of concrete is termed as plastic flow or 'creep'. Creep is the increase of strain in concrete over time under sustained stresses. Creep is proportional to the amount of cement paste present in the concrete and is directly proportional to the duration of the loading. High relative humidity reduces to some extent the creep in concrete. Creep is not much affected by water-cement ratio or the quality of concrete. In the design of pre-stressed concrete structures and in the design of ordinary reinforced concrete structures in the limit state analysis, the effect of creep on the loss of steel stress and on the deflection should be considered. Creep strains attain terminal values in about 5 years, while 75% of total creep occur within the first year or so.

4.5 SHRINKAGE

Shrinkage is the contraction of concrete during drying. Experiments show that shrinkage increases with an increase in the water-cement ratio. Shrinkage is also predominant when fine sand and small-size aggregates are used in concrete. Both these factors are closely associated with the workmanship of the concreting work. The rate of shrinkage is also high in the initial period of hardening of the concrete and the rate diminishes later. Loss of water used in concrete by evaporation into the atmosphere increases the rate of shrinkage. As such a humid atmosphere or a proper curing of concrete during the initial stage of hardening help a lot towards controlling shrinkage. Rapid drying of the concrete surface immediately after the concreting work is over, accelerates the shrinkage, producing differential strain between the upper and the lower layers causing shrinkage cracks.

When concrete is poured in bulk quantity at a place, the concrete may dry non-uniformly. The surface exposed to atmosphere dries fast, releasing rapidly the heat of hydration and is subjected to tension. The inner core of the concrete remains wet, restraining the shrinkage of this layer and is subjected to compression. Shrinkage cracks are produced because of this initial tension in the surface layers of concrete.

Shrinkage stresses can be reduced by proper selection of the water-cement ratio, proper selection of the coarse and the fine aggregates and also by proving shrinkage joints. Shrinkage can be effectively controlled if curing is done in the proper way following the guidelines of the codes.

The shrinkage factor does not come in the initial strength analysis. But the effect of shrinkage resulting in the loss in pre-stress in pre-stressed concrete structures and on deflection in ordinary reinforced concrete structures should be taken into account in the design stage itself.

4.6 CRACKS DUE TO LOCAL RESTRAINTS

Additional restraints, if provided in a structural system, add to the stresses with a strong probability of development of cracks in concrete. Such cracks are noticed in long continuous thin concrete sections, such as, walls, pavements and chajjas, when they are fully restrained at ends. In case of concrete pavements the ill effect of restraints at ends can be reduced by introducing at suitable intervals movement joints and partial construction joints. (Ref. Fig. 4.6).

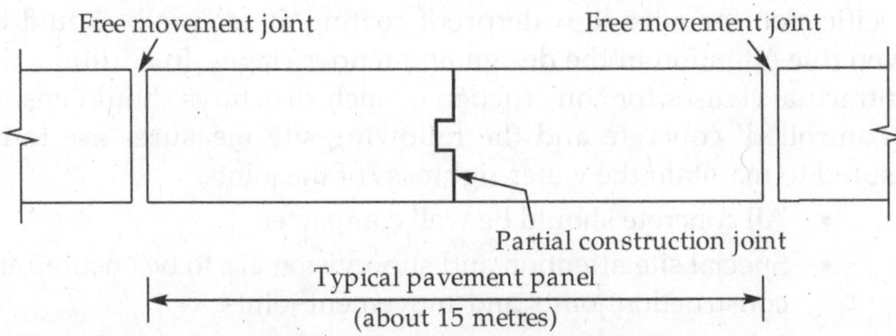

Fig. 4.6 Joints in pavement slab.

In the above case, the restraint will be almost nil at movement joints and greatly reduced at the partial construction joints. For thick slabs and mass concrete blocks the rate of heat loss from the bottom is much less than the heat loss at the top surface, resulting in a differential thermal gradient and will impose additional restraints. To arrest cracks due to such restraints, fabric reinforcements are provided at the top surface with a minimum cover of 40 mm and the minimum reinforcements may be calculated considering that only about 100 mm thick top crust will be critical.

4.7 CRACKS DUE TO WARPING

Even if a thin concrete pavement slab is not restrained at the ends (it happens when the distribution steel is not continuous across the joint or if the construction joint acts as a movement joint), the edge of the pavement slab may be bent upwards ('warped'), if the restraint provided by the base is significant. Cracks are noticed in such cases at the warped ends and these cracks may eventually lead to failure of the slab under wheel loads. (Ref. Fig. 4.7)

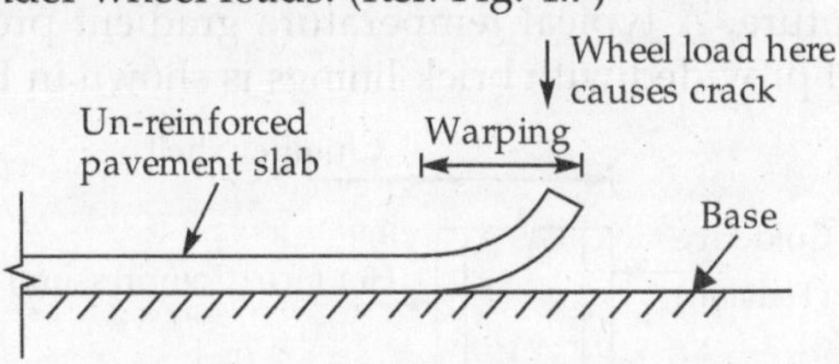

Fig. 4.7 Warping of pavement slab.

4.8 CRACK CONTROL FOR WATERTIGHT CONSTRUCTION

Liquid-retaining structures and building basements are required to be made water-tight for reason of serviceability. Only micro-cracks less than 0.1 mm width are tolerated in such construction. The specification of the materials used, the method of construction, position of construction joints, specification for any special additive needed and specification for outside waterproof coating, if required, should be given due attention in the design and tender stages. In addition, the contractual clauses for construction of such structures should ensure a 'controlled' concrete and the following site measures are to be ensured to maintain the water-tightness of the joints:

- All concrete should be well compacted.
- Special site attention and supervision are to be ensured for construction joints and movement joints.
- Ingress of water due to seepage from outside or foundation bottom should be arrested by sealing the cracks by pressure grouting.

4.9 THERMAL CRACKS IN CONCRETE

A very high temperature gradient across a concrete section may be the cause of cracking in the concrete unless the problem is dealt with at the design stage itself. Mention may be made here the cases of reinforced concrete chimneys and flue ducts through which hot gases are allowed to flow. Under the influence of the flow of such hot gases under steady-state condition, there is compression on the hot face and tensile stress on the cold face (Ref. Fig. 4.8). In the design process these temperature stresses are to be combined algebraically with other stresses due to dead weight, and effects of wind and earthquake and the concrete sections and their reinforcements are fixed accordingly. To reduce the harmful effects of the thermal gradient and prevent thermal cracking, metal or fire-brick linings are usually provided along the hot face. Sometimes gaps are also left between the lining and the concrete to isolate further the concrete from the effects of the high temperature. A typical temperature gradient profile across a chimney wall provided with brick linings is shown in Fig. 4.9.

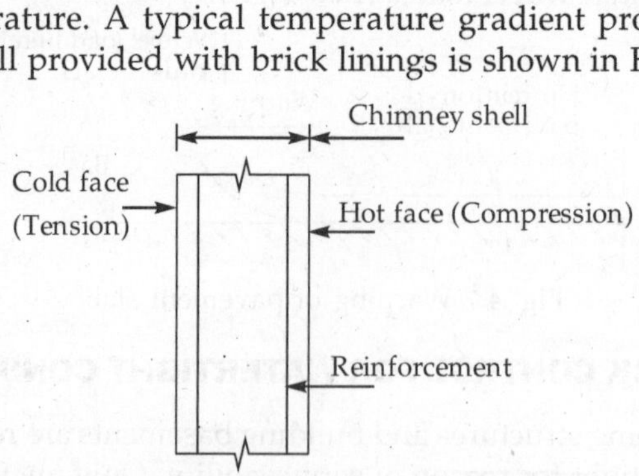

Fig. 4.8 Temperature stresses in a chimney shell.

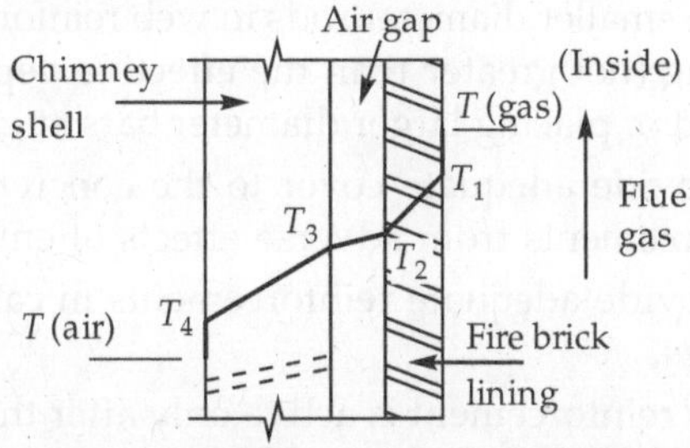

Fig. 4.9 Typical temperature gradient profile of chimney.

Temperature differentials also cause rotation and additional deflection to the structure. In the case of concrete bridge decks, cracks may occur due to thermal gradients and variations during day and night and also seasonal variations during summer and winter.

4.10 DESIGN STRATEGY FOR CONTROL OF CRACKS AND LOCAL DAMAGES

Almost all reinforced concrete structures are now designed by limit state method with use of steel reinforcements in highly stressed condition. However, even under normal working loads, not exceeding their characteristic values, cracks cannot be eliminated altogether from the reinforced concrete sections, unless the design itself is made uneconomical by using steel in a much lower stress range. The primary objective of the designer should therefore be to consider the limit states of cracking and local damages and control the width of the cracks which are likely to be developed. This is necessary not only to retain the general appearance of the concrete but also to protect the reinforcement rods from corrosion. A number of empirical formulae have been developed over the years to calculate in advance the crack widths. However, excessive precision in the crack width calculations do not solve the problem in view of the random nature of the cracks and its wide scatter over the beam section. In order to eliminate or minimize this problem it is the standard engineering practice to adopt the following methods in controlling cracks:

- To use larger number of smaller bars well distributed in the tension region, instead of using smaller number of larger diameter bars.
- To use tension reinforcements in an evenly distributed manner in the tension region to control flexural cracks.
- To use nominal skin reinforcements to control shrinkage cracks in mass concrete structures and machine foundations.

- To use smaller diameter rods in web reinforcements in close spacing (not greater than the effective depth of the beam) instead of placing larger diameter bars at greater distances.
- To provide adequate cover to the concrete to protect the reinforcements from adverse effects of environment.
- To provide adequate reinforcements in case of reversal of stresses.

The shear reinforcement is active only after the shear capacity of concrete is exceeded and diagonal hair-line cracks are formed. Shear reinforcements act as barriers to the extension of the cracks in to the compression zone. As a result, more and more the compression zone can be protected against penetration of the diagonal cracks, if the shear reinforcements are closely spaced.

However, if a beam is overloaded beyond the yield point of the shear reinforcements, shear failure becomes imminent. Such failures should always be avoided by providing adequate extra web reinforcement after correct estimation of the probability of any future overloading.

4.11 SITE MEASURES FOR CRACK CONTROL

Concreting work during summer, if not properly supervised, may invite shrinkage cracks at a very early stage. The development of shrinkage cracks can be effectively controlled during summer by shielding the concrete materials from intense heat of sunlight by erecting temporary canopies over the worksite. To lower the heat of hydration, in critical circumstances, shutters for thin webs of beams may have to be sprayed with cold water even when the concreting work is in progress to avoid the thermal shock at the concrete surface. It is to be noted that the heat of hydration is very high for rich concrete as used for pre-stressed bridge girders. Moreover, since the temperature rise is greater in summer than in winter, the above precautions are all the more necessary during summer concreting work. An effective curing measure should be carried out in all cases, strictly following the norms as per contractual obligations and provisions of codes to minimize both shrinkage and creep strains.

QUESTIONS

1. Explain how homogeneity in concrete is often compromised during concreting and its effect on the behaviour of the concrete member under load.

2. What type of design errors may initiate a sudden failure of a reinforced concrete beam?
3. What is the effect of a large eccentricity of an applied load on a reinforced concrete compression member?
4. What should be the design strategy to ensure a crack-free water-retaining reinforced concrete reservoir?
5. How buckling in a reinforced concrete column can be prevented?
6. Explain why it is not always safe to use reinforced concrete as a tension member.
7. What is the difference between an 'under-reinforced' and an 'over-reinforced' beam section, with respect to their failure modes?
8. Identify the locations where beam sections may fail due to formation of diagonal cracks.
9. How web-shear cracks and flexure-shear cracks can be identified at site?
10. What should be the designer's strategy to avoid bond failure in reinforced concrete members?
11. Write short notes on:
    (*a*) Fatigue failure in reinforced concrete members
    (*b*) Creep in concrete
    (*c*) Shrinkage cracks in floor concrete
    (*d*) Thermal cracks in concrete
12. Enumerate the site measures to control cracks in concrete.

CHAPTER 5

Corrosion and Related Safety Hazards

5.1 INTRODUCTION

Corrosion is generally perceived to be an electrochemical phenomenon which gradually damages metals and alloys when they are exposed to moist atmosphere, aqueous solutions or marine environment. Metals may also be corroded by direct chemical attack in industrial environment. In the construction field, the steel materials in both concrete and steel structures are susceptible to corrosion. In many cases, continued corrosion of vital structural elements during the service life has been found to be the root cause of safety hazards and catastrophic failures. Corrosion appears as a 'silent killer' to structures and propagates in existing cracks of concrete, inside the gaps and holes of expansion joints of bridges, in drain-pipe collars and joints, in honey-combed concrete sections, in thin-walled gutters and in many other elements of a structural system which are exposed to adverse weather conditions or chemicals. Region-wise, corrosion is most prevalent in marine structures and installations along the coastal belts, where the atmosphere is humid as well as saline. The structural distress is accelerated when maintenance is neglected in structures and corrosion is not checked in time. Corrosion accelerates in many cases where, additionally, quality control and good workmanship have not been adhered to during the construction stage. Even otherwise, industrial structures are corroded when they come in regular contact with adverse soil conditions, fumes, gases and chemicals.

Unprotected reinforcement rods of concrete structures and thin sections of structural steelwork are readily attacked and corroded by the moisture present in the air. Iron and steel when exposed to atmosphere are attacked chemically by the moisture resulting in the oxidation of the metal forming reddish-brown rust on the surface. The rust thus deposited on the surface is the product of corrosion, consisting chiefly of oxides, hydrated oxides, hydroxides, carbonates and sulphates of the metal being corroded.

When steel reinforcement rods used in construction works are corroded, the corrosion brings about formation of scales over the surface of the rods and the diameter of the rods increases. If corrosion is allowed to continue over a long period of time, the internal pressure generated due to the swelling of the rods create cracks and fissures in the concrete cover, triggering conditions of further intrusion of water and atmospheric chloride salt inside the concrete and the process of corrosion is accelerated. Such corrosion can also occur if the water used in concreting work contains high concentration of chlorides, sulphates and other harmful impurities.

In coastal areas salinity is quite high and aggressive rusting of steelwork and reinforcement rods of concrete is a common phenomenon. This is because of the presence of a very high concentration of chloride content in the marine environment. This high chloride concentration in the atmosphere is responsible for the formation of rust (which is mostly ferric chloride) in steel causing corrosion of the parent metal. This process is further accelerated in the marine environment due the presence of high humidity in the area.

The process of corrosion is the reverse of the production process of the metal itself. As a result, energy is liberated during the process of corrosion. The extent of corrosion depends on the nature of the environment and the amount and period of exposure of the metal surface to the aggressive environment.

5.2 ELECTROCHEMICAL MECHANISM OF CORROSION

It has already been pointed out that steel, as used in construction work, is corroded through an electrochemical process. When corrosion occurs through an electrochemical mechanism, the area over which the material is attacked is called the anode (steel substrata) and the area from which some substance (surface mill scales) is reduced (to form oxides) acts as the cathode. When the environment contains moisture, it behaves like an aqueous solution around the above cathode and the anode. The combination of the anode, cathode and the aqueous environment constitute a small galvanic cell and corrosion starts with the flow of current in a manner similar to the way current is generated by chemical action in a storage battery on discharge. The process of corrosion continues so long as these factors creating corrosion are active, *i.e.*, so long moisture is present in the environment. There is spontaneous release of energy during the process of corrosion and in the anodic area, which is obviously the area attacked by corrosion, the metal is oxidized and a reddish-brown rust is formed on the surface of the metal. If the rust so formed is spongy, there is a strong possibility of this rust absorbing more oxygen from the moist environment adding to further corrosion. On the other hand, a hard dry layer of rust formed on the metal surface may retard corrosion by forming a protective coating. The process of forming the rust on metal surface is illustrated in Fig. 5.1.

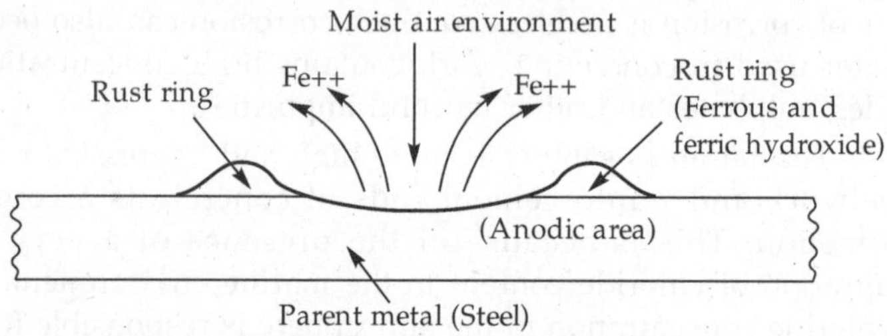

Fig. 5.1 Formation of rust during corrosion.

5.3 COMMON TYPES OF CORROSION

The following types of corrosion are usually observed in the case of steel used in structural steelwork and concrete structures:

5.3.1 Uniform Corrosion

In the case of uniform corrosion, the metal surface is corroded almost uniformly over the entire area. This happens when the metal is under direct attack from acids, which eat and corrode the metal, dissolving it at the same time. In this process the thickness or diameter of the metal reduces gradually until a stage is reached when it loses its load-carrying capacity and fails. Corrosion initiated by acids is noticed predominantly in workshops where acids of storage batteries are handled frequently or in chemical factories or zinc-galvanizing plants. Acid fumes in chemical factories are known to have caused heavy corrosion to steel trusses in many factories.

5.3.2 Galvanic Corrosion

Galvanic corrosion occurs when two dissimilar types of metals (like steel and copper) are joined together and exposed to a corrosive environment. In such cases, the steel acts as anode and the copper as cathode, resulting in corrosion of steel. Galvanic corrosion depends on the electric conductivity of the environment and the ratio of the areas of two metals affected. Galvanic corrosion is likely to create problems in damaged galvanizes sheets, metals provided with electroplated coatings, cladded roof sheets, structures made of metals and alloys of unlike compositions in electrical contact, heterogeneous alloys, soldered and welded structures. Contact between wood and steel material also triggers corrosion in a moist environment.

If dissimilar metals like zinc and steel are in contact, as in cladded sheets, the more active material will provide cathodic protection to the less active metal for a certain length from their point of contact. In the case of zinc and steel, zinc provides the protection to steel. This is the reason of success in providing protection against corrosion in galvanized sheets and galvanized pipes. From experiments a galvanic series of metals (based on their standard oxidation potential) have been fixed from anode to cathode. This is reproduced below:

1. Magnesium
2. Aluminium
3. Manganese
4. Zinc
5. Chromium
6. Steel
7. Nickel
8. Tin
9. Lead
10. Copper

In the above chart, any metal higher in the list will be a more active metal and will be anodic and will provide 'cathodic protection' to any less active metal on the lower rung of the list in a normal environment for some distance from the point of contact. Accordingly, zinc will provide cathodic protection to steel or any other less active metal on the lower rung of the list. For this reason zinc is used extensively for galvanizing of steel sheets, mild steel bolts and other steel products. In the case of zinc and steel, zinc is eventually sacrificed and direct corrosive attack on steel will begin if the protective layer of zinc is damaged at any point.

The above list provides the designer to select proper protective layer for any metal used in construction. The corrosion rate usually increases with rise in the temperature of the environment. As such, corrosion problems are more acute in warmer climates.

5.3.3 Crevice Corrosion

This is observed in a localized form in deep recesses and crevices where oxygen concentrations are usually high. The effect of crevice corrosion is very intense.

5.3.4 Pitting Corrosion

Metal surfaces like plates and angles are pitted due to the presence of impurities and rough spots on the metal. Once pitting starts the process accelerates. Pitting of thin structural sections if left unattended for a long time may lead to perforation of the steel section.

5.3.5 Stress Corrosion

Stress corrosion is the result of corrosion at spots where there is concentration of stress. Suppose a central circular hole of diameter "*d*" is drilled through a plate of width "*w*" and the plate is subjected to a pull "*P*'. (Ref. Fig. 5.2)

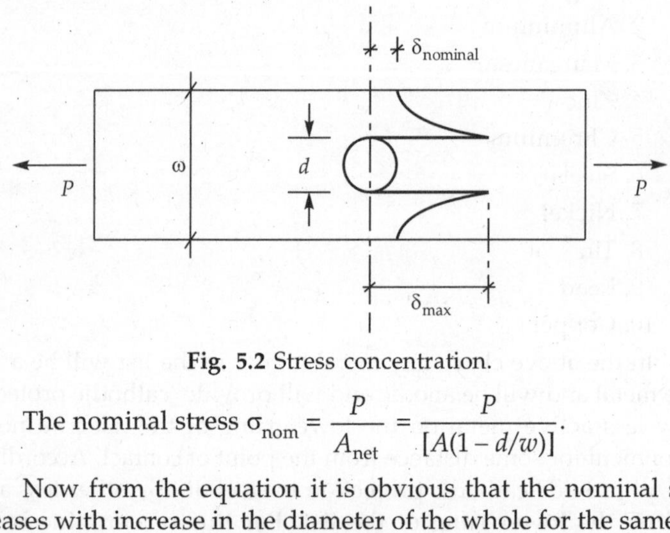

Fig. 5.2 Stress concentration.

The nominal stress $\sigma_{nom} = \dfrac{P}{A_{net}} = \dfrac{P}{[A(1-d/w)]}$.

Now from the equation it is obvious that the nominal stress increases with increase in the diameter of the whole for the same area of the plate. The stress is concentrated at the edge of the hole in the *Y*-direction, where $\sigma_{max} = K \times \sigma_{nom}$, where *K* is the stress concentration factor. It is at this tip of the hole, where the stress attains its maximum value, stress corrosion is manifested and the metal cracks. Stress corrosion also occurs in metals subjected to cold working and quenching during manufacture making the metal more anodic, thus increasing the chance of stress corrosion.

5.3.6 Fatigue Corrosion

When a structural member is subjected to repeated reversal of stress over a period of time, failure may occur even at a stage when the maximum stress does not exceed the elastic limit of the material. Such failures are known as fatigue failures. Again, when a structural member under fluctuating stress is also subjected to sustained corrosion, the member loses its strength very rapidly and it may eventually fail even at a stage when there is no applied stress. This means that, when fatigue is associated with corrosion, no endurance limit can be predicted. These conditions are illustrated in Fig. 5.3.

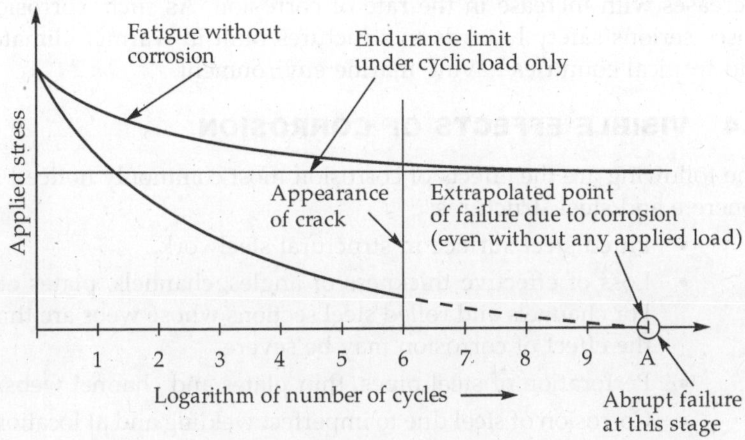

Fig. 5.3 Fatigue corrosion.

From the curves it may be noted that the curve for 'fatigue with corrosion' has a steep fall below the endurance limit (for fatigue only) and it is never horizontal. From the point of initiation of the first crack, if the curve is extrapolated, it will meet the horizontal axis at a point, which indicates the failure condition when the applied stress is zero.

In view of above, for structural members under cyclic loading, fatigue corrosion poses a serious safety hazard as failure may be sudden, when apparently there is no applied load on the member. Generally cracks due to fatigue corrosion start at points of stress concentration at sharp corners, notches and locations where there are sudden changes in cross-sections. These should be avoided during the process of detailed engineering of the structures which are likely to be subjected to fatigue corrosion.

5.3.7 Other Forms of Corrosion

Besides the above cases, metallic structurals may be damaged when corrosion is associated with mechanical wear and abrasion. Cavities on metal surface usually accelerate corrosion. Metals are also corroded and pitted when they come in contact with soils having high acid constituents. Underground pipe lines, conduits and water mains are often damaged in this manner, unless they are given adequate protective covers or coatings.

Moreover, the rate of corrosion increases with temperature. As temperature rises the conductance of the moist environment also increases with increase in the rate of corrosion. As such, corrosion poses serious safety hazards to structures built in warmer climates and tropical countries having marine environment.

5.4 VISIBLE EFFECTS OF CORROSION

The following are the effects of corrosion most commonly noticed in concrete and steel structures:

- Pitted steel surface in structural steelwork.
- Loss of effective thickness of angles, channels, plates etc. For channels and rolled steel sections whose webs are thin, the effect of corrosion may be severe.
- Perforation of steel pipes, thin plates and channel webs.
- Corrosion of steel due to imperfect welding and at locations of stress corrosion.
- Pitting of column bases and reduction in diameter of holding down bolts.
- Corrosion of steel reinforcement rods due exposure to moist atmosphere and seepage of water through cracks in concrete.
- Enlargement of diameter of rods exposed to corrosion, causing cracks in concrete cover and initiation of more ingress of rainwater.
- Spalling of concrete and staining of concrete surface.
- Deposition of rust and scales on reinforcement rods exposed to open weather.
- Cracks initiating failure of thin concrete sections like chajjas and thin walls of water retaining structures.
- Safety hazards due to snapping of tie rods in old jack-arch roofs.

5.5 PRINCIPLE OF CORROSION PREVENTION

Corrosion of steel may be arrested by introducing to the structural system, what is known as 'inhibitors', which may be any suitable substance when added to the environment of steel, would decrease the rate of corrosion. Such inhibitors may be either anodic inhibitors or cathodic inhibitors. Chemicals like chromates, phosphates, silicates etc. are examples of anodic inhibitors to steel. These inhibitors, when added to the steel surface, form a protective coating against corrosion. This principle of using anodic inhibitors has prompted engineers to apply 2 coats of zinc chromate paint to all fabricated steelwork as a standard practice. On the other hand, calcium salt, if added to concrete mix, acts as cathodic inhibitors, diffusing the flow of oxygen, thus reducing the rate of corrosion. However, when concrete is attacked by acid fumes, oxygen itself may act as inhibitors to arrest corrosion. This is because substances that may arrest corrosion in one particular type of environment may stimulate corrosion in a different environment.

The choice of the inhibitors therefore requires considerable knowledge and understanding of the actual state of affairs happening at the spot where corrosion is detected and the cause of corrosion. It is therefore important to prevent localized corrosion or pitting in the first place, instead of trying to bring about a total reduction of corrosion in the system. Structural failures rarely occur due to moderate corrosion, if they are spread over a large area. Failures are more common due to pitting and perforation (of webs of channels and joists or thin plates) due to intense attack in localized areas like inaccessible spots, which are susceptible to the ill effects of aggressive environment to the maximum.

5.5.1 Corrosion Control Measures for Reinforced Concrete Structures

The following precautionary measures should be adopted to arrest corrosion of reinforcement rods and the degradation in concrete:

1. The water used for reinforced concrete work should be free from chlorides, sulphates and other harmful marine salts and samples of water used in concrete should be tested periodically to keep the chemicals and suspended solids within the permissible limits. For Indian conditions the Indian standard code IS:456-2000 stipulates the following permissible limits.

Permissible limits for chemicals and solid in water used for concrete

	Permissible limit (max.)
Organic matter	200 mg/l
Inorganic matter	3000 mg/l
Sulphates	400 mg/l
Chlorides	500 mg/l (For RCC)
Suspended solids	2000 mg/l

Moreover the pH value of water shall not be less than 6 (six).

2. High-Alumina Cement (HAC) may be used in extreme corrosive and marine environment, as HAC is resistant to chemical corrosion.

3. Thermo-Mechanically Treated (TMT) bars or Thermo-mechanically-treated High Corrosion resistant (TMT-HCR) bars may be used as reinforcement.

4. Binding wires should preferably be galvanized.

5. Concrete cover should be at least 75 mm to provide additional safety to the reinforcement rods against corrosion. In marine and coastal areas, the maintenance of an adequate concrete cover should be given due attention during construction.

6. In case of moderate exposure to corrosion, all concrete should be of M-20 grade minimum. Higher grades of concrete should be adopted for sites where the environmental corrosion is more acute.

7. Concrete should be well compacted to make the same as dense as possible.

8. If ordinary Tor-steel bars are used, they should be freed from mill scales, loose rust deposited on the surface. Coats of any oil, paint or soil sticking on the rods must be removed before fabrication is started.

9. In case of sheeting bolts, turnbuckles, tie rods exposed to open weather, the fixtures should be either hot-galvanized or be given protective coats of corrosion inhibitors. Patented phosphate jellies as developed by Central Electro-chemical Research Institute (CECRI) and released by National Research Development Corporation of India may be used for this purpose following the manufacturer's specifications and guidelines.

10. In case the above protective coatings prove to be cost-prohibitive for ordinary concrete work, the standard common practice of giving a cement slurry coating over the bars immediately after cleaning is done. Corrosion during storage can be effectively controlled

in this way. This cement slurry may also be given after using a corrosion inhibitor.

11. The cement surface may be provided with anti-corrosive paint, in case the concrete structure is exposed to any shop-floor acidic exposure.

5.5.2 Corrosion Control Measures for Structural Steelwork

The effect of corrosion on mild steel exposed to moist atmosphere is considered to be mild, when the average rate of metal loss is about 0.12 mm/year and the spread of corrosion is uniform over the entire surface of the material. However, pitting corrosion, crevice corrosion, corrosion of steel in chimney flues and corrosion to steel structures in coastal areas and marine structures (particularly for embedded piles in tidal currents) are usually several times the above rate and the rate climbs to even 0.8 to 1.0 mm per year in many cases. In such cases, it is imperative to keep the rate of corrosion within a tolerable limit so that the structure may not turn out to be unsafe within a few years of its construction.

To keep the corrosion rate within an acceptable limit, the following measures are suggested as a general guideline:

1. The materials selected should be compatible with the environment and corrosion-resistant as far as possible.

2. All steel sections should be allowed extra thickness over the minimum required in structural design to compensate for the anticipated loss of material over the design life of the structure. As for example, there are guidelines in the codes in the design of chimney sections considering the life of the chimney, as any chimney duct is always subjected to intense corrosion during its service life.

3. Detailing of joints should be made keeping access for easy maintenance. Avoid use of back-to-back angles and inverted angles which are likely to retain rain water and initiate corrosion. Holes should be provided in walkway plates for quick drainage of any accumulated rain water.

4. Crevices under bent plates or between overlapping plates should be sealed to prevent ingress of rainwater.

5. Avoid stress concentration or uneven distribution of stresses in structural elements during the design process. Heat treatment of metals used on job should be done as required to relieve the fabricated members of any additional stresses generated during welding.

6. Cracks in welds are major sources of corrosion. In this respect,

the welding guidelines should be strictly followed to avoid such cracks. Proper on-site control should be maintained through radiographic examination to check continuity of welds. In welding work, incorrect profile, craters, splatter, incompletely filled grooves and concave welds are to be avoided, as these are potential spots of corrosion.

7. Use anodic inhibitors for control of corrosion. These include chromates and silicates of sodium and potassium. Select the particular type of inhibitor considering the corrosion environment.

8. Apply protective coating to steelwork. These protective coatings serve as isolating barriers to the steelwork from the corrosive action of moist atmosphere. The protective coatings should be impermeable with good adhesion to the steel material. The performance of such protective coatings depends on the grade of surface preparation, workmanship in application of the coating, thickness provided and correctness in the assessment of the level of corrosion in the atmosphere. Protective coatings are required not only for protection against atmospheric corrosion, but also from shop-floor chemicals, fumes and toxic gases.

To protect steel materials, the following methods are usually adopted:

- Blast-cleaning or wire-brushing the scales
- Application of sprayed coatings
- Hot-dip galvanizing
- Painting
- Encasing by concrete

Blast-cleaning or sand-blasting should be done prior to the start of fabrication and it is to be followed by sprayed coatings of zinc and aluminium. Zinc is widely used, but aluminium sprayed coatings may be necessary in an environment where sulphur compounds are in abundance. For painting it is the most common engineering practice to provide one coat of red oxide or zinc chromate primer of dry film thickness 25 micron (1 micron = 10^{-3} mm) to the fabricated steelwork, followed by 2 coats of synthetic enamel paints (in case of mild corrosive atmosphere) or 2 coats of epoxy-resin chemical resistant enamel paint (suitable for severe corrosion in chemical or marine environment). There are many other types of paints like black paints (for painting underground pipes), chloride rubber paint (for use in industries where acid/alkaline conditions are severe), anti-chlorine anti-corrosive black paint (for drinking water steel tanks) etc. These should be used in specific cases, consulting manufacturer's specifications and method of application.

The encasing of steelwork by reinforced concrete is a very effective method of protecting the same from the corrosive attacks of caustic-soda, acids and other chemicals. Encasing of steel is also effective in marine environment. However, an encasing work adds to the weight of steelwork and its overall cost also, which should be taken into consideration in the design stage.

5.6 CORROSION MONITORING

The condition of an existing structure in a corrosion-prone zone should be monitored periodically to ascertain whether there is any structural deterioration beyond acceptable limit. The purpose of corrosion monitoring is to record the present condition and behaviour of the structure under the influence of corrosion, identify the areas of most active corrosion, recording changes if any, over a period of time and take adequate remedial measures to rectify the defects in order to retain the load carrying capacity of the structure and to avoid any safety hazard.

The following are the broad steps taken in any corrosion monitoring programme:

- Visual inspection to identify the areas most affected.
- Listing the nature and extent of deterioration like, cracks, excessive deflection, stains, lamination, spalling (of concrete cover) etc.
- Assessment of the nature of the corrosive environment.
- Instrumentation by means of resistance probe to quantify the effect of corrosion on each and every structural component and connection, including direct measurement of crack width, excessive deflections (by strain gauges).
- Ranking the corrosion level as mild, severe, most severe, hazardous from safety point of view etc.
- Depending on the above findings, to chalk out remedial measures.
- Implementation of the corrosion protection programme.
- Keeping records for future reference.

In coastal areas, as already mentioned earlier, the level of corrosion is quite high. In marine structures corrosion is particularly predominant at the meeting points of water and atmosphere. Corrosion is excessive at column base plates and holding down bolts in contact with earth and left in unprotected condition. Corrosion due to acid fumes is very common in zinc galvanizing plants, where the thin sections of roof trusses are the most affected by fumes. Moving parts of cranes and derricks under fluctuating loads are susceptible to corrosion. Corrosion effects escape un-noticed in structural joints which are inaccessible. Roof gutters are prone to pitting and perforation due to corrosion unless checked and repaired periodically. Structural sections particularly the thin sections of channels are most affected by corrosion, if they are left in the storage area in un-protected condition for a long time. Sometimes considerable loss is incurred on this account, as the materials are soon found to be un-usable for construction purposes.

The propagation of corrosion is slow but steady in an aggressive environment. The detrimental effect of corrosion is often noticed when it is too late and in many cases complete replacement or emergency repair becomes necessary involving huge cost and interruption in other regular work. A regular maintenance programme, in addition to repair/replacement of corroded parts of a structure, has an important bearing on the prevention of corrosion and safety of the structure during its service life. In this respect proper budgetary support should be given with active participation from the implementing agencies.

QUESTIONS

1. Elaborate the statement: "Corrosion is an electrochemical phenomenon"
2. How does safety of structure is affected due to corrosion in the following cases:
   (*a*) Unprotected reinforcement rods
   (*b*) Steel materials exposed to saline environment
   (*c*) Unprotected steel members exposed to moist environment
   (*d*) Constructions in coastal areas
   (*e*) Industrial structures exposed to harmful corrosive chemicals
   (*f*) Lack of maintenance in thin-walled structural elements
3. What is meant by 'galvanic corrosion'? Explain how zinc provides cathodic protection to steel metal.
4. What is the effect of temperature variations on the rate of corrosion?
5. How corrosion can be detected in steel structural components?
6. What is meant by anodic inhibitors or cathodic inhibitors? How should they be utilized to arrest the corrosion of steel?

7. Describe the corrosion control measures usually adopted in reinforced concrete structures. How corrosion can be prevented in steel structures?
8. What is the usefulness of corrosion monitoring during the service life of a structure?
9. Write short notes on:
   (*a*) Uniform corrosion
   (*b*) Pitting of steel surface
   (*c*) Stress corrosion
   (*d*) Corrosion of steel structures subjected to fluctuating stresses
   (*e*) Effect of fumes of hazardous chemicals on structural steel
   (*f*) Endurance limit against fluctuating loads
   (*g*) Galvanizing of bolts to arrest corrosion

CHAPTER 6

Safety Hazards Due to Excessive Deflection

6.1 INTRODUCTION

The limit state of deflection indicates the eventuality of local damage (or structural failure in extreme cases) due to large deformations occurring to a structure anytime during the construction period or when the structure is used under normal service loads.

Failure or extensive damage may occur if a structural component experiences large deflection incompatible with its strength during transportation, handling or erection. Wrong handling of pre-cast concrete piles, lifting of slender members allowing large free cantilevers or large uncalled-for deflection at the end of bridge girders during cantilever erection are a few examples of such cases.

Excessive sagging of beams may render a floor unserviceable to the user. Sagging of a lintel often causes bending of door and window frames and window grills and also may damage the partitions and finishes, impairing the general look and appearance. In a similar way, excessive deflection of purlins may initiate cracks in the roof sheets, damage to the glazing and other finishes.

Large deflections may occur to vertical upright structures as a secondary effect of differential foundation settlement. This may cause serious damage to the structure.

Corrosion, fatigue or wear and tear may also weaken a structure during its service life, resulting in excessive deflection and eventual failure of the structural system.

In all the above cases, under the influence of excessive deflections, additional internal stresses are developed in the structure and a state of static or geometrical instability may develop. This is a serious hazard scenario, as explained in Chapter 2 earlier, which should be visualized by the designer at the time of proportioning the structural elements and preparing material specifications. Large deflections beyond the limit of tolerance should therefore be prevented by adopting safeguards right in the planning and design stage, considering the load-deflection behaviour of the material used in the structural system, which may comprise steel, concrete or composite materials. Now that more and more slender members are being designed and constructed, considering primarily their limit state of collapse, it has become imperative to calculate the anticipated deflections at critical points of the structure for different critical load combinations during the whole period of the construction and service life of the structure and keep these deflection within the limits of tolerances.

6.2 LOAD-DEFLECTION BEHAVIOUR OF MILD STEEL STRUCTURAL MEMBERS

A typical load deflection curve for mild steel generally used for structural construction work is shown in Figure 6.1. From the curve, it may be noted that the deflection increases more or less linearly as the applied load increases up to the yield load. Thereafter the curve becomes flatter and flatter, indicating occurrence of a large deflection on application of comparatively small load increments, till plastic hinges are developed in the structural system initiating failure of the structure.

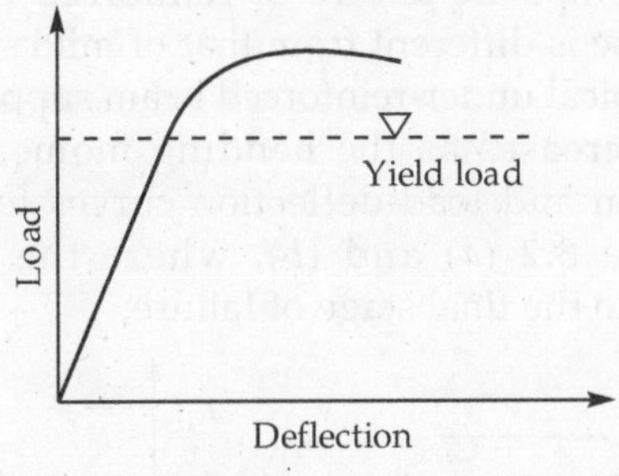

Fig. 6.1 Load-deflection response of mild steel.

In other words, large deflections occur when the actual stresses in a mild steel structural member exceeds the yield stress of the material. This may happen due to various reasons, some of which are stated below:

1. The yield stress may be exceeded due to application of loads larger than the yield load *i.e.*, in common terms, when a member or a structural system is loaded beyond its carrying capacity.

2. The yield stress may be exceeded if the length of a member (either a beam, column or a tie) is too large and the member has a slender cross-section.

3. The yield stress may exceed in case of trussed members, when the span is large, the effective moment of inertia is small (*i.e.*, the members are slender) or the effective depth is inadequate to keep the deflection within the limit of tolerance.

4. The yield stress may be exceeded due to reduction in the effective cross-sectional area of a member due to corrosion and other adverse environmental stresses. This may happen even without any increase in the normal service loads.

It is also to be noted that, at loads greater than the yield load, the structural member does not immediately fail because of the ductile behaviour of mild steel. But the member experiences permanent deformation at this stage and this deformation goes on increasing as the load is increased until the breaking point is reached when failure occurs. It is therefore necessary to ascertain that the deflection in a structural system or in any of its components does not invite permanent deformation at any stage during the construction period or service life.

6.3 LOAD-DEFLECTION BEHAVIOUR OF REINFORCED CONCRETE MEMBERS

Because of the composite nature of reinforced concrete, its load-deflection response is different from that of mild steel. For example, in the case of a typical under-reinforced beam supported at two ends, the curvature increases as the bending moment increases. The moment-deflection and load-deflection curves for such a beam is shown in Figure 6.2 (*a*) and (*b*), where the beam is loaded progressively up to the final stage of failure.

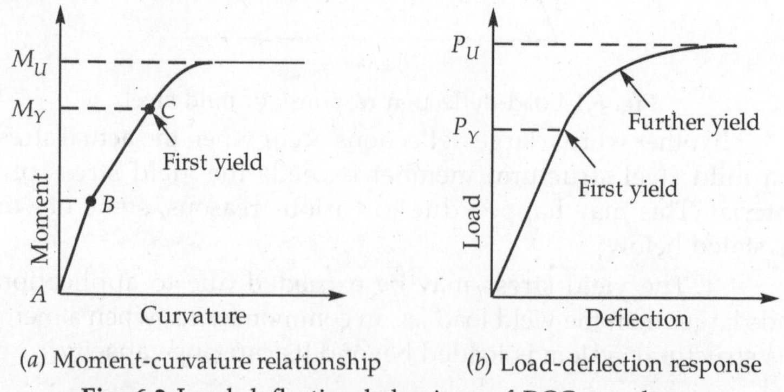

(*a*) Moment-curvature relationship (*b*) Load-deflection response

Fig. 6.2 Load-deflection behaviour of RCC members.

From the curve it is apparent that at the initial stage of loading, the moment-deflection relationship remains almost linear up to the point when the moment increases to a value when initial cracks appear in the tension zone. Thereafter, as the load is increased the moment is also increased and the curvature of the beam becomes more and more pronounced, till a stage is reached when the first yield occurs (indicated by point C in the curve). As soon as the beam starts yielding, large deflections are noticed associated with permanent deformations in the beam. Eventually, with slight increase in the loads, the moment-deflection curve becomes almost horizontal, the deflection becomes excessive and the beam section fails.

6.3.1 Nature of Failures

The failure of a simply-supported beam becomes imminent when the beam behaves as a mechanism with a plastic hinge developed at the point of maximum bending moment in a highly stressed condition. In case of continuous beams, sufficient numbers of plastic hinges will have to be formed on redistribution of moments to convert the beam into a mechanism before the beam finally fails. As such, for the case of indeterminate structures, even after the development of the first plastic hinge some stability can still be maintained, until more hinges are formed to convert the beam to a full mechanism.

However, the time lag between the formation of the first plastic hinge to complete failure is different for under-reinforced and over-reinforced beams. Some time and warnings are available from the point of the first yield to the point of ultimate failure of the beam, if, the beam is under-reinforced and the failure is then termed as ductile failure. On the other hand, if the beam is over-reinforced and is overloaded there is every possibility of a sudden failure of the beam by crushing of the concrete in the compression region. The failure is then termed as brittle failure. Such type of failures occur suddenly without virtually any warning to the user.

The failure is termed as a ductile failure when the **ductility index** (*i.e.,* deflection at collapse/deflection corresponding to first plastic hinge) is greater than 5.0).

On the other hand, the failure is of brittle nature when the ductility index is less than 5.0. No previous warning is noticed in such cases and brittle failures are common when reinforcement percentage is high.

6.4 LOAD-DEFLECTION BEHAVIOUR OF PRE-STRESSED CONCRETE BEAMS

Pre-stressed concrete beams are normally slender and flexible having thin webs and are prone to excessive deflections under load unless the problem is taken care of in the design stage. When a beam is subjected to initial pre-stress, the beam cambers upward and this upward camber increases in course of time due to creep. Later on when the beam carries superimposed dead and live loads, the upward deflection created by the pre-stress is partially or fully overcome. As such, proper attention should be given to the duration of each type of external loads, while calculating deflections for a pre-stressed concrete beam. In most cases, the most significant and bulk of the total deflection takes place while the beam is subjected to dead load plus the sustained part of the live load.

The load-deflection characteristics of a typical pre-stressed concrete beam subjected to camber due to pre-stress is shown below in Figure 6.3.

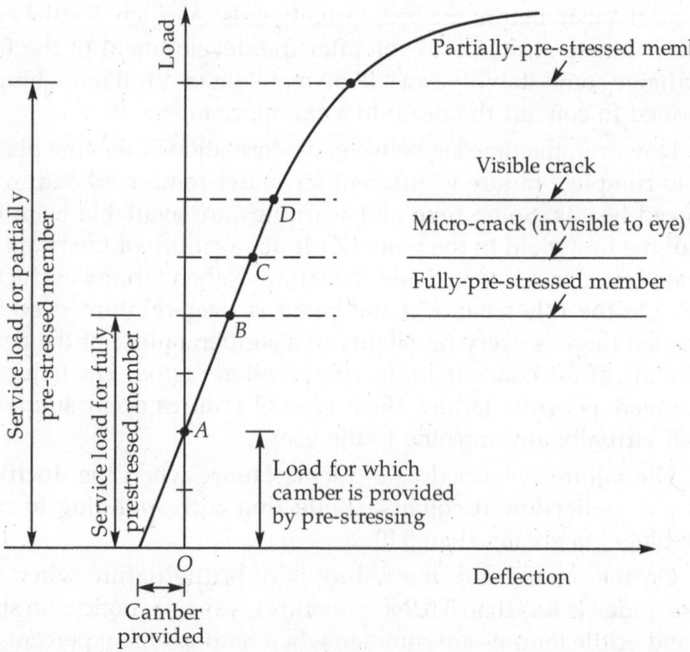

Fig. 6.3 Load-deflection behaviour of pre-stressed concrete member.

From the load-deflection curve it is obvious that the initial camber provided by pre-stressing reduces the net deflection under service load. The point A on the curve indicates the load for which camber is provided by pre-stressing, which may be dead load plus a part of the service load. The net downward deflection at this point is zero. When the beam is eventually loaded with full service load and if the beam is designed as a fully pre-stressed beam, the beam will now have a downward deflection indicated by the point B on the curve. Beyond this stage, micro-cracks, invisible to the eye or visible cracks will appear and the deflections are also high. From the nature of the curve, it is to be noted that the curve is almost linear up to the stage of visible cracking. Beyond this, the deflection increases at a faster rate and the behaviour of the beam is similar to the load-deflection behaviour of a typical reinforced concrete beam.

6.5 CALCULATION OF ANTICIPATED DEFLECTION

The design of a structure is done initially for the most critical limit state, usually the limit state of collapse, considering the values of the characteristic loads, the characteristic strength of materials used in the job and the partial safety factors, as applicable for the load combinations at the particular limit state. The member sections obtained from this initial design exercise are then checked against limit states of serviceability, which includes, among other things, checking of deflections at selected points on the structure, for the most critical conditions likely to occur during the service life.

For structural members carrying vibrating machines, it is imperative to calculate the anticipated maximum static deflection in order to assess the natural frequency of the structural system. In all such deflection calculations the characteristic loads are used directly, without considering any impact factor.

6.5.1. Deflection of Reinforced Concrete Member

In reinforced concrete members, the total deflection is time-dependent and consists of the following parts:

(*a*) Instantaneous deflection under normal service condition due to sustained load and/or heavy short-term load.

(*b*) Long-term deflection due to shrinkage and creep of concrete.

The instantaneous deflection is found out by methods based on the elastic behaviour of the flexural member, considering the time-sequence as well as the relative magnitude of the loads applied during the service condition. The values of the additional long term deflections are usually calculated following the provisions of relevant codes of practices. It is however to be noted that, even after considering so many time-dependent factors in deflection calculations, the error may be as great as 25 per cent. As such, rigorous calculations should be done for long-span structures.

6.5.2 Deflection Limits for Reinforced Concrete Structures

The following limits are generally adopted (with slight variations in different codes of practices) for reinforced concrete members.

- The overall mid-span deflection of reinforced concrete flexural members due to all loads including effects of temperature, shrinkage and creep should not exceed span/250.
- Additional deflection after erection of partitions and application of finishes should not exceed 20 mm or span/350, whichever is less.
- Lateral deflection of tall structures (including piles) should not exceed height/500.

However, for ordinary building structures having short span and light loads, it has been found that deflections are adequately controlled by limiting the span/depth ratio. As such the most convenient approach to control deflection in the design stage will be to calculate maximum deflection for the most critical load combinations and compare with the limiting values specified in the codes. On the other hand, for important members having heavy concentrated loads and long span, it is imperative to calculate deflections at all critical points following the principles of elastic analysis.

6.6 DEFLECTION OF PRE-STRESSED CONCRETE MEMBERS

Most of the pre-stressed concrete members are flexible because of initial and subsequent stages of pre-stressing and pre-stressed bridge girders have very slender webs. These are prone to excessive deflections if not properly taken care of. In addition, when several girders are used for a bridge and they are joined together monolithically by a concrete deck, any excessive deflection in one of the girders will create what is called "differential deflection" on the whole system, which is not at all desirable.

On application of an initial pre-stress to a girder it is common experience that the soffit of the beam shows an upward camber and the dead load is transferred almost entirely at the end supports. The creep and shrinkage effects in concrete ultimately reduces the pre-stress force causing a loss in the pre-stress and a reduction in the camber. Eventually when the girder is subjected to full live and other superimposed dead loads, the upward deflection is wholly or partly nullified. Due to the presence of so many factors, the deflection calculations of pre-stress concrete beams should be done with care.

As a general principle it is customary to add algebraically all incremental deflections that are likely to occur at different periods from the time when the initial pre-stress is applied to the time when, after the final pre-stress, the girder experiences the time-dependent loads, shrinkage and creep effects and changes in material properties. The deflection components thus include the following:

- Short-term upward deflection due to the initial pre-stress
- Downward deflection due to self weight
- Long-term deflection due to loss in pre-stress
- Long-term deflection due to creep
- Deflection due to superimposed load, modified by long-term effect of creep.

The algebraic sum of all the above deflection figures will give the net deflection at full service loading stage. In fully pre-stressed concrete members, at the level of characteristic loads, the deflection calculations are usually done considering properties of un-cracked concrete.

6.6.1 Deflection Limits of Pre-stressed Concrete Members

For pre-stressed concrete members, the final deflection under the effects of creep temperature and shrinkage should not exceed span/250. In addition, when partitions and finishes are installed, the deflection should not exceed span/350 or 20 mm, whichever is less. The deflection due to camber (upward deflection) on transfer of pre-stress should not exceed span/300, if finishes are to be applied. The calculation of deflection at all stages of loadings are a must for all pre-stressed concrete members.

6.7 DEFLECTION IN STEEL STRUCTURES

One of the conditions for limit state of serviceability of steel structures is that the deflection should be so limited as not to impair the strength of the structure or, cause any damage to the secondary members and finishes. For steel structures, deflections are calculated for the most critical combinations of service loads and occasional loads, that may occur during the service period. The deflection is calculated by elastic analysis, using the characteristic load (*i.e.*, partial load factor will be

1.0 always). No impact or dynamic effect will be considered for loads considered in deflection calculations.

6.7.1 Deflection Limits for Steel Structures

The calculated deflection of any structural member should not exceed 1/325 of span. A greater deflection may be allowed if finishes are not damaged and the strength is not impaired.

For crane runway girders, the maximum vertical deflection for dead and imposed loads should not exceed the following limits:

	Deflection
• For manually operated cranes	Span/500
• For EOT cranes up to 50 ton capacity	Span/750
• For EOT cranes over 50 tons capacity	Span/1000

Maximum horizontal deflection due to wind, seismic or other lateral forces should not exceed 1/325 of the height of the column. A greater deflection may be allowed if finishes are not damaged and that the strength is not impaired.

6.8 CONTROLLING DEFLECTION

Large excessive deflections that may occur to a structural system or in any of its components should be assessed in the design stage and designs should be suitably modified if necessary to control such deflection. It is to be kept in mind that it is very difficult to rectify a structure if it is deformed permanently due to excessive deflection. Moreover such permanent deformations are almost always associated with damages to secondary members and finishes and a general degradation in aesthetic qualities.

As discussed in the earlier sections, the span (or height) of a structure, its loading pattern, material specifications, member stiffness and type of structure (steel, concrete, masonry or composite) etc., are contributing factors to creating large deflections either singly or severally. It is therefore necessary to identify and foresee the root causes of any anticipated deflection and take necessary measures in the planning, layout and design of sections. There is no straightjacket rules for doing this job. Only a few principles and methods are stated below.

6.8.1 Changing the Stiffness of the Member

The deflection of a flexural member can be minimized if its moment of inertia is increased. For steel flexural members like plate girders and beams, this can be easily done by adding extra steel material in the form of plates or angles to the flanges. For trussed bridge girders, the effective moment of inertia can be substantially increased by judiciously increasing the depth of the trusses, without crossing the limits of slenderness for the vertical and diagonal members and also by increasing the areas of the top and bottom chords.

For reinforced concrete flexural members like slabs, floor beams or bridge girders, the most easy way to increase the moment of inertia of the member would be by increasing the depth of the member. However, this increases the weight of the member, adding to the deflection and at the same time would decrease the floor height below the soffit level, which may not be acceptable. In such cases adding redundancy or continuity or creating end fixity to the member may help.

The same difficulty arises in case of pre-stressed concrete members if the anticipated deflection exceeds the allowable limit and the problem is compounded as most of the pre-stressed concrete flexural members designed till now are determinate structure without any end fixity or continuity. For such cases excessive deflection can be arrested by suitably modifying the pre-stress force in the design stage.

6.8.2 Adding Redundancy to the Structural System

The deflection at the mid-span of a simply supported beam may be substantially reduced, if partial or full fixity can be developed by proper detailing of the support connections. This can be easily done in both reinforced concrete and steel flexural members. The same effect can be achieved if beams are made continuous.

6.8.3 Optimizing span lengths

Optimizing the span lengths of beams and girders appears to be the best option to control excessive deflection in the service period. However, this has to be attempted right in the planning stage itself. For bridge girders it is extremely important because the whole foundation system, clear waterway and costs are involved in this matter. Before going into detailed design, a proper investigation should be done by doing rough manual calculations to arrive at the most optimum span arrangement, so that clearance during high floods, depth of girders, their deflections and all other associated problems are visualized. In the case of floor slabs, the spacing of columns and beams and their sizes should be optimized so that the deflections do not exceed the allowable limits.

6.8.4 Rearranging Superimposed Loads

In many cases it so happens that heavy machines are placed on a suspended floor in such a way that their supporting beams are heavily loaded and their anticipated deflections would be excessive, unless they are provided with large depths. In such cases effort should be made to relocate and rearrange the machines so as to reduce the beam deflections. Providing additional supports may also help in such cases.

6.8.5 Camber

When large deflections are anticipated (especially in pre-stressed concrete girders and steel bridge girders) because of long span and/or heavy loads, the undesirable effects of large deflections can be avoided by introducing camber (also sometimes termed as pre-camber) to the structure. Such cambers help in reducing deformation stresses when the span is loaded. Cambers are provided to ensure that the structure will retain its theoretical geometric shape under specific loadings for which the camber values are calculated. Cambers are usually restricted to cater for either dead load only or dead load plus partial (50% to 75%) live load. Large cambers are avoided, as they may induce objectionable dynamic response under variable live loads, with the result that secondary members, finishes and partitions are likely to be damaged.

Camber in a pre-stressed concrete girder is provided by initial pre-stressing.

Camber in long-span steel trusses is provided by shortening the tension members and lengthening the compression member to the extent necessary for the load condition for which camber is provided. When such trusses are erected by cantilever erection method, stresses are opposite in the chord and other members. The top chord is then in tension and that requires shortening of the top chord length to control large deflection at the end of the cantilever during the last stage of cantilever erection. This is done by shortening the nominal length of the link members connecting the top chord of the forward span to that of the anchor span without disturbing the cambers already provided to the permanent members.

For roof trusses of shorter spans, a mid-span camber of 1mm per metre length of span is considered to be adequate and no deflection calculation may be necessary, unless the trusses carry heavy loads from monorails.

For long-span reinforced concrete members, it is the general engineering practice to give the forms an upward camber to ensure that the beam does not sag heavily when they are loaded, but such cambers should have proper back-up design. For short-span floor beams of spans 3 metres to 4 metres, no camber is generally provided as deflections under load are almost always within limits under normal floor loads, if the stipulated span/depth ratios are maintained.

6.8.6 Controlling Deflection During Service Period

In-spite of strict compliance to the provisions of the code and proper design and detailing, there are instances of a structural member experiencing excessive deflection during its service period. This may happen due to the influence of several extraneous factors such as:

- Overloading of a structure
- Decay of a structural member due to environmental corrosion
- Unusual wind and earthquake forces not anticipated in the design stage.

Uncontrolled deflection due to the above causes may cause permanent deformation to the structure. If such conditions are allowed to persist, the structure may be rendered unsafe for use, creating safety hazards. If overloading becomes inevitable during some period of its service life, the additional deflection should be controlled by providing temporary supports or by strengthening its members. If there are possibilities of excessive deflection and deformation due to adverse environmental effects, the only remedy will be to arrange for regular preventive maintenance or emergency corrective maintenance to the decaying structure. For unusual wind or earthquake forces, far exceeding the anticipated limits, there is probably nothing can be done to prevent such forces lashing on the structure. However, effort should be made in the design stage to introduce sufficient ductility to the structure, so that damages are kept to the minimum and complete collapse is prevented.

From the above, it is obvious that the task of controlling excessive deflection should be taken up initially at the planning and design stage on assessing the anticipated deflection under service load. Additionally there should be management control in proper handling a structure during erection and also there should be user's initiative to maintain a structure properly during service period. A concerted effort in all these fronts can save a structure or its components from the ill effects of excessive deflection.

QUESTIONS

1. Explain with examples how large deflections are initiated due to corrosion, fatigue, wear and tear, bringing about serious safety hazards to a structural system? When does a structure may fail due to large deflection?
2. What is the effect of corrosion and fatigue on the deflected shape of a structure during its service life?
3. Explain how anticipated large deflections of structural components can be avoided through modifications in the designs?
4. How does excessive deflection bring about static and geometric instability to a structure?
5. Write short notes on the following:
   (*a*) Camber in trusses
   (*b*) Effect of excessive deflections on secondary members and trusses
   (*c*) Ductility Index
   (*d*) Permissible deflection during service life
   (*e*) Time-dependent long-term deflection in concrete beams
   (*f*) Control of deflection in pre-stressed concrete beams
   (*g*) Limit state of deflection
   (*h*) Effect of inadvertent overloading on deflection
6. What is the user's duty in controlling unwanted deflections during the service life of a structure?

CHAPTER 7

Fire Safety

7.1 INTRODUCTION

Fire accidents fall under the category of man-made hazards. Fire hazards may create instability to a structure, even causing a complete collapse of the structural system in extreme hazardous conditions of fire. Usually a fire starts in a limited area and its damaging effects may remain confined to a small area, if the fire is brought under control within a short time. In such cases losses may not be great. However, it so happens, very often, that the fire integrity (*i.e.,* the resistance to fire propagation, heat transmission and spread of hot gases and flames) of the structure is very poor and there is not ample margin or redundancy in the structural system. Also a fire may prolong for a long period in many cases. The overall combined effect may be devastating, causing loss of life and damage to movable and immovable properties.

As no building material is absolutely fire-proof, the designer should visualize in the planning stage the fire hazards likely to be encountered during construction and also during the post-construction service period. The designer should specify the size, dimensions and material specifications in such a way, that the safety of the occupants and users is ensured and damage to structures and its contents are minimized to the extent possible. In this respect, most of the local body regulations insist on fire resistance of buildings in terms of hours, varying from zero to about 4 hours, depending on the use of the building and location with respect to the adjoining existing structures. In fact, fire safety in totality should cover the following aspects:

- Assessment of likely fire hazard and degree of fire resistance required as per fire regulation norms.
- Preventive measures to avoid fire hazard

- Preventive measures against spread of fire
- Adequate provision of emergency exits for occupants
- Installation of fire extinguishing systems
- Emergency plan of rescue operations in case of a fire

7.2 ASSESSMENT OF FIRE HAZARDS

Three types of fire hazards are generally encountered, namely, personal hazard, internal hazard and exposure hazard.

7.2.1 Personal Hazard

In case of a personal hazard during the outbreak of a fire, there are chances of loss of life or injury to the occupants or users. People are often trapped inside a multi-storied building when the main staircase is engulfed by fire and there is no emergency exit. In such circumstances they cannot be evacuated in time and there is every possibility of injury to the occupants with risk to life. Such buildings are considered to have high personal hazard.

7.2.2 Internal Hazard

A building is said to have internal hazard when a fire originating inside the building spreads very quickly from the seat of fire engulfing the whole building. A building stuffed with highly inflammable materials like gas cylinders, paint, jute, timber etc., or constructed with a high percentage of inflammable materials like timber and plastics, is considered to have internal fire hazard. Ducts for air conditioning system also contribute to internal hazard. High internal fire hazards are often closely associated with high personal hazards. Consequently, though highly inflammable materials in large quantities may not be there in theatres, cinema halls or places of public assembly, they are considered to have high risk of internal hazard. On the other hand, a godown stacked with combustible materials will have high internal hazard, but may have low personal hazard, if it is not occupied by persons in a regular manner, except for handling of the contents.

7.2.3 Exposure Hazard

A building is considered to be subjected to exposure hazard, when there is a possibility of the building being engulfed by fire originated from an adjoining building and fanned by wind and flow of hot gases and fumes. Exposure hazard multiplies the losses in a densely built-up area, if the original fire cannot be controlled in time and if the adjoining buildings also have high internal fire hazard.

7.3 FIRE LOAD

The likely intensity of a fire hazard is generally assessed by calculating the 'fire load', which is the quantum of heat in kilocalories (K-cal) which is liberated per square metre of floor area or a compartment due to complete combustion of all the inflammable components and storage contents of the building. The fire load therefore gives an idea of the quantum of combustible material contained inside the building, which is likely to be affected by a fire.

Therefore, fire load

$$= \sum \frac{\text{[Weight of combustible materials} \times \text{Calorific value of the material]}}{\text{[Floor area under consideration]}}$$

and is expressed as k-cal/sqm in metric units or Btu per sft in FPS unit.

Here, the calorific value (or the heating value) of any combustible material is determined in laboratory by burning a one gram sample in a calorimeter. For this purpose, it is the general practice to use the Oxygen Bomb Calorimeter. It is standardized by burning a sample of naphthalene, whose calorific value is obtained from Bureau of Standards.

Sometimes, the fire load is related to the equivalent weight of timber which would be theoretically required to generate the same quantity of heat, assuming the calorific value of timber to be 8000 Btu per pound. In this case, the fire load is expressed as lbs per sft, which is actually the equivalent weight of combustible timber per square foot of the floor area.

Conversions 1 k-cal = 1000 cal = 4186 joules of mechanical energy
1 Btu = 252 cal = 777.9 ft-lb of mechanical energy,

which means, 4186 joules of mechanical energy will be liberated, when converted to heat, the temperature of 1 Kg of water will be raised from 14.5 degree centigrade to 15.5 degree centigrade.

Calorific values of common fuels *Combustible substance*	*Heating value in Btu/lb*
Timber	8000
Anthracite coal	13500
Lignite	6210
Bituminous coal	12330
Coke	13000
Solid fuel mixed with oil	17000
Tar	15000
Alcohol	12390

Conversion: 1 Cal/gm = 1.8 Btu/lb

The temperature-time variation of natural fire at different fire loads of 15 kg wood equivalent per square metre is shown in Fig. 7.1.

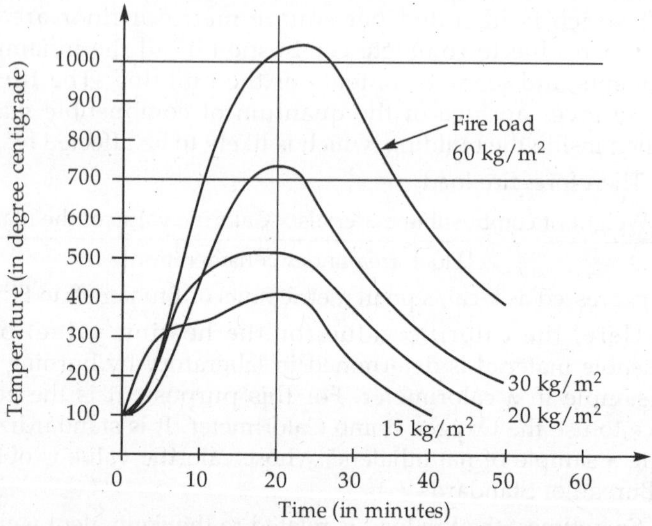

Fig. 7.1 Temperature-time variation of natural fire.

7.4 FLAME TEMPERATURE

A flame is produced through interaction of two or more gases which interact rapidly with emission of heat and/or light. A flame may be either luminous or non-luminous. However, energy is liberated from both of them. In many cases of solid combustible substances such as coke or charcoal, the primary combustion occurs on the surface of the solid. The flame temperature gives the maximum temperature to which a combustible stock is heated by the flame. Theoretical flame temperatures have been calculated for different combustible substances, assuming that there is instant, complete combustion without loss of any heat to the surroundings. However, actual temperatures will always be less than the theoretical flame temperatures, since there will always be some heat loss. Theoretical flame temperatures for a few combustible gaseous fuels are given below.

Gaseous fuel	*Theoretical flame temperature in °C*
Coal gas	2155
Coke oven gas	1888–2127
Oil gas	2188
Natural gas	2060–2116

7.5 IGNITION TEMPERATURE

At ignition temperature a combustible substance ignites and continues to burn without any further addition of heat. This temperature is not definite, as ignition also depends on air pressure, the ratio of combustible gas to air and the size of the compartment and presence of any catalyst, which may lower the ignition temperature. In case of coal, oily rags and some waste products, there may be spontaneous combustion, if heat is slowly dissipated and if there is slow oxidation producing sufficient heat to raise the temperature to the point of ignition.

Grading of buildings by fire load

Based on the anticipated fire load, buildings are usually graded as under:

Type of building	*Expected minimum fire resistance*	*Expected fire load*	*Rating*	*Fire grade*
Domestic buildings, hotels, offices, schools, hospitals, temples, mosques, engineering workshops	1 hour	Not exceeding 2,75,000 k-cal/sqm	Low	4
Trading centers, factories	2 hours	275000–550000 k-cal/sqm	Moderate	3
Godown and similar buildings used for bulk storage of non-hazardous materials and goods	4 hours	550000–110000 k-cal/sqm	High	2
Storage area for hazardous, highly inflammable or explosive substances	6 hours	> 1100000 k-cal/sqm	Very high	1

7.6 FIRE-RESISTANT PROPERTIES OF BUILDING MATERIALS

The fire-resistant properties of a few common construction materials are given below:

Stone. Stone is a non-combustible material, a bad conductor of heat and does not allow spread of fire. But its fire resistance is low, because stone cracks, crumbles, explodes and disintegrates even under a low fire load, if the fire is prolonged. Granite explodes on exposure to heat, limestone crumbles and many other varieties of stones are prone to disintegration when heated and suddenly cooled. Consequently, use of stone materials is limited in fire-resistant structures.

Brick. Brick is a poor conductor of heat and can withstand temperature as high as 1200 degree centigrade for a considerable time under fire exposure. If the mortar strength is high and workmanship is good, brick walls 375 to 500 mm thick built with lime mortar offer excellent safeguard against spread of fire and related fire hazards.

Concrete. Concrete as a material is resistant to exposure to heat and flame, but tends to crack under prolonged exposure. In the case of reinforced concrete, because of its composite nature, the cement, aggregate and the reinforcement rods act differently during fire hazards. While cement initially shrinks on heating, the aggregate expands causing spalling of the concrete surface. These cracks extend rapidly from the surface to the layer of the reinforcement rods and the cover to the reinforcement fails. Reinforcement steel loses about 50% of its strength at normal temperature, when the heat of fire reaches about 500°C and the loss of strength occurs rapidly if the heat of fire is more. The effect is pronounced in the mid-span of beams and slabs, though these beams and slabs do not necessarily collapse, as there is always some fixity at supports and the reinforcements there are at lower temperatures. Because of this the ultimate strength of a beam or a slab under fire load depends on the following factors:

- Adequate cover to reinforcement rods, which checks the spread of the heat
- Quantity of support reinforcement rods and degree of continuity with the adjacent spans.

In the same way a concrete column may buckle under fire load on spalling of concrete and cracking. The buckling is more pronounced in the middle third portion of the concrete column.

Steel. Steel is non-combustible. But it has low fire resistance, because it gets heated rapidly and is a good conductor of heat. There is a marked reduction in the strength of steel, when temperature exceeds 300°C during fire. At 600°C, the yield stress of mild steel reduces to 50% of its value at normal temperature. The fire resistance time of unprotected bare steel sections in common use is only about 15 minutes. However for composite steel sections the fire resistance time increases to about 30 minutes even with a bare steel structural element. This increase in fire resistance is due to the contribution of additional reinforcement bars which are inserted and protected by concrete cover.

For structural steel, the fire rating of 30 minutes may be obtained if the 'section factor' or the 'massivity factor',

$$\frac{F_s}{V_s} < 30 \text{ per metre}$$

where F_s = surface area in square metre of the steel element exposed to fire per unit length

and V_s = volume in m^3 of the steel element per unit length.

However, for standardized steel sections in common use, this condition is rarely satisfied. Hence steel has to be protected if its fire resistance is needed to be increased more than 15 minutes. To achieve a satisfactory result, it is necessary to find out ways and means to:

- alter the section factor
- enhance the stress level
- enhance the grade of steel.

Alternatively, the fire resistance may be suitably increased by adopting redundancy in the structural system, so that adequate safety margin in fire resistance period can be availed during a fire hazard. Continuity or fixity at supports increases the fire resistance of steel beams and columns. A composite floor made of steel beams and concrete slabs or concrete-filled hollow tubular steel sections add to the fire stability beyond 30 minutes.

When fire resistance of steel elements is required to be enhanced beyond 30 minutes, it is the general practice to provide fire protective external barriers to the exposed surfaces of the steel members. A few of the commonly-used fire protection methods are:

- Providing fire resisting paints
- Spraying gypsum, expanded vermiculate or mineral fibres either directly or on a metal lath fixed to the steel.
- Enclosing with gypsum or similar other fire-resistant wall boards
- Encasing the steel structural members with concrete and

nominal reinforcements.

Timber. Timber is a combustible material, which is rapidly damaged by fire, particularly, if the section is slender. But timbers of heavy sections are ignited with difficulty even when they are untreated. Compared to steel beams, large timber beams sawn from dense timber are often more resistant to serious structural collapse in fire hazards. Unlike steel, the expansion of timber when heated is negligible. As a result, timber beams, if simply supported on walls do not push the walls during fire and chances of damage to walls on this account are not very pronounced.

Though timber is eventually completely destroyed on exposure to prolonged fire at temperature higher than 500 degree centigrade, it is rarely found to be necessary to treat it only to improve its fire resistance. In case of timber structures where timber is predominantly used for columns, beams, trusses and floors, more attention should be given to provision of fire-fighting appliances and safeguarding the structure from any inflammable material or accidental fire inside the building.

In earlier times, fire-retardant treatments were usually applied to woodwork meant for construction of ship. In floors made up of timber beams and planks, as in tea garden workshops, it is better to put thicker sections of timber beams at wider spacing than thinner sections at closer spacing.

Cast iron. Cast iron as a material contracts and breaks down in fragments when it is heated and cooled immediately thereafter. Many of the old go-down sheds were made in earlier times of cast iron sections supporting brick jack arches of lime concrete roofs. These cast iron columns, when exposed to fire hazards, have been found to have collapsed during the process of extinguishing the fire, leading to the collapse of the roof structure also. Heating of cast iron followed by rapid cooling is supposed to be the cause of structural failures in such cases. With the advent of steel, cast iron is now rarely used as structural components.

Asbestos cement. Fibrous asbestos is mixed with cement and water and then processed to form asbestos cement. Though asbestos cement has low coefficient of thermal expansion and is relatively incombustible, use of asbestos cement is now prohibited because of its injurious health hazards.

Aluminium. Aluminium is a good conductor of heat and is not at all fire-resistant. Hence its use as roof sheets and side sheets should be limited only to those sheds and buildings, where the anticipated fire load and associated hazards are negligible. Aluminium is extensively used for interior decorations, sliding doors and windows of many office complexes, auditoriums and buildings for public use. However an effective fire fighting system should be developed for these buildings.

Plaster in cement or lime mortar. Lime mortar or cement mortar are non-combustible and renders sufficient barrier to fire risks. Brickwork if constructed with lime mortar can withstand a considerable fire load for a long duration. Plaster in cement mortar gives adequate protection against heat propagation to concrete structural members, if the thickness of plaster is 25 mm or more. Gypsum plaster if used over steel structural elements, offers good fire resistance.

7.7 LIMIT STATES IN FIRE HAZARDS

While designing any structure against fire hazard, two positive limit states of failures should be considered.

- Stability of the structure against complete collapse.
- Fire integrity of the structural system *i.e.,* its capacity to resist fire propagation, heat transmission and spread of hot gases and flames.

In case a fire prolongs for a long time, the ultimate limit state of collapse may reach, when the strength of the fire-affected structural component is reduced below its load carrying capacity. A structure is seriously damaged and approaches a collapse condition, when its limit state of fire is exceeded.

The other limit state, *i.e.,* the limit state of fire spread can be controlled by so designing a structure that its fire integrity is enhanced. It is to be noted that an increase in the fire integrity also halts the approach of the limit state of collapse. As such, planning and arrangement of stocks inside a building, use of proper fire-resistant materials, coupled with good maintenance practice help a lot towards protecting a structure from fire hazards.

7.8 EFFECT OF FIRE ON INFLAMMABLE STOCKS OF MATERIALS

The effect of any fire on inflammable stocks of materials depends on the characteristics of the material, the intensity of the fire load and the duration of the fire. These effects are enumerated below for a few common types of materials which are stocked in store houses.

Materials	*Effect of fire*
Timber	Dry painted wood or sawn timber catches fire very quickly. The effect may be disastrous in the case of forest fires.
Paint, varnishes	Highly combustible: catches fire almost instantly when in touch with flame.
Blasting materials normally used for road work.	Inadvertent explosion may cause fire, apart from explosion-related damages.
Slender steel sections (painted)	Bends on being heated
Oil, turpentine, kerosene oil, petrol, diesel, spirits	Catches fire instantaneously, if contacted with flames.
Oxygen, acetylene gas, LPG etc.	Explodes when the stock comes in contact with flames.
Cotton bales, paper rolls and jute bales	It takes time to extinguish a fire if the stock is large.
Garments	Synthetic garments are more prone to fire than ordinary cotton garments
Furniture	Wooden furniture is prone to complete combustion if they are dry, painted and old.
Fats, waxes, resins, bitumen, rubber etc.	Melts easily under the heat of fire.

In most of the above cases, smoke and noxious gases are emitted during fire, which is fatal to the users of the storehouses and also to the fire-fighters.

7.9 BASIC PRINCIPLES FOR CONSTRUCTION OF FIRE-RESISTANT STRUCTURES

It has already been stated that the fire load of any building comprises mainly of two components, namely, (*a*) heat generated due to complete combustion of all perishable materials stocked inside the building and (*b*) heat generated due to combustion of all inflammable structural components of the building. Obviously, the most ideal solution for fire safety could be attained if a building can be constructed with such materials which would allow a complete burning of all combustible materials stacked inside, without any damage or collapse of any of the structural components. However, no building material is absolutely fire-proof. Therefore such an ideal solution cannot be achieved in practice. As a compromise, therefore, a building or any structure should be constructed with materials of adequate fire resistance and the layout should be so developed that it can exhibit a minimum fire resistance in terms of hours, depending on its occupancy, use and anticipated fire load. For example, a storehouse meant for storing highly inflammable materials should so constructed that it can withstand a minimum fire load of 11,00,000 Kcal per sqm for 6 hours without exhibiting any appreciable damage to property or any risk to life.

7.10 CONSIDERATIONS IN THE PLANNING AND DESIGN STAGE

While the fire load for ordinary residential buildings are low compared to industrial buildings and there is lesser fire hazards because all residences are under the direct control of the owner himself, an ordinary residential brick built house or a low height RCC framed multistory building have low risk from fire hazards. An accidental fire, an electrical short circuit or an inadvertent handling of LPG cylinders often are the primary causes of fire Such mishaps can be averted if the owner is careful and conscious about the use of their kitchen appliances and consequences of a fire. However the situation is quite serious in case of industrial structures, housing store materials of different types. Also they are constructed with materials of very different specifications and the facilities are handled by workers and staff, who may not be careful. Considering all these factors, guidelines have been issued from time to time by regulating authorities and they have also been incorporated in the codes of practices. A few of those guidelines are enumerated below, which should be followed to ensure fire safety of industrial buildings, storage sheds warehouses and other general buildings.

7.11 GUIDELINES FOR FIRE-SAFETY OF INDUSTRIAL BUILDINGS

7.11.1 Location

The storage area should be at least 50 metres away from any railway line, siding or a yard. Highly inflammable or explosive materials, nitrocellulose or jute fibres (having flash point less than 65.5 degree centigrade) should not be stored within residential or crowded urban areas.

The location of the storage sheds and warehouses should have easy accessibility to fire-fighting tenders (they require minimum 3 metre wide roadway alongside the godowns), sources of water supply and safe distance from external fires like furnaces, boilers and chimneys.

7.11.2 Compartments

Each floor of a storage building housing hazardous or inflammable substances should be divided by walls into separate compartments to check the spread of fire. Compartments should be sized as per the following guidelines:

Type of storage	*Maximum size of compartment (floor area)*
A. Shed without sprinkler system	
Single-storey storage building	Not greater than 1000 sqm
Multi-storied storage building	Not greater than 1000 sqm in each floor
Basement	Not greater than 500 sqm
Stair, lifts etc.	To be separated from the main storage area
B. Storage buildings having sprinkler system	Double the areas mentioned above

All these compartments should have solid roof (preferably RCC) and thick masonry walls (at least 250 mm thick). There should be adequate number of fire-proof exit doors (at least two in each floor) and escape routes. The fire-proof doors may be either of the following types:

- Steel plate doors
- Metal cover doors
- Rolling steel shutters

The material specifications, fabrication and installation of such doors should conform to the guidelines laid down by the appropriate local authorities and should be done as per standard engineering practice. These escape doors should lead to corridors, lobbies or staircases, which should have adequate protection against spread of fire. Timber doors should be avoided for compartments storing hazardous materials.

The number of windows should be fixed considering the ventilation required for the material stored. Wired glass panes fixed to steel frames are preferable. No doors and openings are permissible through partition walls separating adjoining compartments. Partition walls are to be provided to segregate or isolate storage spaces from the production area, finishing section, engine room and other storage areas containing hazardous substances.

7.11.3 Height of Storage Sheds

The stack heights inside any storage area should not be so high as to render the stacks unstable and unmanageable during handling. It is the general practice to limit the storage height to 4.5 metres in case of indoor storage, though greater heights may be permissible for non-hazardous materials packed in rectangular shapes which can be safely stacked one above the other.

A minimum clearance of 1 metre should be allowed from the top of the highest storage level to the underside of the roof structure.

It is a good storage practice to introduce a colour band all round the storage godown walls indicating the maximum allowable storage height. When sprinklers are used, the above-mentioned clearance of 1 metre should be between the highest storage level and the underside of the sprinkler system.

For multi-storied storage buildings like cold storages, the height of the building should not exceed 25 metres. Such multi-storied storage houses are to be built only for storing non-hazardous materials like potatoes, vegetables, rice etc. On the other hand, hazardous and extra hazardous goods should be stored only in single storied buildings with heights not exceeding 7.5 metres. Inflammable liquids like kerosene, gasoline, naphtha should be provided with separate outdoor storage facilities with necessary protective arrangements.

7.11.4 Length and Breadth of Storage Sheds

The following general guidelines may be adopted to find out the optimum floor area of a storage shed for effective protection against fire hazards.

1. Internal passages both in the longitudinal as well as in the transverse direction are to be provided at regular intervals, not exceeding 15 metres, so that the total contents of each stack do not exceed 700 cum.

2. A minimum of 2 metre clearance should be maintained in between the walls and the storage stacks. In case the storage area is provided with moving mechanical handling system, the passages should preferably be 2.5 metres wide.

7.11.5 Openings to Walls

1. In case of long rectangular sheds, doors and windows are to be provided to both outer longitudinal and transverse walls at ends of each aisle or passage to facilitate effective operation of water jets in case of emergency.

2. All outer wall openings should have rolling shutters or steel doors wide enough for easy movement of mechanical handling machines. At least two openings should be wide enough for movement of fork lifts and other such mechanical equipments for large stores. Partition walls separating two godowns should be of solid construction with no door or other openings.

3. To minimize accumulation of intense heat and smoke during a raging fire, smoke vents should be provided to roofs of single storey sheds of at least 1 sqm area for each 50 sqm of floor area.

4. All storages should have normal ventilation as required for the comfort of the personnel handling the store materials.

7.11.6 Outdoor Storages

1. When hazardous materials are stored either inside or outside of a storage godown, the outdoor storages should preferably be located at least 15 metres away from the covered godown or warehouse. This provision may be waived or the clear distance may be reduced, if the covered shed is provided with fire-proof doors and shutters. However a minimum distance of 3 metres should always be maintained to facilitate movement of store materials and handling staff.

2. When two warehouses or sheds face each other, the distance between the facing godowns should not be less than 6 metres. If one or both of the godowns contain hazardous materials, the distance between such godowns should be at least 15 metres.

3. Stack height of all outdoor storages should be as low as possible (maximum height not exceeding 10 metres) and the maximum quantity stacked in a lot should not exceed 500 tons.

7.12 GUIDELINES FOR GOOD FIRE-SAFETY MANAGEMENT

In the previous sections it has been discussed how to assess potential fire hazards, fire loads, fire-resistant properties of building materials, effect of fire on inflammable stock of materials and planning considerations for constructing fire-resistant structures. However a good safety management against fire hazards should also include an efficient fire fighting system with adequate machines, equipments and trained staff in order to encounter an emergency fire hazard. To this effect, the following aspects are also needed to be looked into and incorporated in the overall system management.

1. A good and efficient fire-safety management demands that all electrical installations, refrigerating systems and electrical machines, as well as all electrical wirings are well protected against accidental short-circuits, contact with dripping rain water or water from a leaky sprinkler system. All relevant electrical safety regulations and codes of practice should be incorporated alongside general building construction methods to achieve the desired fire-safety in this respect.

2. Adequate number of fire-fighting appliances like portable chemical fire extinguishers (they should be checked periodically and refilled as necessary) and buckets filled with sand are to be installed at regular intervals inside the storage area. It is to be borne in mind that a fire is best tackled at the very onset of the fire when the fire is localized. Ordinary fire extinguishers, if kept in operational mode and if the staff working inside the shed are trained to handle these simple equipments, a greater hazard may be avoided without any substantial loss of assets and storage materials.

3. An automatic fire alarm system conforming to local building by-laws should be installed along with an automatic sprinkler system. These are most helpful for storage spaces which remain closed for most of the time during working hours and rarely visited by people at night.

4. There should be a static water reservoir or a natural source of water like a pond, lake or a perennial river nearby the store buildings in order to meet the demand of water for fire-fighting purpose. For this purpose the demand may be calculated from the following empirical formula, used by US insurance authorities.

$$F = 18 \times C \times A^{1/2}$$

where F = required water in gpm (litre/min/3.78)

1 gallon = 3.78 litres considered here

C = constant varying from 1.5 for wooden structure to 0.6 for fire-resistant construction

A = total floor area in sq. ft (sqm × 10.76)

This demand is to be considered as additional requirement over the daily consumption. The duration of this fire flow is given in the following table:

Demand of water for fire-fighting purpose in gpm	*Duration in hours*
Less than 1000	4
1000–1250	5
1250–1500	6
1500–1750	7
1750–2000	8
2000–2250	9
Greater than 2250	10

The capacity of any storage reservoir should be determined considering the present and future fire flow demand and its duration. Consequently, in a big industrial complex, additional storage facilities may be required for fire-fighting purposes. This demand may be met entirely by pumping out water from deep tube wells or partially from storage reservoirs and balance by pumping. Additional storage facilities, underground or elevated, should be installed in advance to meet emergency demand, which will be an addition to the daily requirement for production and human consumption.

5. For big industrial complexes, where buildings and equipments are spread over a large area, a fire-hydrant system should be installed so that small fires can be tackled easily, without calling big fire-fighting tenders. For this purpose, the spacing and number of fire hydrants are governed by the demand of water for fire fighting, considering a single hose stream having capacity 0.95 cum/min (250 gpm). The minimum area covered by a single fire hydrant is about 40000 sft (3720 sqm) and the required spacing is about 200 feet (60 m). In no case, however, a fire hydrant should be spaced beyond 150 m (500 ft) apart. A normal static pressure of 400-500 KPa (60–75 psi) is recommended for fire hydrants.

Pumps are often used to draw water from fire hydrants through the fire-hose lines. Such motor pumps should have minimum capacity of 1.9 to 5.7 cum/min (500–1500 gpm). Pumps of larger capacities are needed when larger areas are to be included covering community housing. During use, these pumps are connected to the fire hydrants and water is drawn from the hydrant system. A good fire-fighting system usually contains suitably-placed elevated and/or underground water reservoirs connected to the fire hydrant system, with stand-pipe outlets at strategic locations inside the command area.

6. In addition to above, proper house-keeping, surveillance, display boards should be installed indicating what to do in case of a fire, how to call the nearest fire brigade, demarcation of non-smoking zones etc.

7. Lastly, it is necessary to conduct regular fire-fighting drills in large industrial complexes or public gathering areas, so that the fire fighting equipment are in operational mode and the fire-fighting personnel are put on alert. Regular maintenance of fire-fighting equipments, refilling of extinguishers and general vigilance should be a part of an efficient fire-fighting management system.

7.13 FIRE FIGHTING METHODS

As stated earlier, fire is initiated through accidental ignition of combustible materials, resulting in release of heat and flame causing destruction. The presence of air, heat or fuel, either separately or in combination escalate the fire. The combustible materials may be any of the following types:

- Ordinary solid construction materials like wood, plastics, packing materials etc.
- Inflammable liquids like paints, solvents, oil, varnishes, thinners and liquid chemicals
- Live electrical circuits and other electrical equipments connected to live wire.
- Combustible metals like magnesium or titanium.
- Inflammable gases like hydrogen, ammonia, LPG, petrol, furnace oil etc.

The rapidity of spread of any fire depends on the type of the combustible materials affected at a site, their storage environment and the type of construction of the store houses. A fire in the open at a construction site has always a tendency of spreading to adjacent buildings and facilities unless they are contained in an effective way within the shortest possible time. The methods of extinguishing any fire therefore depend on the quick assessment at site the cause of the fire and its damage potential.

Fire may be extinguished by cooling (removing heat), smothering (removing oxygen supply) and starving a fire (stopping supply or removing combustible materials from the spot of fire as quickly as possible). Cooling can be effectively done by using water as coolant. The heat from a fire can be reduced by quick ventilation by opening doors and windows and removing roof slabs above the fire spots. Different types of fire extinguishers are used to smother or blanket a fire in order to starve the fire from supply of oxygen. Lastly, the removal of combustible storage materials from the site helps to reduce the intensity of any fire within a short time. Considering all these factors the following fire extinguishing media are used now-a-days by fire-fighting personnel.

- **Water.** This is the most commonly-used medium of extinguishing a fire. Water extracts the heat and cools the environment. Water jets are used for this purpose with supply from storage facilities or fire hydrant systems. When water is sprinkled on solid combustible materials like wood and pacing materials, the combustible materials are wetted and the temperature falls below their ignition temperature and the fire is controlled.
- **Carbon-dioxide gas.** This is very effective in containing fires in electrical equipments. This is however not very effective in extinguishing fire of solid combustible materials.
- **Foam.** Foam is generated by instant chemical reaction of aluminium-sulphate, sodium bi-carbonate and water, producing carbon-dioxide gas which is helpful in extinguishing a fire. The burning surface can be quickly covered by foam and it is therefore very effective for extinguishing fires in storages containing solvents, paints, oils and varnishes. Foam should never be used over electrical equipments.
- **Dry chemicals.** Sodium bi-carbonate powder mixed with metallic sterates are used as dry chemicals, which are very effective in containing fires of inflammable liquids and electrical equipments.
- **Halon.** Halon is a hydrogenated hydrocarbon gas, which is very effective in breaking the chain reaction from a fire. Halon decomposes into a very poisonous corrosive gas named hydrogen fluoride during use. It is therefore recommended only for use in extinguishing outdoor fires. Only expert trained fire fighters should be allowed to use this chemical, that also by wearing gas masks and taking other body protective measures.

7.14 TRAINING OF CONSTRUCTION PERSONNEL

There is always risk in a fire-fighting operation, however small a fire may be. There are always chances of sudden enlargement of the fire area and also explosion (from chemicals) during fire-fighting operations, if there is an inept handling of the fire. This may cause injury to the fire-fighting personnel. As such an in-depth training is necessary, if major fires are to be handled. For small fires, the staff and workers may be trained to use water or fire extinguishers, which should be made ready for use in times of emergency. Containers filled up with loose sand should be hung from walls at strategic placed at construction sites to extinguish fires as soon as it is noticed. To make an in-house fire-fighting mechanism effective, the following measures should be adopted by the management:

- There should be a fire alarm system at the construction site and the alarm is to be sounded whenever a fire is noticed.
- Immediately after receiving the fire alarm the power supply should be put off from all major equipments.
- Portable fire extinguishers should be put to use with use of sand cover if possible.
- To intimate the fire brigade if there is a big fire.
- Arranging rescue of people trapped in a fire.

It is to be noted that a standard fire fighting strategy should consist of three lines of defensive action, Namely, (*a*) Initial use of portable fire extinguishers (*b*) Use of fire hydrants and automatic sprinkler system, if there is any, and (*c*) Utilizing the services of the trained fire brigade. However, in a construction site, as also in far-off places out of the urban area, the second and the third options may not be available in time and valuable property may be lost due to delay in starting the fire-fighting operations. Moreover, there are always problems faced by the fire brigade personnel in having access to a source of water supply nearby. In view of the above difficulties, **it is always preferable to adopt adequate safety measures at site to prevent fire at any cost.** All the workmen and the staff should be motivated and the project manager should personally see that all combustible construction materials are stored properly, the oil and paints are kept in separate places and explosive materials are stored in specially built storage spaces. Safety drills are needed to keep the staff in readiness all the time. Besides this, all the fire-fighting equipments should be checked and refilled in time. It is to be noted that a little timely attention in these matters may save a lot of money from fire damages.

7.15 ADDITIONAL GUIDELINES FOR DESIGN OF BUILDINGS FOR FIRE SAFETY

The following are some additional guidelines for planning and design of buildings to ensure safety against fire hazards. Two basic principles are to be followed in this respect, namely:

- The architectural layout, entrance and exit locations of the building should be such that the user public can utilize the escape routes during fire and get away from the building as quickly as possible without any loss of life or injury.
- The building structure and the finishes should be built with materials of adequate fire resistance in terms of hours, depending on its occupancy, use and anticipated fire load.

To this end in view, buildings are classified into several categories depending on occupancy, as stated below:

- Residential buildings
- Educational institutions, hospitals and community assembly halls
- Business establishments
- Industrial establishments
- Storage sheds housing mostly non-combustible materials
- Storage sheds housing hazardous chemicals and inflammable liquids

As fire hazards are different in each of the above cases, it would be ideal to segregate them in different zones based on their anticipated fire hazards. While this may be possible while planning for a new township, it is almost impossible to identify fire zone boundaries within an existing building, where some portion of it is used for business purposes, some as storage areas and some for residential purposes as well. This is particularly true in crowded cities where many such buildings are standing for decades and are being used for generations. The safety of the users in such buildings are seriously compromised when hazardous highly combustible materials are stored inside the building and the problem is more compounded when the building is very old, in dilapidated condition and the electrical wirings are fraught with the danger of short circuits any time. The users are also often equally oblivious to their dangers from a fire suddenly started inside the premises. Fire safety inside such types of buildings can only be ensured if the users and occupants are vigilant all the time and maintain basic fire safety norms for their protection.

Suggested fire-safety measures for new buildings

For new buildings, all the above shortcomings can be removed by using the right type of materials in construction and by proper architectural planning to ensure safety of the users from fire hazards. To this end in view, the following safety measures are suggested.

1. For buildings 15 m height or above, non-combustible materials should be used in construction. The internal walls should be of brickwork of minimum thickness 125 mm and the walls around the staircase should be preferably 250 mm thick to ensure a 2 hour fire rating. Hollow masonry walls may be used if the fire is anticipated from one side only. All such internal walls may be provided with 13 mm thick plaster for better performance during a fire.

2. To ensure a **minimum 2 hour fire resistance** the suggested minimum dimensions and concrete cover of structural elements are given below:

Structural elements	*Minimum width*	*Reinforcement cover*
RCC columns	300 mm	40 mm
RCC beams	200 mm	40 mm
Pre-stressed concrete beams	200 mm	70 mm
RCC floors	125 mm	35 mm
Steel columns (encased by RCC) (min dimension 203 mm × 203 mm)		
(*a*) If designed as load-bearing		50 mm
(*b*) Not assumed to be load-bearing but reinforced		25 mm

3. All buildings, irrespective of the type of occupancy, should be planned to satisfy fire safety norms, safety from smoke, fumes and the layout should be such that the building can be vacated by the users immediately after the break-out of a fire without any panic. The local self-government rules, municipal regulations and guidelines of the fire-fighting department should be strictly followed in respect of the following matters.

- Maximum height allowed for the building
- Floor area ratio considering the width of the street and type of occupation
- Open spaces to be maintained for movement of fire-fighting tenders

- Compartmentalization in case of mixed occupancy *i.e.* when a building is used both for business and residential purposes
- Air-conditioning system provided inside the building
- Smoke vents and provision of underground water reservoirs
- Type of doors, windows, glazing and interior finishes used in construction
- Escape routes, staircases, emergency lifts and fire alarms

4. Medium and low-voltage wirings running inside the premises must be of armoured type or run through metal conduits. They should be laid away from any source of fire like oven or gas cylinders. Concealed conduits may also be used for fire safety. All electrical gadgets, meters, distribution boxes and connections to electrical appliances should be properly protected from short circuit and fire hazards following standard electricity rules and regulations. Only approved and dependable appliances and gadgets should be installed.

5. All vertical openings provided in walls for placement of pipes and electrical conduits must be well protected against likely spread of fire from one floor to another.

6. Air-conditioning and ventilation ducts are one the major sources of spread of fire, fumes and smoke, which engulf the whole building in no time, often resulting in death of the occupants due to suffocation. Special attention is to be given to minimize the ill effects of the spread of fire from one floor to another by installing dampers, designed to close automatically in case of a fire alarm. For big departmental stores smoke-sensitive devices should be installed along with air filters and these air handling units for various floors should be separated from one another from fire safety point of view In windowless buildings, smoke vents, designed for natural draft are to be installed.

7. **Selection of wall and ceiling finishes**

The fire resistance ratings of wall and ceiling finishes have important bearing on the overall safety during a fire. A fire may spread very dangerously if the finishes are made of very combustible substances, even if the main structural elements may have good fire ratings. Painted wooden panels, false ceilings made of combustible thin boards and timber doors and windows are the most vulnerable elements in this respect. Finish materials exhibiting very rapid flame spread must not be used in kitchens. Wooden panels joined by bitumen products should also be avoided for the same reason. Wired glass if used, should have a minimum 1/2 hour fire resistance rating. The metal frames, glazing and louvers should be of sufficient strength to have at least 1/2 hour fire resistance. Similar specification should be followed for skylights and monitor openings.

8. **General exit requirements for fire safety**

According to fire safety norms, an exit may be a corridor, internal passage, doorway, internal staircase or a passage leading to an open terrace, roof or the outside street. A horizontal crossover from one building to another adjoining building is also considered to be an exit.

Lifts and escalators should not be treated as fire exits. Small spiral stairs should also not be considered as regular exit.

All exits should be kept neat and clean, free from all obstructions, dumped materials, hazardous chemicals and oils, so that the full area of the exits is available to the occupants during emergency evacuation.

No exit should be utilized for living purpose, be rented for storage of materials and should not be illegally encroached upon by the occupants and these exits should preferably not be kept under lock and key, unless the keys are in charge of security guards on duty and readily available in times of emergency.

All exit points should be properly illuminated. This is particularly important for exits from assembly halls, auditoriums and other public institutions.

The staircases should be preferably of reinforced concrete and should be wide enough for quick evacuation of occupants, particularly for educational institutions and cinema halls.

All exits should be so arranged that they are accessible without passing through other occupied units.

The number of occupants should be pragmatically assessed by the designer to decide upon the number of exits required in a particular building.

The location of the staircases should be so fixed that the occupants may not have to travel/run more than 20-25 metres to reach a staircase in case of a fire alert. As a general guide, it is suggested that at least two staircases should be provided when the floor area exceeds 500 sqm. The design of the staircases, their width, tread, rise, landing dimensions, headroom, handrail details etc. should follow the norms laid down by the municipal authorities.

7.16 SUGGESTED FIRE PROTECTION FOR OLD EXISTING BUILDINGS

In almost every city in the world there are old buildings which are being used for residential, office and business purposes for generations. Many of the old buildings have also been declared as heritage buildings by the municipal corporations, as these buildings are associated with many illustrious persons, national leaders and many of such heritage buildings are of historical importance and exhibit superb architectural facades, All these buildings are needed to he protected from fire all the time. It is obvious that the present consciousness about fire hazards were not prevalent at the time when these buildings were built. But one thing is certain that many of these buildings have stood the test of time against fire hazards and therefore it is incumbent on the present generation to protect these buildings from fire hazards, when they are being used by the owners and the general public. With this end in view there are many rules and guidelines issued from the government authorities from time to time. Some of these are mentioned below:

1. Whenever any repair, addition or alterations are to be done to such buildings, a thorough in-depth study should be made of the structural system of the existing building and the additions, alterations should match with the old ones, Even the materials used for repair work should match with the materials used in the old ones.

2. No major structural changes should be attempted unless it is absolutely necessary for the safety of the old building. All new additions should match with the old system as far as possible.

3. All materials used for repair or renovations should be of sufficient fire resistance in terms of hours as necessary in the particular building.

4. The present users should be properly cautioned about fire hazards due to storage of combustible materials inside these buildings. There should be periodic checks by the concerned authorities and stringent legal actions should be taken against habitual offenders.

5. Many of such old buildings are very large in floor area and the staircases are often found to be quite narrow for proper accommodation of the present number of users. Additional entrance and exit facilities should be built for these buildings. This is more applicable for old temples, mosques and other buildings of historical importance which are visited by hundreds of people everyday.

6. There should be fire alarm systems and security guards to check and prevent any fire hazard.

7. Sufficient quantities of water or a regular water body should be made available to tackle any emergency situation. In short, all these buildings should also be provided with modern fire-fighting arrangements to the extent possible in any particular site,

8. For old buildings, where priceless paintings and other artifacts are displayed for the public view and there are streams of visitors everyday to have a look at them, it is of paramount importance to protect the building, as well as the displayed objects from the onslaught of fire. There are stringent rules and regulations specific for such cases, which should be followed.

9. Inside temples, where candles are regularly used during worship, proper cover is to be provided to prevent any spread of fire. It is a very common mishap that a small fire breaks out somewhere inside such confined places and the fire spreads very rapidly due to wrong-handling of the situation and panic is created among the general public. This should be prevented at all costs, in order to save the building and the public.

QUESTIONS

1. What are the possible reasons of an outbreak of fire inside a building? How a building and its inhabitants are affected by internal fire hazards?
2. How buildings are engulfed in fire due to exposure hazards? What is the effect of an exposure hazard on the inhabitants in a densely-populated area?
3. Define 'fire load'. What is the unit of fire load? How the fire load is assessed for a storage area containing various types of combustible materials? How buildings, godowns and storage areas are rated as per their fire loads?
4. What is meant by ignition temperature? How is it differentiated from the flame temperature?
5. Name a few fire-resistant building materials which can be used for construction of the main frame of buildings in a cost-effective manner? What is the difference in fire resistance between a material which is non-combustible and a material which is a poor conductor of heat? Explain why stone material, being both non-combustible and non-conductor of heat, is not suitable for fire resistant structures? What are the advantages and disadvantages of brick and steel in such cases?

6. What is meant by the limit state of fire hazard? How is it related to the limit state of collapse?
7. What is meant by fire integrity? What is its relation with the limit state of collapse of a structure?
8. What is the effect of fire on structures made of timber or slender steel sections? How do concrete structures respond to fire loads? How unsafe can be a storage area containing paint, varnishes, jute bales, wax and bitumen, if proper fire protection is not provided?
9. What are the personal risks of fire fighters during a fire-fighting operation?
10. How the spread of fire can be checked in a building which is meant for storage of hazardous or inflammable materials?
11. As no building material is absolutely fire-proof, what should the most practical approach in constructing fire-resistant structures?
12. What are the guidelines for fixing the location, size, height for storages meant for stacking highly inflammable materials?
13. What precautions should be taken to build outdoor storages for hazardous chemicals?
14. What is the function of a sprinkler system in preventing fire spread? What should be the maximum size of compartments in a single-storey shed having a sprinkler system?
15. How effective are the steel plate doors, rolling shutters and steel windows in dividing storage areas into compartments? How the partitions are to be designed to check fire spread?
16. What should be the maximum storage heights and side clearances for proper house-keeping considering fire hazards?
17. How openings should be located on roof to check accumulation of heat in case of a fire inside?
18. Explain the effectiveness of the following appliances in a fire-fighting system:
    (*a*) Portable fire-extinguishers
    (*b*) Fire-alarm system
    (*c*) Static storage reservoir
    (*d*) Inter-connected fire hydrants
19. How the water demand is assessed for fire-fighting purposes? How the fire hydrants should be arranged inside industrial complexes for this purpose?

20. Write short notes on the use of the following in fire-fighting systems:

(*a*) Ladders

(*b*) Nets for rescue operations

(*c*) Pumps

(*d*) Stand-pipe outlets

21. How the organization should be geared up in a factory establishment to combat fire hazards?

22. What steps should be taken to avoid fire hazards in old buildings?

CHAPTER

8

Safety against Noise Pollution

8.1 INTRODUCTION

Sound waves may be divided into three ranges, namely,

- the infrasonic range
- the audible range and
- the ultrasonic range.

Audible sounds in detectable frequency domain have frequencies ranging from 20 cycles per second to 20000 cycles per second.

Audible sounds have pitch like quality when frequencies range from 20 cycles per second to 12000 cycles per second.

An infrasonic wave is a mechanical longitudinal wave having frequency below the audible range.

When a sound wave has frequency higher than the audible range it is called 'ultrasonic' sound.

One example of an infrasonic wave is the earthquake wave, which is of tremendous interest to the construction engineer. As these waves are generated from large sources, they often develop tremendous energy on the earth surface to destroy life and property. Audible sound, on the other hand, is pleasant to the ear, when the pitch is not too high and the sound waves are periodic, as in the case of musical notes and sweet human voices.

Noise is created primarily from audible sound waves, when these sound waves are non-periodic in nature and the intensity is too high. Noise is also created on superposition of periodic waves and when a large number of such periodic wave components overlap with each other at the same time.

Therefore, when sound is generated by irregular non-periodic vibrations in the audible range and if it is loud and random in nature, we may call it a noise. The source of a noise may be any of the following:

(*a*) aerodynamic, from air-cooled engines and jet-propelled aircrafts,

(*b*) mechanical, from operation of machines, gear boxes and alternators

(*c*) rolling noise from vehicular traffic.

A noise is also felt if a sound is continued without any respite, as in the case of prolonged hooting of a car horn. An old machine often creates a noisy atmosphere when it is run. In a shop floor when several such machines are run at a time, the noise created is often intolerable to the people working around. They become inattentive to their work, cannot communicate freely with others and often meet with accidents in work places. An extremely noisy environment is often a precursor to accidents during erection of structural steelwork, as workers' attention is diverted and they cannot follow instructions correctly. Excessive noise also reduces efficiency and productivity of workers and they may become hard of hearing on prolonged exposure to such noise.

Noise is generated from vibrations, derived from the mechanical energy of the source. When such noise is generated within a confined room having little or no openings, reverberations may occur due to repeated reflection of the sound waves. This creates additional disturbance to the workers, if the reverberations are allowed to persist for long. In such cases, noise control is necessary so that the acoustic load on the building is kept to the minimum.

8.2 SOUND PRESSURE AND INTENSITY

The base level of sound intensity is generally taken as 10^{-16} watts per sq. cm that is approximately the lowest level of intensity for audibility, corresponding to acoustic pressure of 0.000204 dyne/sq. cm in air at 20 degree centigrade. The faintest sound that can be detected by a good ear creates such pressure. On the other hand, for ordinary conversations the sound pressure is about 1 dyne/square cm. When the pressure increases to about 200 dyne/square cm, the sound is painful to the ear.

However, instead of expressing the sound intensity in absolute terms, it is the general practice to express it as **'decibel'** units in which the relative intensity of sound is expressed with reference to a base level (usually taken as 10^{-16} watts per sq. cm).

Accordingly, if I_1 is the base level intensity and I_2 is the intensity of another sound, the relative intensity in decibel is given by $10 \times \log_{10} I_2/I_1$.

When expressed in terms of sound pressure, as intensity is square of pressure, the relative intensity in decibel is given by $20 \times \log_{10} p_2/p_1$, where p_1 is the base level pressure and p_2 are the pressures of another sound.

From the above expression, it can be shown that, if the sound intensity at its source (*i.e.*, the value of I_2) is doubled, there is only an increase of about 3-decibel units from the base level.

An increase of one decibel represents an increase in the sound intensity to the order of 26%, which is about the smallest change a human ear can detect. There are several methods of measuring the noise level at a particular place, depending on the type of instruments used for the purpose. Mention may be made here of sound level meter, octave band analyzer, magnetic tape recorder, pen recorder and statistical analyzers.

8.3 LOUDNESS OF SOUND

The loudness of sound depends not only on the intensity (or pressure), but on the frequency also. A noise is generated from a broad spectrum of multi-frequency sound waves, which is not linearly proportional to its intensity. Moreover, loudness depends on how a particular person receives a sound as sensitivities vary from person to person. For that reason, a given sound is found to be enjoyable to the person who creates it, but to another person it appears to be intolerably noisy. For a normal human being, a sound having frequency within the range of 20 cps to 20000 cps is audible. As such, any cluster of unwanted disturbing vibrations within the above useful frequency band would appear to be loud and noisy.

8.4 EFFECT OF NOISE IN WORK PLACES

In construction sites and fabrication shops, the environment often becomes noisy due to noises created by old machinery, by people talking loudly from a distance, due to hauling of machines on metal road, due to impact noises created during piling operations and various other factors. A noisy environment, thus created, affects in many ways the progress of the work of other people in the vicinity and invites safety hazards with loss in productivity. Intense noise creates irritability to workers and long term exposure may lead to hearing impairment and nervous disorders. Exposure to high-intensity noise is considered an occupational hazard with adverse effect on normal speech also. An unprotected ear cannot withstand noise level more than 135 dB or an instantaneous sound of more than 150 dB intensity. As the ill effects of noise on the olfactory organs are cumulative, workers at sites should not be exposed more than 60 dB intensity of sound, average 8 hours a day for 40 hours a week.

The circumstances which may lead to a health hazard due to noise should therefore be identified for every construction site, as noise level vary from site to site depending on the location, environment and the construction machinery used on job. Workers in the construction industry are exposed to the following types of noises:

- Jack hammers and compressors in pavement breaking jobs
- Noise from mixer machines and needle vibrators at concreting sites
- Noise from hammers and grinders at fabrication shops
- Noise from pile driving operations in foundation work
- Noise from moving machinery at industrial establishments
- Noise from earth-moving machines, compaction and impacting machines
- Impulsive noise from explosives in road and embankment work

Though it is often argued that noises emanating from construction sites are of short duration, occurring at a particular site, it is to be noted that the construction workers engaged in these jobs are almost always exposed to such safety hazards, so long as they are associated with the construction work.

8.5 EXTERNAL NOISE FROM RAILWAY TRAFFIC MOVEMENTS

The movements of railway traffic create both vibration and noise. Though the ground-borne vibration is generally accepted by the general public, the peak noise generated by the passing trains is disturbing, particularly at dead of night for the people residing near the track. Disturbing noise is also created during shunting, track maintenance and long whistles. Trains moving at very high speeds, more than 80 km per hour create a high-level aerodynamic noise. The usual rail noise level increases by a few db on a concrete tracks and by more than 10 dB on ballast-less tracks on a steel deck. High embankments and buildings shield areas behind, but intensify the noise in front of them. It has been observed that a barrier 2 metre high and as long as that of a train reduces effectively the peak level of noise. Welded rails reduce noise to a great extent.

8.6 EFFECT OF NOISE ON PHYSICAL AND MENTAL HEALTH

A noise at 100^+ dB, people become stressed mentally, their physical control over activities lessen if such noise persists for long, though he may regain his normal faculties within a short time once the noise stops. At noise level 150^+ dB, permanent damage may happen to the olfactory organs, if such high level noises are repeated.

Loud continuous noise reduces the efficiency of a worker, he may overlook warning signals and he is likely to commit mistakes, which may turn to be fatal. Communication becomes difficult when noise frequencies happen to coincide or interfere with the frequency of verbal communication. People residing or working in the vicinity of airports are often disturbed by acoustic loads generated by jet-propelled aircraft engines. Acceptable noise levels for different locations are given below:

Location	*Acceptable noise levels (db)*
Rural areas	25–35
Urban residential areas	35–45
Urban business areas	45–50
Industrial areas	50–65

8.7. NOISE THRESHOLD LIMITS

In consideration to the above factors, various national codes have specified the permissible time limit corresponding to the threshold noise levels. A typical specification is given below:

Sound level (db)	*Permissible duration in a day (hours)*
70	no limit
80	16
85	8
90	4
95	2
100	1
105	1/2
110	1/4
115	1/8

When at any particular place, the noise comprises of two or more periods of permissible noise exposures at different decibel magnitudes, their combined effect should be such that,

$$\frac{C_1}{T_1} + \frac{C_2}{T_2} + \dots + \frac{C_n}{T_n} \text{ should not exceed } 1.0$$

where $C_1, C_2, \dots C_n$ = Duration of a particular noise level in a day
and $T_1, T_2, \dots T_n$ = Corresponding permissible duration in a day

So, if in a work area, noise levels are 85 db for 2 hours and 90 db for 6 hours,

then, $\frac{C_1}{T_1} + \frac{C_2}{T_2} = \frac{2}{8} + \frac{6}{4} = 0.25 + 1.5 = 1.75$ which is much greater than 1.0.

This exceeds the permissible limits. Hence noise is to be controlled in this particular case.

8.8. NOISE CREATED BY IMPACT

For noise created by repeated impacts, as in the case of pile-driving operations, the noise level should preferably not exceed 120 dB and the interval should be not less than three seconds. When several rigs operate at a time, it is however really difficult to maintain this limit of three seconds without slowing down or delaying the operation of one or two rigs.

8.9. CONTROL TECHNIQUE FOR REDUCING NOISE LEVEL

There are three spots where noise should be controlled:

- At source
- Along the transmission path
- At the receiving end

8.9.1 Noise Control at Source

Noise should preferably be controlled at source, where it is produced. This is probably the best solution of noise control. These include several measures, such as:

- Dynamic balancing of the rotating machinery parts, by adjusting the mass distribution of the rotor (either by addition of weight or removal of material). The addition of material is done by addition of wire solder, addition of bolts and washers or welded weights. The correction by removal of weights is done by drilling, milling, shaping and grinding (sometimes by trial and error method). A schematic diagram is shown in figure 8.1 to explain the principle of dynamic balancing.

- Reducing frictional forces between machine parts by greasing
- By resorting to vibration isolation, as shown in figure 8.2.

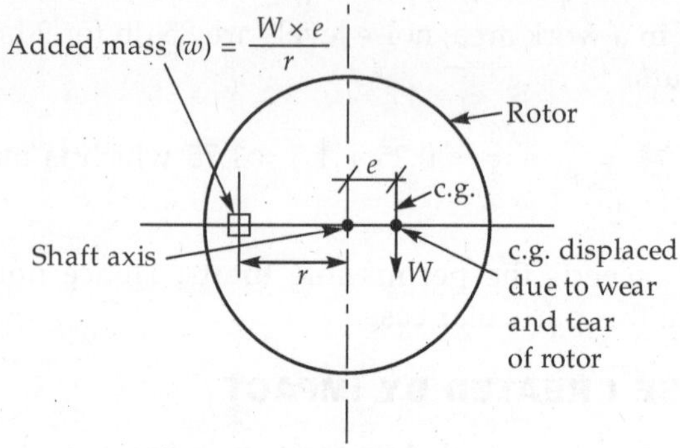

Fig. 8.1 Dynamic balancing.

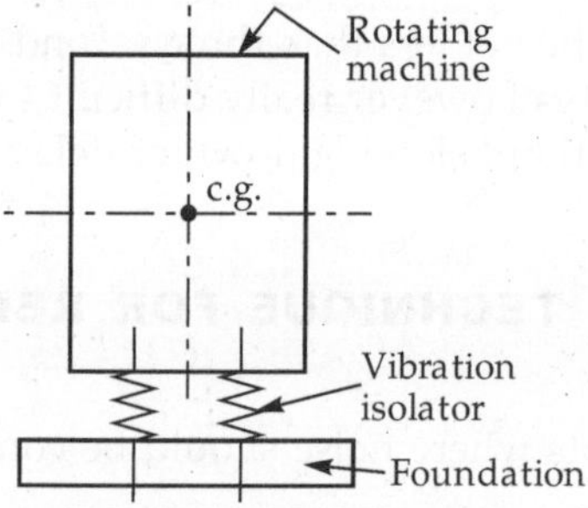

Fig. 8.2 Vibration isolation.

8.9.2 Noise Control along Transmission Path by Noise Barriers

Noises can be controlled along the transmission path, if effective noise barriers are erected. Such noise barriers are very much in use now-a-days along roads where there is heavy density of noisy traffic. Noise barriers are primarily of two types, namely, (*a*) reflective type and (*b*) sound absorbent type. The reflecting type of barriers deflect the noise back to the direction of its source and its transmission through the barrier is minimized. On the other hand, in the case of sound absorbent barriers, there is a dampening of sound due to porosity of absorptive materials used, like, thermocol boards, mineral wool, wood and jute fibre, perforated steel sheets etc. Earth mounds, timber partitions, steel perforated sheets, concrete walls and brick walls are most commonly used as noise barriers. Providing double walls with annular air gaps in between are very effective in arresting noise pollution. Now even transparent polycarbonate sheets, glass or acrylic sheets are also used for the same purpose and these offer in addition good visual appearances. If the top level of the noise barrier is properly curved, a good amount of sound waves may be diffracted also from the top edge of the barrier. The effectiveness of a noise barrier is shown in figure 8.3. Here the noise is reduced, because of the path length difference of $A + B - C$, which is the extra distance the sound travels due to installation of the noise barrier.

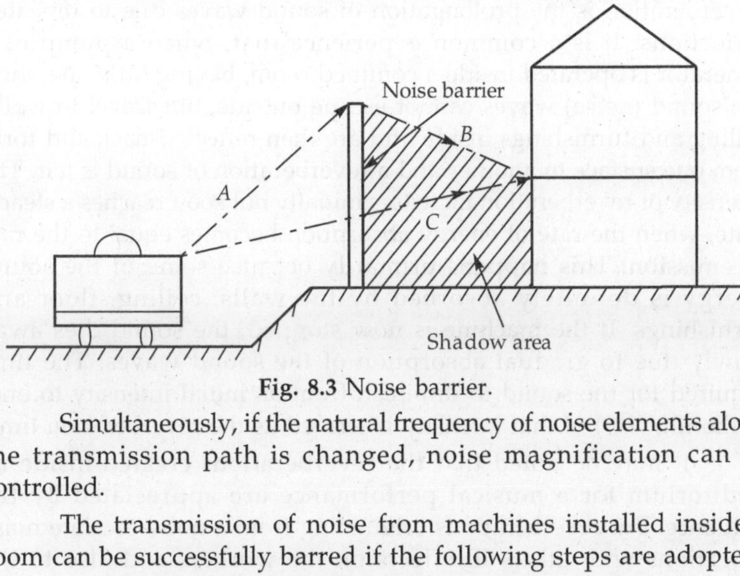

Fig. 8.3 Noise barrier.

Simultaneously, if the natural frequency of noise elements along the transmission path is changed, noise magnification can be controlled.

The transmission of noise from machines installed inside a room can be successfully barred if the following steps are adopted:

- By erecting double walls with air cavity in between
- By installing absorbent materials over the internal wall surfaces and the ceiling
- By installing doors and windows using noise absorbent materials over wood
- By keeping the doors and windows shut during operation of the machine

8.9.3 Noise Control at the Receiving End

At the receiving end, noise can be controlled by use of ear protective measures and prevention against noise exposure by providing protective enclosures around the work place and rearranging the sitting arrangements or by suitable alteration of work place layout.

In addition, changes in the layout of machinery, putting absorptive material guards and partitions at the receiving place and enforcing discontinuities in the noise path would help in noise control. If the room is large, effort should be made to relocate the machine in one corner and provide adequate noise barriers there to control noise. Wooden paneled doors, open windows and provision of absorbent materials on wall and ceiling would certainly help in this matter.

8.10 REVERBERATION OF SOUND AND RELATED SAFETY HAZARDS

Reverberation is the prolongation of sound waves due to repeated reflections. It is a common experience that, when a pump or a generator is operated inside a confined room, having little openings, the sound (noise) waves cannot escape outside, but travel to walls, ceiling and furnishings inside and are then reflected back and forth from one surface to another and a reverberation of sound is felt. The intensity of reverberation increases initially but soon reaches a steady state, when the rate of energy absorption becomes equal to the rate of emission. This happens primarily because some of the sound energy is definitely absorbed by the walls, ceiling, floor and furnishings. If the machine is now stopped, the sound dies away slowly due to gradual absorption of the sound waves. The time required for the sound to diminish from its initial intensity to one-millionth/(10^6) of that intensity is termed as the reverberation time.

It may be noted that the reverberations created inside an auditorium for a musical performance are appreciated by the audience. But reverberations originating from a noise escalate noise vibrations with all its ill effects on the workers and also to the machinery and structures. To get respite from the ill effects of noise reverberation, the optimum period of dieing out the noise reflections *i.e.*, the reverberation time should be brought down to the level of 1 to 2.5 seconds. This can be done in two steps, namely:

Step 1: Assessing the anticipated level of reverberation.

Step 2: Increasing the absorption level of sound by suitably altering specifications of wall and ceiling surfaces, floors and furnishings.

8.10.1 Assessment of Reverberation Time

The reverberation time is directly proportional to the volume of the confined place or room where the noise is produced and inversely proportional to (*a*) velocity of sound and (*b*) total absorption by walls, ceiling, floor and furnishings inside the room. The reverberation time (t) is given by:

$$t = \{2.303 \times 6\} \times [1/k],$$

where $1/k = \text{Constant} \times \dfrac{V}{C \times A}$

where the constant = 4.0

V = volume of the confined place in cubic feet

C = velocity of sound in air = 331.5 m/sec = 1087.32 feet per second

A = total absorption inside the confined place, expressed as 'sabines', (one sabine being defined as the absorption of sound through an open window one square foot in area) = sum of absorptions of interior surfaces and furnishes, where the absorption of each material is the product of its exposed area in square feet by the absorption coefficient (α).

The absorption coefficients of different materials are given below:

Material	*Absorption coefficient* (α)
Open window	1.0
Brick wall	0.03
Carpet	0.04
Cotton curtains	0.05
Felt	0.707
Glass	0.02
Wood	0.06
Plaster	0.03
Adult person	4.0 per person
Seats	0.30 per seat
Cushioned seats	1.0 to 2.0 per seat

From the above table it is obvious that open windows offer maximum absorption, as noise waves falling on the open windows escape outside and are never reflected back.

Putting the values of constants in FPS units,

$$\mathbf{T = 0.05 \times [V/A]} \textbf{ expressed in seconds}$$

Example. *A room 10 feet × 12 feet × 11 feet high is provided with brick walls and RCC roof with a wooden door 3 feet × 7 feet and two windows each 3 feet × 4 feet size. The inside walls and ceiling are plastered by cement mortar. A captive generator is proposed to be installed inside the room. Calculate the expected maximum reverberation time (a) when the door and both the windows are closed and (b) when the door is closed but the windows are kept open. It is assumed that the floor and the ceiling have the same absorption characteristics.*

Solution.

V = volume of the room = 10 × 12 × 11 = 1320 cubic feet

Absorption areas (A)

Item	*Area in sft*	*All openings closed*	*Only windows open*
Walls	484	0.03 × 484 = 14.52	14.52
Ceiling	120	0.03 × 120 = 3.60	3.60
Floor	120	0.03 × 120 = 3.60	3.60
Door	21	0.06 × 21 = 1.26	1.26
Windows	24	0.06 × 24 = 1.44	1.0 × 24 = 24.00
Total absorption		= 24.42	46.98
Reverberation time (t) = 0.05 × V/A			0.05 × 1320/46098
		= 0.05 × 1320/24.42	= 1.40 seconds
		= 2.70 seconds	

Hence the expected maximum reverberation time is 2.70 seconds.

8.10.2 Increasing the Absorption Level of Noise

From the above calculations it is evident that openings have an important bearing on the reverberation time. It is always advantageous to keep all doors and windows open while a machine is being run inside a room, so that noise generated from the machine escapes to outside atmosphere reducing both the loudness of audible sound and reverberation. It may also be noted that the reverberation time depends on the size and volume of the room and the absorption characteristics of the materials and furnishings inside and does not depend on the operational frequency of the machine. As such, the specifications of the wall and floor finishes should be examined and suitably modified and more absorptive materials should be used so that the reverberation time is reduced.

8.10.3 Ill Effects of Noise Reverberation

The most prominent ill effect of prolonged noise reverberation is noticed in case of very old structures. In old dilapidated buildings, having little or no maintenance, plasters occasionally peel off from the walls and ceiling and they are subsequently affected by the adverse effect of corrosion and decay. People working inside feel uneasy when there is prolonged noise reverberation. Sophisticated electronic equipments and computers are likely to be affected because of associated vibrations. Parallel walls provided with reflective materials often generate "standing waves" generated from noise reverberations, which refuse to die out.

For a better building acoustic it is therefore essential to assess in the planning stage the expected range of reverberations when a number of machines have to be run inside a confined workshop area and take necessary steps to minimize reverberation as far as possible.

QUESTIONS

1. What is the difference between a musical note and noise? Explain how noise at work place may create safety hazards.
2. What is the audible range of noise? How noise is created from different sources?
3. What is the base level of sound intensity for lowest audibility? What is the base level of sound intensity for ordinary conversations? How much does it differ from high-pitch noises?
4. Explain the term 'decibel' and explain how decibel units are used to express relative intensity of two sound levels? Prove that, if the sound intensity at its source is doubled, there is only an increase of about 3-decibel units.
5. How noise from a running machine can be controlled at source?
6. How effective are noise barriers alongside highways?
7. Explain how continuous noise reverberations may create safety hazards inside old buildings, housing running machinery. How such reverberations can be minimized?
8. Write short notes on:
   (*a*) Noise threshold limit in work places
   (*b*) Noise isolation
   (*c*) Acoustic load
   (*d*) Noise absorption
   (*e*) Effect of rolling noise from rail traffic
9. What are the likely ill-effects of noise beyond threshold limit on the physical and mental health of people at workplaces?

CHAPTER 9

Safety against Mechanical Shock and Vibration

9.1 SAFETY AGAINST MECHANICAL SHOCK

Mechanical shock is defined as a non-periodic excitation, generated in the form of a pulse, step or transient vibration. There are elements of suddenness and severity usually associated with mechanical shock. Any structure subjected to a severe mechanical shock exhibits significant relative displacements and/or unwanted vibration. It is to be noted that mechanical shock is different from electric shock or psychological (traumatic) shock, though a mechanical sock may trigger an electric shock due to short-circuit or may cause serious trauma to the people affected by damages caused by a mechanical shock. In the following sections the term shock will be used to denote mechanical shock only for reason of brevity.

9.2 TYPES OF SHOCK (OR MECHANICAL SHOCK)

Shock is created by several types of external applied forces, such as:

- Impact or impulsive force
- Forces generated by collision of rigid bodies
- Forces created from blasts or explosions
- Shock waves due to ground motion

Mechanical shock in any of the above forms may create safety hazards to structures and sometimes have devastating effects on people in the vicinity, unless adequate protective measures are taken.

9.3 CHARACTERISTICS OF SHOCK MOTION

A common characteristic of all types of shock motions, as listed above, is that there is an element of suddenness in their application with the generation of a significantly large inertia force on the structure in the immediate aftermath of the shock. Consequently there are changes in the velocity, displacement or natural frequency in the structural system. Accordingly a shock is defined as velocity shock, displacement shock or frequency shock or combined multiple shocks.

9.3.1. Velocity Shock

A velocity shock produces an instantaneous change in the velocity of the target on which the shock is applied and is measured by the change in the velocity. As the duration of this velocity change is very small (to the order of a few milli-seconds), this type of shock is purely impulsive in nature. The acceleration generated from the impulsive force during this small fraction of time is transformed entirely as inertia forces to the structural components and is absorbed in the structural system depending on the flexibility and structural strength. The velocity-time and the force-time diagram depicting a velocity shock is shown in Fig. 9.1 (*a*) and (*b*). A classic example of a velocity shock is the case when a smooth sphere collides with another smooth sphere along the line joining the centers of the spheres. Refer Fig. 9.1 (*c*).

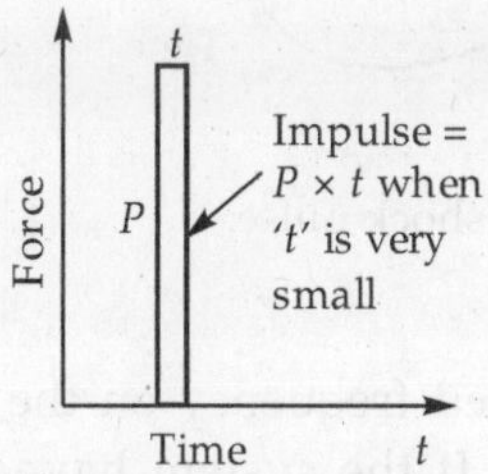

(*a*) Impulsive force causing a velocity shock

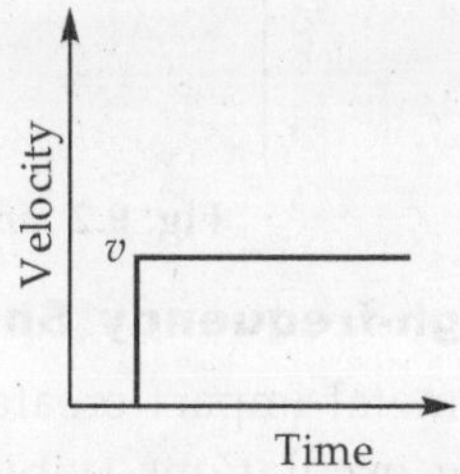

(*b*) Instantaneous change in velocity during a velocity shock

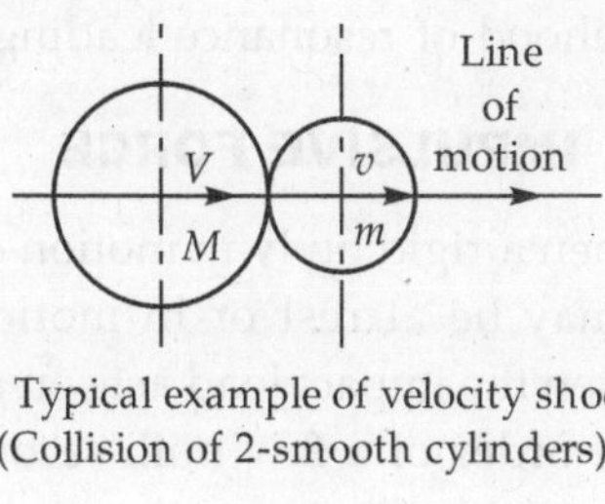

(*c*) Typical example of velocity shock (Collision of 2-smooth cylinders)

Fig. 9.1

Now, if V and v are the velocities of mass M and m at the time of contact and, if V' and v' are their velocities after collision, then by the law of conservation of energy,

Change in momentum

$$= M (V - v') = m (v' - v)$$

In the case impulsive forces the change of momentum is finite, but the displacement during the extremely short interval of application of the force is negligible. Whatever displacement occurs to the colliding bodies occur after the collision due to velocity change.

9.3.2 Displacement Shock

When a shock pulse is sino-soidal in nature (as in the case of a operating rotary machine), the velocity change in the first half of the cycle is cancelled during the second half-cycle and, as a result, the position remains the same as it was prior to the application of the shock pulse. (Refer Fig. 9.2)

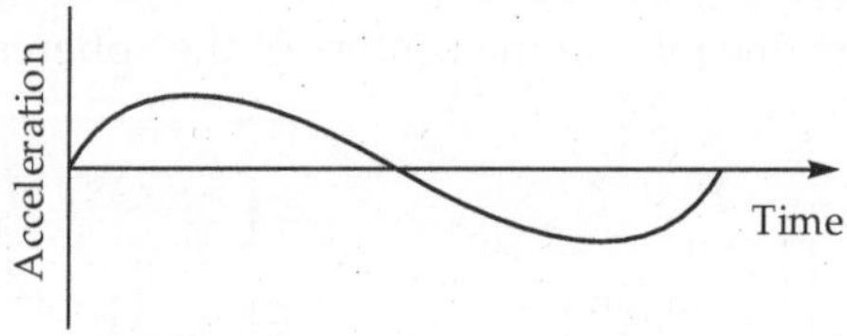

Fig. 9.2 Sino-soidal shock pulse.

9.3.3 High-frequency Shock

Metal-to-metal impact creates induced frequency on the structure exhibiting oscillations (vibrations). If the system have damping characteristics, such oscillations die out rapidly. Otherwise, if the oscillations created converge with the natural frequency of structural system, there is likelihood of resonance leading to safety hazards.

9.4 IMPACT OR IMPULSIVE FORCE

An impact occurs when a rigid body in motion collides with another rigid body, which may be at rest or in motion. The impact is of impulsive nature, when the impact load acts on a small area in a very short duration to the order of a few milli-seconds. Impacts may be 'accidental', occurring without any notice or 'induced' *i.e.*, known beforehand and considered in the structural design of equipments, structural components and their supports.

The occurrence of accidental impacts cannot be eliminated altogether, but with advance precautionary measures their occurrence and damaging effects can be minimized. The most common types examples of accidental impacts are stated below with suggestions for avoiding them.

Nature of accidental impacts	*Suggested precautionary measures*
1. Accidental fall of objects like loose brick, bolts, nuts, spanners etc., from height.	Use safety net below working platform.
2. Accidental rolling of loose boulders and rock from hill top on vehicles and people below.	Avoid steep slope, erect boulder catchers, restrict construction work on hill top.
3. Sudden drop or swing of heavy load during lifting, because of mechanical fault in lifting. devices, worn-out equipments and ropes or due to negligence.	Compulsory periodic checking of wire ropes and other lifting devices and rectify defects. Engage skilled workers in mechanical handling jobs.
4. Sudden collapse of walls, floors or roof of old buildings and structures.	Arrange periodic inspection of old structures, regular maintenance. Retrofit, modify and strengthen, as needed. Demolish if rehabilitation is not possible.
5. Accidental collision	Adopt preventive measures as necessary.

Accidental impact is also associated with blasts, explosion, missile and aircraft strikes on buildings and structures and fall of meteorites. Buildings for residential and public use (*i.e.,* excluding structures for nuclear installations and strategic requirements) are seldom designed to withstand such impacts to avoid prohibitive cost of construction. Instead, it is the common practice to classify all structures according to their importance and utility value and adopt adequate safety factors in the design, so that damages to life and property are minimum during such accidental impacts. However any structure is always exposed to accidental impacts like impact from meteorites, though the probability of such a strike is very low.

Induced impacts, on the other hand, cannot be avoided as the occurrence of such impacts is certain. It is essential to correctly estimate the impact load, the duration and frequency of such impacts and the type of the impact. These are to be taken into consideration in the design of structures with adequate safety factors. A few common types induced impacts are stated below:

- Impact caused by rolling loads like moving vehicles on a bridge
- Impact transferred on soil-foundation system by impact machines such as hammers, drop-weights, crushers etc.
- Impact transferred on piles during pile driving operation
- Impact caused by high-speed water jets on impact or velocity turbines

9.4.1 Effect of Impact on Structures

All impact loads are transient loads acting momentarily on the 'target', which may be stationary or moving slower than the 'missile' causing the impact. An impact is considered a 'hard' impact, when the target is damaged more than the missile. Conversely, an impact is soft, which causes less damage to the target and more to the missile. In other words, if the missile is more rigid than the target, a substantial image may occur to the target. It may therefore be concluded that the damage potential of an impact depends, not only on the energy transferred during impact, but also on the relative rigidities of the missile and the target.

The effect of impact on steel and concrete structures varies widely because of the inherent material characteristics. While steel, being a ductile material, often shows only permanent deformation (excessive deflections in the case of beams, plates and shells), the damage potential to a concrete member is more, because of the brittleness of concrete.

A soft impact on a RCC beam may create only an initial shock, which may spall the concrete cover. On the other hand, a hard impact will create shock waves penetrating deep inside the concrete, resulting in cracking and eventual collapse.

A soft impact on a steel structural member may create only a dent at the point of impact. But in case of a hard impact, a steel member may deform permanently without collapse due to ductility of steel. But the joints of steel members are likely to be hit most, as they are usually not so flexible as the member itself, particularly if the joints are welded. As such, for the same member section a welded member is more prone to damage due to a hard impact than a member bolted at ends.

For accidental impacts it is not expected that a structure will be designed extra strong at prohibitive cost to remain 100% safe against all sorts of possible impacts at all times during construction or in its service life. However, a realistic estimation of all possible accidental impacts should be done and structures should be strong enough to withstand soft impacts that have usually more probability of occurrences. Additionally it is preferable to set up adequate safeguards in the structural system so that energy transference due to impacts is minimized to the extent possible. This is usually done by introducing shock absorbers, shock isolators and similar other energy absorbing devices.

On the other hand, induced impacts cannot be avoided, as in the case of hammer foundations, forging machines and pile driving. For all such cases a proper assessment should be made to find out the following data:

- Nature of the impact
- Duration and frequency of the impact
- The pulse shape and force of the impact
- Energy transferred to the structure or to the soil-foundation system
- Likely response behaviour of the proposed structure

Proportioning of structural members subjected to impact and vibration is usually done by increasing the dynamic load by a suitable percentage and added to the dead load to find an equivalent static load. A constant working stress as applicable for the dead load is allowed in the design.

Thus equivalent static load

= Static load (as per the most critical combination of static and dynamic load)
+ Impact factor
× (Dynamic loads producing impact and vibration)

The impact factors for various types of dynamic loads are specified in Indian Standard Code of Practices, some of which are listed below:

	Structural types carrying dynamic loads	*IS Code reference for impact factors*
1.	For design, manufacture, erection and testing (structural portion) of cranes and hoists	IS: 807-1976
2.	For building structures and foundations supporting lifts, hoists and machinery producing impact and vibration	IS: 875 (Part 2)-1987 IS: 2974 (Part 1 to 4) - (also manufacturer's specifications)
3.	For design of road bridges and culverts	IRC: 6-2000
4.	For design of steel pedestrian bridges	IRC: SP-56-2000
5.	For design of railway bridges	Indian Railways Steel Bridge Code and foundation code

However for design of structures and foundations subjected to dynamic loads and vibrations due to earthquake ground movements, wind, storm and gusts, a detailed analysis is recommended in codes to take care of the complexities of such loads.

9.4.2 Impact Due to Collision

Collision is generally perceived as a violent crash when a moving rigid body collides with another rigid body which may be at rest or in motion.

Collision is always followed by impact, vibration creating safety hazards to structures, property and human lives.

9.5 SAFETY HAZARDS DUE TO VEHICULAR COLLISION ON ROADS

Road accidents involving collision with moving vehicles are very common in our road transport system. Every year more than 60000 people lose their lives and about 3,00,000 persons suffer minor to near fatal injuries and the casualty figures are increasing every year. Rash driving, collision with vehicles running in the same lane from the other direction, attempt to overtake from the wrong side, overtaking in an inappropriate moment, sudden application of brakes to save cyclists and pedestrians, bad illumination at night and bad road conditions are some of the major factors contributing to increasing number of accidents with loss of lives and property. Sometimes a particular stretch of a road becomes more accident-prone due to cumulative effects of several factors mentioned above. It is therefore necessary to remove the bottlenecks in the highway network and devise ways and means to ensure safety of the road users. The following are some of the most commonly adopted measures that should be considered in this respect.

- Separate lanes for slow moving vehicles and demarcated lanes for cyclists and pedestrians are a must to reduce vehicular collisions
- Proper road signs for both the moving vehicles and pedestrians at crossings
- Provision of footpaths in crowded areas
- Removing all obstructions from the existing footpaths
- Installing traffic signals at important crossings and monitoring the same
- Pedestrian refuges at vulnerable pedestrian crossings
- Improving road conditions, filling up potholes and providing drainage
- Providing fencings and crash barriers alongside major highways
- Providing footbridges and/or subways at cross roads with high pedestrian traffic.
- Strict enforcement of traffic regulations, drivers' training and checking of vehicles
- To check overloading of vehicles
- Awareness campaign of road users

From the above long list, it is evident that vehicular collisions can be avoided only if concerted efforts are given by all concerned road users and the administration and if adequate road safety measures are considered right from the planning and design stage.

9.5.1 Safety Hazards Due to Collision inside Work Places

The condition is somewhat different inside work places at construction sites. Here collision related accidents occur due to several reasons such as:

- Accidental flying off of machine parts from a running machine and hitting persons nearby.
- Rolling of a heavy object along a slope and hitting below. This happens occasionally while loading and unloading logs from lorries.

- Accidental collision of a vehicle with permanent structures inside a factory complex. This happens if the clearance for negotiating a vehicle round a corner is inadequate or, at times, when the driver is unmindful and negligent.
- Accidental swing of loads while being lifted by wire ropes.

In all such cases it will be seen that lack or absence of supervision, lack of maintenance of vehicles and equipments are the main factors contributing to such safety hazards and effort should be made to eliminate them.

9.5.2 Safety Hazards Due to Ship Collision

Collision of floating vessels with bridge piers and superstructure often creates serious safety hazards, which need to be considered in the design stage. Such collisions occur primarily due to lesser headroom under the bridge during high tide, strong undercurrents around the pier or inefficient negligent handling of the vessel.

There are instances of shipping vessels hitting the underside of a bridge during high tide. One such instance is that of an accidental collision of the mast of a vessel hitting the underside of the deck of Howrah Bridge at Calcutta a few years back during high tide, as a result of which the mast of the vessel got stuck to the bridge bottom and a portion of the underside structural members got damaged. It was not possible to extricate the vessel easily due to the high tide and ultimately the mast had to be cut off to release the vessel. This incident happened because the vessel tried to negotiate below the bridge at a spot where the clearance was not adequate. There is record also of moving vessels hitting a railway bridge pier, damaging the pier and superstructure and twisting the railway track. These are cases of accidental collisions. On the other hand, a collision is allowed to occur in a controlled manner whenever a vessel is berthing to a jetty. This is done to ensure the safety of the jetty and its supporting structures.

In all the above cases, the kinetic energy of the floating vessel is transferred as an impact force and dissipated to the bridge pier or the fender system in various manners like:

- Conversion of kinetic energy to potential energy for gravity structures
- Through compression, bending, shear and/or torsion in case of elastomeric fender system
- Conversion of kinetic energy to friction
- Permanent deformation of fenders of expendable type

The magnitude of the impact force depends on several factors like: mass and velocity of the vessel, angle of impact, wind current, wave action etc. For evaluating the damage potential of a ship collision it is essential to assess the likely magnitude of the kinetic energy and the corresponding impact force transferred to the pier or the fender system.

The kinetic energy absorbed by the pier or the fender system is usually calculated by the following formula:

Kinetic energy (E)

$$= (\tfrac{1}{2} \times m \times v^2) \times C_1 \times C_2 \times C_3 \times C_4$$

where m = mass of the vessel = vessel displacement tonnage/g $= DT/g$

v = velocity component normal to the pier, varying from 1.0 to 3.0 m/sec.

C_1 = reduction coefficient accounting for vessel rotation during impact, varying from 0.5 to 0.8

C_2 = coefficient for added entrained mass of water in front, usually taken as 1.05

C_3 = shape factor for pier, varying from 0.8 to 1.0
For solid piers and bulkheads = 0.8
For piers shorter than the vessel length = 0.9
For pile-supported jetty and dolphins = 1.0

C_4 = stiffness coefficient for hull and fender system, varying from 0.9 to 1.0

For calculating the corresponding impact force transferred to the pier, the following empirical formula is generally used:

Maximum and minimum impact force ($P_{max/min}$)

$= (0.88 \times (dwt)^{1/2})$ plus/minus (50%), expressed in Mn

where dwt is approximately = 0.75 × displacement tonnage of the vessel $= 0.75 \times DT$

Since kinetic energy is equal to work done and if all other losses are neglected,

K.E. = Average impact force × damage length (Refer Fig. 9.3)

Or, $E = \tfrac{1}{2} \times P_{max} \times$ damage length

Or, damage length anticipated $= E/[1/2 \times P_{max}]$

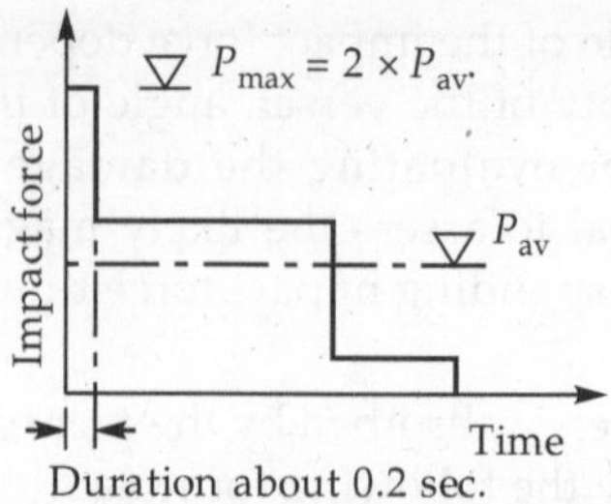

Fig. 9.3 Impact due to ship collision.

While a floating vessel collides with a bridge pier at an angle (Refer Fig. 9.4), the longitudinal component of the force parallel to the face of the pier causes damage to the pier surface due to friction and rubbing.

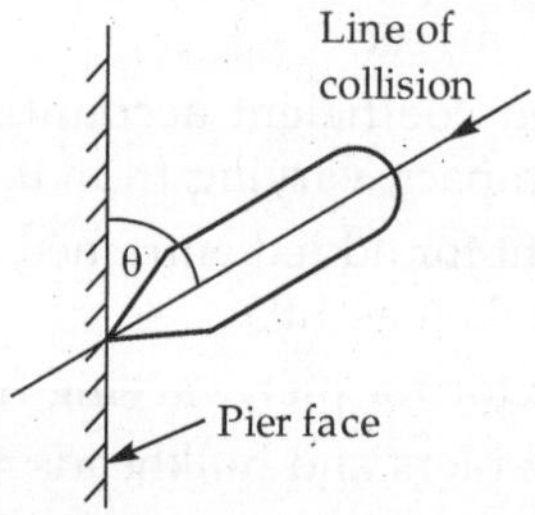

Fig. 9.4 Floating vessel colliding with a bridge pier at an angle θ.

This frictional force (F)

$$= \text{Coefficient of friction } (\mu) \times \text{maximum normal impact force } (P_{max})$$

$$= \mu \times [0.88 \times (dwt)^{1/2} \times 1.50]$$

where μ = coefficient of friction as under:

Steel to steel = 0.15

Steel to concrete = 0.35

Steel to wood = 0.65

dwt = displacement weight of the floating vessel in tons

While designing the fender system, the pier is considered to be rigid and its deflection is neglected, except in the case of fenders connected to single pile substructure, as in the case of lighting towers usually supported on big diameter single piles.

Example 1. *Calculate the impact force and kinetic energy transferred to the fender system when a floating barge of displacement weight 1800 t hits a round bridge pier normally at a velocity of 2.0 m/sec. The force acts* *for a short duration and there is no damage to the foundations except for spalling of concrete and dislocation of the superstructure slightly. Calculate also the theoretical damage length of the pier.*

Solution. For the barge,

$dwt = 0.75 \times$ displacement weight

$= 0.75 \times 1800t = 1350t$

Impact force $= 0.88 \times (dwt)^{1/2} + - 50\%$

$= 0.88 \times (1350)^{1/2} + - 50\% = 48.5/16.17$ MN

Kinetic energy transferred

$= ½ \times (1800/9.81) \times (2.0 \times 2.0) \times 0.5 \times 1.05 \times 0.8 \times 0.9$

$= 138.72$ MN-m

Since the duration of the impact is very small,

Average impact force $= ½ \times P_{max} = ½ \times 48.5 = 24.25$ MN

Theoretical damage length on pier

= (Kinetic energy transferred)/(max. impact force)

= 138.72/24.25

= 5.72 metres. **Ans.**

This value may be checked from the damage caused to the pier to ensure the correctness of the assessment of the impact.

Example 2. *Calculate the extent of damage that may occur to the pier mentioned in example 1, if the velocity of approach is 1.5 m/sec.*

Solution. Maximum impact force, as above = 48.5 MN

Kinetic energy transferred in the present case

$= ½ \times [(1800/9.81) \times (1.5 \times 1.5) \times 0.5 \times 1.05 \times 0.8 \times 0.9]$

$= 78.0$ MN-m

Hence the anticipated damage length in this case

= 78.0/48.5 = 1.61 metres **Ans.**

Please note that the overall berthing coefficient in the above example

$= C_1 \times C_2 \times C_3 \times C_4$

$= 0.5 \times 1.05 \times 0.8 \times 0.9$

$= 0.378$ (approximately 0.40)

i.e., about 40% of the total kinetic energy is absorbed by the pier. Some designers take the value of overall berthing coefficient as 0.50 for preliminary design of the pier and fender system.

9.5.3 Safety Measures Suggested to Avoid Ship Collision

Accidental collisions by floating vessels with piers, waterfront structures and port facilities may be avoided by taking suitable protective measures such as:

- By adopting suitable protective measures around the piers and structures
- By providing suitable fender system to the jetty structures
- By providing better piles to those structures that are supported on piles
- By providing a rigid bulkhead to take the collision impact
- By demarcating specific lanes for movement of vessels of different displacement tonnage
- Introducing guidelines for safe negotiation of vessels
- Introducing night signals
- Design of the jetty fender system to take the desired impact from vessels likely to be berthing there.

9.6 SAFETY HAZARDS DUE TO BLASTS AND EXPLOSIONS

Blasts and the related hard impacts and collateral damage to structures and human beings are frequently encountered in work places, in residential homes and construction sites. We often associate blasts with only sabotage and arson. But blasts and explosions may also happen due to many other reasons, some of which are mentioned below:

- wrong handling of equipments like boilers
- wrong storage of hazardous explosive materials
- Carelessness on the part of the people concerned
- Wrong handling of explosives used for rock excavations
- Inadvertent mixing of cold water to highly heated steam
- Bursting of LPG cylinders at home due to negligence in handling
- Bursting of oxygen cylinders at work site

Blasts are almost always followed by deafening noise, fire, impact due to the blast and damage to structures and human beings. Blasts also happen if hazardous chemicals get ignited inadvertently.

It is to be noted that, all kinds of blasts and explosions should be avoided and workplaces and structures should be as safe as possible for the safe working and use of all concerned.

9.6.1 Types of Blasts

Blasts may be classified into three broad categories, such as:

- Underground blast
- Blast inside a closed chamber
- Blast in open air

Underground blast. In well sinking operations, underground blasts are done in certain circumstances in a controlled manner to expedite sinking of an well, when all other regular methods of well sinking fails because of adverse soil conditions. Such underground blasts induce excitation in all directions below ground and the intensity of the blast is directly proportional the amount of charge put in. To ensure safety of the structure underground, the velocity generated by the underground blast should not exceed 50 mm/sec for soft rock and 70 mm/sec for hard rock. The anticipated velocity is calculated from the following empirical relation:

$$V = C \times [W^{2/3}/d]^{1.25}$$

where V = velocity in mm/sec

C = soil coefficient (800 for soil and soft rock and 1400 for hard rock)

W = weight of the charge in kg of TNT

d = distance of charge in metres from the point of blast

The above velocity should not be allowed to exceed the allowable limit for the safety of the structure underground.

Blast inside a closed chamber. Blasts of LPG cylinders in residential places, blasts of oxygen cylinders, blast of chemicals in workplaces and mine blasts are common examples of internal blasts. An internal blast increases the temperature inside the closed chamber, resulting in an instant increase in the air pressure, obeying the gas laws. An internal blast is mostly followed by propagation of fire and gaseous fumes, which cannot be immediately controlled because of its suddenness. The extra pressure generated lingers inside the closed space, the duration of which is somewhat longer than that of a blast in open air. As a result, damages to property and burn injury to the people around are always extensive in an internal blast. The pressure is eventually released through vents and openings if there are any. The cooling effect of the confining walls also helps in reducing the blast pressure.

Since the damage potential of an internal blast is very large, stringent preventive measures are to be taken in residential homes, hospitals, schools and work places. Open flames from candles, negligent smoking or a simple electric spark may create an internal blast, if there are leaks in the containers of the combustible materials or if the gas outlets are kept open inadvertently. Stringent safety measures are to be taken by all users to prevent accidental internal blasts and connecting valves and gadgets are to be checked periodically without fail. Manufacturers' safety manuals should be followed and warning notices are to be displayed prominently at work places. All combustible materials should have proper storage facilities as per standard practices.

Blast in open air. The shock waves generated by an open-air blast moves at supersonic speed and the effect on a structure is maximum at the spot, nearest to the origin of the blast. Consequently the effect varies from point to point and extents of damages also vary from one part of the structure to another part. The shock wave is reflected away from the structure that causes a reverse shock wave. An open air blast is accompanied by a wind gust, which causes intense dynamic pressure in the form of a pressure bulb on the structure, though its duration may be short-lived, as an open-air blast decays exponentially with time. Leaving aside sabotage, an open air blast can originate due to negligent handling of equipments, like boilers or during the transportation of combustible materials like petrol, diesel and LPG. Accidental collision of such transport vehicles with other modes of transport have caused serious deadly open air blasts in many cases.

Blasting during rock excavation. Excavation work in hard rock is often expedited by blasting. However there are safety hazards in rock blasting unless stringent precautionary measures are adopted. Some of these measures that are contractually obligatory on the part of the contractors are stated below:

- The contractor should have a valid blasting license and he should engage competent licenced blaster to do the job.
- All area inside a 200 metre radius from the blasting point should be cleared of all persons not related to blasting and this area should be demarcated by red flags.
- Firing points should be covered by MS plates with adequate dead weight over the same.
- No more than 6 holes are to be set off at a time and all charges are to be placed firmly by wooden tampers only. The charges must not be rammed or pounded.
- Holes for the charges should be drilled by pneumatic drills and charges are to be fired electrically from a distance.

- No blasting work should be done within 30 metres of any existing structure without examining the fallout of such operations
- No blasting is permitted within 24 hours of any concreting up to a distance of 100 metres.
- Blasts should tally with the number of charges placed. If they do not tally, the misfired charges should be located within ½ an hour after blasting and this unexploded charge should be blasted by drilling a new hole not nearer than 600 mm from the misfired charge and exploding a new charge.
- Adequate storage facilities are to be provided for the explosives.
- No explosive should be brought at site of work in excess of what is actually needed for a particular firing operation.
- Safety in blasting operations should follow the guidelines given in IS: 4081-Safety code for blasting and related drilling operations.

9.7 SAFETY HAZARDS DUE TO GROUND MOTION

Ground motions caused by earthquakes also induce shock waves on a structure. As the time, duration and intensity of an earthquake cannot be predicted with certainty even with the help of the most sophisticated instruments, damages caused by an earthquake cannot be prevented altogether. Effort therefore should be given to minimize the damages to life and property by proper proportioning of structural components considering the most likely intensity of earthquakes that may have to be encountered at a particular place. There are guidelines in national codes giving maps of seismic prone zones based on data collected from previous earthquakes and their statistical analysis. Structures are to be designed considering their importance, height and required safety for a particular structure. This aspect will be discussed in more details in a separate chapter.

9.8 SAFETY AGAINST VIBRATION

All types of shock waves create vibrations in a structure. Vibrations are also transmitted from running machines, vehicles and locomotives. Intense vibrations are often felt from the noise created by a jet aircraft flying low over a building. Operators experience vibrations through their hands when they operate power tools and riveting appliances.

When all such vibrations are transferred to structural components and their foundations, to equipments positioned nearby and to other sensitive instruments, there is likelihood of damages if the vibrations cross the threshold limits of tolerance. Vibrations may affect vital organs of human beings if they are exposed to intolerable vibrations frequently or for long durations.

All equipments and their supporting structures should therefore be designed to withstand a reasonable level of vibration so that they can be safely used without any undesirable consequences

9.9 MECHANICS OF VIBRATION

Vibration in a structural system involves a complex interaction of externally applied oscillations with the inertia of the structure, its elastic rebounding capacity and damping due to friction and material characteristics. There is also an additional interaction with the soil mass below a foundation below the foundation, when a foundation supports a vibrating machine. When a system vibrates freely, it tends to vibrate at one or more of its '**natural frequencies**'. If there is an imposed excitation, the system then undergoes a '**forced vibration**' or forced oscillation. Again, when the imposed excitation is periodic and continues over a long period of time, the system oscillates under a '**steady-state**' condition. '**Resonance**' occurs when such a steady-state oscillation coincides or comes very near to the natural frequency of the system. A resonance is accompanied by large amplitudes and internal stresses, leading to failure of the structural components in extreme cases. Even if there is no structural failure, the application of an oscillating force may magnify the normal static deflection significantly and damage the finishes and minor components.

9.10 NATURAL FREQUENCY

The natural frequency of a structural system is the frequency of its free vibration, which occurs when the structural system is free from all restraints or excitation. The degree of freedom in a structural system indicates the number of independent displacements which are possible in absence of any externally applied loads (which include moments, torsion and oscillatory loads also). A block foundation supporting a machine may be visualized as having 6-degrees of freedom, having 6 natural frequencies, each one corresponding to each of the degrees of freedom or mode of vibration. (Refer Fig. 9.5).

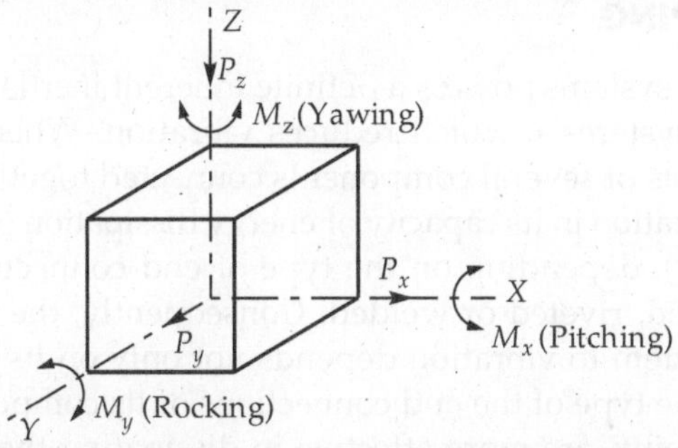

Fig. 9.5 Six degrees of freedom of movement of a block foundation

It may be noted that 2 or modes may be 'coupled' together during the operation of a machine or they may be 'de-coupled' also. There are separate natural frequencies for each of the individual modes of vibration and also separate natural frequencies for the coupled modes. That is, a system may have a number of natural frequencies at which the system may oscillate even in the absence of any external force.

9.11 RESONANCE

Resonance occurs when the operating frequency of a machine coincides with any of the above natural frequencies of its foundation system. The natural frequency of vibration of a floor system may contain a wide range of frequency spectrum because of its structural arrangement. Consequently it is likely that, when such a floor supports a number of vibrating machines, one of their operating frequencies may coincide with any one of the natural frequency of the supporting system. In case of a rigid floor supported by rigid supports, the amplitude of vibration may be small, but the vibration may damage the settings of machine tools and computerized measuring instruments. On the other hand when vibrating machines are installed and operated on foundations on ground floor, a part of the underlying soil also vibrates along with the machine. This soil-structure interaction may sometimes disturb the bearing capacity of the soil which should be considered at the design stage.

The oscillations created by a machine vibrating in a steady-state condition are instrumental to the transfer of a temporary storage of strain energy in the vibrating structural components. In case of resonance condition, the accumulation of this strain energy eventually may lead to such a high level that the machine parts may be seriously damaged.

9.12 DAMPING

All structural systems possess a definite inherent inertia and property of material hysteresis, which reduces vibration. When a structural system consists of several components connected together, it exhibits a marked variation in its capacity of energy dissipation (or, 'damping', as it is called), depending on the type of end connections, whether they are bolted, riveted or welded. Consequently, the response of a structural system to vibration depends not only on its mass/inertia, but also on the type of the end connections of its components. Bolted and riveted joints are more effective in dissipating the stored strain energy of vibration, because they permit slippage at joints. The damping effect of welded joints is less than that of a bolted or riveted joint, but more than a solid piece unit. Again, the damping characteristics of a rigid-jointed concrete structure are different from a steel structure Typical values of effective damping are given below for different types of construction.

	Type of construction	*Effective damping (η) (fraction of critical damping)*
Steel:	One piece unit	0.01
	Welded assembly	0.02
	Riveted assembly	0.03
	Bolted assembly	0.04
Concrete:	Rigid frame	0.05

Effective damping (η) is a fraction of critical damping, which is the minimum damping required by a vibrating unit to return to its initial position without oscillation. The inverse of the fraction of critical damping ($1/\eta$) is proportional to the amplification at resonance condition. The value of $1/\eta$ gives an idea of the severity of resonance and related safety hazards. From the above table, the relative damping response of different structures can be visualized and the designer may modify the design and end connections to suit the required objectives. This modification can be done in several ways. A few of the most popular methods are listed in the following section.

9.13 METHODS OF CONTROLLING RESONANCE VIBRATION

The safety hazards from resonance vibration can be tackled through appropriate combination of several steps during the design stage, as explained below.

1. Resonance in a structural system may be avoided by adjusting the size, dimension and weight of the equipment and its supporting structures, including the weight of the foundation, so that the calculated natural frequency of the structural system is at least 20% away from the operating frequency of the machine. That is,

f_n should be beyond the spectrum 0.8 f_{op} to 1.2 f_{op}.

where f_n = calculated natural frequency of the system
and f_{op} = operating frequency of the machine.

As for example, if the operating frequency of a machine is 1500 rpm, the natural frequency of the support system should be either less than 0.8 × 1500 = 1200 rpm or more than 1.2 × 1500 = 1800 rpm. In general it may be pointed out that, heavier the foundation, less will be the natural frequency. Consequently the designer will be tempted to adopt as heavy a foundation as possible, which would involve cost. The cost becomes prohibitive if several machines are to be installed in such a manner. On the other hand, a light-weight foundation may have its natural frequency well above the operating frequency, but it may not be admissible to reduce the weight of a foundation beyond a certain limit for other reasons. Under this constraint it is advisable to choose the base area, the overall weight, the bearing area provided for the machine considering the dynamic response of the soil underneath. A few trials may have to be made in this regard to arrive at a cost-satisfactory solution satisfying the functional requirements.

2. Resonance condition in a structural system is often avoided by introducing vibration isolators (also called vibration mounts) in order to put an impedance to free transference of vibration from the machine to the support structures.

3. In many cases resonance is avoided by introducing in the structural system any one or more of the following energy dissipation devices such as:

- Auxiliary mass dampers
- Dynamic balancing of the rotating parts of the machine, particularly for old ones
- Inserting viscous damping materials sand-witched between the rotating parts and their supports

9.14 VIBRATION ISOLATORS

All vibration isolators are basically resilient supports available in the market in various shapes and sizes and are used to control and isolate shock and vibration. Vibration isolators are also called vibration mounts. The main purpose of using such isolators are:

- To isolate the supporting structure or foundation from shock and vibration originating from external dynamic disturbances
- To protect sensitive equipments and accessories which are prone to damage or failure due to external vibrations. The selection of a vibration isolator depends on the correct identification of the nature of the dynamic disturbing force which are again classified into 3 categories, namely:
- **Periodic vibration** which may be of continuous sinusoidal type or acceleration at discrete frequencies.
- **Random vibration** created out of vibrations having different frequencies, direction of application and different amplitudes (also having phase differences)
- **Transient vibration** created by shock, which produces a sudden non-periodic effect which suddenly changes the velocity, acceleration and displacement.

It is to be noted that vibration amplitudes are usually less than shock amplitudes. Consequently, a small isolator may suffice to control vibration, whereas, a larger one with more internal free space, may have to be chosen for absorbing shocks.

9.15 MATERIALS USED IN ISOLATORS

Different types of resilient materials are used in the manufacture of isolators. A particular isolator is called by the type of material used. Common types of such isolators are:

- Elastomeric isolators
- Plastic isolators
- Metal springs
- Air (pneumatic) springs

The stiffness and damping characteristics of any isolator determine the effectiveness of the isolator to isolate shock or vibration.

9.15.1 Elastomeric Vibration Isolators

Rubber is both elastic and viscous and is termed as elastomer in the raw state. When rubber is vulcanized, additional chemical bonds impart stability, strength and resilience. Elastomers may be of natural rubber or synthetic (artificial) rubber compounds. Some of the common elastomers which are used as vibration isolators are:

- Natural rubber
- Butyl rubber
- Neoprene
- Poly-ethylene-propylene
- Polysulphide
- Silicone rubber

Natural rubber is very popular as shock and vibration absorbers for machines because of its inherent resilience and low cost. Rubber has low modulus of elasticity and can withstand a deformation as large as 1000 per cent. It also exhibits substantial internal damping and a great capacity of withstanding high stresses and storing energy. The inherent damping property prevents excessive vibration amplitude at near resonance condition. Rubber does not corrode and does not require lubrication under vibration. However the use of natural rubber is restricted sometimes due to its limited resistance to hydro-carbons, ozone gas and high ambient temperature.

On the other hand, synthetic elastomers (like neoprene and Butyl rubber) have a wide range of static and dynamic properties and have greater resistance to heat, oxidation, hydro-carbon oils and are widely used for high vibration damping. On the whole, Butyl rubber is a good general purpose synthetic rubber which may be used as vibration isolators.

While selecting any particular elastomer isolator, screening should be done by ascertaining the solvents and gases to which the isolator is likely to be exposed during normal operating condition, as also the static and dynamic properties. This is very important when elastomer isolators are used inside chemical factories.

From the cost view-point, it may be mentioned that silicone rubber is much more costly than other types of elastomers. But silicone rubber is remarkably effective over a wide temperature variation (ranging from – 54 degree centigrade to + 177 degree centigrade). By comparison, neoprene rubber's use is limited to – 40 degree centigrade to + 90 degree centigrade only. However silicone rubber has inferior strength, tear resistance and abrasion resistance, which limits its use in many cases. A few of the common elastomer isolators are shown in Fig. 9.6.

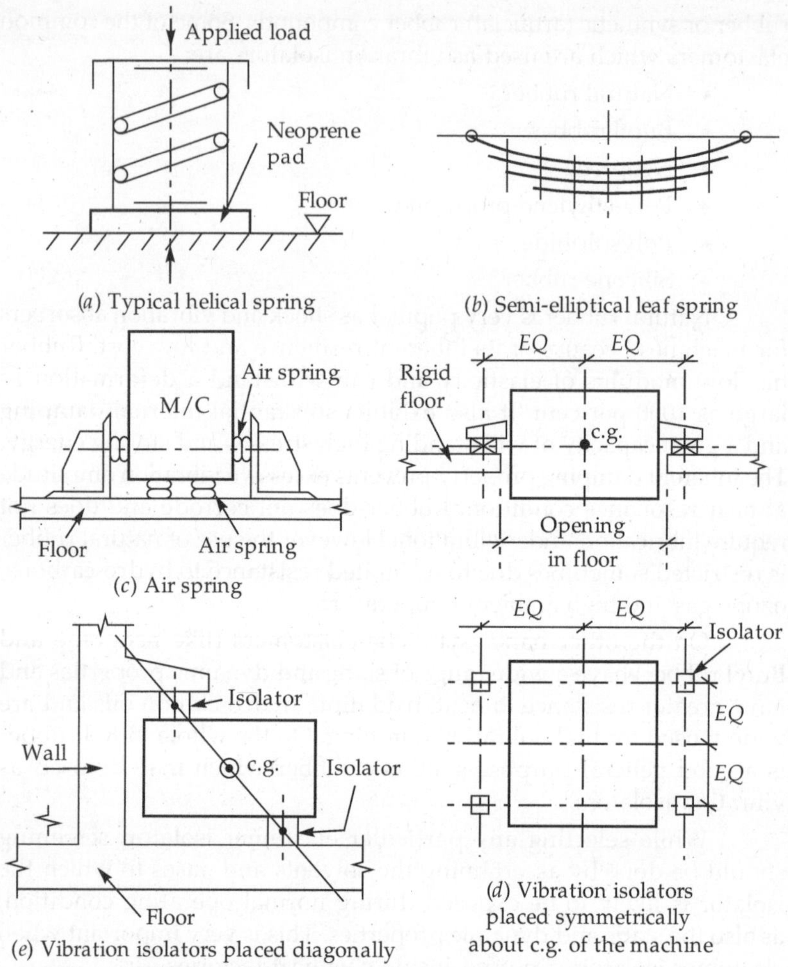

Fig. 9.6 Examples of typical vibration isolators.

9.15.2 Plastic Isolators

Plastic isolators are manufactured by bonding rigid thermoplastic polystyrene (for structural strength) and thermoplastic elastomer butadiene styrene (for resilience). Plastic isolators perform excellently under dynamic loads and exhibit good dimensional stability and tolerance. Major disadvantages are: lesser structural strength than metallic isolators, limited temperature range (– 40 to + 82 degree centigrade) and creep deformation. Thus for ambient room temperature and light loads (both static and dynamic), plastic isolators are used extensively, as costs are less.

9.15.3 Metal Isolators

Metal springs are used for shock and vibration control below heavily-loaded steel wagons, transport vehicles and impact machines. There are various types of metal springs like, helical springs, rings, conical bevel discs, wire-mesh springs and leaf springs.

9.15.4 Air or Pneumatic Springs

Gas is used as the resilient material in pneumatic springs. When air is used, it is called as air spring. Air has adequate low stiffness which is necessary for vibration isolation. At the same time, air can be compressed to the pressure necessary to withstand the machine load. However, the main difficulty in adopting air springs as vibration isolators is that air must be suitably contained in a sealed pressure vessel with provision for releasing and refilling. In-spite of these difficulties, pneumatic shock absorber is normally used in landing gears of airplanes to cushion the shock during landing. The main features of the strut of a simple landing gear are shown in Fig. 9.7. During touchdown, the wheel exerts through the oil piston an upward force on the strut which is greater than the weight of the airplane, thereby compressing the entrained air in the upper chamber of the strut. The net effect is that the kinetic energy generated from the touchdown of the airplane is quickly dissipated through the shock absorber. Similar shock absorbers are also used in heavy-duty cranes.

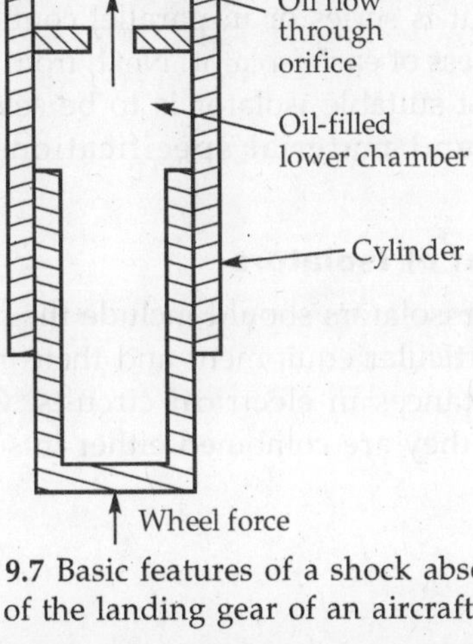

Fig. 9.7 Basic features of a shock absorber of the landing gear of an aircraft.

For machines air springs are available commercially in different sizes and shapes catering for the shock loads ranging from as low as 10 *Kg* to as high as 45 tons, suitable for temperature range – 40 to + 83 degree centigrade. By proper selection of air springs, the natural frequency of the machine support system can be brought down to as low as 1 Hz. When air springs are used in the transverse direction as shock absorbers for laterally applied forces, the natural frequency varies from zero to 3 Hz. The natural frequency of an un-damped air spring is given by:

$$F_n = \delta^{-1/2}, \text{ where, } \delta = \text{static deflection in cm.}$$

9.15.5 Strategy for Selection of Isolators

While selecting an isolator an unusual high safety margin by increasing (or over-specifying) the anticipated load complicates the connections and increases cost. All isolators should be environment-specific and should be compatible with the applied load characteristics. For this purpose, while specifying or procuring vibration isolators, effort should be made to collect the following information:

- Static loads of the different parts of the equipment, its base area and position of center of gravity of the loads.
- Quantifying anticipated dynamic loads, which may be periodic, random or transient (shock).
- Expected temperature range between ambient condition and operating condition.
- Isolation efficiency demanded from the isolators. Normally 70% to 90% efficiency is desirable.

From the above information, it is to be decided whether the isolators will be put is series or in parallel configuration and what should be the stiffness of each isolator. Next, from the manufacturer's catalogue, the most suitable isolator is to be selected, whose load-rating, stiffness and material specifications match with the requirement.

9.15.6 Placement of Isolators

The specification of isolators should include the number of isolators needed for any particular equipment and their mode of placement. Usually, like resistances in electrical circuits, when a number of isolators are used, they are combined either in series, parallel or in combinations.

Isolators in series. In a series arrangement (Refer Fig. 9.8), each isolator carries the total load. If the equipment is supported by *'n'* isolators, each having stiffness, *'k'*, then the combined stiffness of *'n'* isolators in series = k/n.

When there are, say, 3 isolators,

Combined stiffness = 1/3rd × stiffness of a single isolator.

And, static deflection = 3 × deflection of a single isolator.

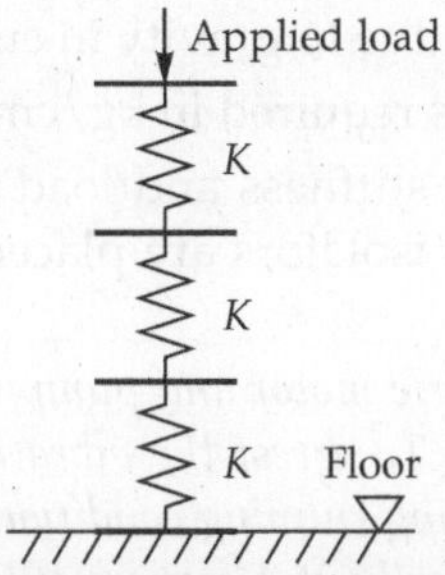

Fig. 9.8 Isolators in series.

Isolators in parallel. When the isolators are put in parallel (Refer Fig. 9.9), the equipment load is shared among the isolators, so that each isolator carries a part of the total load. If there are *'n'* isolators (in parallel), each having stiffness *'k'*, the combined stiffness is given by $n*k$. When 3 isolators are put symmetrically about the center of gravity of loads, and each isolator is of the same stiffness, then the combined stiffness = 3 × the stiffness of each isolator and the static deflection is the same for each isolator. Commonly, isolators are placed in parallel configuration.

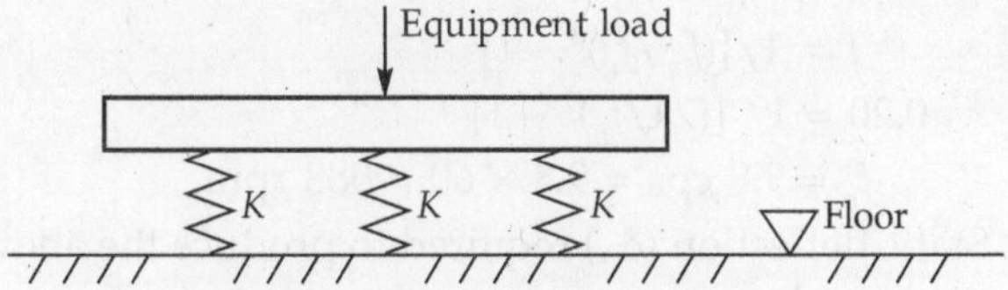

Fig. 9.9 Isolators in parallel.

The following equations are used in this regard:

1. Transmissibility of vibration
   = 1 – (isolation efficiency required, expressed in percentage)
2. Calculate the system natural frequency from the equation:

$$T = 1/[(f_{op}/f_n)^2 - 1]$$

where f_{op} = operating frequency in cps

and f_n = system natural frequency in cps.

3. Calculate static deflection from the equation:

$$f_n = 300/[\delta_{st}]^{1/2}$$

where f_n = system natural frequency in cps.
and δ_{st} = static deflection in cm.

4. Calculate total stiffness required (k) from the equation:

$$f_n = [1/2\pi] \times [(k \times g)/W]^{1/2}$$

where w = weight of equipment in kg
g = acceleration due to gravity in cm/sec^2
k = total stiffness required in kg/cm.

5. Determine the stiffness and load carried by each isolator, considering whether the isolators are placed in series or parallel on in combination.

Example. *An electric motor and pump assembly is rigidly fixed to a common steel base plate. To arrest the vibration from being transmitted to the concrete pedestal during running condition of the motor, it is proposed to fix 4 isolators symmetrically at 4 corners of the base plate. Calculate the capacity and stiffness of the isolators, if a vibration isolation efficiency of 80% is to be achieved.*

The total weight of the pump assembly = 75 kg.

And the operating frequency of the motor = 1440 rpm.

Solution

1. Transmissibility of vibration
= 1 – isolation efficiency required = 1 – 0.80 = 0.20

Operating frequency, f_{op} = 1440 rpm = 24 cps.

2. Natural frequency fn of the isolated system

$$T = 1/[(f_{op}/f_n)^2 - 1]$$

or $$0.20 = 1/\ [(24/f_n)^2 - 1]$$

or $$f_n = 9.8 \text{ cps} = 9.8 \times 60 = 588 \text{ rpm.}$$

3. Static deflection (δ_{st}) required to produce the above natural frequency is given by:

$$f_n = 300/[\delta_{st}]^{1/2}$$

or $$588 = 300/\sqrt{\delta_{st}}$$

or $$\delta_{st} = 0.26 \text{ cm.}$$

4. Corresponding spring constant (k) of the combination of 4 isolators is given by:

$$f_n = [1/2\pi] \times [(k \times g)/W]^{1/2}$$

where $f_n = 9.8$ cps

$W = 75$ kg

$g = 981$ cm/sec^2

k = total stiffness in kg/cm

Putting the values, $k = 290$ kg/cm

Hence, stiffness required by each isolator (placed in parallel in this case)

$= 290/4 = 72.5$ kg/cm **Ans.**

5. Load to be transmitted by each isolator, (assuming total load is shared equally by the isolators) $= 75/4 = 18.75$ kg. **Ans.**

9.15.7 Safety Guidelines for Installation of Isolators

An improperly installed isolator may not perform well and costly equipments may be damaged, even if the selection of the isolators has been proper. The following guidelines should be followed for safe and trouble-free installation of the isolators and trouble-free operation of the equipment:

1. The isolators should not be overloaded. Overloading shortens the life and disturbs the vibration isolation efficiency.

2. The vibrating equipment should not have any contact with another similar equipment or any of the shed structure components. Adequate clearance from all adjacent structures should be maintained.

3. The isolators should be so placed that the center of gravity of the loads and that of the isolators coincide.

4. Arrangement of isolators should be such that the static deflection is the same for all the isolators. If one side of the equipment is exceptionally heavy, the isolators on that side should have a higher spring constant, so that deflections of all the isolators are more or less the same.

5. Excessive deformation, tilt etc., of the isolators should be avoided.

6. If a machinery installation comprises of several rotating components, each having different natural frequencies, then each must be considered separately and the natural frequency of the isolator should be 20% lower than the lowest frequency in the system.

7. Manufacturer's specifications should be followed during installation of the isolators at site.

9.16 AUXILIARY MASS DAMPERS

When the vibration amplitude of an operating machine is very high, it may not be possible to reduce the transmissibility of vibration to a satisfactory level by vibration isolators only. In such cases auxiliary mass dampers are often attached to the vibrating equipment itself to dissipate the energy of vibration at source itself. An auxiliary mass damper usually consists of small metal elements, tungsten powder or steel shots sealed in a container, which is connected to the vibrating equipment. When the equipment is in running condition, the machine vibration is counter acted by multiple collisions of the metal elements inside the sealed container, producing a damping effect on the system due to conversion of mechanical energy to heat. The relative motion and the friction between the metal elements inside the container absorb to a great extent the incipient vibration of the machine itself.

9.17 BALANCING OF ROTATING MACHINES

High-speed rotating machines often exhibit vibrations beyond tolerable limits due to effects of mass imbalance. The problem becomes acute, as the rotating parts become old, worn-out and mis-aligned. As a result, the supporting structures including isolators and dampers, if they are already installed, are subjected to extra load over that considered in the design. The source of such imbalance may be traced to the following sources:

- Lack of symmetry in the rotor (Fig. 9.10).
- Non-homogeneity in the material used, blow holes etc., causing variations in the density of the material of the rotating parts.
- Axis of rotation not coinciding with the principal axis of the rotor (Refer Fig. 9.11). The magnitude of the unbalance force *'F'* being equal to:

$$F = M \times e \times \omega^2$$

where M = mass of the rotor

e = radial distortion of the axis of rotation from the principal axis

ω = rotational speed in radians/sec.

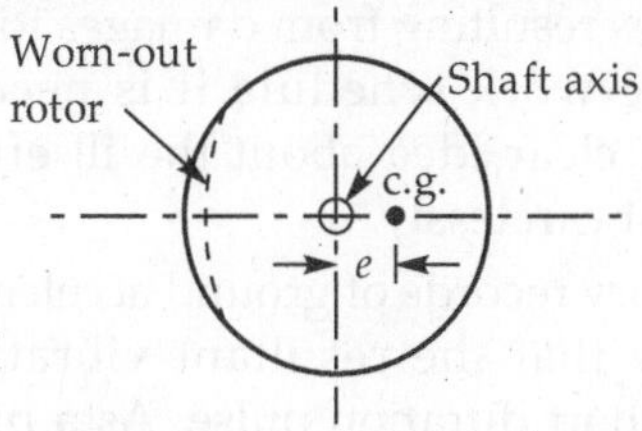

Fig. 9.10 Unbalance due to lack of symmetry of rotor.

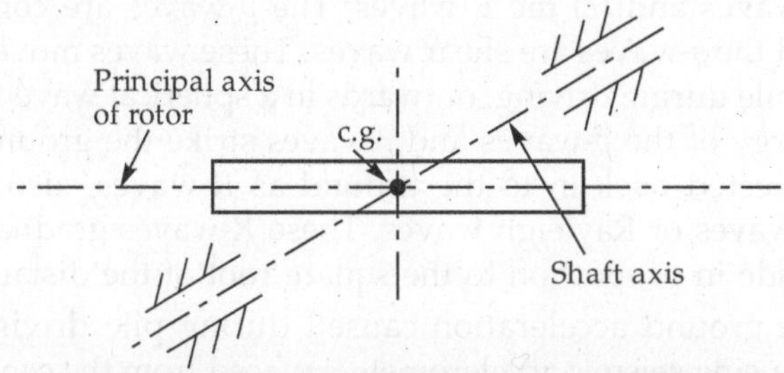

Fig. 9.11 Unbalance due to axis of rotation not coinciding with the principal axis of rotor.

Many of the above imbalances may occur due to defects in the manufacturing process. Again, manufacturing tolerances often allowed in normal cases may also create imbalance in the rotating parts afterwards. Fabricated components like fans often gets distorted during service period, when they are old and worn out. To rectify all these defects, it is the usual practice to take out the unbalanced rotating parts and tested by balancing machines that use various types of sensing elements to detect the quantum and the angle of imbalance. The imbalance, thus identified, is usually corrected either by (*a*) addition of extra weight to the rotor or (*b*) by removal of material from the rotor body by drilling, milling, shaping or grinding, as necessary. By drilling about 1/10th of the imbalance can be corrected. Addition of extra weights, if estimated accurately and properly positioned, can reduce imbalance to about 1/20th of the original value. If the imbalance cannot be brought down below the tolerable limit in the first attempt, a second correction is often needed.

9.18 VIBRATION CAUSED BY PILE DRIVING

Pile-driving causes ground acceleration both vertically and longitudinally, which are likely to damage structures in the vicinity of the pile driving work. On many occasions the vibrations cause cracks in buildings nearby and residents are very much disturbed if pile-driving operations are continued late night. Work is often stalled because of court cases resulting from damages to structures. To avoid interruptions in the work schedule it is necessary for the field engineers to have a clear idea about the ill effects of pile driving operation carried out carelessly.

The time-history records of ground acceleration caused by pile-driving work show that the resultant vibration is of impulsive dynamic nature of short duration pulse. As a pile is driven into the ground, three types of waves are propagated, namely (*a*) the p-waves, (*b*) the *s*-waves and (*c*) the *R*-waves. The *p*-waves are compression waves and the *s*-waves are shear waves. These waves move from the tip of the pile during driving, outwards in a spherical wave from. Part of the energy of the *p*-waves and *r*-waves strike the ground surface and is reflected back in to the ground as *R*-waves, also called as reflected waves or Rayleigh waves. These *R*-waves gradually decay in amplitude in proportion to the square root of the distance.

The ground acceleration caused during pile driving can be measured using seismic accelerometers placed from the centre of pile at a distance of 5*D* to 25*D*, where *D* is equal to the diameter of the pile. The recorded data are then analysed by finite element method to calculate the variation of the peak acceleration with the depth of penetration of the pile.

There are serious potential dangers to the safety of adjoining structures from the impact of pile driving, particularly if the adjoining buildings and structures are old and are in a dilapidated condition. There are chances of differential settlements due to changes in the soil pore pressure and, in extreme cases, partial or complete collapse of structures.

As already stated, pile driving causes ground accelerations both vertically and longitudinally, the vertical vibration being more predominant than the horizontal one. From experimental study it has been observed that the ground acceleration has a frequency band of 9.4 Hz to 51.5 Hz. Any structure in the vicinity of the pile driving activities having natural frequency falling within this range is likely to exhibit resonance vibration and related damages. The safe limit to damage to property is usually taken as the particle velocity of 50 mm per second calculated from spectrum analysis.

The ground acceleration caused by pile driving is more severe if piles are driven in sandy soil layers. Vibrations usually densify a find sandy soil layer and there may be significant differential settlement to the adjoining structures, if they are not adequately protected. Flexible structures are likely to be damaged more by concrete piling work. On the other hand, rigid structures are more affected by driving of steel piles.

If there are chances of damage to adjoining structures due to pile driving operations, the following protective measures are suggested:

- To relocate the piles at a safe distance.
- To modify pile driving methods to reduce vibrations, by adopting screw piles instead of driven piles.
- To redesign the foundation of the new structure avoiding piles if possible.

QUESTIONS

1. What is a mechanical shock? How it is created and what are it's manifestations on a structural system?
2. Explain how different types of shocks are absorbed by a structural system. What types of mechanical shocks are responsible for the following effects on a structural system?
   (*a*) Instantaneous change in velocity
   (*b*) Sinusoidal change in velocity
   (*c*) Sudden displacement
   (*d*) Oscillations
3. What is an impact force? How does it affect the safety of workers at worksites? What measures should be taken to prevent safety hazards from impact?
4. What is meant by a soft and a hard impact? Under what conditions a structure may be damaged by a hard impact? What are the safety hazards for a rigid structure due to accidental collisions? How a flexible structure is likely to behave under similar conditions?
5. Under what circumstances impacts are purposely induced on structural components at site? How safety hazards from such induced impacts are to be minimized?
6. How structures may be damaged due to accidental collisions? What safety measures should be adopted to avoid vehicular collisions on road? How the workers are to be protected from collision impacts at work places?
7. Explain how bridges may be damaged due to accidental collisions from moving vessels. What safety measures should be taken in the design stage to avoid such collisions?

8. What is a fender system? How does it minimize the ill-effects of impact during berthing of vessels at jetties?
9. Mention the circumstances when a structural system may be seriously damaged by accidental blasts. What may be the effect of a blast on human beings? What is the difference between a blast occurring inside a closed space and a similar blast occurring in open air? What kinds of security measured are needed when rock excavation is done by blasting?
10. What is the difference between a free vibration and a forced vibration?
11. What is meant by the natural frequency of a structural system? How the natural frequency is disturbed by resonance and what is the influence of structural damping on the resonance frequency of a system?
12. Write explanatory notes on the following:
    (*a*) Critical damping
    (*b*) Effective damping
    (*c*) Amplification at resonance vibration
    (*d*) Effect of structural inertia on its response to external vibratory forces
    (*e*) Safety hazards due to resonance vibration
13. What is meant by energy dissipation devices and what is the usefulness of such devices?
14. What is the function of a vibration isolator in machine foundations? Explain how they can be fruitfully used to control transmissibility of vibration from the machine to the foundation.
15. Write short notes on the following:
    (*a*) Elastomeric isolators
    (*b*) Springs used as vibration isolators
    (*c*) Material specifications for an elastomeric isolator
    (*d*) Pneumatic isolators
16. How the isolators should be placed under a vibrating machine?
17. What is the use of auxiliary mass dampers? Explain how the vibration of an old machine can be reduced by balancing the rotating parts of the machine.
18. What precautions should be taken when placing vibrating machinery on suspended floors? Explain how imbalance of the rotating parts may create safety hazards in such cases.

CHAPTER

10

Safety against Natural Calamities—Earthquake

10.1 SAFETY HAZARDS DUE TO EARTHQUAKE

In India on 26th January, 2001, when all states were preparing for celebration of the 52nd Republic day with the usual fanfare, a severe earthquake of 7.7 intensity struck at 20 Km north-west of Bhuj, Gujrat. The effect was so devastating that, within 3-4 minutes, several cities and towns like Bhuj, Anjar, Gandhidham, Sukhpur, Ladai, Kotlar and their adjoining areas were razed and flattened to the ground leaving:

- A death toll of 30,000 people
- Injury to about 1.50 lakh people
- 2-lakh people homeless
- 2.29 lakh houses completely destroyed
- 21000 cattle dead
- Property loss to the extent of ₹ 21,000 Crores.

There were damages to buildings even 300 Km away at Ahmedabad city. Tremors were felt at far-away places also in Delhi, Chennai, Karachi, Peswar, Afganisthan, Bhutan and Bangladesh.

A brief chronology of major earthquakes that have hit the Indian subcontinent since early nineteenth century is given below:

S. No.	*Date*	*Place of occurrence*	*Magnitude*	*Death toll*
1.	16th Jan, 1819	Kutch, Gujrat	8.0	2000
2.	10th Jan, 1869	Cachar, Assam	7.5	not known
3.	12th June 1897	Shillong, Assam	8.77	not known
4.	4th April, 1905	Kangra, H.P.	8.0	20000
5.	15th Jan, 1934	Bihar-Nepal border	8.3	14000
6.	15th Aug,1950	Arunachal Pradesh	8.5	1532
7.	21th Aug, 1988	Arunachal Pradesh	6.4	1003
8.	30th Sept, 1993	Latur, Maharastra	6.3	10000
9.	26th Jan, 2001	Bhuj, Gujrat	7.7	30000

The earthquake of 1897 in Shillong is said to have cast its spell over an area of radius 2000 Km and is identified to be the greatest earthquake in recent history. Among devastating earthquakes outside India, mention may be made of Japan quake of 1891 (7.9), Columbian earthquake 1906 (8.6), Sarikm Japan earthquake of 1933 (8.3), Tangsha, China 1976, Algeria 1980, South Italy 1980, Chillian earthquake 1985 and Mexican earthquake 1985.

Earthquakes are unpredictable. Scientists, even with their most sophisticated instruments have not been able to predict precisely the exact place of occurrence, time and intensity of any future earthquake. However, scientists, geologists and engineers have been doing extensive studies on the magnitude and intensity of recorded earthquakes and have compiled in-depth reports on the damages caused by such earthquakes. The analysis of these reports reveals that earthquakes have recurred again and again repeatedly, sometimes at almost regular intervals in different parts of the globe under specific geological conditions and structures have collapsed or have been damaged in varying degrees, whenever they have exhibited low energy-absorbing capacity. This has led to the development of seismic zoning and guidelines for design and construction of earthquake-resistant structures.

10.2 BASIC CHARACTERISTICS OF AN EARTHQUAKE

Earthquakes occur either due to movement of earth's crustal plates against each other (plate tectonics) or due to movement of faults underground. Other causes are seismic sea waves (caused by submarine quakes), volcanic eruptions, disturbance due to collapse of cave roofs, extremely heavy surcharge load from man-made water reservoirs or even powerful man-made explosions. However, movements of faults are responsible for most earthquakes. Such movements cause displacement of one side of a fault relative to the other, either horizontally, vertically or obliquely. The most immediate effect is stretching and/or compression of the earth's crust, releasing a tremendous amount of energy, which spreads through the earth's crust and tremors are then felt. Most of the major earthquakes have originated either from the thrust due to plate movement or relative movement of the fault planes. It is to be noted that the earthquake in the Run of Kutch in 1819 as well as in 2001 originated from re-activated movements of the existing East-West faults in the Kutch region.

10.3 MAGNITUDE OF AN EARTHQUAKE

The magnitude of an earthquake, a concept developed by Charles Richter in 1930, is a measure of the strain energy released during an earthquake at its origin below the earth's surface, called the focus. On the other hand, the epicenter is the point on the earth's surface just above the focus. The magnitude M is a number, obtained from the equation:

$$M = \log A/T + C_1 (\Delta, h) + C_2 + C_3$$

where A = amplitude in thousandth's of a mm.

T = period of seismic wave propagation in seconds

C_1 = correction factor for epicentral distance (Δ) and focal depth (h)

C_2 = correction factor applied at the particular seismological observatory.

C_3 = regional correction factor

Earthquakes below magnitude 2.5 are termed as very mild tremors, whereas major earthquakes have magnitudes 8.5 and more.

Now-a-days with the invention of more sophisticated seismographs, magnitudes are also calculated as Local Magnitude (M_L), Body Wave Magnitude (M_B), Surface Wave Magnitude (M_S) and Seismic Moment Magnitude (M_W). Among these, strong earthquakes are better measured by the Seismic Moment Magnitude method, where seismic moment is a measure of strain energy released on rupture of fault surfaces. Here, the seismic moment, M_0, is given by:

$$M_0 = G \times U \times A$$

where, G = modulus of rigidity (3×10^{10} N/sqm for crust)

U = longitudinal displacement of fault in metres.

A = fault area (length × breadth) in sqm.

The magnitude of the earthquake (M_W) is then calculated from the equation

$$M_W = 2/3 \times \log_{10} M_0 - 6.0$$

The values of the earthquake magnitudes, calculated by different available methods, vary slightly for light tremors, but converge for large earthquakes *i.e.* for magnitudes greater than 6.0.

10.4 RELEASE OF ENERGY DURING AN EARTHQUAKE

During earthquakes large quantity of energy is released, the quantum of which is dependent on the magnitude of the earthquake and is estimated using the formula:

$$E = 10^{4.8 + 1.5M} \text{ in Joules}$$

(1 Joule = energy equivalent to work of 1 Newton-metre)

A nuclear explosion of one megaton releases an energy of 5×10^{15} Joules, which, if equated in the above equation reveals that it is equivalent to energy released by an earthquake of magnitude 7.3.

Again, it is interesting to note that, if the magnitude of an earthquake increases by a single unit (say if it increases from 7.0 to 8.0), the energy release is magnified by 32 times.

On the other hand, the energy release of an earthquake of magnitude say 7.0 will be 1000 times the energy released by an earthquake of magnitude 5.0. This is the reason why damages are so high and devastating, while an earthquake of high magnitude strikes a region.

10.5 INTENSITY OF AN EARTHQUAKE

The location at which an earthquake originates under the earth's surface is termed as the '**focus**' and the point on the surface directly above the focus is called the '**epicenter**' of the earthquake. The severity of an earthquake and consequent damages are more pronounced in places around the epicenter of the earthquake. The effect gradually decreases as the distance of a place increases from the epicenter. As a result, for the same earthquake, people experience severity and damages in varying degrees at different locations depending on the distance of the place from the epicenter. The intensity of an earthquake is a measure of the severity of an earthquake at a particular place. On the other hand the magnitude indicates the total energy released by an earthquake. As a result, the bigger the magnitude of the earthquake, the larger will be the area covered by the same intensity.

Attempts have been made to express quantitatively the intensity of an earthquake by a single numerical value in a graded scale. The most popular one used nowadays is the Modified Mercalli Intensity Scale (MMI Scale), proposed by Newman in 1954. An abbreviated version of this scale is given below, in which the intensity scale is graded into 12 categories depending on the effects, damages and changes occurring in the surroundings.

Intensity	Defined characteristics
I	**Insignificant:** detected only by sensitive instruments
II	**Very light:** felt only by persons at rest in upper floors of buildings
III	**Light:** small vibratory motion for stationary automobiles
IV	**Moderate**: rattling of doors and windows, walls may creak, noise produced by moving objects
V	**Slightly strong:** felt by all, cracking of plaster, breaking of dishes and window glass, panic in general public, disturbances in trees, telephone poles noticed
VI	**Strong:** people are frightened, run outdoor, falling plaster, toppling of chimneys, some damage to non-seismic-resistant structures
VII	**Very strong:** People running outdoors, considerable damage to poorly built structures, some damage to seismic-resistant buildings, chimneys broken, tremor felt in moving vehicles.
VIII	**Destructive:** serious damage to structures in general, falling of houses, monuments, panel walls thrown out, changes in pond/well water levels.
IX	**Ruinous:** serious damage even to buildings of good design and construction, structures thrown out of alignments, foundations damaged, ground cracks, U/G pipe lines seriously damaged
X	**Disastrous:** only seismic-resistant structures remain standing, collapse of all wooden houses and ordinary masonry structures, rails bent, landslide, rise in water level
XI	**Extremely destructive:** collapse of all masonry structures, bridges destroyed, ground fissured, general panic and almost total destruction all round.

XII **Catastrophic:** total destruction of all structures, waves on ground surfaces and topography changed.

In India, depending on the records of previous tremors, the country has been divided into four zones (II, III, IV and V) with seismic intensity termed as low, moderate, severe and very severe with appropriate zone factors allocated to each of them. (The erstwhile Zone I has been included in Zone II in the recent revision)

10.6 DAMAGE POTENTIAL OF AN EARTHQUAKE

The damage potential of an earthquake depends on several factors, namely, magnitude, intensity, duration and variation in the geological strata.

Magnitude of an earthquake: Higher the magnitude, higher is the damage potential.

Intensity of an earthquake: From study of recorded earthquakes, it is learnt that the origin (focus) of most of the earthquakes are located at four distinct seismic belts around the world, namely, (*a*) at ocean bottom, (*b*) island arcs (*c*) arc-shaped mountains and (*d*) interiors of continents. Obviously these seismic belts or active seismic zones are not evenly distributed over the globe. But regions nearer to these seismic belts are prone to be hit hard, as and when there are major earthquakes in these regions.

Variations in the geological strata

The intensity of an earthquake is sensitive to the variations in the underlying geological strata through which the earthquake waves pass. As a result intensity felt from the same earthquake may be different even at places equidistant from the epicenter.

Duration

Earthquake tremors consist of both short-period and long-period waves. Short period tremors die out first. Since they do not travel a long distance, damages, if any, due to short-period tremors are mostly localized. On the other hand, at far-away locations from the epicenter, the proportion of long waves predominates over any remnant short waves. Thus at distant locations from the epicenter, long waves have more damage potential.

Earthquakes create ground motions and vibrations of variable frequency, amplitude and duration. Moreover, the ground motion is of random nature and exhibit complex reactions to earthquakes in different geological environments. To bring all these variables within the ambit of a single quantifiable unit, it is the common practice in structural analysis and design, to express the intensity of an earthquake by the maximum acceleration it produces at a particular place. This is based on the hypothesis that the 'maximum' acceleration generated from an earthquake determines the most likely critical damaging effect on building structures, particularly if the structure is rigid. However, for flexible structures like chimneys, narrow tall buildings and long-span bridges, a more appropriate approach would be to adopt the so-called **'Response Spectrum Method'**, which takes into account the deflection and the vibration factors.

Ground acceleration records have been compiled for a large number of strong-motion earthquakes with the help of Mass-spring Seismic Transducers. The output data is plotted with time (in seconds) along the X-coordinate and ground acceleration (a/g) as the ratio of acceleration due to gravity along the Y-coordinate. Integrating numerically the acceleration function, thus obtained, with respect to time, the curve for ground velocity is obtained. Again, by integration of the velocity function with respect to time the displacement of the ground is obtained. These integrations are usually done with necessary base line corrections with the help of special software.

Figures are available, which show the recorded data of the well-known devastating El Cento, California earthquake in 1940 and the curves generated show the calculated values of the ground velocity and ground displacement. For this particular earthquake, the maximum acceleration is 0.32 g, and the calculated maximum velocity and displacement were found to be 35 cm/sec and 21 cm respectively. It is to be noted that these maximum values may not occur at the same time. But the maximum values of acceleration, velocity and displacement give a fairly good idea of the damage potential of such an earthquake. In this connection, it is of particular interest to note that walls crack when the velocity is about 2.4 cm/sec and walls collapse when the maximum velocity is about 4.7 cm/sec.

Distance

The intensity of an earthquake decrease with increase in distance from the focus. The variation of earthquake intensity with distance is shown in Fig. 10.1.

Again, the larger the distance of the location from the focus, the striking angle of the earthquake force go on decreasing. Consequently, the vertical component of this force goes on decreasing with increase in the horizontal component and the effect of the horizontal force becomes more significant. (Refer Fig. 10.2)

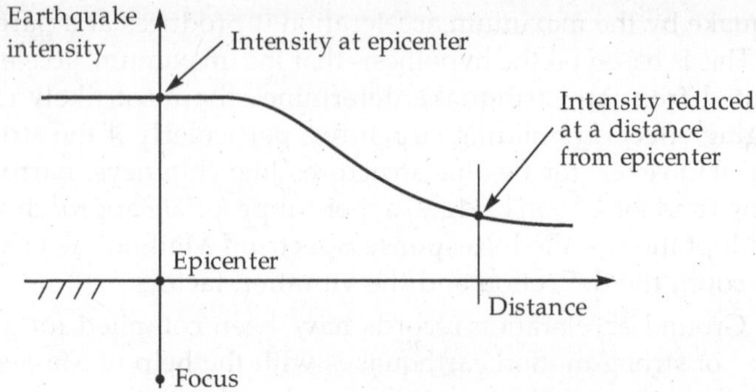

Fig. 10.1 Variation of the intensity of an earthquake with distance from the epicenter.

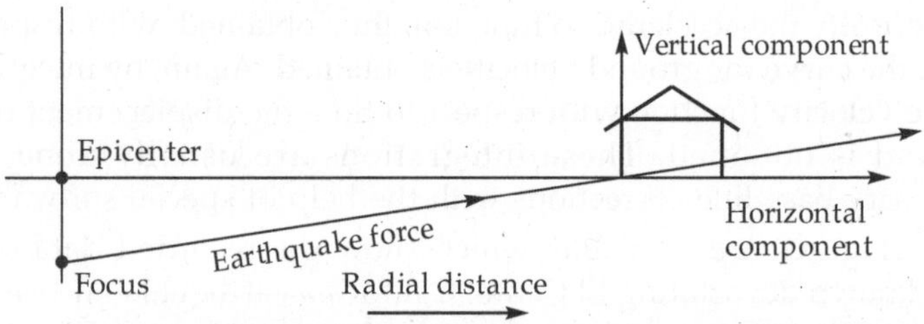

Fig. 10.2 Components of earthquake force.

Usually, the vertical component of an earthquake force is taken as 10% of the horizontal component.

10.7 TOPOGRAPHICAL CHANGES DURING EARTHQUAKES AND THEIR EFFECT ON STRUCTURAL SAFETY

The topography and soil characteristics are altered in various ways during earthquakes causing structural damages to buildings, bridges and other infrastructure facilities. From study of post-tremor soil investigations and records (sometimes historical records) of evidences of earlier earthquakes, scientists and engineers have identified a number of typical ground and structural failure patterns caused by ground movements and vibration. These are discussed below.

Soil Liquefaction

The ground vibration created by an earthquake often leads to the densification and compaction of foundation soil with development of excessive pore pressure. As a result, the soil below the foundation behaves like a heavy fluid, crating sand boils. As it happens, trapped water inside the soil mass moves to the ground surface and the soil loses its original shear strength, resulting in substantial reduction in its bearing capacity. When the foundation soil is cohesionless, loosely-packed or mixed with silt and gravels having low plasticity, the above phenomenon of soil liquefaction is more pronounced. Massive settlement, bearing failure of foundations, collapse of side slopes of embankments and structural damages are results of soil liquefaction. Liquefaction coupled with ground displacement and foundation settlement is observed along coastal lines in many parts of the world during major earthquakes.

When loose saturated sandy soil or finely-grained soil of very low plasticity is subjected to cyclic dynamic loads or shock loads in an un-drained condition, the soil often loses its shear strength and behaves like a liquid. This phenomenon is also due to soil liquefaction. If heavy rotating machines are installed over cohesionless, loose, saturated, sandy soil, there always remains a strong possibility of heavy settlement and/or differential settlement endangering the safety of the equipment, if the soil underneath is fully saturated and un-drained.

During earthquakes, liquefaction-induced settlement often becomes one of the major causes of disaster. Excess pore pressure is built up during the liquefaction process and the shear strength of soil may be reduced to almost zero. In this condition when there is shaking or movement of the ground due to earthquake, structural deformation and failure are almost inevitable. In many cases severe damages have been noticed in dock, harbour and off-shore structures due to earthquake-related liquefaction of soil

For the safety of structures, particularly machine foundations, the probability of liquefaction of soil should be investigated by studying the settlement properties of soil and proper protective measures should be taken, like, providing good drainage of soil below the machine foundation or replacing the settlement-prone soil by cohesive clayey soil of appropriate dynamic properties.

Ground Motion

All structures are shaken during an earthquake with possibility of safety hazards to life and property. Strong ground motion generated during an earthquake may cause unacceptable undulation in floor and surrounding ground, failure of pavement subgrade, lateral displacement of boundary walls, embankments and retaining walls and serious damage to stone masonry, mud-walls and poorly-built brick masonry walls built without cross diaphragm walls or bands. Damages to underground oil pipe lines, cable ducts and lateral shifting of isolated footings not held by cross tie beams are also observed, whenever there is strong ground motion during an earthquake.

Ground cracking

Long, wide, horizontal cracks are often seen to have developed in the immediate aftermath of an earthquake, contributing to damages in pavements, abrupt fall in water levels in ponds and reservoirs and even release of trapped water from underground layers.

Ground settlement

Earthquakes also contribute to damages due to ground settlement, mine subsidence and differential settlement of foundations. The damaging effects of ground settlement are more pronounced if buildings are built over soft compressible soil or filled-up ground without resorting to any pre-consolidation, stabilization or piling. Buildings and structures constructed over reclaimed land (from water bodies) are also prone to settlement damages during earthquakes. Ground settlement also causes drag (negative friction) on existing piles, resulting in substantial reduction in their load-carrying capacity.

The substrata under foundations are considered to be divided into 3 distinct categories, so far as their response to the ground motion during an earthquake is concerned. These are: (*a*) rock or hard soil (*b*) medium soil and (*c*) soft soil. The seismic force hitting a structure depends not only on the intensity of the earthquake at that location (or in other words the maximum acceleration), but also on the instantaneous changes in the topography and soil characteristics. These factors together with the importance of the structure itself, are usually taken into account in the national codes while designing earthquake-resistant structures.

10.8 RESPONSE MECHANISM OF STRUCTURES

How a particular structure will react when an earthquake hits it, depends on several structural characteristics, namely:

- Rigidity or flexibility of the structure as a whole
- Ductility of the structural components and the connections and their capacity to resist seismic forces without undergoing irreparable damage to life and property.
- Damping characteristics of the structure as a whole, which determines the energy-absorption capacity of the structural system.

For the same horizontal seismic force, a rigid structure deflects less than a flexible one. As a result, a rigid structure absorbs more energy than a flexible structure. Theoretically an infinitely rigid structure has the same response as the maximum ground acceleration produced during an earthquake. Moreover, stiff structures, being in general heavier and more massive than a flexible one, is likely to attract more horizontal force. However, a heavy structure designed for a large horizontal seismic force, will not necessarily have greater margin of safety than a similar structure having flexibility. In other words, by using the same seismic coefficient value for different types of structures, the designer cannot be sure that they have the same resistance against earthquakes, in case they are designed with different sets of allowable stresses. A structure designed by working stress method would have a different degree of resistance against earthquakes, when it is designed by limit state method, though seismic coefficients used may be the same in both cases.

10.9 DETERMINATION OF THE DESIGN SEISMIC FORCES

As per provisions of the revised BIS Code no: IS-1895 (Part I)-2001: Criteria for earthquake resistant design of structures,

$$\text{Design seismic base shear } (V_B) = A_h \times W$$

where A_h = design horizontal acceleration spectrum value, considering the fundamental natural period of vibration, Zone factor (considering the maximum considered earthquake MCE and the service life of the structure), Importance Factor and Response Reduction Factor (considering ductility/brittle deformation, damping characteristics of the proposed structure and the prevalent soil conditions)

And W = seismic weight of the structure.

Values of the above coefficients have been given in the above code of practice for easy reference. Similar values are available for other countries in their respective national codes.

The Response Reduction Factor mentioned above is based on the concept of the probability of energy-dissipation of the structural components. The Response Reduction Factors also consider the damping characteristics of the material used in the structures. It may be noted here that the energy transfer decreases with increase in the external damping. If necessary, in the design stage, additional damping devices may have to be introduced through installation of viscous or frictional devices at critical locations of the structure to achieve a satisfactory performance level during earthquakes. In the above seismic codes, the problems of differential settlement and torsion have also been taken care of through provisions of additional appropriate clauses.

10.10 BASIC CRITERIA FOR DESIGN OF EARTHQUAKE-RESISTANT STRUCTURES

From economic point of view, it is not justifiable to design buildings, bridges etc with provisions of large reserve strength so that the structures can withstand, without any damage, the onslaught of the strongest earthquake ever possible. It will be sheer wastage of money to build all structures extra strong to meet such conditions of high-level seismicity, if the probability of return of the strongest earthquake during the service life of a structure is very low. In view of this, the principal objective of the earthquake-resistant design has been to proportion the structural elements and their connections for two distinct hazard scenarios.

1. For moderate intensity earthquakes the structure should be able to withstand the seismic shock without any significant damage. The stresses of the structural components should obviously be within the elastic range.

2. For strong-intensity earthquakes, some damages to the structure will be tolerated, but the structure should not collapse and there will be no loss of life. To ensure this condition, it is necessary to utilize the ductile behaviour of the material used and design the structure with adequate flexibility to deform without serious damage or collapse and the absorbed seismic energy is dissipated mainly through cracking and yielding, avoiding a sudden brittle failure. To satisfy this condition, the designer has to take recourse to the Response Reduction Factors, explained in the previous section and proportion the structure accordingly.

10.11 BASIC PRINCIPLES FOR DESIGN OF EARTH-QUAKE-RESISTANT STRUCTURES

Soil-structure interaction

The response of a structure to seismic shock and vibration depends on the nature of the soil, type of the foundation and superstructure, besides the intensity and duration of the ground motion. It is to be noted that the Indian Code of Practice IS: 1893 (Part I)-2002 specifies the design forces to be considered in the design of structures built either on rock or soil, which do not settle or liquefy or lose their shear strength due to landslide. Consequently, it is implied that, while calculating the design seismic forces it should be ensured that the structure is built either:

- On rock
- Or, on non-compressible soil
- Or, on soil which does not liquefy *i.e.* the soil should maintain cohesiveness and should not be loosely packed or mixed with silt.
- Or, on soil not likely to be affected by landslides.

If the reports of soil investigations and ground topography points to any deficiency in this respect, proper remedial measures are to be taken like, soil stabilization, provision of retaining walls for landslide-prone areas or adoption of deep foundations in place of shallow foundations, so that the superstructure load is transferred to a good load bearing strata.

Design of superstructure considering flexibility and ductile material of materials

As reinforced concrete structures are in general heavier than a steel or composite structure, a reinforced concrete structure (or pre-stressed concrete structure) attracts more seismic force. However this does not mean that a reinforced concrete structure is more unsafe than a steel structure. Stability against earthquakes depends on the spare capacity available to the structural system for absorbing seismic energy as the structure starts yielding (or deflect) with cracking and failure of joints. At this stage the ductility or flexibility of the structure is more important than the question whether the structure is heavy or light.

An earthquake creates vibration in several modes (Ref. Fig. 10.3).

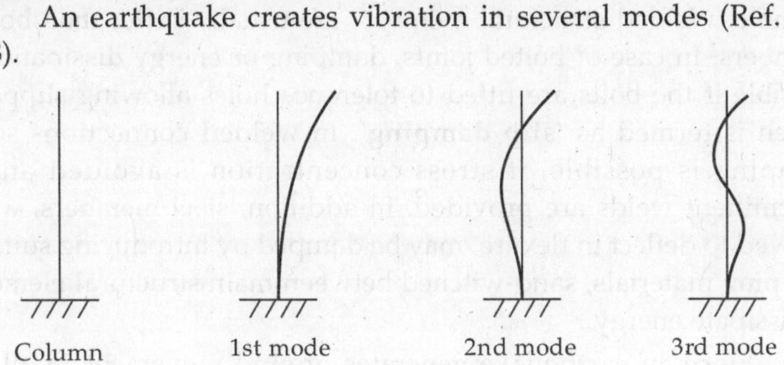

Fig. 10.3 Deflected shapes of column

The response of a structure is different in different modes of vibration. If earthquake tremors strike a structure repeatedly within a very short period of a few seconds, all the above modes of vibrations usually overlap. In that case the response coefficients for each mode should be calculated and the resultant is found statistically by the root-mean-square method. But, in most cases, the 1st mode (also called the fundamental period of vibration) is the deciding factor for the stability of a structure, because of the large deflection generated in this mode. This deflection again depends on the amount of inherent ductility in the structural components and flexibility provided in the design of their end connections.

In reinforced concrete members ductility can be assured by providing closely-spaced transverse reinforcements in the form of ties and stirrups to confine the concrete at the time of yielding. These transverse reinforcements should be complimented with provision of adequate amount of longitudinal steel, so that the member can deflect, sustaining large strains, even if the concrete cover is spalled off and cracks appear in the concrete member. However it should be ensured that the vertical load-carrying capacity (dead load and live load) is not reduced and buckling of longitudinal reinforcements are prevented by providing intermediate ties at suitable levels. In the design stage, the potential locations of forming plastic hinges should be visualized and the detailing should be done accordingly.

In the case steel structures, there is inherent flexibility in the system, because of the ductile properties of steel. However, for a steel structural system the capacity to absorb seismic energy can be augmented, if the joints are designed as flexible, to the extent possible, considering the functional requirements of the structural system as a whole. Welded structural members are usually stiffer than bolted members. In case of bolted joints, damping or energy dissipation is possible if the bolts are fitted to tolerance holes allowing slippage, which is termed as **'slip damping'**. In welded connections some damping is possible, if stress concentration is avoided and if intermittent welds are provided. In addition, steel members, when allowed to deflect in flexure, may be damped by introducing suitable damping materials, sand-witched between main structural elements to dissipate energy.

Since an earthquake generates ground movement in all the planes, a structure may be shaken, shifted, tilted or rotated. Consequently, an earthquake produces not only horizontal or vertical shear, but also torsional moments. Torsional moments are produced when a structure has no symmetry in plan, as in the case of L-shaped buildings or small annex buildings structurally connected with a large one (Ref. Fig. 10.4). In such case the torsion is caused by the eccentricity of the resultant seismic shear acting on the foundations with the center of gravity of the structure itself. For overturning moment, example may be cited for earthquake shear forces acting transverse to a trussed bridge span causing overturning moment about the bearings. In all such cases the effects of seismic loads are to be algebraically added to the effects of gravity loads, following provisions formulated in codes. If the structure is meant to be designed as a flexible structure so that inelastic deflection is allowed to avoid collapse, the connections are also to be designed accordingly, taking into account the effect of all gravity loads and seismic effects.

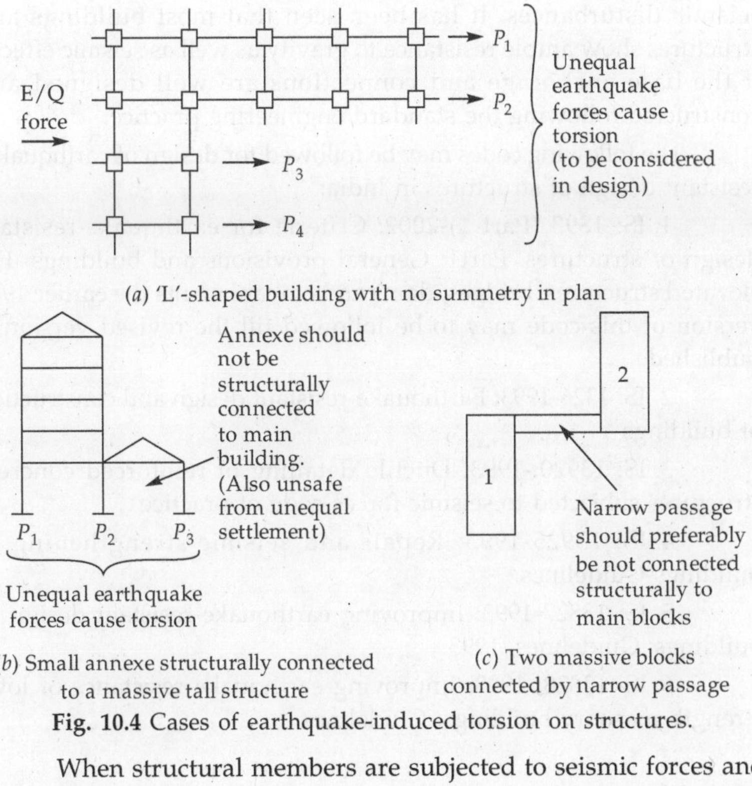

(*a*) 'L'-shaped building with no summetry in plan

(*b*) Small annexe structurally connected to a massive tall structure

(*c*) Two massive blocks connected by narrow passage

Fig. 10.4 Cases of earthquake-induced torsion on structures.

When structural members are subjected to seismic forces and their components in different orthogonal directions are calculated, the overall effect (response) may be computed by either of the following methods:

Method no. 1: Compute response for each direction separately and then take the square root of the sum of squares of the stresses produced in each direction as the combined response.

Method no. 2: Consider 100% seismic force in one direction with 40% of the forces in the other two orthogonal directions. Add the absolute values of these forces to get the resultant force in a structural system in any particular direction, computing the stresses corresponding to the combined effects.

In general, the method no. 2 gives a conservative result.

Adequate attention is to be given in the detailing of earthquake-resistant connections, for which the codal provisions are to be strictly followed. In addition, material specification, quality of fabrication and workmanship during construction are also equally important to ensure adequate performance of the structure during seismic disturbances. It has been seen that most buildings and structures show ample resistance to gravity as well as seismic effects, if the base anchorage and connections are well designed and constructed following the standard engineering practice.

The following codes may be followed for design of earthquake-resistant design of structures in India:

1. IS: 1893 (Part 1)-2002: Criteria for earthquake-resistant design of structures. Part1: General provisions and buildings. For elevated structures, bridges, dams and embankments the earlier 1984 version of this code may to be followed till the revised version is published.

2. IS: 4326-1993: Earthquake-resistant design and construction of buildings

3. IS: 13920:-1993: Ductile detailing of reinforced concrete structures subjected to seismic forces-code of practice

4. IS: 13925-1993: Repair and seismic strengthening of buildings-Guidelines.

5. IS: 13827-1993: Improving earthquake-resistant design of buildings: Guidelines, 1993.

6. IS: 13828: 1993: Improving earthquake resistance of low-strength masonry buildings: Guidelines.

10.12 STANDARD ENGINEERING PRACTICE FOR DESIGN OF EARTHQUAKE-RESISTANT STRUCTURES

Considering all the aspects of seismic forces, soil-structure interactions and type of structures, well-knit standard engineering practices have been developed over the few decades and they have been incorporated in building codes of different countries for planning and designing earthquake-resistant structures to ensure reasonable safeguard against loss of life and property. Though the provisions vary from one country to another depending on the intensity of earthquakes anticipated at various locations, there are common ground principles for design of earthquake resistant design of structures in every country. Some of these important common features are stated below:

Reinforced concrete framed buildings

1. All RCC building frames should be symmetrical in plan as well as in elevation with dead load of the building more or less evenly distributed, so that the earthquake forces acting on the structural frame do not have any large eccentricity with respect to the center of gravity of the building mass. Irregular buildings (Ref Fig 10.4) attract additional torsional moments and shear, which should be considered in the design of building elements.

2. Soft storey in multistory buildings should be avoided. (Ref. Fig. 10.5)

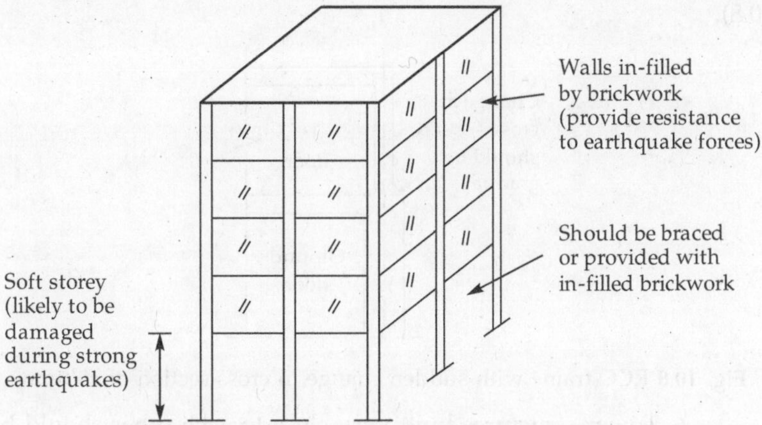

Fig. 10.5 Soft storey in multi-storied buildings.

3. Shear walls should be placed symmetrically in a judicious manner to take care of ductile deformations in the post-elastic stage. (Ref. Fig. 10.6)

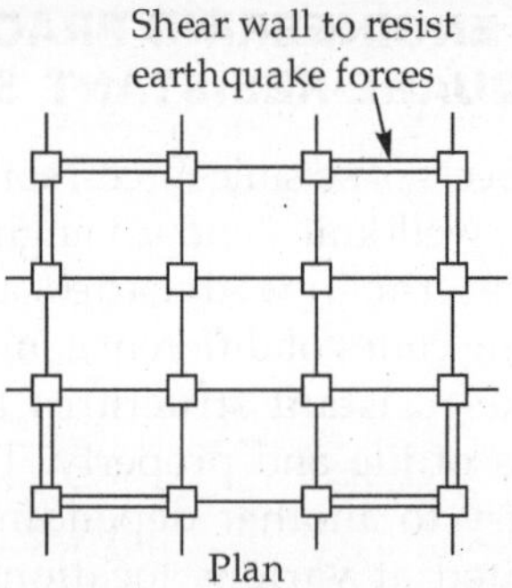

Fig. 10.6 Preferred position of shear walls in multi-storied buildings.

4. Large openings in masonry walls should be avoided. (Fig. 10.7)

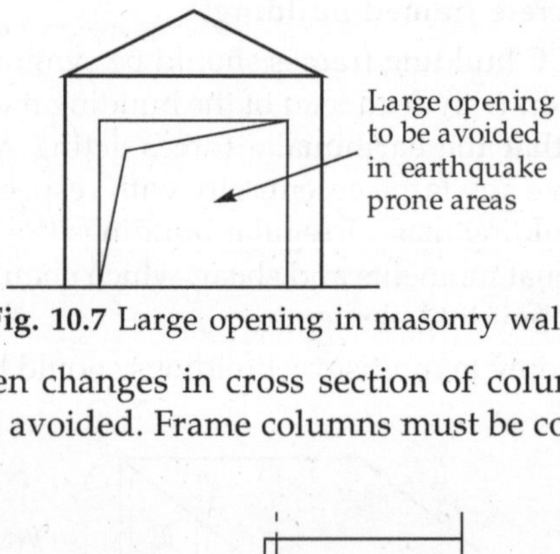

Fig. 10.7 Large opening in masonry wall.

5. Sudden changes in cross section of columns in building frames are to be avoided. Frame columns must be co-axial. (Ref. Fig. 10.8).

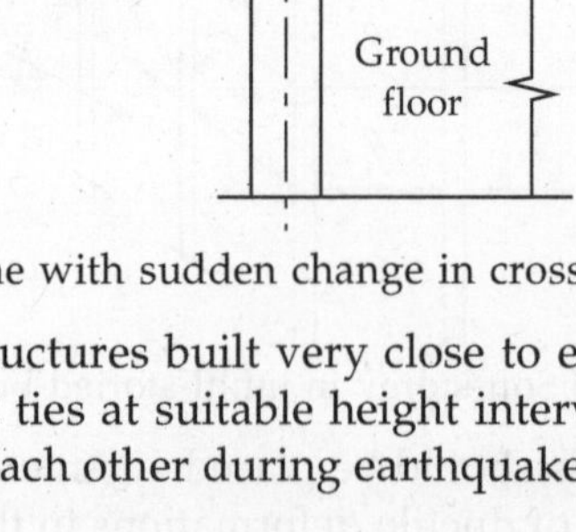

Fig. 10.8 RCC frame with sudden change in cross-section of column.

6. Tower structures built very close to each other should be provided with RCC ties at suitable height intervals, so that they do not pound against each other during earthquakes. (Fig. 10.9).

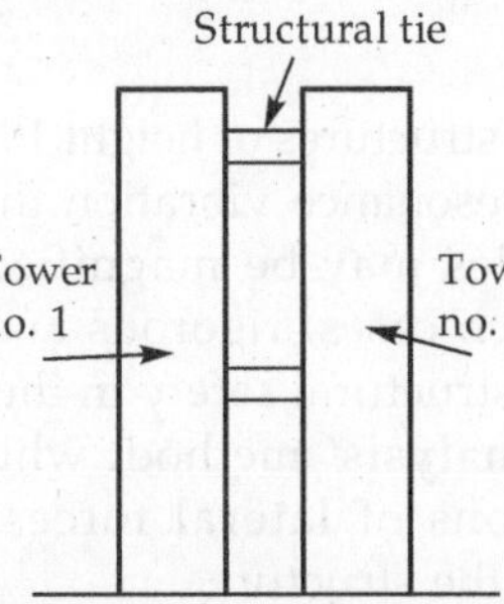

Fig. 10.9 Structural tie to connect closely spaced tower-like structures.

7. All RCC building frames are to be firmly tied together and stiffly braced in such a way that the whole building would tend to move as a single unit during earthquakes.

8. Massive big buildings should not be structurally connected with a small annex. (Refer 10.4 '*b*'). Small corridors one storey height connected structurally to two multistory buildings are susceptible to cracks and damages during earthquakes. (Refer Fig. 10.4 '*c*')

9. Sufficient space should be allowed between adjacent buildings to avoid pounding of one with another due to different amplitudes. A minimum gap of 150 mm to 200 mm should be given and the gap should be filled in with compressible substance.

10. A strong-motion earthquake is often followed by outbreaks of fire in the air-condition ducts, explosion of gas cylinders and other inflammable items stored inside the building. Proper fire safety norms are to be followed to mitigate such post-tremor fire safety hazards.

11. An earthquake usually has a natural period of vibration ($t = 1/f$, where f is the natural frequency) of 1.0 to 2.5 seconds. Multistory buildings, on the other hand, normally exhibit the following variations in their natural periods.

Storey height	*Natural frequency*
2	0.2
5	0.5
10	1.0
20	2.0

30	3.0

In view of above, structures of height 10 storey and above have a strong possibility of resonance vibration during earthquakes and the vibration amplitudes may be magnified beyond the limit of structural safety. In such cases, rigorous analysis is to be done to examine the margin of structural safety in the inelastic stage, by the so-called **'Push-over-analysis'** method, which takes into account incremental applications of lateral forces and the consequent progressive yielding of the structure.

12. The detailing of all structural members like columns, beams, ties, bracings etc should follow the norms and guidelines given IS: code number IS: 13920: Code of practice for ductile detailing of RCC structures subjected to seismic forces.

13. Foundations for RCC framed buildings in seismic zones are to be designed for vertical loads and checked for earthquake forces. Usually such foundations are designed as isolated/combined footings, pile foundations or RCC raft foundations or well foundations depending on the type of structure, local soil conditions and imposed loads.

Masonry structures

Low-rise (up to three stories) masonry buildings are usually constructed with bricks having compressive strength of 5 KN per sq mm joined by cement mortar of 1:4 to 1:6 mix. Such type of masonry structures exhibit poor response to earthquake forces, though the horizontal and vertical mortar joints offer some damping effect. Response of masonry structures to seismic forces would be better, if, (*a*) the masonry walls are reinforced with horizontal RCC bands or lintels, or, (*b*) reinforced with horizontal RCC bands and vertical bars at corners or at joints of cross walls.

Un-reinforced masonry is brittle with natural frequency ranging from 0.1 second to 0.8 second and its load carrying capacity reduces substantially, whenever cracks develop due to earthquake forces. Corners of un-reinforced masonry tend to separate during earthquakes developing wide cracks and the structural behaviour changes from a box section to individual cantilevers. At that point the rigidity of the whole structural system is lost leading to collapses in many cases.

The brittle behaviour of un-reinforced masonry walls may be modified advantageously if the masonry is reinforced horizontally or both horizontally and vertically as mentioned above. The vertical reinforcements resist bending, adding ductility to the structural system to avoid complete collapse. On the other hand, the box action with high rigidity is ensured by introducing horizontal reinforcements in the form of continuous band lintels.

Methods of reinforcing masonry walls

The following methods are usually adopted in reinforcing masonry walls:

Hollow-brick reinforced masonry

In places, where good quality hollow bricks are available, the masonry walls are built with hollow bricks in cement mortar joints and the hollows are grouted with vertical reinforcements. In addition, small diameter (8mm diameter) horizontal reinforcements are also placed in the mortar joints at suitable intervals to generate horizontal shear resistance. Additional vertical steel as bundles may also be placed at wall joints to add to the rigidity of the structural system. This type of reinforced masonry is recommended for regions of low to moderate seismic disturbances.

Solid brick reinforced masonry

In places of moderate to high seismicity, masonry structures are built with solid bricks in cement mortar 1:4 mix and reinforced by both horizontal and vertical RCC bands so that the walls act together as a box. This type of structural system is essentially a reinforced frame with in-filled masonry. In multistoried frames, such RCC vertical ties should be integrally connected to the floor slabs, so that the floor slabs may act as horizontal diaphragms and horizontal forces are transferred through box action of the RCC ties and verticals. The above arrangement is recommended in Zones III, IV and V, which are likely to encounter moderate to high intensity earthquake forces.

In-filled masonry structures are built to increase the rigidity in frames. However, the in-filled walls are to be so oriented that there is no substantial addition to torsional moments due to shifting of the center of rigidity of the frame as a whole. In the same way, opening locations should be symmetrical to avoid torsional moments. Partial in-fill between columns should be avoided. All reinforcements should be grouted in the walls and the reinforcements should be evenly distributed. The spacing of such reinforcement rods may be 300 to 450 mm vertically and 400 to 500 mm horizontally.

When masonry walls are part of the load-bearing structural system, the walls should have as small openings as possible and the openings should be symmetrically placed. Usually it is taken to be granted that the total length of any structural masonry wall, resisting seismic forces, should be more than 200 mm per sqm of plinth area, *i.e.* for a plinth area of 100sqm, the total length of such walls should be at least 20 metres. All walls in upper stories should be placed concentrically over the walls of the lower stories without any eccentricity. It is preferable to provide RCC beams over masonry walls and these beams should be cast monolithically with the floor slab. The vertical reinforcements of the masonry walls should be anchored inside the RCC peripheral beams. It is preferable to provide reinforced strap footings below masonry walls, so that the footings can withstand differential settlements and variations in loadings.

Steel structures

Steel structures should be designed and proportioned in such a way that the whole structure acts as a single unit space frame under load. They should have adequate flexibility for yielding and plastic deformation without any substantial loss of strength during earthquakes. Brittle fracture leading to sudden collapse is not allowed in earthquake-resistant design of steel structures. However, local damage due to yielding and/or buckling may be allowed, so long there is no threat to life. The beam and column sections are to be so proportioned that, under earthquake forces, yielding due to formation of plastic hinges occurs only in beams away from the beam-column moment connections. From observations it has been established that, in steel moment-frame connections, plastic rotations of about 0.02 radians may be allowed without any significant loss in the structural strength.

Concept of structural fuse

To achieve the above objective, it is the standard practice to adopt and use the R-factor as recommended in the code of practices. In addition, certain specific structural components and their connections may be identified and designed as structural fuses to allow dissipation of seismic energy by in-elastic yielding. All other components are then designed as per capacity design concept for gravity and earthquake forces in the elastic range. That means, while the components designed as structural fuses may collapse due to in-elastic yielding, other components would still remain in the elastic range without any significant loss in gravity load-bearing capacity. To avoid loss in life and property therefore the identification of the locations of structural fuses in the whole system is very important.

In addition, the following aspects are to be strictly followed in the design of earthquake-resistant steel structures, which it may be noted, have much similarity with the methods suggested earlier for design of earthquake-resistant RCC structures.

1. The structural system should have a regular configuration, preferably symmetrical about the center line about all the planes.

2. There should be uniformity in the stiffness or margin of safety in the structural components proportional the earthquake and gravity loads.

3. Discontinuity in structural system should be avoided.

4. In case of multi-storied structural frames, there should be uniformity in the ratio of lateral load to the tributary mass, where the tributary mass is the mass of that portion of the frame supported above the lateral force under consideration.

5. Ordinary moment frames (OMF) under little or moderate seismic forces, may be designed as a stiff structure which is strong against gravity loads and lateral forces, but with lesser ductility. On the other hand, for structures in zones of high seismicity, special moment frames (SMF) are to be adopted with moment resisting connections capable of a minimum level of rotational capacity. Help of special analytical tools/software should be taken to achieve this objective.

6. Splicing of columns in structural frames should be located preferably within the middle one-third of the storey height and the splice should have sufficient capacity to resist earthquake-induced shear in both the orthogonal directions.

7. All bracings should be concentric to allow for inelastic deformation responses under moderate to high intensity seismic disturbances.

10.13 CONSIDERATION FOR THE WEAKEST LINKS IN THE DESIGN OF EARTHQUAKE-RESISTANT STRUCTURES

From study and observations of damages caused to structures during earlier earthquakes, it is seen that an earthquake always hits the weakest link in the structural system first. Examples of such weak links are:

- Mortar joints in brickwork
- Plaster and floor finishes
- Projected balconies in buildings
- Bearings of bridges

- Structural components affected by corrosion or having inadequate sections.

Mortar joints in brick walls

Seismic forces are resisted effectively by the brick material, but mortar joints fail due to large strains caused by seismic forces, thereby rendering brickwork as a whole vulnerable to earthquakes. Even in reinforced masonry walls, mortar joints remain the weakest link in the whole process of transferring the inertia forces due to earthquake. For this reason, to develop better cohesion between bricks and mortar and to have increased shear strength of masonry, it is recommended that the compressive strength of mortar should neither be less than 10 N/sq mm, nor greater than 20 N/sq mm, as determined by prism test. This corresponds roughly to cement mortar (1 cement:3 sand) *i.e.* mortar type H1 as per IS: 1905-1980- Code of practice for structural safety of buildings: masonry walls.

Plaster and floor finishes

It is often the practice to use irregular-sized bricks for brickwork in masonry structures or for in-filled masonry walls in reinforced concrete/steel frames. The inside plaster becomes thick due to the irregular size of the bricks, as it is the standard practice to construct brickwork with outside faces of the bricks flush. Ceiling plaster may also be very thick if the soffit of the roof becomes uneven due to bad workmanship. In such cases, large chunks of plaster are likely to be dislodged even during moderate earthquakes causing injury to the inhabitants. Such types of safety hazards may be avoided, if plasters are made as thin as possible, by using regular sized bricks in walls and by maintaining proper levels in the roof slabs. Also, suspended ceilings, if used, should be made of light-weight materials and they should be strongly tied and anchored to the main structural system. Similarly, multi-layered ornamental plasters should be avoided in high-intensity seismic zones.

Projected balconies in buildings

Projected balconies, parapets, walls and chimneys are badly hit during earthquakes. The weakest links of these structural components are their connections to the supports or foundations. It is however better to avoid projected structural elements in high seismic zones. However, if they are unavoidable, proper care should be taken in the detail engineering stage to provide adequate anchorage to the supports and foundations. Guyed chimneys are preferable to the free-standing ones in this respect. Vertical cantilever boundary walls may be provided with suitable counterforts at suitable intervals. RCC cantilever slabs must be anchored securely to the main framework through adequate reinforcements.

Bearings of bridges

From the point of view of transfer of seismic inertia forces, the bearings of bridges should be treated as a weak link most vulnerable to displacement, distortion and failure during any major earthquake. The bearings transfer all the dead loads, live loads and also incidental loads from wind or earthquake forces. The term load should be treated here in a broader term including all gravity load, horizontal shear, torsion and overturning moments. While adequate factor of safety can be allowed to member stresses in superstructure and they may designed with a reasonable safety margin, still, there remains the possibility of the whole superstructure being dislodged, tilted, overturned or shifted from its specified location, if earthquake forces are not restrained adequately at the bearing level. To prevent such safety hazards additional fixtures are installed at the bearing level. These are:

- Seismic restrainers
- Seismic isolators
- Structural fuse
- Shock transmission units

Detailed discussions on the method of manufacture, fabrication or design of these items are outside the scope of this book. However the basic considerations from safety point of view behind the use of these items will be presented in the following sections.

Seismic restrainers

The purpose of installing seismic restrainers in bridges is to arrest horizontal movement (dislodging) of the superstructure. These restrainers may be either rigid concrete blocks, also called 'reaction blocks', protruding from the pier cap (Refer Fig. 10.10 '*a*') and butting with the bridge girders or flexible ones composed of pre-stressed cables tieing the superstructure with the pier cap. Box girders are often provided with 'projected support diaphragms', which are locked in a specially designed recess on the pier and rested on elastomeric bearings to resist only the rotation, but allow no side shifting. (Refer Fig. 10.10 '*b*'). In steel bridges, seismic restrainers take the form of vertical brackets connected to the girder ends and firmly fixed to the pier cap by anchor bolts. (Refer Fig. 10.10 '*c*').

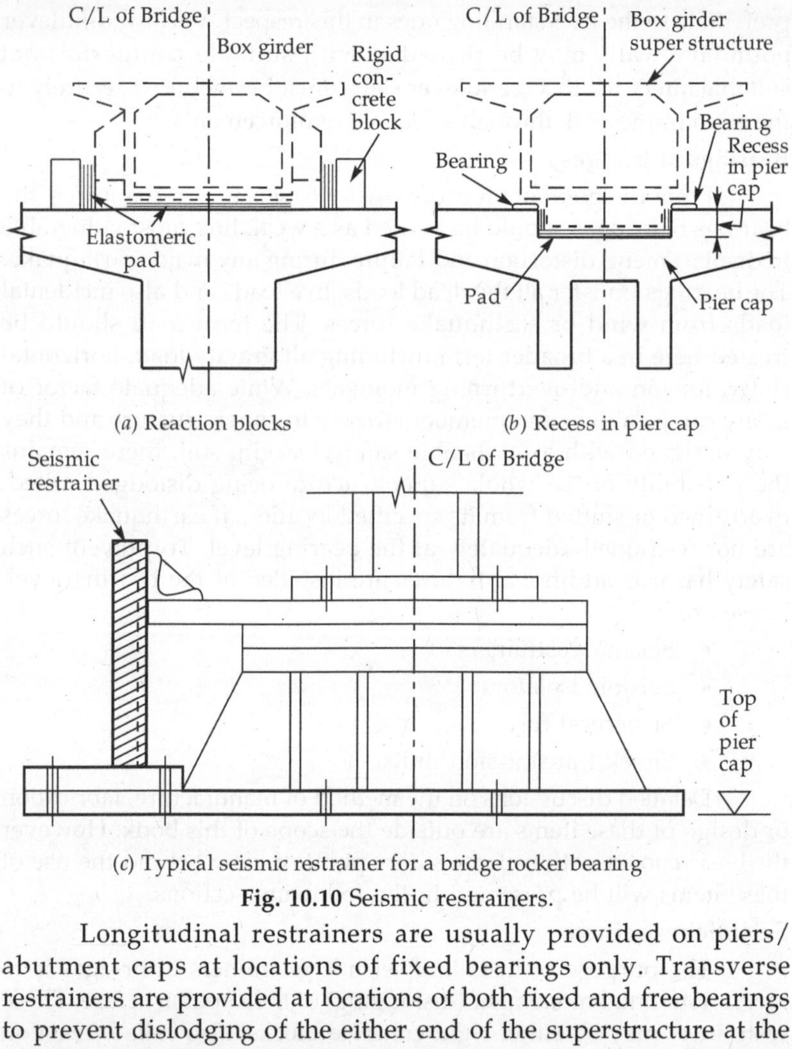

(*a*) Reaction blocks (*b*) Recess in pier cap

(*c*) Typical seismic restrainer for a bridge rocker bearing

Fig. 10.10 Seismic restrainers.

Longitudinal restrainers are usually provided on piers/ abutment caps at locations of fixed bearings only. Transverse restrainers are provided at locations of both fixed and free bearings to prevent dislodging of the either end of the superstructure at the bearing level. These restrainers also help in increasing the damping of the structural system. They also withstand impact forces and pounding during earthquakes and reduce chances of local damage.

Uplift of superstructure during earthquakes is usually prevented by the dead weight of the superstructure, which should have adequate factor of safety against vertical component of the earthquake forces. In critical cases, vertical pre-stressing combining pier/abutment with the superstructure may be done, so that the weight of the abutment/pier is also activated when uplift forces act on the system.

Adequate seating of the bridge girders over the bearings (particularly elastomeric bearings) ensures that friction is developed between the girder and the bearing. This friction acts as partial restrainers in the horizontal plane and reduces the load on the seismic restrainers. In view of above, good workmanship is a must when lowering the bridge girders on the elastomeric bearings. In zones of very low seismicity, however, friction developed at the bearing level may be adequate for safety and seismic restrainers may not be necessary. However, for zones III and above, seismic restrainers are a must to ensure structural safety of the superstructure.

Seismic Isolators

Seismic isolators are devices to reduce the seismic force induced at a particular level. Elastomeric bearings (Refer Fig. 10.11) transfer the vertical loads from the superstructure and act also as seismic isolators, as they induce flexibility reducing the seismic force response. For this purpose, special type of elastomeric bearings called Lead Rubber Bearings (LRB) (Refer Fig. 10.12) and High-Damping Rubber Bearings have been introduced as bridge bearings in many countries. The LRB bearing is also very effective as shock isolators, as vertical lead plugs are embedded inside the LBR bearings during its manufacture and these lead plugs act as isolators very efficiently. The seismic shear is transferred from the superstructure to the substructure through bolts.

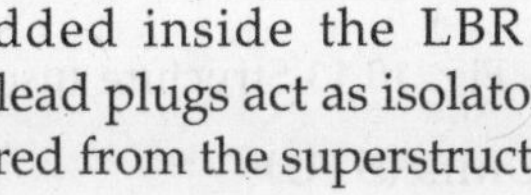

Fig. 10.11 Reinforced elastomeric bearing.

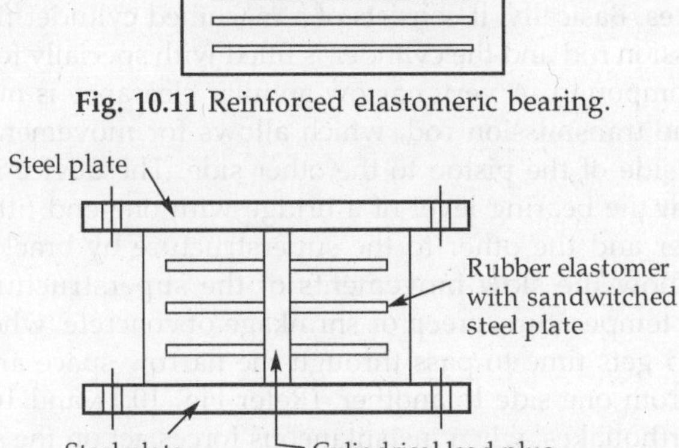

Fig. 10.12 Lead Rubber Bearing (LBR).

Structural fuses

It has been mentioned earlier that, in steel framings certain non-important members are identified and designed as structural fuses to dissipate the seismic energy by in-elastic yielding. In earthquake-resistant design of bridges also, significant local damages can be accepted in certain structural components and these may be allowed to act as structural fuses. Such structural elements are the dirt walls behind the abutments, a specified portion of the bridge deck or the expansion joints. The overall safety off the structural system can be assured if the above parts fail or allowed to be 'blown off' during earthquakes ensuring safety to other components. A typical example of structural fuses is given in Fig. 10.13.

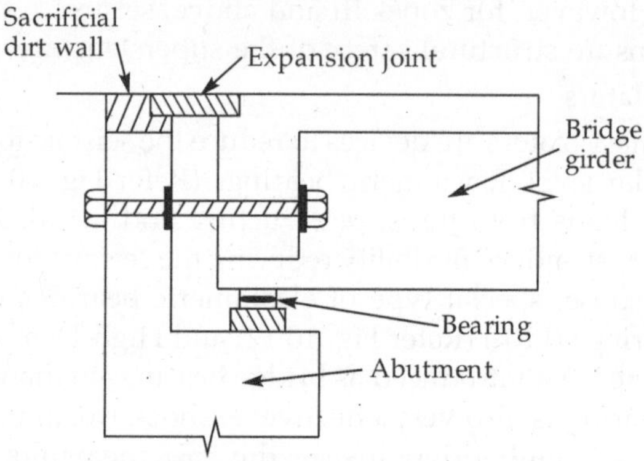

Fig. 10.13 Structure fuse.

Shock Transmission Units (STU)

A Shock Transmission Unit (STU) is essentially a device which provides resistance to the instantaneous loads generated during earthquakes. Basically, it consists of a machined cylinder fitted with a transmission rod and the cylinder is filled with specially formulated silicone compound. A very narrow annular clearance is maintained around the transmission rod, which allows for movement of fluid from one side of the piston to the other side. The device is usually attached at the bearing level of a bridge with one end fitted to the bridge pier and the other to the superstructure by brackets. Such devices allow the slow movements of the superstructure due to change in temperature, creep or shrinkage of concrete, when the in-filled fluid gets time to pass through the narrow space around the cylinder from one side to another. (Refer Fig. 10.14 and 10.15). But during earthquakes, when instantaneous forces act on the structural system, such movements are restricted, as transfer of the in-filled fluid is not possible within the short duration of the application of the seismic forces and the piston and the cylinder is virtually locked. If shock transmission units are fixed to free bearing locations, these devices help to distribute the earthquake forces to piers which were not resisting the earthquake loads beforehand. In such retrofitting measures, the shock transmission units help in utilizing the unutilized structural capacity of structural components during an earthquake.

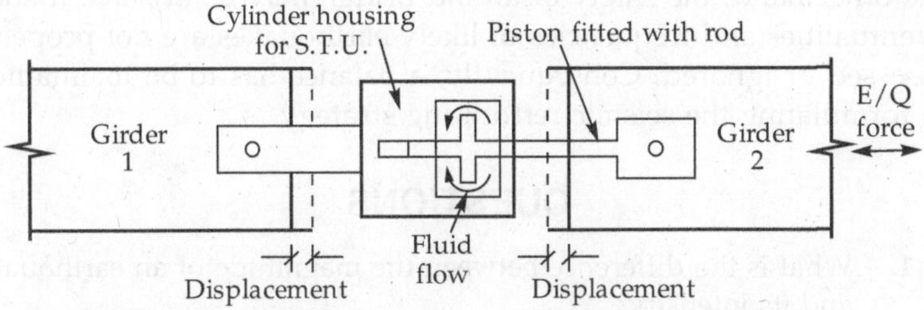

Fig. 10.14 Basic components of a typical shock transmission unit.

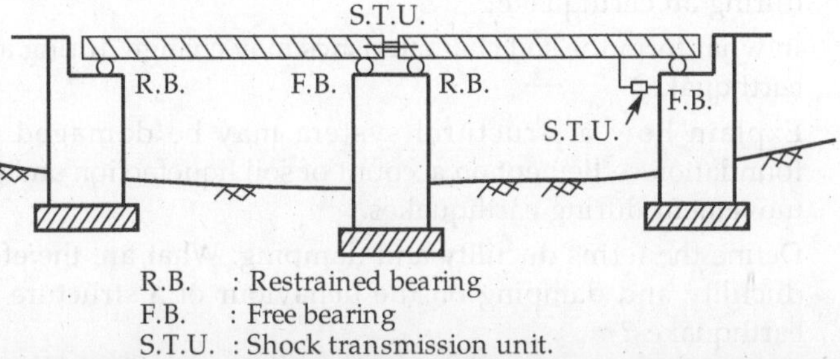

Fig. 10.15 Typical arrangement of shock transmission units in simply supported Girder bridge system.

10.14 SEISMIC RETROFITTING OF OLD BRIDGES

Old existing bridges are needed to be strengthened for improving their dynamic response during earthquakes. With periodic review and ongoing revisions of seismic zones, it has become necessary now to identify old bridges which have reduced seismic response as per the current measures of seismicity and these bridges should be strengthened in order to have better response to seismic vibration and shock. The retrofitting work of such bridges usually revolves around the following planning and design aspects.

- Strengthening the foundations to improve ductility
- Providing seismic restrainers at suitable locations to prevent dislodgement

Each case should be examined individually and retrofitting measures for any particular bridge are to be adopted considering the residual design life of the bridge, the probability of exceeding earthquake of any particular intensity and the return period of such earthquakes during its residual design life. Enormous costs are involved if the damage potential of any future earthquake having a large intensity is to be covered trough the retrofitting measures. On the other hand, the safety of an old bridge may be at stake if such eventualities and frequencies of likely earthquakes are not properly assessed or ignored. Consequently, a balance has to be maintained in formulating the seismic retrofitting strategy.

QUESTIONS

1. What is the difference between the magnitude of an earthquake and its intensity?
2. What are the factors responsible for major damages of buildings during an earthquake?
3. In what form the soil characteristics may change during a strong earthquake?
4. Explain how a structural system may be damaged due to foundation settlement on account of soil liquefaction and ground movement during earthquakes.
5. Define the terms ductility and damping. What are the effects of ductility and damping on the behaviour of a structure during earthquakes?
6. What are the advantages/disadvantages in introducing the following in a structural system in resisting earthquake forces?
   (*a*) Soft storey in a multistory building
   (*b*) Large opening in a wall
   (*c*) Abrupt change in a column section
7. What is the function of a shear wall in a multi-storey RCC framed building? How should they be placed?
8. How vulnerable are masonry structures during earthquakes? Suggest how masonry walls should be reinforced to resist earthquake forces.
9. Write explanatory notes on the following, mentioning their usefulness in resisting earthquake forces:
   (*a*) Seismic restrainers
   (*b*) Seismic isolators
   (*c*) STU
   (*d*) Anchorage for chimneys and vertical cantilever retaining walls
10. Using the empirical formula $E = 10^{4.8 + 1.5M}$ in Joules, for calculating release of energy during an earthquake, show that the energy release is magnified by 32 times, if the magnitude increases by only one unit.

CHAPTER 11

Safety Against Wind Hazards

11.1 INTRODUCTION

All structures above ground are subjected to wind loads in addition to gravity loads. With advances of modern urbanization, it has become the order of the day to build tall, vertical structures in the form of tall multistoried buildings, power transmission towers, microwave communication towers, tall chimneys, high-rise industrial structures, overhead water tanks and off-shore platforms. On the other side of this spectrum of high-rise structures, there are the low-height pitched roof, village hutments and temporary structures built to support the main structural system during construction. These structures are also equally hit by wind forces and badly damaged very often. Again, there are innumerable medium to long-span bridges situated high above the ground in open terrain. All these structures are subjected to varying degrees of both steady and/or turbulent wind throughout their physical life, depending on their height, base area, and shape and also terrain characteristics. The design of such structures against wind depends not only on the correct assessment of the wind load, but also on the correct formulation of material specifications and ensuring adequate safety against all possible wind-related safety hazards.

11.2 WIND VELOCITY

Wind is generated from the movement of air from high to low atmospheric pressure. At high altitudes, between 300 metres to 600 metres, wind blows fairly at a constant velocity without any hardly any hindrance from ground surface and is called **'gradient wind'.** Below that range of height, the wind flow is disturbed by ground obstructions and turbulence is created. This layer is known as the **'boundary layer'** for wind flow. Wind velocity may have longitudinal, lateral as well as vertical components. Each of these components again comprises of two components, namely, **'the mean wind velocity'** which is a quasi-static component and a **'fluctuating velocity'**, which is a dynamic component. (Refer Fig. 11.1).

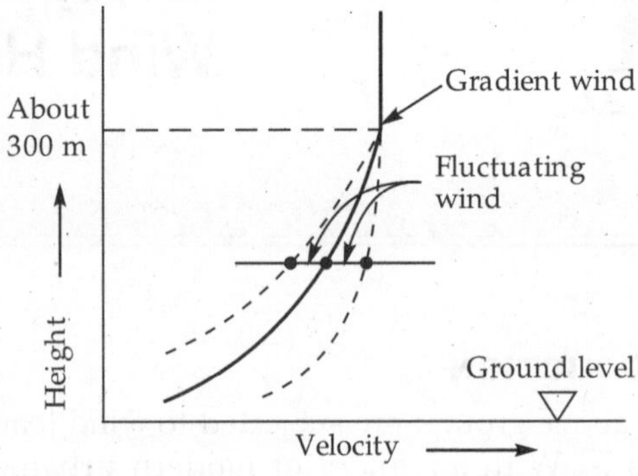

Fig. 11.1 Components of wind velocity.

Thus, $V(t) = V_{mean} + v(t)$

where V_{mean} = mean (time-averaged) wind velocity

$v(t)$ = fluctuating velocity component of wind

11.2.1 Mean Wind Velocity

The mean wind velocity is generally determined by averaging wind speeds over a period of 10 to 60 minutes and is considered adequate for engineering purposes and gives reasonably steady mean values. The mean wind velocity varies with height and also changes significantly and sometimes abruptly depending on the terrain, surface and roughness. In hilly areas, the wind velocity gets reduced near the valley, but accelerates at hill top. The mean velocity component of the wind force tends to produce a steady displacement (deflection) in a structure.

11.2.2 Fluctuating Component of Wind Velocity

The fluctuating component of wind velocity is random both in time and space. It is also sometimes termed as 'gust' wind, which increases or decreases the wind velocity from its mean value and lasts for a short period of about 1–2 minutes. When a structure is exposed to wind, the above fluctuating component of wind velocity creates a time-variable oscillation (deflection) of the structure. Such wind-induced oscillation is random in nature and it is difficult to predict the exact time of its occurrence and likely magnitude. However, for structural design purposes, a simple codal provision has been made with the introduction of the concept of **'Basic Wind Speed'**, which is based on the peak gust velocity averaged over a short-time interval of about 3 seconds, at 10 metre height above ground and worked out for a return period of 50 years. The basic wind speed applicable for important cities and towns are incorporated in the national codes, which are periodically revised as per results of statistical analysis of continuous wind velocity records maintained at meteorological stations. Basic wind speed for other places can be found out by interpolation between isopleths (lines of equal wind speed) drawn usually at 2 metres per second interval on the map prepared by meteorological stations.

11.2.3 Design Wind Speed

For design of structures, the basic wind speed is further modified to obtain the design wind speed at any height for a particular structure as under:

$$V_z = V_B \times K_1 \times K_2 \times K_3$$

where V_z = Design wind speed at any height in m/sec

V_B = Basic wind speed in m/sec

K_1 = risk coefficient

K_2 = factor for terrain, height and type of structure

K_3 = topography factor

And, design wind pressure (p_z) at any height above ground level is given by:

$$P_z = 0.6 \times V_z^2 \text{ N/m}^2$$

where V_z is in m/s and 0.6 is the coefficient depending on atmospheric pressure and air temperature in Indian condition. IS: 875-(Part 3)-1975 gives detailed guidelines for design of structural elements like walls, roofs, buildings with large openings, open air structures etc. of different shape and size, using the above design wind pressure.

The above design approach is quasi-static in principle and gives satisfactory results for rigid structures of small heights, which do not have a tendency to oscillate under the influence of wind turbulence. In most such cases the design is done for dead load and live load and the sections are checked for additional stresses developed due to the horizontal and vertical components of the wind force.

11.3 DYNAMIC STABILITY OF SLENDER STRUCTURES UNDER WIND FORCES

For slender structures which have tendencies to oscillate under strong wind, the safety and stability cannot however be assured by adopting only a quasi-static approach as described above. Under this category come the tall buildings, tall chimneys, medium to long-span bridges, particularly suspension bridges, cable-stay bridges and communication/ transmission towers. The stability calculations of all such structures should take into account the turbulent characteristics of wind flow and the likely aerodynamic response of the structure, which depends on the mass, flexibility, natural frequency, geometric shape and damping characteristics of the materials used in the construction. In such cases the aerodynamic responses which are to be investigated are the following:

- **Buffeting:** oscillation of the structure at the leeward side, when two similar structures are built side by side.
- **Vortex shedding:** creation of transverse oscillations due to cross-wind flow, particularly in lightly-damped structures.
- **Flutter:** resonance created due to coupling of frequency modes during flow of cross wind.
- **Gust:** producing sudden local pressure.

11.3.1 Buffeting

Wind tunnel tests conducted on the aerodynamic behaviour of tall chimneys reveal the following results regarding buffeting effect of wind.

(*a*) Due to buffeting effect, the leeward chimney exhibits much larger amplitude than the windward chimney.

(*b*) The buffeting effect is maximum at 1/3rd height from top, when the center to center distance between the windward and the leeward chimney is limited to 5-times the diameter of the chimneys.

11.3.2 Vortex Shedding

When wind flows past cylindrical structures like tall chimneys of round shape, vortexes are formed (shed) on the leeward side, creating significant cross-wind motions. (Refer Fig. 11.2).

The over-all effect may be critical if the frequency of vortex shedding comes close to the natural frequency of the structure itself. Unlined welded steel chimneys and lightly-damped slender tall structures are prone to resonance vibration due to vortex shedding. This may create safety hazards in extreme circumstances. Wind tunnel tests reveal that, when there are more than one stack constructed side by side, the leeward chimney exhibits larger oscillations if there is resonance due to vortex shedding.

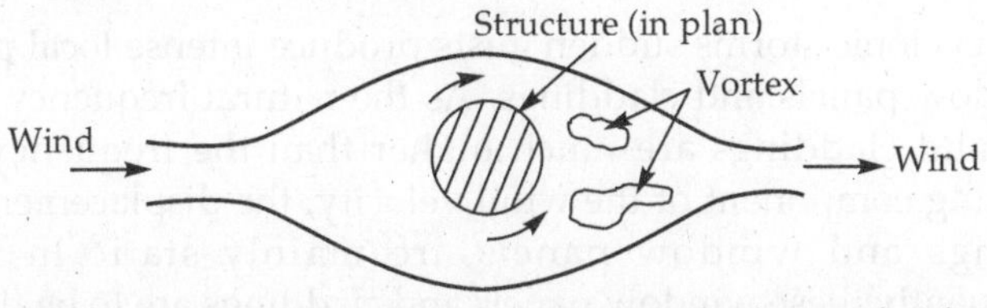

Fig. 11.2 Formation of wind vortex on the leeward side.

Unlike the gust factors, vortex forces originate in the leeward side of a tall structure and acts in the across-wind direction. The dominant frequency of vortex shedding f_v is given by:

$$F_v = S \times \{V_{mean} / D\} \times H_z$$

where S = dimensionless constant called Strouhal number (0.20 to 0.25 for structures circular in plan and 0.25 for rectangular shaped structures)

V_{mean} = mean wind velocity

D = width of the frontal area.

Resonance occurs when this vortex frequency coincides with the natural frequency of the structure itself.

11.3.3 Flutter

For long-span bridges, particularly for suspension bridges, 'flutter' of the bridge deck is another serious wind-related safety hazard. Mention may be made here of the failure of the Tacoma Narrows suspension bridge in 1940 in USA. It is known that, in the absence of wind, the torsional frequency of a typical suspension bridge is always greater than its fundamental natural frequency in the vertical mode. As the wind blows, the torsional frequency is reduced,but the vertical frequency remains unchanged. As the wind blows harder and harder, a critical stage is reached when the torsional frequency becomes equal to the vertical natural frequency and then resonance is initiated. This phenomenon is called 'flutter'. To avoid this undesirable aerodynamic disturbance causing structural instability, the designer has to choose the deck system and its stiffening arrangements in such a manner that, the critical wind speed at which flutter initiates, remains always greater than the design wind speed. The stiffness of the deck and its support system are to be adjusted to avoid flutter. Additional damping devices are also used to prevent the occurrence of flutter, by way of effectively arresting energy transfer from one mode of oscillation to another.

11.3.4 Gust

During cyclonic storms sudden gusts produce intense local pressure on window panels and claddings. As the natural frequency of such panels and claddings are much higher than the frequency of the fluctuating component of the wind velocity, the displacement of the claddings and window panels are mainly static in nature. Consequently these window panels and claddings are to be designed for the expected maximum pressure given by the equation:

$$P_{max} = p \times G$$

where p = mean pressure

and G = gust factors (peak load/mean load) as given in national codes.

Hangers of suspension bridges are often subjected to across-wind vibrations/oscillations called **'singing'**. Same kinds of oscillations are also felt in cable stays. For long cable stays, oscillations are also caused by wind coupled with rain. To overcome such undesirable oscillations, auxiliary cables are often provided for long stays along with damping devices.

11.4 DYNAMIC STABILITY FOR TALL BUILDINGS

For tall buildings whose heights are more than 5 times the minimum lateral dimension or whose first mode fundamental natural frequency (f_n) is less than 1.0 Hz, the structure is considered to be flexible. In such cases the dynamic effects of wind-induced oscillations are to be critically examined. For moment-resisting multi-storied frames without shear walls, $T = 0.1n$, where T is the fundamental time period in seconds (*i.e.*, $T = 1/f_n$) and n is the number of stories including basement. From the equation it is evident that, from multi-storied frames more than 10-storey height, cross turbulence may create galloping, flutter, ovaling or unsteady wake-flow and these may be critical for aerodynamic stability of tall buildings. Analytical methods should be adopted or wind tunnel tests may be conducted for investigations in this regard.

11.5 DYNAMIC STABILITY FOR TALL STEEL STRUCTURES

All-welded steel structures have low damping ratio (sometimes less than 0.005) and exhibit strong oscillations during fluctuating wind.

Such safety hazards are noticeable in free-standing towers, steel chimneys and masts. Moreover, dynamic instability may occur sooner than desired, if the welded structural components have flaws in their connections, notches or attachments. In such cases the welded members may cross their fatigue limit, even if the actual wind speed is much less than the 'design wind speed'. To avoid such mishaps, it is required primarily to design and detail the welded joints properly following the provisions of the codes and standard engineering practice, so that early fatigue failures are avoided.

11.5.1 Design for Safety Against Wind Forces

Unlike earthquake forces, the wind forces are more or less deterministic and it is now possible from the past records available to anticipate in advance during the planning stage itself the safety hazards likely to be encountered due to strong winds. The codal provisions also give excellent guidelines in this respect. As such, it is the designer's responsibility to introduce in the structural system adequate provisions for resisting the most critical wind forces. To achieve this objective, the wind load should be calculated for:

1. The structure as a whole, applying force coefficients as applicable to the particular structure as per provisions of the code.
2. Individual structural elements like roofs, walls considering the pressure differences between the opposite faces of such elements.
3. Individual structural units like glazing, fixtures and ridges against local suction due to wind.

The connections and the bracing system should be adequate for transference of the wind loads so calculated. In this connection special attention should be given to ensure safety against the fluctuating dynamic component of the wind. This can be achieved by any of the following means:

- By introducing indeterminate bracing system to control to-and-fro oscillations due to fluctuating wind.
- By providing helical strakes to cylindrical welded structures like chimney stacks to break down the fluctuating wind effect
- By modifying suitably the aspect ratio (height: least lateral dimension) of the structure at the planning stage
- By introducing, if necessary, auxiliary mass dampers attached to the main structures and tuned for out-of-phase vibration

- Designing welded structures as space frames and detailing the joints accordingly.

11.6 WIND DISTURBANCES DURING CONSTRUCTION STAGE

Medium to long-span steel bridges are often erected at site by free cantilever method, when the whole span is progressively erected member by member, using a previously-erected span as anchor span with the help of an erection crane erected on the top chord of the forward span. The erection crane is moved forward as the erection work proceeds and almost the whole span cantilevers out in the last phase of the erection, till the forward end reaches the next pier or abutment. Though the erection work is usually done at site under strict supervision in controlled condition when the wind velocity is low, the aerodynamic stability and safety of the whole system should be critically examined even when the crane is not working and the erection work is halted. Suitable stays, guys, receiving brackets and temporary supports should be provided to avoid additional torsional stresses and consequent flutter due to fluctuating wind and gust forces.

11.7 SAFETY HAZARDS UNDER EXTREME WIND CONDITIONS

Extreme wind conditions beyond those stipulated in the codes are often manifested in several parts of India, particularly along the coastal belts. These appear in different forms, namely:

- Cyclone
- Thunderstorm
- Tornado

11.7.1 Cyclones

Cyclones are intensive low-pressure systems originating in tropical latitudes, mostly between 6°–20° North and 6°–20° South. Cyclonic wind moves anti-clockwise in the northern hemisphere and clockwise in the southern hemisphere. They originate from oceans around the world and are named differently as:

- Cyclone: in the Indian ocean
- Hurricane: in the Gulf of Mexico
- Typhoons: in the China seas
- Willy-willies off the coast of Australia

Tropical cyclones in India are almost always very strong and they are associated with torrential rain. The center of the storm (or the 'eye', as it is called) is confined to a small area about 18–20 Km across, very calm of light wind. Beyond that region, whirlwind moves with terrific force, sometimes attaining a velocity of 150–200 Km/hour or even more, associated with torrential rain and thunderstorm. In India, cyclones usually originate from the Bay of Bengal and in the Arabian Sea during the months of April to June. and also during October to December. As a cyclone moves into the mainland, the coastal areas experience violent wind, heavy rainfall and tidal waves, creating floods or flood-like situations with safety hazards to life and property. Every year losses in infrastructure due to cyclonic devastations cost the exchequer crores of rupees, which becomes very difficult to replenish.On an average, one or two cyclones may be expected in Andhra, Orissa and West Bengal coasts every year in the pre-monsoon period. The cyclonic storms lose their strength as it moves inland. Therefore the infrastructure facilities built inland India are generally not very much affected by the cyclones.

Early warnings of cyclones are usually broadcast from meteorological stations, indicating their expected speed, direction of movement and intensity. Studies on the effect of cyclones on micro-wave towers reveal that tower members are subjected to almost 30% higher stresses in case of cyclones, compared to the stresses generated corresponding to wind speed at 10metre height as prescribed in the codes. Alongside, it is recorded that cyclonic wind speeds have exceeded the non-cyclonic wind speeds by 36.4% in West Bengal, 70% in Andhra Pradesh and 64% in Konkan and Tamil Nadu.

11.7.2 Thunderstorms

As against cyclones, which originate from oceans, thunderstorms are local storms generated from cumulonimbus clouds followed by lightning and thunder. Torrential rain and lightning strikes are the main safety hazards of thunderstorms. Sometimes thunderstorms are preceded by dust storms and hail storms. Such phenomenon is of short duration, but thunderstorms are often violent, such as the Nor'westers of West Bengal. The horizontal wind velocity may reach as high as 75 m/sec, which is substantially higher than the highest basic wind speed for normal wind prescribed in the Indian code.

Both cyclones and thunderstorms are non-stationary in nature and their paths are also not well defined. But it is fairly well established that cyclonic storms generate from the sea and it strikes the coastal areas in full fury with turbulent high wind associated with heavy rainfall. The cyclonic storm loses much of the energy as it moves inland. Consequently, all structures, major, minor or temporary, which are built in the coastal areas should be safe-guarded with adequate factor of safety against cyclone-related damages. The provisions in the Indian code IS: 875 (Part 3)-2002 specifies a basic wind speed of 50 m/sec for coastal districts, considering gust wind and, at the same time, indicated a wind velocity of 80 m/sec for cyclonic storms, thunderstorms, dust storms and vigorous monsoons. This leaves to the discretion of the designer to specify as to what should be the reasonable design wind speed for structures in coastal area. Damages observed in Andhra Pradesh, Orissa and West Bengal cyclones clearly indicates that the statutory wind speed, considering only the mean and the fluctuating component of the wind is not adequate for safety of structures during cyclones. Moreover, fatigue factors contribute to the early failure of steel structures and their connections, when high-velocity cyclones hit them. Due to this reason, roof sheets often fail at dynamic loads much lower than their static load carrying capacity. American code ACI-1976 indicates the following regional multiplying factors for structures to cater for such eventualities.

	For velocity
Normal (non-cyclonic)	1.0
Intermediate	1.225
Tropical cyclones	1.517
Severe tropical cyclones	1.817

11.7.3 Tornado

Tornadoes are swirling low-pressure localized wind vortices rising from the ground surface and moving at terrific speed of even 100–120 m/sec. A tremendous vertical suction is produced by a tornado, which uproots trees, destroys buildings and often lifts and throws at a distance entire roof structures. Tornadoes are short-lived, existing rarely more than 30 minutes or so, sometimes for a few minutes even. The wind moves clockwise in a tornado-hit vortex area with immense velocity. Tornadoes are about 200–300 metre wide and therefore it leaves a trail of destruction along that strip of land, over which it moves. Tornadoes are common in the Mississippi Basin and so far, they pose as the most destructive wind force in the world. Tornadoes are also encountered in India in several places, though their time of appearance is quite arbitrary and un-predictable.

Fortunately, tornado-related disasters are localized and limited in area. But, even in this limited area, the wind vortex creates immense chaos, producing excessive low pressure around buildings. As a result, buildings often tend to collapse outwards, because the internal pressure inside the building becomes much greater than the pressure outside. Safety measures against tornadoes should ensure a sturdy robust construction, proper anchorage of structural components, particularly load-bearing columns and providing extra wind ties or wind girders to resist the vertical and radial uplift forces.

Based on the past records of tornado-related damages in USA and Canada, Newark (1991) has developed a design basis for fixing the tornado wind speeds in five Fujita scales (F_0-F_4), commonly referred to as 'Newark Scale'. An abridged version of the *F*-scale values is given in the following table for reference of the readers.

Design parameters	*F-scale values*				
	F_0	F_1	F_2	F_3	F_4
Median damage length (km)	0.5	1.6	3.5	10.9	22.2
Max. rotational speed (m/s)	31.9	49.7	69.7	91.7	115.6
Dynamic wind press (KPa)	1.32	2.50	4.28	6.77	10.14
Change of static pressure (KPa/sec)	2.31	2.08	1.96	1.86	1.78
(1 KPa = 100 Kg/sqm)					

From the above table it is obvious that the damage length increases with the increase in the maximum rotational speed and the dynamic wind pressure of the tornado. Also, it cannot be predicted accurately the exact path of a tornado or time of its occurrence, except that certain regions in each country experience tornado-related disasters more often than in other places. As such, there is utter uncertainty in this regard and only a probabilistic approach may be taken in the design of structure and a rapid warning system should be organized to intimate people in case of any imminent disaster, so that their lives can be saved and they can move either to basements of their houses or to other safe places.

QUESTIONS

1. What is meant by gradient wind? How is it distributed near the ground surface?
2. Explain what is meant by quasi-static and dynamic components of the wind velocity. What types of displacements are caused by these wind components to structures over-ground?
3. What is the relevance of assessing the basic wind speed for structural designs? How the randomness of wind forces are periodically incorporated in the national codes?
4. Explain how the design wind speed is calculated at different heights of a tall structure? How the risks from wind-related damages and topographical factors are considered in the assessment of he above design wind speed?
5. Explain how buffeting, vortex shedding, flutter and gust may cause dynamic instability to tall slender structures.
6. What should be the strategy for designing a structure against wind loads? How wind loads should be combined with other loads?
7. In what circumstances a structure under construction may be rendered unstable due to wind disturbances? What precautions should be taken at site to avoid wind-related mishaps during construction?
8. Write short notes on the following, with special reference to Indian conditions:
   (*a*) Cyclone
   (*b*) Thunderstorms
   (*c*) Tornado
9. How the powerful dynamic wind pressure generated during a tornado movement may be assessed from observed damages with the help of Newark scale?
10. What type of safety features should be incorporated in the design of structures to have reasonable protection against tornado-related disasters?
11. Explain how slender structures should be protected from damages from storms or cyclones.
12. Identify the zones in India which are almost regularly affected by strong wind forces, cyclones and thunderstorms. How the safety and security of the people in these areas should be assured? What is the social effect of wind-related damages to the people residing in temporary hutments in coastal areas of India?

CHAPTER 12

Safety against Natural Calamities–Landslide

12.1 INTRODUCTION

In geological terminology landslides are movements of solid rocks, weathered material or loose earth along weaker planes of hill slopes. In case of clays such sliding often occurs along a circular plane, known as the slip circle and the mass rotates along this curved plane. The dislodged materials accumulate down at the bottom of the hill slope creating huge masses of slumps and destroying life and property along its path. Landslides are often activated during monsoon or immediately after heavy rains, when the hills are surcharged with water and internal cohesion of the soil is very low. When solid rocks move down during landslides, the slide occurs along the cracks, fissures and weak planes already existing within the rock mass. In high mountain regions, huge masses of ice, snow and rock often flow downwards as avalanches. The movements of avalanches are often associated with mudflows. Mudslides may be the outcome when molten lava materials roll down the slopes of a volcano. Such volcanic outbursts also occur when volcanoes under the sea become active and, in extreme cases, they create huge wave fronts, called 'tsunami', which lashes on the sea shores. All these are natural phenomenon that often create safety hazards coupled with loss of human lives and property.

There are many cases where geological factors have been found to be the prime critical factor for landslides. The Vaiont dam disaster in 1963 in Italy may be cited as an example in this regard. In this case unstable geological conditions created such a huge landslide in the reservoir area that the ensuing slide pushed waters over the high dam. The dam withstood the thrust of water but the floodwaters downstream killed over 2000 people with enormous loss of property and other infrastructure.

Similarly, earthquake-induced landslides have occurred in the Ningxia province of China in 1920 causing deaths of more than 100000 people. Slope failures during earthquakes have also been encountered recently: at Loma Preta in 1989, at Northbridge in 1994, at Kobe in 1995 and also at Kashmir in 2005.

In India, landslides are frequently encountered in the mountain slopes of the Himalayas, as the geological structure of the rock there is young, unstable and fractured in many places. Moreover the rainfall intensity is quite high and landslides are also triggered by seismological disturbances. During monsoon, the shear strength and cohesive strength of the soil in this region decrease considerably when devastating landslides cause road blockades and damage to the road and railway infrastructure. In fact some regions are perpetually prone to landslides that require extraordinary annual expenses for clearances of debris and restoration work. Such landslides are very active in the Kullu-Manali-Leh valley in hilly region of Himachal Pradesh and also in the Darjeeling- Kalimpong-Gangtok region.

Landslides may be triggered due to uncalled-for human activities like construction of heavy buildings over unstable hill tops or disturbing the natural hill slopes to construct roads and railway lines.

The stability of hill slopes is also affected due to slide of debris along slope, fall of boulders, erosion and chemical weathering of rocks. Limestone cavities often trigger a slope failure. In high-intensity rainfall areas, gully formations accelerate the erosion of the hill slope. Wider gullies often lead to flow of rainwater over the road surface damaging the road and the shoulders.

In hilly areas cuttings are done along hill slopes to build roads and railway tracts. These cuttings are essentially excavations that are left open permanently for the above projects. Cuttings have to be done also for open mines, for construction of deep foundation pits and also for stone and sand quarries. To maintain the required profile of these cuttings it is imperative to maintain stability of the side slopes of the cuttings and precautions are to be taken to that effect as per design and specifications. However, in spite of all precautions taken from time to time, it is a common experience that side slopes of cuttings lose their stable position and huge mounds of earth containing loose boulders, rock pieces and loose soil come down all on a sudden below from the top and create safety hazard to moving vehicles with loss of lives and property.

Landslides also happen at bridge sites close to newly constructed un-consolidated high embankments due to slip circle failures. In extreme cases there are reports of lateral shift in the abutment well due to such embankment failure. Movement of vehicles and construction of buildings and structures on the top of cuttings also contribute to the safety hazards related to landslides.

12.2 CAUSES OF LANDSLIDES

The movement of loosened earth during landslides occurs under gravitational pull and the intensity increases when the materials in the slopes are surcharged with rainwater or moisture. Landslides are also frequent in those hilly areas where the rock formations are not hard and consolidated and are prone to be loose on seepage of rain water during the heavy monsoon rains. Land slides also happen in those areas where the slopes of the cuttings are quite stiff. The major factors that may cause landslides may therefore be attributed to the following:

- Geological formation of the hill slopes
- Geological structure of the rocks
- Ground water conditions prevailing at the time of the landslide
- Moving vehicles on top of loose slopes
- Imposition of heavy loads due to construction (often unauthorized) of buildings and other structures or dumping of construction materials on top.
- Erosion at the toe
- Ground movement due to earthquake

Any one or more of the above may be responsible for a particular landslide. Therefore it is necessary to identify the factors causing landslides at a particular place and then find out ways and means to minimize the related safety hazards.

12.3 GEOLOGICAL STRUCTURE AND FORMATION OF ROCKS

The probability of occurrence and damage potential of a landslide in hilly areas depend to a great extent on the geological structure and nature of the rocks.

12.3.1 Igneous and Metamorphic Rocks

Hill slopes made up of igneous and metamorphic rocks like, granite, basalt, gneiss, quartzite etc, are generally found to be stable, Even an almost vertical slope can be maintained in such cases. However, the presence of faults, deep fissures and shear zones may render even such solid rocks unstable. The following preventive measures should be taken in such cases.

- The rock slopes may be cut and dressed along their planes of weakness.
- Accumulation of ground water may be avoided by proper drainage.
- Extremely weak cracks and fissures may be grouted with concrete with admixtures.

12.3.2 Sedimentary Rocks

Thick layers of sedimentary rocks made up of sandstone, limestone, laterite, coal etc are stable against landslides more or less permanently, if properly maintained and looked after. However the stability of cuttings through sedimentary rocks depends on the slope of the bedding planes to a great extent. If the beds are more or less horizontal and are made up of compact massive rocks, steep slopes will remain stable. If the rock mass is made up of horizontal sediments traversed by joints, the slope can be stabilized by reducing the gradients followed by proper drainage.

Again, when the sedimentary rock beds are inclined, *i.e.* they have a certain 'dip', the cutting slopes may be inclined along or against such dip of the beds. The slope is unstable when the sedimentary beds dip towards the cutting wall at an angle less than the inclination of the cutting slope. On the other hand, the slope is generally stable if the beds dip away from the cutting walls. Typical cases of stability of hill slopes for road-cuts in hilly areas are shown in Fig. 12.1.

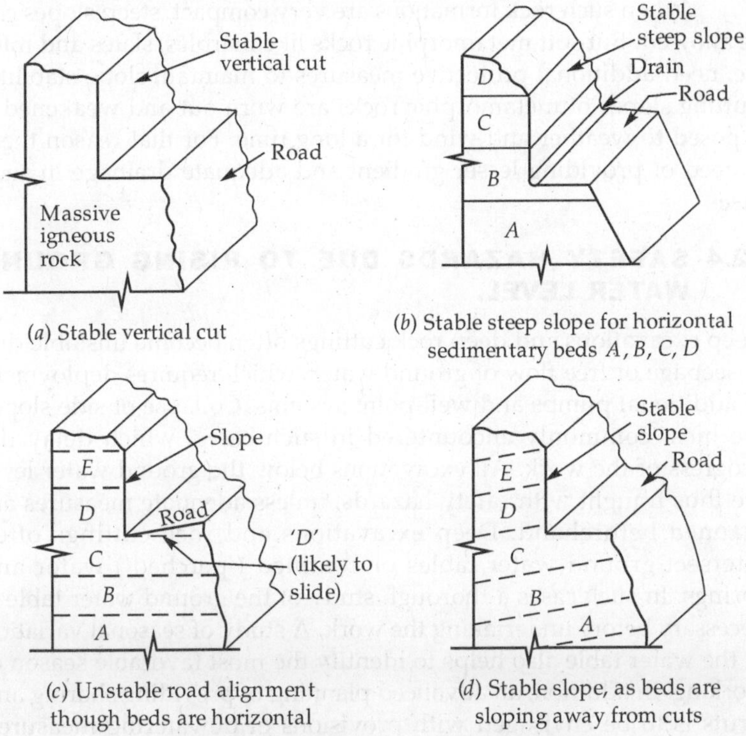

Fig. 12.1 Typical cases of stability of hill slopes for road-cuts in hilly areas.

12.3.3 Argillaceous Rocks

Argillaceous rocks are essentially sedimentary rocks but made up of particles of very fine grain size. Shale, clay stone and mudstone etc. fall under this rock category. These rocks are inherently weak and soft. Steep slopes through these rocks are likely to be unstable, particularly during heavy rains. In such cases the stability of slopes can only be maintained by reducing the cutting slopes and providing adequate drainage.

12.3.4 Metamorphic Rocks

Metamorphic rocks on earth have been formed of minerals under superimposed conditions of high temperature and pressure. It may be mentioned that, out of all the three types of rocks namely, igneous, sedimentary and metamorphic rocks, the crust of the earth abounds in the presence of metamorphic rocks due to constant reform or metamorphism under temperature, pressure and chemical reactions.

When such rock formations are very compact, steep slopes can be allowed. But soft metamorphic rocks like marbles, slates and mica etc. need additional protective measures to maintain slope stability. Cutting slopes of metamorphic rocks are worn out and weakened if exposed to weather and wind for a long time. For that reason there is need of providing lesser gradient and adequate drainage in such cases.

12.4 SAFETY HAZARDS DUE TO RISING GROUND WATER LEVEL.

Deep excavations and deep rock cuttings often become unstable due to seepage or free flow of ground water, which requires deployment of additional pumps and well-point systems. Collapse of side slopes are most commonly encountered in such cases, which delay the progress of the work. All excavations below the ground water level are thus fraught with safety hazards, unless adequate measures are planned beforehand. Deep excavations and rock cuttings often intersect ground water tables or confined ('perched') water and springs. In such cases a thorough study of the ground water table is necessary before undertaking the work. A study of seasonal variation in the water table also helps to identify the most favorable season of working. In addition, an advanced planning of providing shoring and struts is to be envisaged with provisions of dewatering measures. Seepage of water along cutting slopes in hilly areas can neither be avoided, nor be obstructed. As such, it will be prudent to allow the seepage water to flow along pre-determined drainage paths to the point of natural springs nearby.

From economic point of view, safety breaches due to landslides and collapse of side slopes during deep excavations have adverse bearings on the local and regional economy. Important arterial roads and railway lines often remain disconnected for a long time due to landslides. Worksites become paralyzed due to sudden side collapses during excavations. Human lives are also lost and running projects are delayed in many circumstances. Even completed projects like high embankments are damaged often due to instability and failure of side slopes. It is therefore extremely important to consider right at the planning and design stage all aspects of any landslide or side collapse that may be encountered in any hilly road or high embankment project.

In the planning and design stage a thorough field study, survey and site investigation should be done to find out the following data and, on analyzing those data, suitable preventive measures should to be taken:

- Topographical features of the proposed alignment
- Extent of rock joints, fissures, folds and faults
- Composition and type of the rock
- Orientation of the bedding plane and dip of the rock beds
- Rock Quality Designator (RQD) of the rock formations
- Plant varieties in the locality and their effectiveness in arresting landslides

12.5 LANDSLIDE HAZARD ZONATION (LHZ) MAP FOR LARGE PROJECTS IN HILLY AREAS

For large developmental projects like hilly roads running through hill tracts of unknown geological features, it is the common practice to conduct Landslide Hazard Zonation (LHZ) mapping of the project area to ascertain the factors and probabilities of landslides and their likely adverse effects on the project infrastructure. This investigation is usually focused on the finding field data on the following causative factors of slope instability.

- **Lithology:** to know the probabilities of soil erosion
- **Rock structure:** to ascertain the position of faults and discontinuities
- **Slope characteristics:** to know the variations in slope and contour
- **Local relief of the hills:** to demarcate the low medium and high relief zones
- **Land use:** to indicate the extent of forest cover and agriculture
- **Hydro-geological factors:** to identify the flow pattern of groundwater

For a particular zone where the above survey is conducted, ratings are given against all the above six causative factors on the basis of their significance in causing instability to the hill slopes. Based on these factors, a Landslide Hazard Zonation (LHZ) map is prepared, indicating on the map Zones of landslide vulnerability, as under:

- Very high hazard zone
- High hazard zone
- Moderate hazard zone

- Low hazard zone
- Very low hazard zone

Though such possible landslide hazards cannot be quantified in numerical terms from such mapping process, which largely depends on the experience and detailed observation of the surveyor, from this LHZ map a more or less clear idea can be formed about the extent of the project area likely to be affected by landslides and the intensity and adverse effect of such landslides. Accordingly preventive measures can be incorporated in the design of the infrastructure.

12.6 SUGGESTED METHODS OF CONTROLLING LANDSLIDES

The following are some of the measures generally adopted to control landslide:

- Cutting of the hill slopes at their **normal angle of repose** as far as practicable
- Providing a protection on the road side in the form of a **breast wall**
- Providing a **toe wall** on the river side
- Providing **river training work**
- Providing proper **drainage**
- Providing small **culverts** where natural streams are running without obstructing their flow
- Providing **retaining walls** (either of stone masonry, brick or RCC) along hill slope to retain earth from sliding
- Proving **proper slope to the roadway** to drain out water as quickly as possible
- **Grouting of cracks and fissures** with cement grout to protect the slope from erosion from seepage of rain water.
- Providing reinforced **anchor blocks or netlon mesh** or coir matting to the retaining walls for stability
- Providing **weep holes** in retaining walls by 50 mm/75 mm dia PVC pipes @ 6 m c/c and @ 1.5 m along height to release excessive hydraulic pressure behind the retaining walls
- **Avoiding avalanche prone areas** for road or railway projects

- **Forestation** in the landslide prone areas by vegetation turfs.
- **Slope treatment** by jute mesh/ coir mesh or geo-textile materials.
- **Avoiding blasting operations** during construction in landslide-prone areas.
- Providing adequate shoring to **prevent collapse of sides** during excavation work

A few of the above measures are indicated in Fig. 12.2.

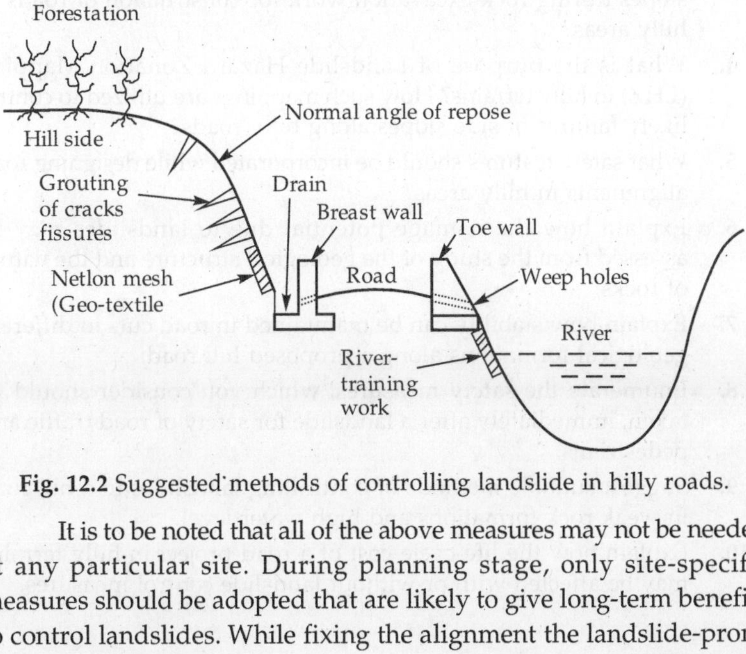

Fig. 12.2 Suggested methods of controlling landslide in hilly roads.

It is to be noted that all of the above measures may not be needed at any particular site. During planning stage, only site-specific measures should be adopted that are likely to give long-term benefits to control landslides. While fixing the alignment the landslide-prone areas should be identified and a very rough estimate should be done to find out the life cycle cost of constructing the additional infrastructure to control landslides and the recurring costs to maintain the same during the whole service life. In many cases, it may be found to be worthwhile to divert the alignment itself incurring an initial extra cost, instead of inviting safety hazards in landslides and going through the trouble of removing from time to time huge amount of debris and repair the road or railway tract in a most unfavorable working condition.

QUESTIONS

1. Why landslides are treated as serious safety hazards for structures in hilly terrains? How the local people are affected by landslides?
2. What types of geological formations and ground water conditions trigger landslides along hill slopes? How torrential rain or a strong earthquake may aggravate the safety hazards?
3. What should be the basic guidelines to maintain stability of hill slopes during rock excavation work for construction of roads in hilly areas?
4. What is the purpose of Landslide Hazard Zonation Mapping (LHZ) in hilly terrains? How such mappings are utilized to control likely failures of side slopes along hilly roads?
5. What safety features should be incorporated while designing road alignments in hilly areas?
6. Explain how the damage potential due to landslides may be assessed from the study of the geological structure and the nature of rocks.
7. Explain how stability can be maintained in road cuts in different geological formations along a proposed hill road.
8. Enumerate the safety measures, which you consider should be taken, immediately after a landslide for safety of road traffic and pedestrians.
9. Suggest suitable methods of controlling landslides in a hill road in weak rock formations and high water level.
10. Explain how the life-cycle cost of a road project in hilly terrains may be affected with or without landslide control measures.

CHAPTER 13

Safety against Natural Calamities–Flood

13.1 INTRODUCTION

Flood is the result of inundation of a widespread area by overflow of water from river basins and tidal flow in coastal areas. The main reasons for flooding of any particular region may be traced to several factors, such as:

- Heavy rainfall in the river catchments
- Man-made obstructions to normal flow of water
- Mal-functioning of the river-valley projects
- Secondary effect from other natural calamities like earthquake

The flood situation worsens when more than one or two of the above factors hit a particular place. Safety and security of people are badly affected during flood rendering them homeless and destitute. Tangible assets like roads, railways, bridges, industrial establishments and utilities are also equally affected, damaged and destroyed by flood.

Heavy rainfall

In tropical countries like India, during monsoon, when both ground percolation and evaporation in the atmosphere are very low, heavy rainfall in the upper catchments of any river system is usually followed by flood in the plains along the lower reaches of the rivers. Normally there is little discharge in the rivers during the dry season, but shortly after heavy rains, the rivers flow in spate, overflowing the banks, flooding adjoining areas, often sweeping away roads, railways and bridges and simultaneously inundating towns and villages. In this process, the seasonal intensity of rainfall precipitation, the steepness of slope in the catchment area, the impermeability of the river bed and lack of forest cover are also contributing factors to high flood discharge. Excessive localized rains in the plains or melting of glaciers due to the effect of global warming also trigger flood.

Man-made obstructions

Apart from the above natural causes, man-made obstructions often create flood in urban and suburban localities, by:

- Accumulation of rain water in big cities devoid of effective drainage facilities
- Obstruction to natural drainage by railway or road embankments.
- Inadequate cross-drainage like culverts
- Unplanned urbanization blocking open space, filling natural water bodies and choking of the storm water drainage system.

The water-logging of the Kolkata basin every year during monsoon is the most striking example in this regard. The city area has natural slope from west to east, but this natural gradient is obstructed by high river embankment on the west side and a recently-built road embankment (Eastern Metropolitan Bypass) along the eastern side periphery of the city. Practically all the storm water channels in this city are century-old and are clogged. Besides this, the natural outfall of this storm water is to the Bidyadhary river, which is also blocked by unplanned housing on its bed. The Tolly's nallah on the southern side of the city is also not capable of carrying any substantial quantity of storm water. All these have been the major contributing factors for the city's flood during monsoon every year. The same condition exists in Mumbai due to choking of the Mithi river, which is the main drainage outlet for the city.

Mal-functioning of river-valley projects

Extensive floods coupled with flood-related erosion occur also due to mal-functioning of the river-valley projects. The main reasons for this malfunction of the river-valley projects are:

- Silting of reservoirs behind dams and barrages, resulting in reduced storage capacity of the reservoirs.
- Simultaneous silting of the river beds downstream of these dams and barrages during dry periods when the velocity of flow is low.
- Breaching, erosion and overflowing of river embankments during monsoon periods flooding the adjoining areas due to the above causes.

The flood condition often worsens on sudden release of enormous quantity of water continuously for days together by opening the lock gates to save the dams from excessive built- up water pressure. The regions downstream of the dams and barrages are worst hit in this process.

Secondary causes for flood

Other natural calamities like earthquakes, cyclones or typhoons also create floods. It is well known the quantum of devastations caused to several south Asian countries due to Tsunami in the wake of several strong-intensity earthquakes in the year 2008. Cyclonic storms moving from the Bay of Bengal to inland India are almost always associated with heavy rains causing localized floods in places where the drainage system is already poor or non-existent.

13.2 EFFECT OF FLOOD

As extensive areas are flooded, buildings, infrastructure and industrial installations are damaged and in extreme cases such facilities may remain unserviceable for a long time. Mention may be made in this regard to the following damages:

- Damage by subsidence of road and railway network
- Breach of embankments causing flood
- Washing away of bridge approaches
- Scour around bridge piers, causing tilt of the piers
- Dislodgment of bridge superstructure
- Destruction of power grids
- Damage to under-ground facilities
- Prolonged inundation of cultivated land, causing loss and failure of crops
- Destruction of mud houses and thatched roofs in countryside.
- Damage to floors affected by flood water
- Settlement of floors and shallow footings
- Damage to temporary structures
- Loss of life

Major floods seriously retard the regional economic activities. Occurrence of such floods in the same region again and again every year drives the inhabitants to destitute conditions with collapse of the socio-economic order, forcing the affected people to migrate from one place to other. Mention may be made here of the recent Koshi flood disaster. In 2008, there was a breach in the eastern afflux bund on Koshi at Kushaha.in Nepal. The breach created a very wide gap and the mighty Koshi river flowed over 993 villages, scattered in five districts of North Bihar for almost 10 months, killing 527 people and rendering over five million people homeless.

13.3 FLASH FLOODS IN HILLY AREAS

In hilly areas flash floods often carry a high discharge much above the estimated value along with large boulders and wooden logs. These logs with their branches get tangled with the handrails and the deck structure, of bridges adding to obstructions. In many cases such obstructions develop a serious situation when the regular flow of the channel is completely blocked and the river is seen to have changed its course by washing away part of the approaches. In such cases it has been necessary to build temporary Bailey bridges to maintain the road traffic after the flood recedes.

Flash floods often create havoc and bring in financial loss at bridge sites, if construction equipments and materials are left unprotected on the river bed in the open during floods. To avoid such disasters, it is absolutely necessary to have a clear contingency plan to wind up the site and remove all equipments and materials to safe places well in advance. In case a concrete superstructure is concreted over staging erected on the river bed, the work of the particular span should be commenced well in advance so that there is ample time available to the workers to remove the staging from the river bed after the stipulated curing time is allowed to the green concrete to harden. It is better not to take any chances in this respect assuming that floods may not occur in any particular period of time of the season, unless there is reliable information to the contrary.

13.4 SAFETY MANAGEMENT AGAINST FLOODS

A natural phenomenon like flood cannot be prevented fully, but effort should be made to control the flood to ensure the safety and stability of structures and keep in good and serviceable condition the roads, railways, bridges and other infrastructure facilities. Flood control in a broader perspective usually demands the following measures.

- De-silting of rivers, reservoirs and canals
- Providing guide-bundhs and repairing the old ones
- Adequate river-training work at bridge sites
- Providing adequate cross drainage systems for road and railway embankments

- Fixing the spans of the new culverts, bridges and all cross-drainage works, considering the discharge, velocity of flow and the depth of scour at the site.

Hydrological study for flood control projects

To avoid safety hazards and to mitigate the disastrous effects of flood, a comprehensive hydrological study should be carried out covering the following aspects of flow characteristics of any flood-prone river:

- Size of the catchment area, which can be calculated from toposheets of 1:2500 scale. From these topo-sheets, the slope of the terrain, soil characteristics, nature of the river (meandering or otherwise), vegetation, forest cover and land use can also be ascertained. Imageries from Google Earth digital terrain maps are available now-a-days, which helps in the preliminary investigation stage.
- Rainfall characteristics and rainfall data in the catchment area, flood history of the particular river, flow characteristics (perennial or seasonal).
- Particulars of the tributary rivers and their flow characteristics.
- Run-off data.
- Sedimentation data.

Often such data are available from central government and various agencies of the state governments, where regular records are maintained. However, in case of small tributaries and for the rivers flowing through the hilly regions, such records may not be available. In such situations detailed on-spot hydrological studies are needed to gather all the necessary information. For hydraulic design of bridges, dams, spillways etc, the most important input is the flood peak and its frequency. To ensure safety of these structures against any serious damage from the fury of flood, the magnitude of the peak flood is assessed using several alternative methods, like, the rational method, the empirical method, the unit-hydrograph technique and the statistical method of flood frequency studies.

13.5 FLOOD SAFETY FOR BRIDGES AND RIVER-TRAINING WORKS

In cases of all major floods, the bridges, their approaches, the river embankments and the river-training works are worst hit and are often washed away. Large tracts of adjoining land are submerged under flood water with damage to human settlements, cultivations and industrial structures. To avoid such mishaps, it is necessary to conduct proper hydrological and soil investigations and determine as accurately as possible the waterway needed for free passage of the flood water under the bridge. To this effect, the following data needs to be collected at the planning stage itself:

- Peak flood discharge at the bridge site and its return period.
- High flood level
- Clearance needed for free flow of water during the peak flow
- Likely scour depth at pier locations.
- Likely sedimentation during the lean season
- Likely change in the flow pattern of the river upstream or downstream of the bridge site.
- Likely effect on the future flow pattern of the river on construction of the bridge and river-training works.

When a **new bridge** is to be constructed the designer should fix the waterway and the number of spans and their lengths considering all available data collected for the purpose. The main concern of the designer should be to ensure that the free flow of flood water is not restricted beyond tolerable limit enhancing the scour around the piers and the river should also not overflow its banks or damage the approaches. Though empirical formulae and design methods have been developed to solve the problem and software packages are also available, it will be prudent on the part of the designer to apply his mind and sound judgment in this respect. It is to be borne in mind that each river has its own characteristic flow pattern, which should be studied in details through site investigations and past records as available. A design based purely on guess work may lead to uneconomic design or unsafe design.

If an **existing bridge is to be widened** (for increased traffic) or **partially reconstructed** (due to flood damages), the designer is compelled to provide the existing waterway, unless the existing bridge is wholly dismantled and re-built. But additional spans may be constructed in specific cases so that the discharge during the high flood is not restricted at the bridge site due to constriction of the waterway and the river continues to flow during the flood without causing heavy scour. On the other hand, undue widening of the waterway under the bridge would only increase the cost and invite heavy sedimentation during the lean season. The formation of hydraulic jumps in the upstream of a river in a steep hilly region should always be avoided.

The **sedimentation rate** is very high for rivers in the deltaic regions (like the Ganges and the Mahanadi delta) due to decrease in the velocity of flow and the rivers change its course very often. Such rivers are called 'meandering' rivers and huge land masses, called 'deltas' are formed at the confluence of these rivers with the sea (Refer Fig. 13.1 and 13.2)

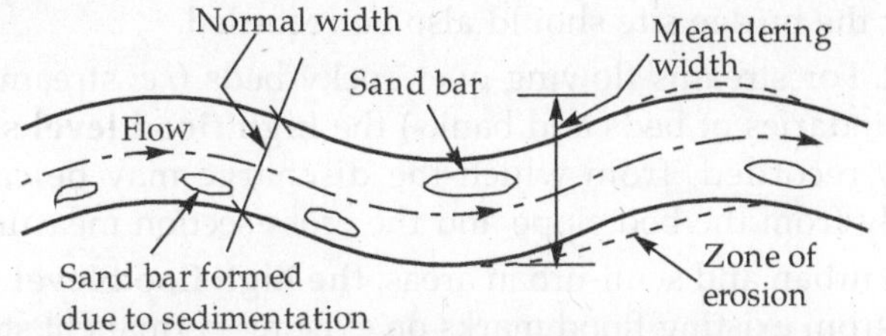

Fig. 13.1 Typical flow pattern of a meandering river.

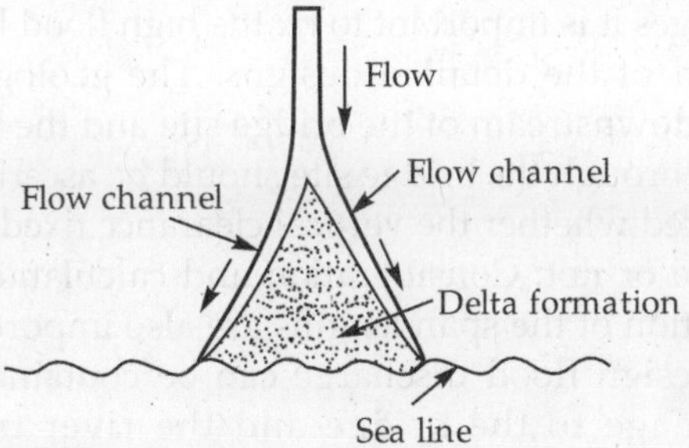

Fig. 13.2 Formation of delta at coastal zones.

The location of the bridge site should be carefully decided in these areas. Some rivers in the deltaic regions also exhibit a strong back flow causing water-logging and inundation of large areas in the upstream locations. In such cases the flow can possibly be maintained in a steady state only by regular dredging of the river channels, as is being done at the Haldia Port.

To divert the flood flow away from an eroding river bank, **spurs** are often constructed protruding inside the river. Such spurs are also buttressed by **flood embankments** built inside the main land away from the embankment line to check the subterranean flow from the river during the time when the flood recedes and the embankment erosion is very heavy. Such embankments have been constructed in the district of Maldah in West Bengal, though its success is not full-proof due to the intense scour of the river Ganges flowing nearby.

13.6 GUIDELINES FOR DESIGN OF BRIDGES FOR FLOOD SAFETY

Keeping in mind the above broad perspectives, the following guidelines should be followed in the design of bridges for flood safety.

1. **The cross section** of the river should be measured and recorded upstream and downstream of the bridge site at a distance of 150 metres for small catchments (less than 2.5 sq. Km) and 300 metres and above for larger catchments. The meandering pattern, if any near the bridge site should also be recorded.

2. For streams flowing over rocky beds (*i.e.* streams having rigid boundaries of beds and banks) the **high flood level** should be carefully recorded, from which the discharge may be calculated accurately from the bed slope and the cross-section measurements.

In urban and semi-urban areas, **the high flood level** may also be fixed from existing flood marks on existing permanent structures, which are clearly noticeable immediately after a flood.

For bridges it is important to fix the high flood level judiciously before the start of the detailed designs. The geological conditions upstream and downstream of the bridge site and the likely discharge of flood water through the bridge site should be ascertained properly. It is to be checked whether the vertical clearance fixed for a particular site is adequate or not. Consideration and calculations of the scour depth and fixation of the span lengths are also important in deciding whether the design flood discharge can be contained without any excessive damage to the bridge and the river training works. Available data from other sites may also be consulted in this regard.

3. **Design discharge for alluvial streams.** Fixing design discharge should be based on sound economy and waterway needed. Generally, rivers flowing over alluvial soils are wide and shallow. Such rivers exhibit meandering tendencies to a great extent. These rivers always tend to scour the bed during flood and get silted up after the flood, till a 'stable' condition of non-silting and non-scouring condition is reached. All these rivers are termed as 'regime' channels and are regarded as stable. Empirical equations like Lacey's equations are usually applied to calculate the regime cross-section, regime velocity and slope, the regime width and the normal depth of scour (depending on the silt-factor of the materials deposited on the river bed). The linear waterway for a bridge across a wholly alluvial stream should be equal to the width required for 'stability', *i.e.*, to acquire a regime condition given by Lacey's equation.

4. **Linear waterway.** Provision of unnecessary extra linear waterway does not help much. On the contrary, it increases the cost of the bridge itself and also increases the cost of the river-training works. Again if the linear waterway is constricted under the bridge, safety hazards due to erosion of embankments become a distinct possibility. Consequently, it will be appropriate to fix and provide a linear waterway which is optimum for the particular bridge site. For streams not wholly alluvial or for streams having rigid boundaries (in hilly regions), the linear waterway should be made equal to the width of the river at high flood level. The linear waterway at a bridge site is often constricted greatly (Refer Fig. 13.3).

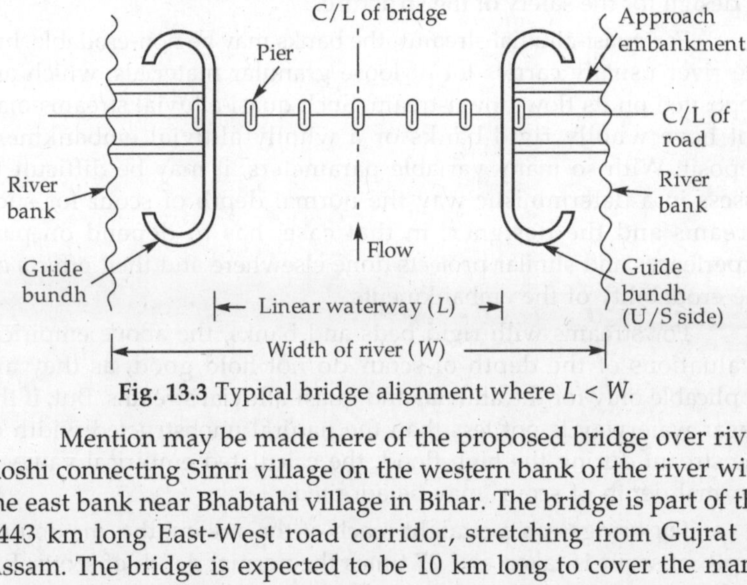

Fig. 13.3 Typical bridge alignment where $L < W$.

Mention may be made here of the proposed bridge over river Koshi connecting Simri village on the western bank of the river with the east bank near Bhabtahi village in Bihar. The bridge is part of the 3443 km long East-West road corridor, stretching from Gujrat to Assam. The bridge is expected to be 10 km long to cover the many flow channels of Koshi and the flow of the river will be constricted within two km only in the middle portion. Extensive embankment work is planned upstream to contain the flow of the river during the peak floods. The success of flood control upstream of the river depends on the effectiveness of the stability of these embankments.

5. **Maximum depth of scour.** A correct assessment of the depth of scour has to be made before the selection of the type of foundation and the structural design of the foundation elements. The safety of the foundation and the superstructure is seriously compromised if there is a serious mistake or error in assessing the depth of scour. Previous records, if available, help in this matter. But this should be corroborated from soil investigations and collection and evaluation of the data collected.

Alluvial streams are said to have 'normal depth of scour', when they attain stable conditions in flow. However, such ideal conditions are seldom found in alluvial streams, which exhibit meandering tendencies (Refer Fig. 13.1). As such it is the standard engineering practice to calculate the 'maximum depth of scour' and fix the depth of foundations accordingly by applying empirical formulae which are suggested by various codes and official guidelines. Again this depth of scour is dependent on the variability of the linear waterway under the bridge. If for other site constraints the linear waterway under the bridge is kept less than that required for regime condition, the scour depth will be more than the normal value, which should be considered in design for the safety of the structure.

For quasi-alluvial streams, the banks may be non-erodable, but the river usually carries lot of loose granular materials, which are deposited on its flow downstream. Such quasi-alluvial streams may not have wholly rigid banks or a wholly alluvial embankment deposit. With so many variable parameters, it may be difficult to assess in a deterministic way the normal depth of scour for such streams and the designer, in that case, has to depend on past experiences and similar projects done elsewhere and their effects on the erodability of the embankments.

For streams with rigid beds and banks, the above empirical evaluations of the depth of scour do not hold good, as they are applicable only for the alluvial and quasi-alluvial streams. But, if the linear waterway is not less than the natural unobstructed width of the stream during the high flood, the calculated empirical value of 'normal depth of scour' may be adopted.

For bridges on a straight reach of the stream, the 'maximum' depth of scour is taken as 1.27 times the normal depth of scour. For bridges on curves or over streams having cross or diagonal currents, the maximum depth of scour is taken as 2-times the normal depth of scour.

6. **Fixing the depth of bridge foundation.** The primary objective of assessing the normal depth of scour and the maximum depth of scour is to determine the minimum depth of the bridge foundation, which is safe for the bridge during the whole period of its service life. Considering all aspects of the problem, it is the standard practice to take the foundation (which may be a well foundation, raft or a pile foundation) to a depth of 1.33-times the maximum depth of scour. For non-erodable beds, however, the foundation may be secured even at a lesser depth. (Refer Fig. 13.4).

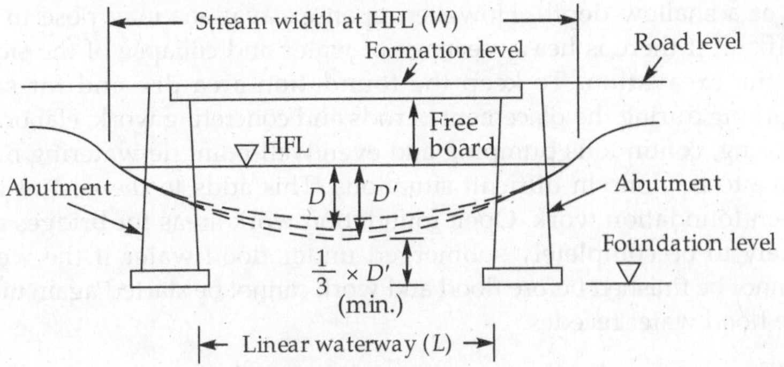

D : Normal depth of scour

D' : Maximum depth of scour

Fig. 13.4 Typical single-span bridge.

7. **Span arrangement.** The span arrangement should preferably be fixed in such a way that the cost of the superstructure is equal to the cost of the substructure, satisfying at the same time all the above variable parameters. However, such ideal conditions are seldom attained in many cases and each bridge should therefore be designed separately on merit only, considering all the above hydrological factors, bed conditions, scour levels, soil characteristics and the actual cost of construction.

8. **Choice of the foundation system.** The choice of the bridge foundation system will have a very profound influence on the overall performance and structural response of the bridge as a whole. As such, due attention should be given to find out the most suitable foundation type for a particular site in order to have proper safety against flood, earthquake, current and wind forces in addition to the superstructure dead and live loads. Bridge foundations, as adopted in different site conditions, may be classified under three distinct categories (Refer Fig. 13.5), namely:

- Open foundations
- Pile foundations
- Well and caisson foundations

Open foundation

Open foundations are the simplest and often most economical, when the ground is firm or rocky at shallow depths. Open excavation is done up to the required depth in such cases and the foundation is laid there. Under this category come the spread footings, raft slabs or masonry over a thick RCC base. Small and minor bridges may be provided with shallow foundations when rock is available at surface or at a shallow depth. However, open excavations may pose to be difficult if there is heavy seepage of water and collapse of the sides of the excavation. To keep the foundation area dry and for safe working during the placement of rods and concreting work, elaborate shoring, continuous pumping and even well-point de-watering may have to be done in difficult situations. This adds to the cost of the open foundation work. Open foundation work areas for bridges are likely to be completely submerged under flood water if the work cannot be finished before flood and work cannot be started again until the flood water recedes.

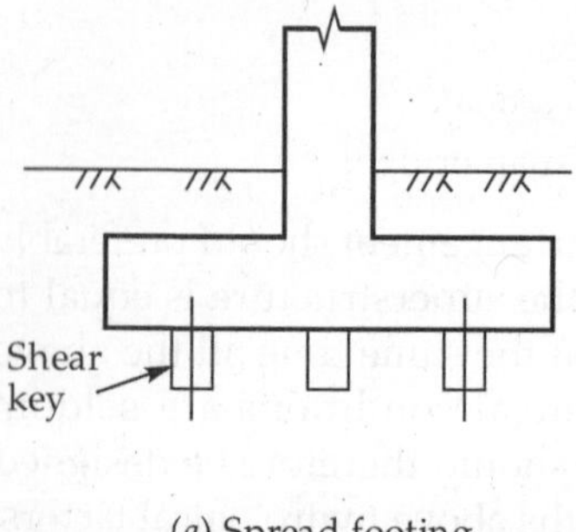

(*a*) Spread footing

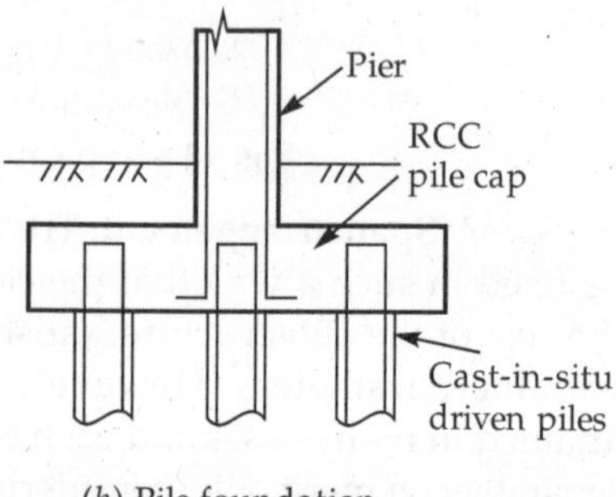

(*b*) Pile foundation

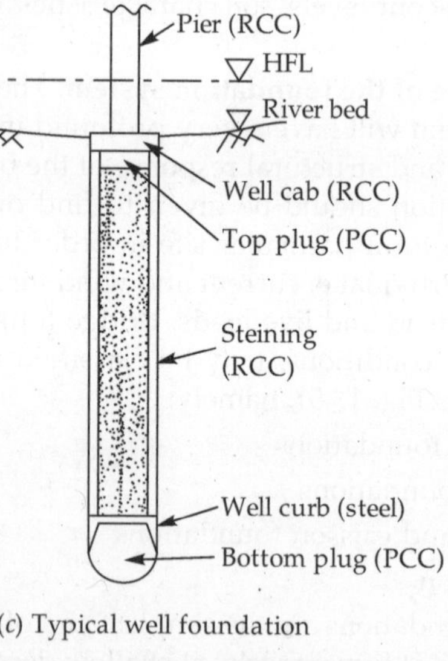

(*c*) Typical well foundation

Fig. 13.5 Typical foundation alternatives for bridges.

Pile foundation

According to the material used for piling work, piles are termed as timber piles, steel piles and concrete piles. While timber piles are used predominantly for temporary structures in bridge construction work, the main superstructure is often rested on large diameter (1.2 metre and more) concrete piles or caisson piles. According to use, piles are classified as vertical load bearing piles, batter piles, fender piles, sheet piles etc. Piles may be solid circular, tubular or even octagonal. For major bridge work, small diameter piles are not suitable because of its slenderness. As a result, large diameter piles have to be adopted for bridge foundation work, which needs deployment of sophisticated pile driving machinery and rigs. Again the deployment and movement of heavy pile-driving machinery on the river bed in flood-prone sites needs advance planning to ensure the safety of the costly equipments. Pile foundations are most suitable where mechanization is possible and soil conditions are favourable for piling work.

Well foundations

A typical well foundation consists of a steel cutting edge connected integrally to a well curb and a steining which is built in stages as the muck inside the well is dredged out till the well is sunk up to the foundation level. The well is then plugged at the bottom with a concrete 'bottom plug', the inside of the steining is then filled partially or fully by sand and a top plug is put in place and the well cap and the pier are built thereafter.

The dredge hole of an well is made big enough for easy working of the grabs during the sinking operation and the annular steining wall is designed to have the required thickness (1.2 metres or more) to overcome the soil friction without much of sinking effort or additional load of kentledge. As such the wells become quite massive and are not economical for minor bridges where open foundations or piles may be more suitable. The depth of well foundations in scourable river beds should be fixed considering the normal scour depth, the local scour likely around the pier and the grip required below the maximum scour depth.

A comparative study of usefulness of different types of foundations reveals the following facts:

1. Compared to piles, annular wells have a large section modulus with a minimum cross sectional area. Wells can resist large horizontal forces and vertical loads. But they attract at the same time more earthquake forces because of the heavy weights of the wells.

2. In high scourable river beds, wells are more suitable than piles when the unsupported lengths of the foundation is considerable.

3. Piles driven inside the river bed are likely to be damaged by large floating boulders and trees rolling with the water during a flood. Wells are the most suitable option in such cases.

4. The load bearing capacity of a well at the foundation level is much more than a pile due to the large bearing area of a well. Wells are therefore more stable.

5. Piles cannot be driven easily through large boulders and logs which are often buried inside the river bed. It is rather easy for a massive well to push through these obstacles. In extremely difficult situations, these boulders can be removed by chiseling, blasting or by sending divers inside the well to remove these.

6. If the foundation has to be taken to a great depth due to subsoil or ground conditions, well foundations offer the most satisfactory solution, though wells are generally more costly than a pile foundation.

7. In case wells are sunk by dewatering or pneumatic process, a visual examination is possible to examine the nature of the founding strata. Even when wells are sunk by dredging, a continuous monitoring and examination of the soil strata is possible. In case the founding strata is found to be unsuitable, the wells can be taken to a greater depth if necessary.

8. Open foundations at shallow depths are economical, but may involve dewatering problems in sandy river beds where seepage of water is very high. Also if there is heavy scour in the bed during floods, shallow open foundations may create safety hazards. Well foundations, though costly, may pose to be a better solution in such cases. On the other hand open foundations are simple in design and easy to construct and the work can be inspected for all the time.

9. The construction process and the choice of a particular type of bridge foundation also depend on the nature of the river flow, the return period of major floods and the depth of water in the river during the construction period. In many cases it may have to be necessary to construct islands at well positions and place the cutting edge over the well in dry condition. At sites where the velocity of water is very high and the depth of water is considerable, islands may not be a feasible solution. Steel cassions are adopted with their heights at least 1/3rd more than the depth of water.

13.7 FLOOD SAFETY FOR HYDRAULIC STRUCTURES

In the design of major hydraulic structures like dams and spillways, the safety of the structure against the fury of flood should be given due priority over costs involved, as safety hazards (like dam-bursts) for these major structures may bring untold disaster to millions of people and infrastructure. For these structures, a detailed flood-frequency study is done and the peak floods and their return periods are assessed from statistical analysis using the Gumbel's distribution for prediction of maximum rainfall and flood peaks. In this respect, the inflow design flood for safety of dams is taken as under. As there is a natural and inbuilt uncertainty of failure in these structures, the risk, reliability and safety factors are also analyzed.

Class	*Gross storage in Mm*^{3}	*Inflow design flood for safety*
Small	0.5 to 10	100 year flood
Intermediate	10 to 60	Standard Project flood
Large	> 60	Probable maximum flood

The standard project flood takes into consideration severe combination of meteorological and hydrological factors applicable to the region. Extremely rare combinations are excluded. The probable maximum flood is the extreme flood that is likely to occur in a region, as a result of the rarest combination of meteorological and hydrological factors.

13.8 FLOOD EROSION

Erosion of the banks is another safety hazard which is noticed when the flood begins to recede. The width of the river gets wider and wider every year due to erosion of the banks after the floods and the depth at the same time reduces on silting in many places. This phenomenon compounds the safety hazards for the people and the establishments in the vicinity of the river banks.

The phenomenon of flood erosion is manifested in several ways, namely:

- Erosion due to rainfall
- Erosion due to river current
- Erosion due to standing waves on the seaside
- Erosion from flash floods

While a devastating flood damages buildings, bridges and other infrastructure all on a sudden, if they are unprotected, safety hazards due to erosion creep into the landmass surreptitiously, engulfing forest covers, construction works, human settlements and cultivable lands. To mitigate damages due to soil erosion, it is necessary to protect the landmass through adequate protective measures. A sustained effort in river-training work is needed to contain the erosion within an acceptable limit and this needs proper budgetary support and involvement of the authorities concerned. These include:

- Construction of river embankments, guide bundhs, spurs and afflux bundhs
- River protection work at bridge sites and at locations of sharp river bends, where erosion is predominant
- Use of geo-synthetic materials for bank protection
- Constant vigilance during and after floods
- Repair and maintenance of existing erosion control mechanisms and their strengthening, as necessary.

The main objective of adopting the above control system is to '**contain**' the landmass, '**reinforce**' the same and '**separate**' it from the onslaught of the flood and to '**drain**' out rain water into the river during heavy rains. A few standard methods of river-training works are shown in Fig. 13.6.

Use of geo-synthetic products for erosion control

Geo-synthetic products are made almost entirely from polymers or polypropylene and the products are available in the market termed as "Geo-textiles', 'Geo-grids", Geo-nets', Geo-membranes', and Geo-pipes (PVC or HPPE pipes), depending on their specific applications and performance characteristics.

Geo-textiles are synthetic polymers derived from crude oil and natural gas. They exhibit a high level of durability and resistance to degradation in adverse soil conditions. Geo-textiles are of two general categories: woven and un-woven. Woven geo-textiles are widely used for erosion control. These are woven filaments, manufactured by weaving extruded filaments (either single or in groups, called multi-filaments) together to form the geo-textile fabric. This material is often used also as reinforcements to the soil mass in erosion control applications.

Geo-grids are grid-like polymer materials made by punching holes in sheets of high-density polyethylene sheets or by weaving and coating high-strength polyester yarns. Geo-grids are appropriate for soil reinforcement in erosion control works and are also used on asphalt pavements cracked due to thermal stresses and fatigue.

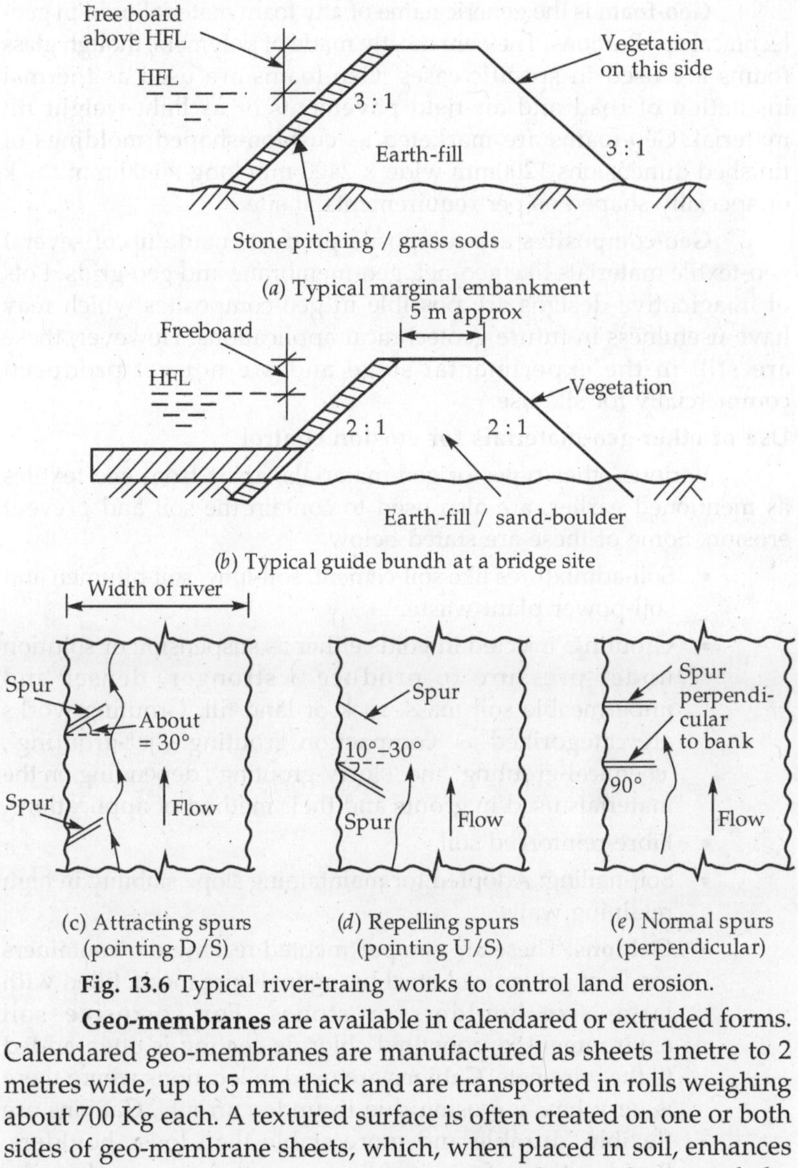

Fig. 13.6 Typical river-traing works to control land erosion.

Geo-membranes are available in calendared or extruded forms. Calendared geo-membranes are manufactured as sheets 1metre to 2 metres wide, up to 5 mm thick and are transported in rolls weighing about 700 Kg each. A textured surface is often created on one or both sides of geo-membrane sheets, which, when placed in soil, enhances the interface friction between the geo-membrane sheets and the adjoining soil mass.

Geo-nets are tight nets of closely-spaced ribs made of extruded molten polymer through slits. Geo-nets have parallel set of ribs overlying similar parallel set of ribs at different angle to form a tight net. Geo-nets are most suitable for in-plane drainage.

Geo-foam is the generic name of any foam material used in geo-technical applications. They are mostly made of polymers, though glass foams are used in specific cases. Geo-foams are used as thermal insulation of road and air-field pavements or as light-weight fill material. Geo-foams are marketed as cushion-shaped moldings of finished dimensions 1200mm wide × 2400 mm long × 600 mm thick or specially shaped as per requirements at site.

Geo-composites are composite products made up of several geo-textile materials like geo-net, geo-membrane and geo-grids. Lots of imaginative designs are possible in geo-composites which may have usefulness in future geotechnical applications. However, these are still in the experimental stage and are not yet produced commercially for site use.

Use of other geo-materials for erosion control

Various other types of geo-materials, apart from geo-textiles as mentioned earlier, are also used to contain the soil and prevent erosion. Some of these are stated below:

- Soil-admixtures like soil-cement, soil-lime, soil-bitumen and soil-power plant waste.
- Grouting: injected in voids either as suspension or solution under pressure to produce a stronger, denser and impermeable soil mass, rock or land-fill. Grouting works are categorized as 'compaction grouting', 'jet-grouting', 'chemical-grouting' and 'slurry-grouting', depending on the materials used in grouts and their method of applications.
- Fibre-reinforced soil.
- Soil-nailing: Adopted for maintaining slope stability in high retaining walls.
- **Gabions:** These are compartmented rectangular containers made of galvanized-steel hexagonal wire mesh, filled with large size boulders or stones. For corrosive soil environment, a polyvinyl chloride coating is often added to the wire nets. Gabions are used in locations where there is very heavy erosion due to undercurrents. Gabions are flexible, durable and more stable than loose boulders. Besides these factors, plant growth is ensured in the sediments which are deposited inside the boulder fills, adding to the efficiency in the erosion control mechanism.
- **Jute geo-textiles** are woven for use in road embankments in cohesive soils. Non-woven jute geo-textiles are used

mostly for protection of concealed drains emba... Some varieties of jute geo-textiles ar... lso us... separation and filtration. For slope stabiliza..., wove... geo-textiles are treated with bitumen. ...ter mini... operations, jute geo-textiles are also used for er...ion contro... and stabilization of land slopes.

Soil bio-engineering techniques for erosion control

The soil bio-engineering technique aims at the maximum use of vegetation and living plants to control erosion and protect the embankment by imparting stability to the slopes. Two types of plant species are generally used for this purpose, *i.e.* Herbaceous vegetation and Woody vegetation. The herbaceous vegetation is most suitable for protection of the slopes of the embankments. It resists the impact from heavy rains and run-off and enhances the shear strength and cohesion of the soil. The woody vegetation comprises of trees which give canopy protection to the ground and their roots act as soil anchors. As the roots of these trees draw moisture and water from the soil for their growth, they help in increasing the shear strength of the soil. These roots also add to the stability of the slopes, as the ground ball developed by the fine roots acts as counterweight, which may be even 6-8 times the weight of the branches above ground for some species. Usually three types of root systems work efficiently in this regard, namely:

- Sinker root system
- Tap root system
- Heart root system

Out of these three types, the heart root system is the most effective medium of maintaining slope stability, so far as anchoring is concerned, because the roots of this system form a huge bulk with the soil. The presence of the roots also increases the shear strength of the soil and the ground is also anchored at the same time. While selecting the species for soil conservation, it is to be borne in mind that trees are about 2 times more resistant than grassy vegetation and the roots of bushes are twice as strong as the trees. However, once such trees are allowed to grow for embankment protection, they should not cut down, as, in that case the roots will decay, leaving cavities in the embankment fill, thus initiating internal erosion and piping failure. (Refer Fig. 13.7)

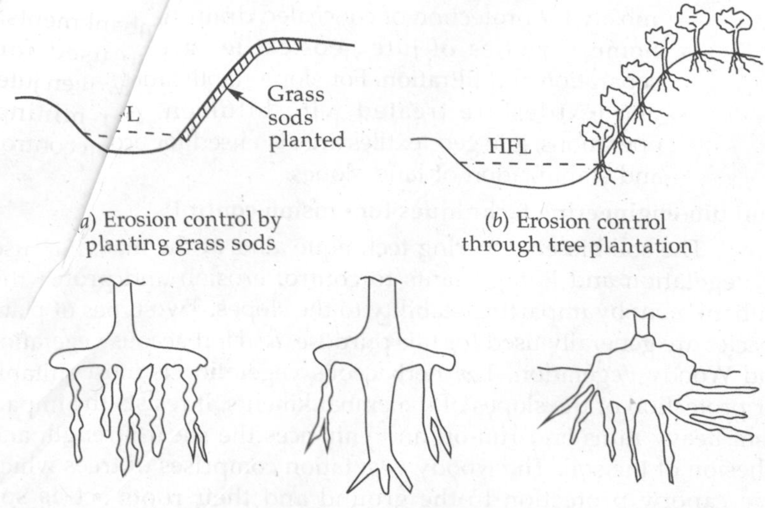

(*a*) Erosion control by planting grass sods

(*b*) Erosion control through tree plantation

(*c*) Sinker root system

(*d*) Tap root system

(*e*) Heart root system

Fig. 13.7 Erosion control through soil-bio-engineering techniques.

In the above sections, several methods have been discussed for soil erosion. However, the selection of any or combination of the erosion control techniques depends on the functional requirement and serviceability, which can be assured only after detailed landscape study, nature of the soil- fill in the embankment, level of soil erosion, availability of a suitable species of plant, costs involved if geo-textiles are used and the life-cycle cost of any particular erosion control technique. While the use of geo-textiles may give immediate results, their replacement may be a deterrent from cost point of view. On the other hand, planting of grass and trees along the embankment takes a rather long time to produce any satisfactory result. But the replacement is rather easy and it is eco-friendly. For this reason, soil bio-engineering techniques are gaining popularity day by day among environmental scientists, soil technologists and engineers, because of its eco-friendly appeal in spite of its being labour-intensive.

13.9 WATER-LOGGING DUE TO FLOOD

In flood-prone areas, due attention should be given to the probability and extent of likely damages which may occur to the equipments, machinery and materials during the construction period. The plinth level of all new permanent structures should be fixed after proper investigation about the level of inundation during floods and the likely frequency of occurrence of such floods in the region.

For industrial complexes, due attention should be given to avoid inundation of the costly machinery during floods or water-logging. If necessary, the plinth level should made high to clear the water-logging effect. In many situations it may be worthwhile to install the running machinery on the first floor and keep the ground floor free from heavy machinery. Similarly, warehouses and cold storages should not be built in areas affected by prolonged water-logging every year, unless they are given adequate protection against flooding of the floor.

In urban areas, the drainage system should be de-silted and kept operative during heavy rainfall. The existing arrangement may be augmented by addition of more pumping facility in order to pump out accumulated water from the roads as quickly as possible. In addition, all buildings, utilities and other structures should be repaired and made serviceable immediately after a flood or water-logging of streets. All these require proper planning and budgetary supports from the concerned authorities.

APPENDIX 13/1

Guidelines for the design of small and minor bridges to ensure flood safety

1. Estimating design flood discharge

Rainfall records are available from government authorities at different strategic locations in the catchment areas of major rivers in India. These records are generally reliable, if they are regularly updated. But flood records downstream may not be available in many cases. In such cases, when fixing the linear waterway for bridges and culverts, the Indian Roads Congress, SP-13 provides excellent guidelines for design of small bridges and culverts. It recommends that flood discharges should be estimated in three different ways initially.

(*a*) Using rational formulae for peak run-off from the catchment area u/s of the bridge site. This takes into consideration the intensity, distribution and duration of the rainfall in the catchment area and also the nature, slope and the permeability of the catchment.

Peak run-off from catchment area

$$Q = 0.028 \times P \times A \times I_c$$

where Q = maximum run-off in cum per second

A = Area of the catchment upstream of the bridge site in hectares (1 hectare = 10000 sq metres) assessed from measurement of the catchment area u/s of a bridge site from topo-sheets.

I_c = critical intensity of rainfall in cm per hour

P = coefficient depending on the characteristics of the catchment area

Values of 'P'

Bare rocks and pavements	0.90
Rock in wooded areas	0.80
Plateau	0.70
Clayey soil	0.60 to 0.50
Sandy soil	0.20 to 0.10

For catchment areas greater than 10000 hectares, the calculated run-off may be further reduced by a factor (0.75 to 0.60), considering the spread of the storm over the whole catchment area. This factor takes into account the time taken by the runoff from distant places to reach the bridge site.

(*b*) Estimating the flood discharge from the velocity and the cross-sectional of the stream measured at the bridge site. The Manning's formula is used here for calculating the velocity on the basis of hydraulic mean depth, slope of the stream and the rugosity coefficient of the river bed.

$$Q = A \times V$$

where $V = [R^{2/3} \times S^{1/2}]/n$ (Manning's formula)

where A = cross section in sq metre

V = velocity in metre per second

R = Hydraulic mean depth = (cross sectional area)/(Wetted perimeter)

S = slope of the river bed, measured over a reasonably long reach

N = rugosity coefficient, varying from 0.025, 0.035 and 0.075 for straight,winding and very weedy natural streams.

(*c*) The flood discharge is to be estimated from flood marks on any existing structure nearby. The standing wave, afflux etc are considered here and the discharge is calculated using weir formula or orifice formula, depending on the value of the discharge. Alternatively, for minor bridges and culverts, the Dickens formula is widely used also.

Dicken's formula: $Q = C \times M^{3/4}$

where, Q = peak run-off in cum per second

M = catchment area in sq km.

C = 6.0 for north-Indian planes

11–14 for north-Indian hilly regions

14–28 for central India

22–28 for coastal Andhra and Orissa

This is however a very simplified solution which may not yield accurate results, as the flood-frequency is not considered. In addition, there are host of other empirical formulae, which should however be used only in appropriate cases.

The recommended rule for fixing the design discharge is:

(*a*) The values in all the above cases are to quantified and calculated in same units, so that they may be compared.

(*b*) The highest of these values may be taken as the design discharge (Q), provided it does not exceed the next highest discharge value by not more than 50%. If it exceeds by more than 50%, then the value should be restricted to that limit.

2. Calculation of the normal depth of scour

(*a*) For alluvial streams flowing in regime condition, the normal depth of scour (D) is calculated from the Lacey's equation:

$$D = [0.473 \times Q^{1/3}]/f^{1/3}$$

where Q = design discharge, as calculated earlier

F = silt factor $= 1.76 \times \sqrt{m}$, where, m = mean diameter of particles in mm

= 0.50 for fine silt

= 1.00 for standard silt

= 1.20 for medium sand

= 1.50 for coarse sand

For a stable alluvial stream, flowing in regime condition, the stable width (W) can be taken as equal to the wetted peremeter (P)

i.e. $$W = P = 4.8 \times Q^{1/2}, \quad \text{when } L \not> W.$$

If the linear waterway under a bridge L is kept less than the regime width (W), *i.e.* if the waterway is constricted under the bridge, then the normal depth of scour should be multiplied by a factor $[W/L]^{0.61}$, to account for the increase in the depth of scour at the bridge location. In that case, the revised depth of normal scour (D') will be :

$$D' = D \times [W/L]^{0.61}$$

where W = regime width of the river
and L = designed waterway.

(*b*) For quasi-alluvial streams, when the width of the stream is very large, compared to its depth, the wetted peremeter is approximately equal to the width of the stream and is not affected seriously by any variation in its depth. Assuming that the slope remains constant, the normal depth of scour may be calculated, in such cases, from the following equation:

$$D = [1.21 \times Q^{0.63}]/[f^{0.33} \times W^{0.60}], \text{ when } L \nless W$$

Again, if the linear waterway at the bridge site is kept less than its width (*i.e.* if $L < W$), then, the above value of normal depth of scour will be multiplied by the factor $[W/L]^{0.61}$ as before.

3. Maximum depth of scour (D_m)

Recommended values of D_m:

(*a*) For straight reach:

$$D_m = 1.27 \times D$$

(*b*) For sites with diagonal currents and multi-span sites:

$$D_m = 2 \times D$$

(*c*) For bridges where the linear waterway (L) provided is less than the regime width (W):

$$D_m = D \times [W/L]^{1.56}$$

4. Depth of bridge foundation (D_f)

Guidelines for determining the appropriate founding level of a bridge, when the stream is free to scour and there is no provision of any bed floor.

(*a*) For erodible beds

D_f should be 1.33 × maximum scour depth (D_m), subject to a maximum of 2 metres for arch bridges and 1.2 metres for other bridges.

(*b*) For non-erodible beds (hard beds)

D_f should be equal to: D_m + 0.3 metre for rock

And, D_m + 0.6 metre for other hard beds

(*c*) In all cases, the soil pressure at the founding level must be within the allowable bearing capacity at that level. This should be determined by soil investigations.

5. Minimum vertical clearance needed to be provided under the bridge

The following minimum vertical clearance should be maintained, unless required otherwise due to specific site constraints like clearance needed for the mast of a vessel moving under the bridge.

Discharge Q in cumec	*Minimum vertical clearance in metres*
30 to 300	0.900
300 to 3000	1.200
above 3000	1.500

6. Fixing span lengths

For the span length to be economical from the cost point of view, the cost of the variable parts of the superstructure should be equal to the cost of the subs-structure. For small bridges in hilly regions, it is better to have no intermediate piers, which may obstruct the flow of the stream and the span should be from bank to bank. For major bridges, if the required linear waterway (*L*) is less than the economical span length, as defined above, the bridge should preferably have a single span. On the other hand, when the linear waterway (*L*) is more than the economical span length (*S*), the number of spans (*n*) should be equal to: $n = L/S$ and '*n*' obviously should be a whole number, preferably odd. Moreover, the span lengths are to be suitably arranged so that there is least obstruction to the flow, even if the span arrangement is un-economical from the cost point of view.

For major bridges, which are subject to very heavy flood discharge in the alluvial plains, detailed soil investigation work should be carried out before fixing the basic parameters of the bridge, considering all aspects of the scour problems, site facilities available for well sinking work, bed characteristics, nature of flow and sound economics. In this it is advisable to have bore holes at all the prospective pier and abutment locations in order to get a representative picture of the soil characteristics at the bridge site. Similar soil investigations should also be done at all other feasible alternate site locations for the bridge.

7. Afflux

The afflux at a bridge is the heading of the flowing water during a flood on its upstream side due to constriction of the flow down the bridge (Refer Fig. 13.8).

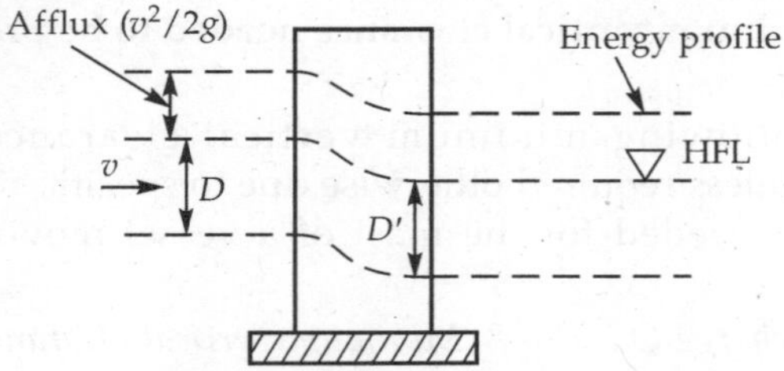

D : Normal depth of scour
D' : Maximum depth of scour

Fig. 13.8 Scout levels and afflux at pier location.

It is measured by the difference in water levels upstream and downstream of the bridge. The more the linear waterway is constricted the more will be the afflux. The afflux creates an additional pressure on the embankments due to rise in water level during floods. In many locations embankments have to be raised by constructing what is called 'afflux bundhs' to ensure safety from breach and overflowing of the embankments. Ideally a stream should not be constricted by the bridge and river training works. But in cases of many minor and major bridges flowing through flood-prone alluvial planes, the river becomes very wide with comparatively shallow depths. In such cases the width eventually becomes much greater than that required for 'regime' flow. When bridges are to be constructed across such rivers, the existing width of the bridge has to be narrowed down and intermediate piers have to be constructed also for reasons of economy and convenience of construction. Both the banks, upstream and downstream of the bridge alignment should then be protected by adequate protective measure to ensure safety against breach, overflowing and erosion of the embankments. This becomes an important part of the flood safety measures at any major site where the river is meandering in flow.

8. Overtopping of embankments during high floods

At places where the velocity of the stream is not very high and the depth is shallow compared to its width, there is every possibility of spillage of flood water and overtopping of the banks during flood. To prevent this, the embankment or the road level over the embankment should be at least $V^2/2g$ or $V^2/19.6$ metres higher than the H.F.L. from the point where the overflow is likely to start and V is the velocity of the stream during high floods. Detailed topographical survey is needed for embankment safety management in such cases. This is all the more necessary because flood protection measures by constructing embankments entail a huge investment from the exchequer.

In many cases relief culverts are constructed to force the overflow backinto the main stream. However, care is to be taken to ensure that there is no ponding effect upstream of these relief culverts, which may trigger erosion on the downstream side of such flood protective measures. If necessary provision of baffle walls should be provided downstream of these culverts to dissipate the energy of the falling water and the velocity should be controlled through construction of properly-designed expanding flumes.

For more details regarding the design of bridges against flood safety, the reader is advised to refer to The Indian Roads Congress Special Publication no: 13 and other relevant codes.

QUESTIONS

1. What are the main environmental and man-made safety hazards which contribute to heavy floods in any particular region? Describe how the flood situation at a particular place may worsen due to simultaneous occurrence of several such safety hazards.

2. How man-made obstructions may worsen a flood situation?

3. Indicate how the continued mal-functioning of a river-valley project may create safety hazards to the life and property downstream of any such project?

4. What are the economic and social fall-out of a major flood?

5. Write short notes on the following:

(*a*) Flash flood

(*b*) Necessity of river-training works

(*c*) Hydrological study for flood control

(*d*) Necessity of cross-drainage works across road and rail embankments

6. What type of field data should be collected during planning stage to ensure flood safety for bridges?

7. Explain the effectiveness of spurs to resist the onslaught of flood water.

8. What is meant by the following terms and explain how these are related to assessment of flood damages:

(*a*) High flood level

(*b*) Linear waterway

(*c*) Discharge of flood water through a bridge

(*d*) Maximum scour depth

(*e*) Afflux

9. Explain how span arrangements influence the depth of bridge foundations and the cost of river-training works. What are the main factors governing the choice of a bridge foundation system?

10. A reinforced concrete road bridge is to be constructed across a river 300 feet wide from bank to bank. The middle part of the river is perennial, the bed is erodable, so also both the banks. To fix the span lengths the following alternatives have cropped up during preliminary discussions. Without going through any detailed calculations, please chalk out the likely advantages and disadvantages for each of the following suggested alternatives from the point of view of the overall cost of the bridge, free flow of the river during heavy floods and the cost of the river-training works:

Alternative 1: Single span 300 ft long

Alternative 2: One central span 150 feet with two side spans each 75 feet long

Alternative3: Two spans each 150 feet long

Alternative 4: Three spans each 100 feet long

Alternative 5: One central span 200 feet only, with approaches extended by 50 feet inside the river bed on each side with necessary river-training works

List the field data which should be collected before starting the preliminary project report for such a project.

11. What are the major safety hazards due to flood erosion? How these hazards can be mitigated by using geo-synthetic products? What type of geo-synthetic products should be used for control of embankment erosion?

12. What is meant by soil bio-engineering technique as adopted for erosion control? Write short notes on the usefulness of the following root systems and the efficacy in erosion control:

(*a*) Sinker root system

(*b*) Taproot system

(*c*) Heart root system

CHAPTER

14

Safety in Material Handling and Transportation

14.1 INTRODUCTION

Transportation and handling of materials are very critical components of material management in any construction project. To augment the supply of materials and maintaining the right stock all the time, right from the start of construction to the completion of the project, it becomes necessary to keep the supply system safe and hazard free. Transportation of materials and equipments are also to be done during winding of the site after completion of the project.

Briefly, transportation and material handling are involved in the following cases:

- Carriage of raw materials like coarse and fine aggregates from the quarries/procurement site to the place of work
- Carriage of structural steel, cement, bricks etc from their respective place of production to the site of work
- Carriage of fabricated steel products and precast RCC products fron their place of fabrication to site of work
- Carriage of all sundry store materials, consumables, petrol, diesel, paint, timber, glass, bolts, shuttering materials etc as required for any particular project

In addition, there may be occasions when machines and heavy equipments may also have to be transported and ready-mix concrete may have to be transported to site for concreting programmes.

All the above items and many more that may be required for construction work, are needed to be loaded, unloaded and handled manually or by mechanical means. The timely completion of any project depends largely on a safe accident-free transportation and material handling system, apart from other management functions in this regard. It is therefore imperative for the project manager to anticipate the likely safety hazards in this area of project management and take suitable measures to avoid accidents which may disrupt the project.

14.2 CAUSES OF ACCIDENTS IN TRANSPORTATION AND MATERIAL HANDLING WORK

Accidents may happen due to the following causes:

1. Mechanical fault in the vehicle used
2. Operator is inattentive
3. Operator takes chances while negotiating through narrow space or through crowd
4. Operator is inexperienced to run a particular type of transport vehicle
5. Wrong or inept handling of heavy material or hazardous material
6. Stacking of material in unsafe stacks not in stable equilibrium

The immediate effect of an accident may be delay in material procurement, loss/damage to costly materials, injury/death to the operator, helper of to any third person and lastly a dislocation in the supply chain.

14.3 SAFETY CONSIDERATIONS FOR MANUAL HANDLING OF MATERIALS

Though mechanization is very much popular now-a-days for stacking, loading and unloading of bulk quantities of different types of materials like coal, iron ore, cement, steel etc., still in a wide spectrum of medium and low budget construction contracts, material handling is done manually. Consequently, safety hazards related to manual operations are a reality and the associated problems are to be addressed properly.

In the case of lifting a load manually, the greater is the lever arm (*i.e.* the distance of the lifted object from the foot), the more is the effort required to lift the load, putting more pressure on the spinal chord of the person engaged in the lifting operation.. Most commonly reported mishaps during manual handling of loads relate to strain or injury to the spinal chord and nerves. To avoid this, the lifting point of the load should be as close the body as possible and the height of the same should preferably be near to the finger level of an adult person during carrying. This is the most optimum height to shift any load manually. The hand-carry method with equal loads in each hand is a good practice, provided the combined weight does not exceed the carrying capacity of the person concerned. Again it is to be noted that weights of 20–25 kg loads can be easily carried and shifted manually, provided the packets are properly sized with provision of handles and rollers. For shifting of pellets, cement bags, sand bags etc from one place to another inside the construction site, it is safe and user-friendly to utilize hand-carts or wheel barrows.

On the other hand, machines and equipments may be shifted manually with the help of rollers and other tackles over a level ground safely without much manual effort, provided personal safety is maintained and the machine is evenly placed over the rollers. The weights of pre-cast RCC slabs are usually made not more than 100 to 120 kg each so that not more than 4 persons are required to lift the slab and put the same in position. In such cases, for safe and easy handling, the size and weight of the finished slabs are most important.

For hauling men and materials for repair and inspection work along the railway track, trolleys fitted over dip-lorries are still widely used. It is to be borne in mind that an easier way to handle a load is also the safe approach.

Stacking of jute bales and packets is usually done with help of fork lifts, which move along the floor. Manual handling is limited to only arranging these materials properly so that the stacks are not tilted and become unstable. For stack heights greater than 2.0metres, ladders should be engaged for safety of the workers.

In the building industry, it is still the common practice to handle green concrete manually for carrying, lifting and laying in place, though controlled concrete transported from the nearest batching plants are also used in places where such batching plant facilities are available. Even in the latter case when batch concrete is used, the laying and spreading jobs are done manually in most cases. Proper working platforms with ladders and handrails should be provided in all such cases for reasons of safety. For high rise buildings the safest procedure should be to use lifts to raise the green concrete boxes to the required level and then spread the same manually. Otherwise the staircases should be finished simultaneously so that the green concrete can be lifted manually. This is however possible only when the building is only 5–6 storey high. Shuttering boards, reinforcement rods can however be safely hauled to upper floors up to 2–3 storey high with the help of wire ropes and pulley.

For indoor repair and renovation work the materials used are usually not very heavy. They are joined together in small pieces. As such all such materials are manually handled. However, special precautionary measures should be taken when handling acids, paint, varnishes and glass.

Some tools and tackles are used for manual handling of materials. They should be made available to the workers for convenience and safety in doing the job. A few of them are mentioned below:

- Shovels
- Pick-axes
- Crow-bars
- Rail tongs
- Lifting jacks
- Movable ladders
- Ropes and slings
- Pipes
- Sal balla stout members
- Max pullers
- Metal hooks
- Wheel barrows
- Dip lorries
- Rail pieces
- Small timber derricks with all fittings
- Other items as required for any particular job

14.4 MECHANIZED MATERIAL HANDLING INSIDE CONSTRUCTION SITES AND FABRICATION SHOPS

Inside the premises of big construction sites and fabrication shops where it is required to handle bulk quantities of materials everyday it becomes necessary to install mechanized material handling systems like belt conveyors (Refer Fig. 14.1). Undoubtedly they add to the efficiency in the material handling job. But at the same time the introduction of sophisticated machines and handling systems may create safety hazards unless they are taken care of properly. In such cases, mention may be made of the following equipments that are frequently used at construction sites and fabrication yards:

- Electric Overhead Traveling (EOT) crane
- Gantry cranes

- Fork Lifts
- Tower cranes, hoists and derricks
- Traveling jib cranes
- Mobile cranes

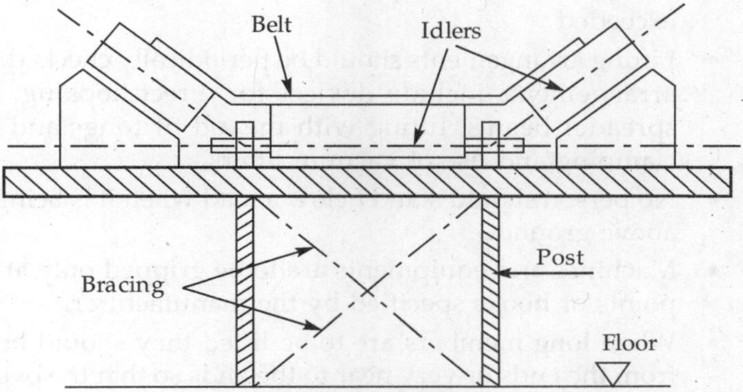

Fig. 14.1 Belt conveyor

Electric Overhead Traveling (EOT) Crane (Refer Fig. 14.2)

EOT cranes are engaged in construction sites and fabrication yards where materials, both heavy and light ones are needed to be shifted from one end of the work place to another regularly as per demands of the fabrication and construction work involved. EOT cranes are mostly used indoor, but are often extended outdoor also to facilitate unloading of raw materials and loading finished items. These are also used for handling of equipments during erection, shifting and dismantling. In steel producing sections and in foundry shops it is a common sight to see molten slag and iron being lifted from electric furnace crucibles in specially-designed containers, shifted to another corner of the factory and poured in molten condition inside pattern boxes.

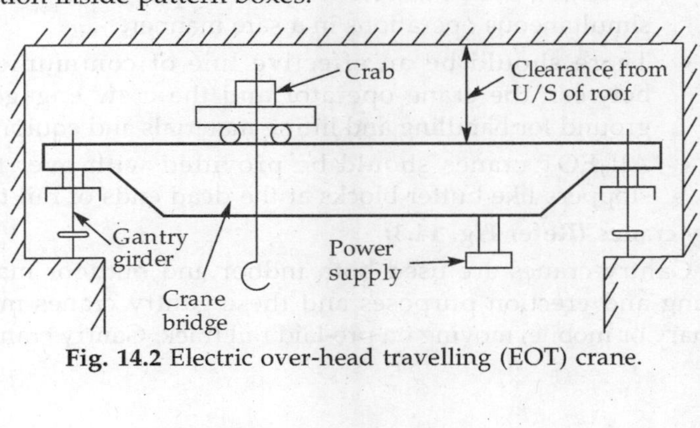

Fig. 14.2 Electric over-head travelling (EOT) crane.

The manufactures of the EOT cranes supply general safety guidelines for erection, operation and maintenance of such cranes. However at construction sites additional site-specific safeguards are needed to be adopted. Some of these are mentioned below:

- The rated lifting capacity of a crane should never be exceeded
- Lifting arrangements should be periodically checked. These arrangements include devices for direct hooking, slings, spreader beams, lifting with the aid of tongs and grabs, clamping and use of vacuum lifters.
- No person should stand below a load when it is being lifted above ground.
- Machines and equipments are to be gripped only at lifting points or hooks specified by the manufacturer.
- When long members are to be lifted they should be lifted from the ends or very near to the ends so that the overhang stresses do not exceed the permissible limits. This is particularly important when handling pre-cast pre-stressed concrete poles
- It is always safe to attach auxiliary ropes to the material or equipment to be lifted to prevent any inadmissible swing during lifting operation.
- Effort should be made to lift a load in such a way that its center of gravity coincides with the center of the lifting arrangement.
- Additional personal safety is a must when handling molten materials or hazardous chemicals.
- When two cranes are engaged at a particular construction site, they should be spaced more that two radii of 'reach' apart, so that sufficient space is provided for their simultaneous operations in a safe manner.
- There should be an effective line of communication between the crane operator and the crew engaged on ground for handling and lifting materials and equipments.
- All EOT cranes should be provided with over-travel stoppers like buffer blocks at the dead ends of rail tracks.

Gantry cranes (Refer Fig. 14.3)

Gantry cranes are used both indoor and outdoor material handling and erection purposes and these gantry cranes may be stationary or mobile, moving on pre-laid rail track. Gantry cranes are used mainly at storage depots and pre-assembly areas of construction sites. They may be designed for large lifting capacity with sufficient stability. However, their mobility is somewhat restricted compared to an EOT crane.

While handling materials and equipments with a gantry crane the same safety precautions are needed as for EOT cranes. As such they are not repeated here.

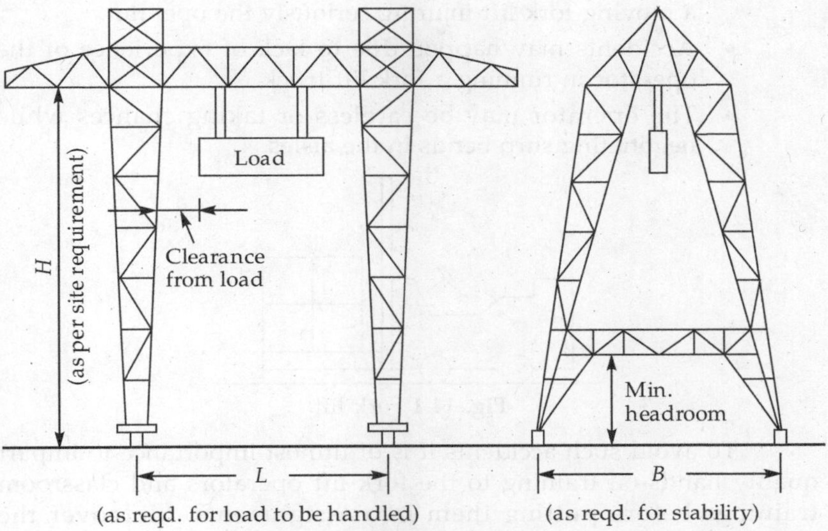

Fig. 14.3 Gantry crane.

Fork Lifts (Refer 14.4)

Fork lift trucks are extremely useful and popular in handling of containers, pallets and small-sized packets, paints and various other materials that are required for construction work. Fork lifts are seen to be moving in almost all storage depots with or without loads through aisles. However in spite of advantages in using fork lifts, statistics show that fork lifts often invite accidents and safety hazards to the people around these machines. The most common forms of safety hazards encountered in the operation of fork lifts are mentioned below:

- An employee accidentally stepping in front of a running fork lift, even in unloaded condition, is liable to be seriously injured. Often pedestrians get trapped between running fork lifts and stationary stacks of materials.
- A fork lift may push a loaded container to a person.
- A load falling from the fork on a person standing nearby.

- Due to mechanical fault, the operator may not be able to slow down or stop the vehicle in time.
- Accidents may happen when a moving fork lift rams into another moving fork lift.
- Sometimes the operator forgets to jam the wheels during unloading causing serious mishaps.
- Due to instability in the material stacks, loads may fall on a moving fork lift injuring seriously the operator.
- Accidents may happen due to lack of experience of the operator in running a fork lift truck.
- The operator may be careless or taking chances while negotiating shrp bends in the aisles.

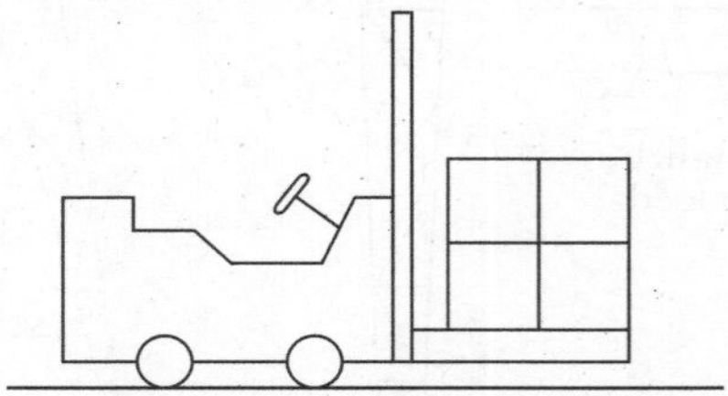

Fig. 14.4 Fork lift.

To avoid such accidents it is of utmost importance to impart quality hands-on training to the fork lift operators and classroom trainings before putting them into assignments. Moreover the operators should be motivated to look after the fork lift trucks. In addition there should be adequate monitoring and supervision to enforce safe work practices in the place of work. In this respect the supervisor should attend to the following safety hazards.

- The fork lift traveling high with improperly secured loads
- The operator is carrying passengers on the fork lift
- The loads are stacked improperly on the fork lift.
- There is not adequate counterbalance
- Lack of periodic maintenance

In short, the safety in the movement of fork lifts should not be taken as granted, considering that it is easy to operate a fork lift truck.

Tower cranes (Refer Fig. 14.5)

Tower cranes are used for erection of high-rise structures and apartments. These are provided with lifting booms to lift and move loads horizontally. The horizontal boom of the tower cranes should be tied to firm supports when not in use to provide stability against wind forces.

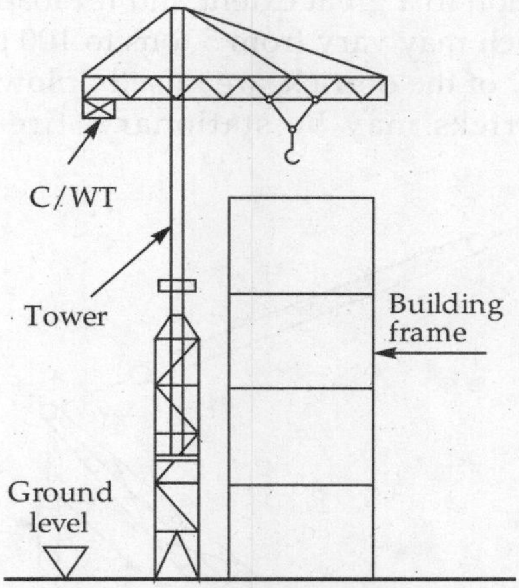

Fig. 14.5 Tower crane.

Hoists (Refer Fig. 14.6)

Materials are often lifted to upper floors during the construction of high-rise buildings with the help of climbing hoists, that moves vertically from one level to another. For providing stability to such hoists, the main frame of the hoist is supported at intervals to the building frame.

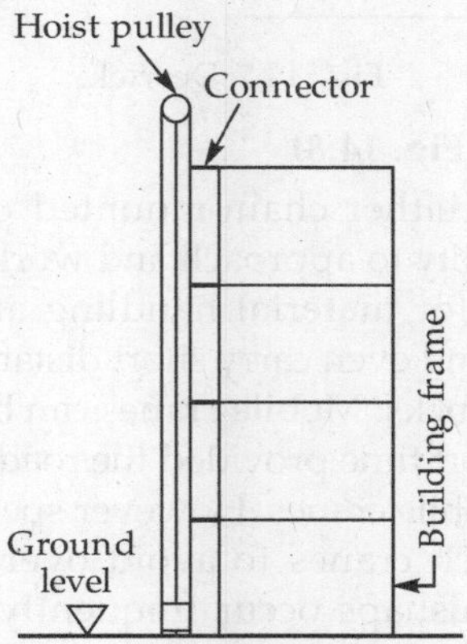

Fig. 14.6 Hoist.

Derricks (Refer Fig. 14.7)

A derrick is a strut supported at its top with wire rope guys and is meant for lifting and lowering materials and equipments.

Though theoretically only three guys at 120 degrees apart may be required for keeping the derrick pole straight, not less than six guys are normally used. Greater number of guys also permit inclining the strut in any direction to a great extent and lift loads from a distance. The lift loads, which may vary from 5 tons to 100 tons depending on the lifting capacity of the derrick, are raised or lowered by a hoisting mechanism. Derricks may be stationary, tire-mounted or rail mounted.

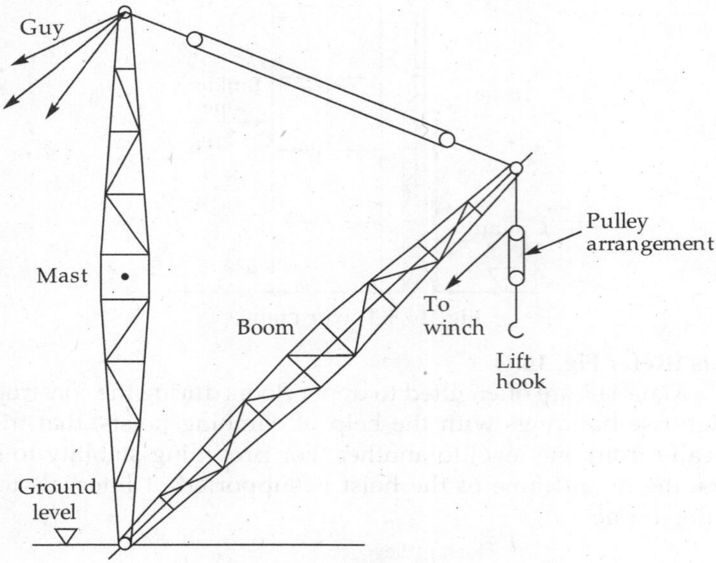

Fig. 14.7 Derrick.

Mobile cranes (Refer Fig. 14.8)

Mobile cranes, either chain-mounted or on wheels are very popular for their mobility to approach and work in difficult places and are extensively used for material handling and lifting of erectable members, equipment and even carry short distances with the lifted load to place the same on trucks. Mobile cranes can be moved from one site to another in a very short time provided the road condition is conducive to the movement of mobile cranes. However special attention should be given while using such cranes to avoid overturning during lifting operations, as such mishaps occur frequently in absence of proper supervision in handling such types of cranes. Sometimes, the back of the crane is supported by sleeper cribs while the crane is operated. Special purpose steel mats are also kept ready for easy movement of mobile cranes when these are deployed on slushy ground or on soft river beds. In spite of all the above difficulties a mobile crane is of much use simply because of its mobility.

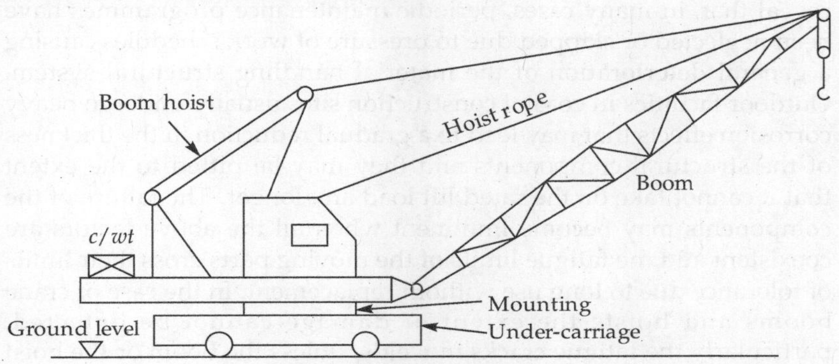

Fig. 14.8 Mobile crane.

Traveling Jib cranes (Contractor's type)

Traveling jib cranes mounted on rail track are used for erection work at construction sites. The major safety hazards of using such cranes are overturning during loading and overturning due to strong wind during erection work. When such type of cranes are used for cantilever erection of bridges and the crane is mounted on rails fixed on the top chords and moves forward inside the river spans, any mishap due to overturning of the crane is unwanted. To avoid this, it is the standard practice to put adequate calculated counterweight on the back of the crane platform to prevent overturning during lifting operations. Sometimes the main frame of the crane platform is kept tied to the permanent structure for the same purpose. The best way to prevent overturning due to strong wind would be not to do any erection work under such conditions and make programme of erection work at suitable time of the day when the wind is not strong enough to cause any damage by overturning the crane.

14.5 SAFETY HAZARDS IN USING OLD MECHANICAL HANDLING SYSTEMS

It is a common knowledge that the efficiency of a machine gets reduced over time due to continuous use. It is no different in the case of mechanized mechanical handling systems. The lifting power of a crane or a hoist may be seriously affected leading to safety hazards due to several factors such as:

- lack or absence of maintenance
- environmental corrosion and
- fatigue of the structural components.

Investigations of failures or near-failure conditions of various types of mechanical handling systems, particularly outdoor cranes, reveal that, in many cases, periodic maintenance programmes have been neglected or skipped due to pressure of work schedules causing a general deterioration of the material handling structural system. Outdoor facilities in coastal construction sites usually undergo heavy corrosion effects that may lead to a gradual reduction in the thickness of the structural components and they may be pitted to the extent that it cannot take on the rated lift load any longer. The failure of the components may become imminent when all the above factors are coexistent and the fatigue limits of the moving parts cross their limits of tolerance due to long use without replacement. In the case of crane booms and hoists the extent of damage cannot be detected, particularly the fatigue cracks in welds, unless the boom or the hoist is lowered for a close view shutting down the facility.

Under the above circumstances the project manager sometimes puts restrictions on the operation of cranes, either by lifting loads lesser than the rated lift load or lift rated loads at greater boom inclinations. Though from safety point of view this may appear to be correct, this should be treated only as stop gap arrangements, as operators may forget or deviate from the restrictions due to complacency over a period of time and may operate the crane at greater loads causing accidents. Moreover, lack of repair, replacement of parts and periodic maintenance may further reduce its already-reduced load carrying capacity causing accidents during operation.

Maintenance manuals prepared by the manufacturers provide excellent guidelines for periodic and preventive maintenance programmes and they should be followed scrupulously.

Electrical safety

Mechanical handling systems are often run by electric power and therefore electrical safety should also be ensured. The electric power supply of an EOT crane is usually 440 V-3-phase-60 Hz AC, supplied to a cable that is either looped or fed from a retractable spring-loaded feeding drum. Electrical shock from such a power supply may paralyze or cause death to a person. An electric shock is a function of current flow as well as the voltage. The longer the current flows through a human body the greater is the shock suffered. Again, an instantaneous high voltage shock is also fatal. Electric shocks paralyses the nervous system, interferes with the regular breathing mechanism due to contraction of the chest muscles and the rhythm of the heart beats are blocked. Flow of heavy current increases the body heat and burn injury from electric shocks is also common. The resistance of a human body comes primarily from the skin. But wet skin is 100 times less resistant to electric current than the dry skin.

Considering all the dangers and safety hazards from unattended electric supply lines and the connections, the power supply system should kept in order by taking the following safety provisions by engaging people who know the job and have license.

- All switch gears, switches and cables should be free from any leakage and their material and specifications should conform to the power supply requirements
- All electrical systems should be provided with ground-earth systems with proper specifications and capacity.
- Proper protection against rain should be given to outdoor electric supply facilities
- Provision of circuit breakers and ground fault systems for protection against short circuit.
- Additional protection of the electric supply system if hazardous chemicals are handled.

14.6 SAFETY HAZARDS IN TRANSPORTATION OF MATERIALS

For any construction project materials are mostly carried to the site of work by truck transports from the nearest railhead, port or quarries, mines and production centers of finished goods. Dump trucks (Refer Fig. 14.9) are extensively used for transportation of materials from one end of the site to another and also for removal of surplus earth after excavations.

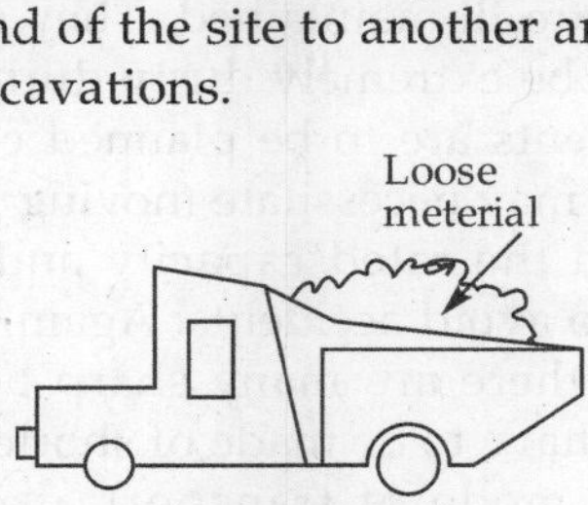

Fig. 14.9 Dump truck.

In any construction project the timely completion of the project depends to a large extent on the timely supply of construction materials and replenishment of the inventory. This can be made possible by maintaining strict safety norms in truck movements that depend on several site-specific factors, namely:

- Type of materials to be transported for a particular project
- Choice of the appropriate type of transport to carry those materials
- Condition of roads
- Efficiency and training of drivers and other related staff

The type of materials to be transported usually consists of loose materials like stone chips, sand and gravel, packaged material like cement, paint and store items, heavy fabricated steel materials, equipments and liquid petroleum products. Recently controlled concrete is also being transported in specially-designed vehicles from the nearest batch production centers to the site of work within a stipulated time to avoid consolidation of concrete on the way.

The choice of a particular vehicle for carriage purpose depends on the unit load of the materials to be shifted, its specification and size. While loose materials like stone chips, sand and gravel can be loaded in a truck of any capacity, transportation of fabricated steel items may need trailers (Refer Fig. 14.10) of specific lengths, instead of ordinary trucks to accommodate the fabricated items.

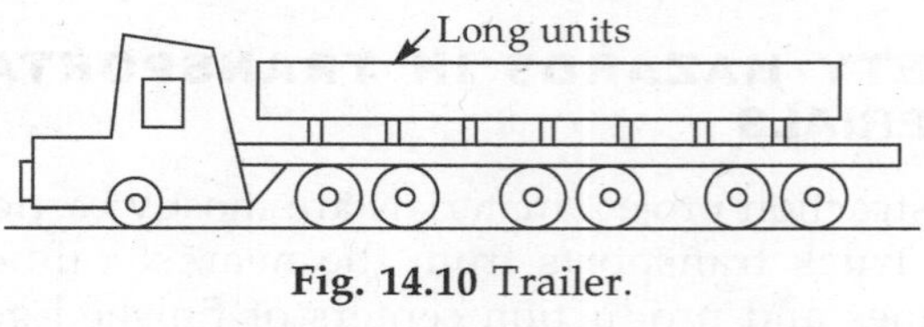

Fig. 14.10 Trailer.

Sometimes the roads leading to the construction sites are not fully developed and are ill-maintained. They remain slushy during monsoon and turn to be extremely dusty during the winter season. All vehicular movements are to be planned considering the actual road condition which may necessitate moving industrial trucks with loads much less than the rated capacity and if necessary speeds should be restricted to avoid accidents. Again, for construction sites in hilly areas where there are many sharp bends on the way the fabricated items may have to be made of shorter lengths to negotiate such bends and the mode of transport also has to be selected accordingly.

In any construction site, all construction materials and inventory items are needed in a phased manner, depending on the programme and the progress of the work. Equipments are also to be brought to site as per predetermined time schedule. Accordingly, the choice of a particular type of transport and their numbers required in different phases are decided following the material procurement schedule. Even if the job of material transport is offloaded to external agencies, transport planning is a must for all big construction sites.

The timely and safe delivery of all types of construction materials and equipments depends on the condition of the roads and driver's training and efficiency to carry on his duties in a systematic way avoiding accidents and mishaps.

Safety hazards in road transportation due to tyre failure

Previous records show that around 60% of the vehicular accidents on Indian highways involve heavy vehicles and a large number of reported (and also un-reported) accidents relate to pedestrians, cyclists and two-wheelers. It is recorded that road accident fatalities in India amounted to 64000 in 1994 with 312080 persons injured during this year itself. Road traffic accidents have since increased year after year and are more frequent on the National Highways, though these highways comprise only 2% of the total road length in India. While investigating the root causes of all these accidents, it is found that the deterioration in the tyre condition and low riding qualities of the road surface have important bearing on the safety of the vehicles, on the safety in transportation of materials and also on the safety of other travelers and pedestrians. A tyre failure of the front wheel of a load-carrying vehicle is often the prelude to serious accidents and related damages.

The function of a typical tyre of a heavy vehicle is to transfer the load to the pavement over its area of contact and it also provides cushion and grip against skidding, shock and vibration. Mainly three types of tyres are used for road transport, namely, (*a*) Tube tyre, (*b*) Tubeless tyres and (*c*) Studded tyres. High-pressure tube tyres (maximum pressure of about 5.6 kg/sqm) are used in commercial vehicles and are robust in construction. Tube-less tyres (with pressure up to 7.0 kg/sqm) are also used in trucks and buses. These are basically light-weight tyres, which performs well on road surfaces in cool conditions and are resistant to nail puncture in most situations. On the other hand, the studded tyres are very special type tyres, to which studs are anchored in the tread. These studs provide better traction capacity in snow-capped roads.

Tyres should be 'balanced', both statically and dynamically to avoid wobbling of the wheels and maintaining good steering. The treads should be so designed that it runs on wet surfaces and slushy roads without skidding. The ribs should also be so designed that the wear and tear of the tyre is uniform. Each tyre should be checked before use to ensure proper inflation. Over-inflation weakens the chord and under-inflation causes severe flexing due to deflection under load. Tyres should not be subjected over-loading, which reduces its normal mileage and reduces its effective service life. (Refer Fig. 14.11).

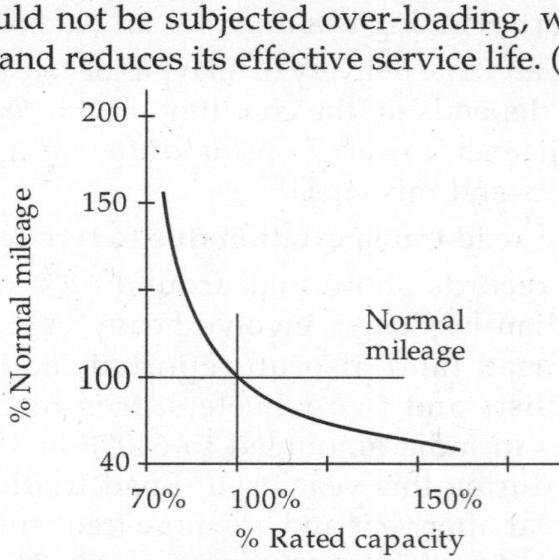

Fig. 14.11 Effect of over-loading on mileage covered by a tyre.

Another major problem frequently encountered in the safe use of any tyre is the overheating of the tyre. Major causes of overheating of the tyre in running condition are:

- Under-inflation, as explained above
- Over-speed
- Sudden application of brakes and sudden start of the vehicle
- Continuous running without stop
- Bad road conditions
- Misalignment of the wheels, damaging the tyres
- Blistering of the road surface (for flexible pavements) and over-heating (for concrete pavements)

Wear and tear of tyres

The wear and tear of tyres is accelerated due to bad road conditions. The wear of a tyre can be quantified by measuring the weight loss or decrease in the thickness of its crown. The wear and tear of a tyre may be traced to several factors, namely:

- Wear due to continued abrasion with the road surface
- Wear due to fatigue
- Wear due to blistering
- Wear due to roll formation

To minimize wear and tear of vehicle tyres, the pavements (whether they are flexible pavements or rigid pavements) should be designed to develop the optimum friction for smooth passing of the vehicles. By optimum friction, it means that the friction developed should neither be too low, which may cause skidding, nor too high to cause abrasion to the tyres. Apart from low friction, skidding may also occur due to oil-spill over the road surface or due to a slushy road surface. The skid resistance (μ) is calculated from the following equation after measuring with the help of instruments at site the force (*F*) required to pull a **'locked'** tyre carrying a known vertical load (*W*) on a wet pavement.

$$F = \mu \times R \text{ (Refer Fig. 14.12)}$$

where R = the reaction from the vehicle = W.

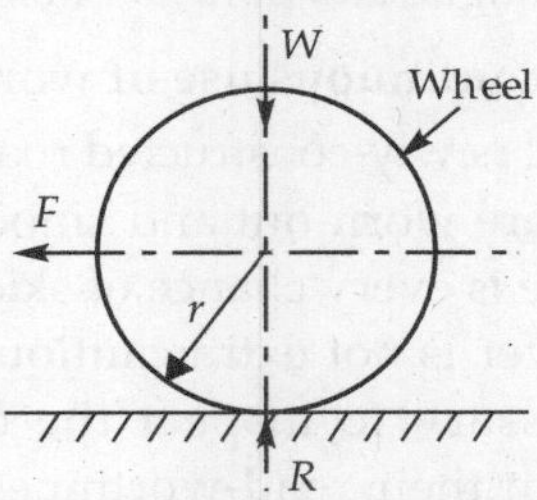

Fig. 14.12 Road surface friction.

Please note that the initial force required to pull a vehicle (F_1) is different from the above value and is given by the following relationship.

$$F_1 = [\mu_1 \times R]/r$$

where R = reaction as before = W (applied load)

r = radius of the tyre

μ_1 = coefficient of rolling friction, when the vehicle is about to move

The above relationship indicates that the force required to pull any vehicle is lesser as the radius of the tyre (*r*) is made bigger.

The chances of skidding are more at sharp bends, particularly if the vehicle runs at a high speed and safety is seriously endangered if, additionally, the road surface is oily or slushy. On the other hand, when the coefficient of friction is more than 1.25, tyres are subjected to abrasive wear and tear. Below this limit, there is no appreciable abrasion with the road surface, but the tyre may be subjected to fatigue wear, causing smearing and cracking from continuous long use. (Refer Fig. 14.13). Abrasive wear of tyres is also caused by continued impact of tyres with sharp corners of aggregates protruding from ill-maintained concrete pavements.

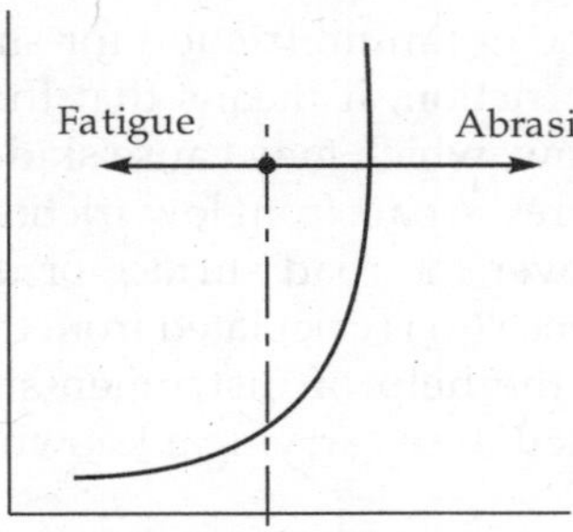

Fig. 14.13 Fatigue and abrasion in vehicle tyres.

Safety hazards due to continuous use of worn-out tyres

Even on a normal newly-constructed road surface, a vehicle may skid, if the tyres used are worn-out and smooth. When the speed of the vehicle is high, there is every chance of skidding or overturning at sharp bends, if the driver is not extra cautious. To avoid mishaps in such cases, it is necessary to inspect the condition of the tyres periodically to ascertain their road-worthiness. At the initial stages of wear and tear, a tyre may be re-treaded or repaired and used again for some time, before it is replaced by a new tyre. Re-treading should be attempted only to those worn-out tyres, which have some residual fatigue life. On the other hand, a tyre whose fatigue resistance potentiality is used up, no attempt should be made for re-treading or repair. Such tyres should be replaced by new ones for reasons of road safety. In any case, no tyre should be re-treaded more than twice during its service life.

The rate of wear of an old tyre depends on the pavement roughness, degree of curves negotiated, the condition of the vehicle springs and the driver's driving habits.Fatigue is accelerated when the load is very heavy causing a large deflection to the tyre casing and the road surface temperature is high.

The expected tyre life is usually specified by the manufacturer for normal road and driving conditions. As a general rule, the life of a tyre is reduced by 50% when the speed is doubled, by 20% during hot weather and by about 25% due to overload. The tyre life is also reduced when a vehicle is used in hilly terrains with pavement grades more than 6%. Considering all these factors, management decisions should be taken for the most optimum time for retreading/repair or replacement of a tyre for safe running of the vehicles meant for carrying and transporting construction materials and equipments.

14.7 SAFETY GUIDELINES IN TRANSPORTATION OF MATERIALS AND EQUIPMENTS

There are three distinct work areas where accidents happen in whole process of transportation jobs at construction sites, namely:

- During loading
- During transportation
- During unloading

In order to maintain regular and uninterrupted transportation activities it is necessary to assess the likely safety hazards and enforce strict safety regulations and guidelines and try to monitor on a regular basis the performance in this sector. In this regard The Occupational Safety and Health Administration (OSHA), (created in USA under The Williams Steiger Act, 1970) had prepared important guidelines, that are being revised and modified regularly in that country to enforce safety in transportation of various types of materials by industrial trucks. The most salient features of that guideline and other safety precautions normally adopted are worth mentioning here for the benefit of the reader.

Safety during loading operation

The following aspects should be looked into during loading of industrial trucks:

1. Trucks should be loaded within its rated load carrying capacity

2. Loads should be arranged and fixed in such a way that the stacks are stable

3. Equipments should be rested on firm supports and rigidly tied with ropes and other attachments as necessary.

4. Multi-tier loads should not have heights infringing with over-head cables and cross-bars at railway gates en-route to the destination.

5. Trucks loaded with attachments like derricks and winches should be treated as partially-loaded truck when not handling a load.

6. Tilt of loads must be avoided during multi-tier loading, particularly for manually operated handcarts. (Refer Fig. 14.14)

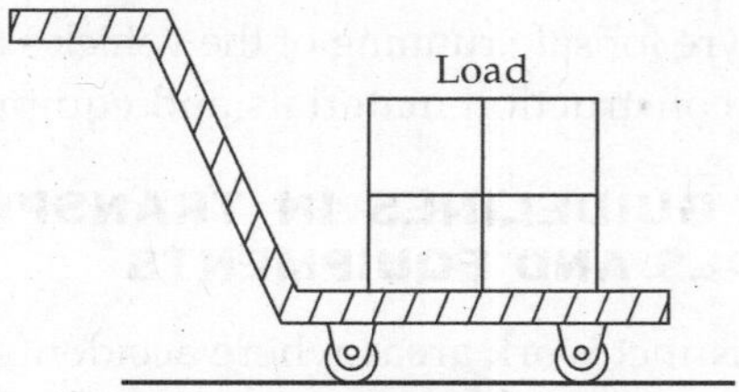

Fig. 14.14 Hand-cart.

7. All loading activities should be carried by skilled personnel, who should be supplied with necessary tools and tackles like pulleys, wire ropes, slings and other tools required normally for handling a load manually.

8. Loading operation for heavy machines and equipments should be done under close supervision of supervisory staff.

9. When mechanical loaders are used for loading loose materials like iron ore, coal ash, stone chips etc care should be taken so that the loader does not hit the truck causing damage.

10. Personal safety must be maintained during all loading operations. This is particularly important when revolving jib cranes are operated. (Refer Fig. 14.15)

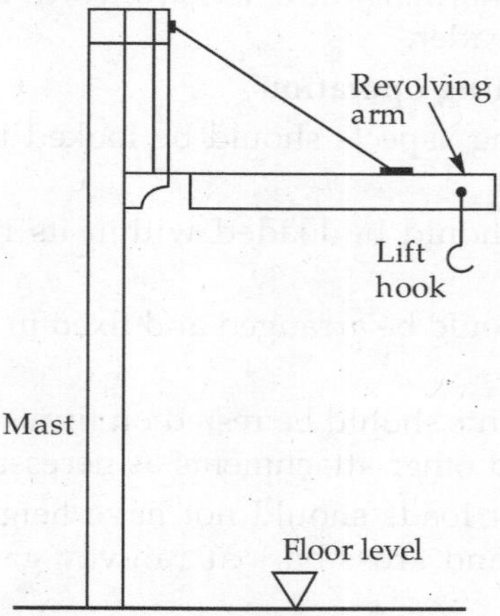

Fig. 14.15 Revolving jib crane.

11. When mechanized equipments like EOT cranes or fork lifts are engaged for loading purposes all safety norms as required for mechanized handling of materials should be followed.

12. Wheels should be jammed or locked when a truck is parked on an inclined road. Brakes should be set and wheel blocks should be in place while loading a vehicle.

13. A supervisor should treat a loaded vehicle to be unattended if the operator remains more than 25feet away even if the vehicle remains in view or if the operator himself is out of view from the loading point.

14. Sufficient headroom and safe distances are to be maintained from permanent structures during loading operations.

14.8 SAFETY DURING TRUCK MOVEMENT

Safety during movement of transport trucks lies almost entirely on the driver of the vehicle concerned and also on the alertness of other drivers on the roadway. The foremost of the rules that are to be followed in this connection are stated below.

1. All traffic rules laid by the authority should be observed.

2. Speed limits as indicated on different road sections are to be maintained.

3. Fire tenders, ambulances and other vehicles on emergency duty should be given the right of way. Right of way should be strictly observed while driving along hilly roads.

4. No overtaking should be attempted on bridge sections.

5. Operators should be extra careful while driving at night.

6. Industrial trucks carrying heavy loads protruding at the back should have proper red signals at the end. They should have visual conspicuity borders (retro-reflective markings) on the body at rear and sides for vehicles exceeding 7.5 t and for trailers whose length exceeds 8m.

6. The driver should slow down at road intersections, at sharp bends, at wet patches on roads and at spots where vision is obstructed by bill boards and other vehicles in front.

7. Stunt driving must be avoided.

8. All motorized trucks that have to enter elevators or other closed work areas must enter with the load in the forward position.

9. When parking loaded trucks at railway sidings, a clearance of at least 8feet from the rail center must be maintained.

10. While ascending or descending steep grades in excess of 10%, loads should be positioned on the upgrade side. Speed should be strictly controlled while negotiating grades.

11. The driver should have proper license to operate heavy vehicles and he should be assisted by an assistant all along the journey. The journey period on long distances should be so planned that the driver may get time for rest and food.

12. Night parking of loaded vehicles should be done at designated places only.

14.9 MAINTENANCE PROGRAMME FOR INDUSTRIAL TRUCKS

A safe journey needs a vehicle well maintained and in safe operating condition. As a result, a vehicle should be put temporarily out of service if mechanical defects are noticed or if periodic maintenance becomes due. The project authority would only invite potential safety hazards if the vehicle is continued to run for the sake of achieving programmes and schedules. A vehicle should be sent to workshop for maintenance under the following conditions:

- When the fuel tank is leaking
- If defects in the brake system or cooling system is reported
- If the electrical system needs repair
- If any mechanical part needs immediate replacement
- If the battery needs charging or replacement
- If the fuel system needs remodeling as per statute regulations
- If a fire hazard is anticipated in the fuel and ignition system.
- If the vehicle needs general cleaning and overhauling

Separate log books should be maintained for each vehicle in which the maintenance and repairs done should be chronologically recorded along with mileage covered and fuel consumptions.

14.10 DRIVER'S TRAINING

The operator must have adequate training in handling an industrial truck engaged in transportation of various types of materials from one place to another as per requirements at site. Besides administrative guidance and class room lessons a trainee should have hands-on experience in the following aspects:

- Inspection: The operator should have the basic training to detect likely defects just by walking round the vehicle and during start-up.
- The trainee should know the rules for a safe start-up.
- The trainee should undergo adequate practical training to run a vehicle in a safe manner.

- The trainee should have general guidelines about what to do in case of an accidental fire (use of fire extinguishers on board the vehicle).
- The trainee should have practical training in loading operations, fixing and tying heavy loads and equipments on board and parking rules.
- The trainee should be given license only after his job-oriented performance is found to be satisfactory.

14.11 SUPERVISOR'S ROLE IN TRANSPORTATION ACTIVITIES

In the whole sphere of transportation by industrial trucks the supervisor has the responsibility to identify the critical areas where his intervention is necessary, in order to improve safety conditions within the construction site area and also outside. His main objective should be to prevent accidents by timely interventions, rather than post-accident review and fault-finding.

QUESTIONS

1. Explain how accidents may occur during transportation and handling of construction materials and fabricated items.
2. Write briefly about the safety measures needed to be adopted during handling of green concrete and hot bituminous materials.
3. Under what circumstances old material handling equipments may become unsafe for regular use?
4. Why electrical safety is considered to be so important in material handling work? What electrical safety measures should be taken inside a fabrication shop while handling steel materials by mechanical means?
5. Explain how bad reconditioned tyres lead to road accidents. What other factors are also responsible for frequent road accidents?
6. What are the causes of wear and tear of tyres? How skid resistance for any road surface can be experimentally determined at site? Why the continuous use of worn-out tyres may cause accidents even on a newly-constructed road?
7. What safety measures should be taken while loading and stacking materials on trucks? How the safety of the workers may be assured during loading and unloading of materials and equipments?
8. Write briefly about the safety rules to be followed during truck movements both inside and outside work places.

9. Explain why regular maintenance of hauling equipments is needed for smooth accident-free operations.

10. What is the role of the supervisory staff during loading and unloading of construction materials and handling equipments?

11. Write short notes on the following items, mentioning their applicability and usefulness in material handling operations:

(*a*) Belt conveyor

(*b*) EOT crane

(*c*) Fork lift

(*d*) Gantry crane

(*e*) Derricks and hoists

(*f*) Tower crane

(*g*) Mobile crane

CHAPTER 15

Safety Practice During Construction

15.1 INTRODUCTION

For timely completion of complex large projects the project managers now-a-days are deploying extensively different types of equipments and machinery along with labours, both skilled and unskilled. Mechanization backed by advanced technology is the order of the day for controlling costs as also for constructing special structures of innovative designs. However in the rush of work pressure, carelessness and sometimes complacency creep in and serious accidents happen at work sites causing injury and death to workers followed very often by damage to valuable machinery and disruption in the work schedule. In many cases, long-drawn legal disputes arise that delay the progress of the work inordinately.

Past records indicate that the rate of accidents in the construction industry is three times more than the rate in the manufacturing sector. It is also a fact that, on an average, one in six persons engaged directly in construction activities become victims of accident-related injuries. In view of above it is absolutely necessary to devise ways and means for deployment of machinery and work force at construction sites enforcing safe work procedures.

The types and shapes of the foundations and superstructures vary in their design for different types of structures like buildings, bridges, tall structures, industrial structures and utilities depending on their loads and functional requirements. Their methods of construction also differ widely depending on whether the construction is done manually, in a semi-automatic manner or by engaging fully automatic equipments. In most cases a mix of various methods are adopted to suit site conditions, availability of skilled labour and equipments and financial capability of the constructor. However, in spite of wide differences in the methods of construction, there are certain basic work items like excavation, concreting, steelwork, masonry work etc that are common to most of the above-mentioned constructions, though the volume of work involved may be radically different in each case. Consequently the concept of safety in construction work should start with analyzing the safety hazards normally encountered in the implementation of the above-mentioned work items and finding ways and means to solve them. Considering the above facts, safety measures required for executing these most common items of work would be discussed in the following sections.

15.2 EXCAVATION

A civil construction work usually starts with earthwork in excavation that involves the following operations:

- Excavation of the trench or pit
- Shoring of sides, in case there is possibility of side collapse
- Dewatering/bailing out water from the pit or the trench
- Maintaining the stability of the sides and bottom till the foundation work is completed
- Backfilling of the trench pit afterwards
- Disposal of the surplus earth to specified locations

For very small projects involving a few shallow spread footings, the volume of the earthwork may not be much for each individual footing. In most of such cases earthwork is still done manually, engaging small diaphragm pumps, hand pumps or diesel pumps. Safety is more or less assured if the workmen are alert and skilled for the job. However, the case is not so easy for very large-volume excavation work in which various other aspects need to be looked after for safe execution of the work item. They are mentioned below.

Area of the pit to be excavated and the depth of excavation: The volume and complexity of excavation work increase with increase in the plan area and the depth of excavation. An increase in the depth of excavation poses more safety hazards compared to only an increase in the plan area.

Nature of the soil likely to be encountered during excavation work: An excavation work may have to be done either in a soft soil, or in hard soil or rock. Again the rock may be disintegrated or solid.

The excavation is easy for soft soil, but it has a tendency to collapse. On the other hand, blasting may be required for excavation in very hard soil and rocky strata. Both require additional safety measures for the safety of the workmen and the work area.

Water table likely to be encountered during excavation work: When the water table is high and almost near the ground surface, keeping the excavated pit dry for foundation work becomes an additional headache for the project manager. The problem of side collapses becomes more and more acute as the excavation progresses and there is high seepage of underground water through the open-cut slopes. Workers may even get buried if side collapses remain unattended for long in deep excavated pits. Seepage of water and heaving of soil at the bottom surface of the excavated pit often threatens to complete collapse of the excavation work, unless they are arrested in time.

Special arrangements of dewatering like well-point dewatering system may have to be installed when traditional dewatering by pumping out water from sumps located near the pit becomes ineffective. Dewatering can be minimized if the area of excavation is reduced by side shoring or sheet piling. Dewatering is always followed by side collapses if the sides are unprotected and the soil is sandy or mixed with gravels, which becomes very loose when the water level inside the pit is lowered on dewatering. Deep excavation works near coastal areas are therefore always hazard-prone.

Chances of flooding of the pit during work: Additional protection of the excavation area is needed, if the excavation is done on river beds for bridge works and that puts extra pressure on the financial outlay. Complete wash-outs of all site installations due to flash floods are not uncommon in hilly areas and 'terai' regions.

Excavations in different site conditions are shown in **Fig. 15.1**.

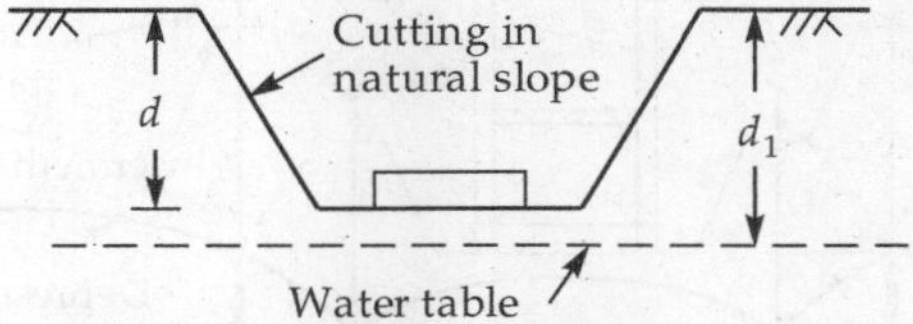

(*a*) Most ideal condition in excavation work:
Cuts in natural slope with depth of excavation (d)
less than the depth of water table (d_1)

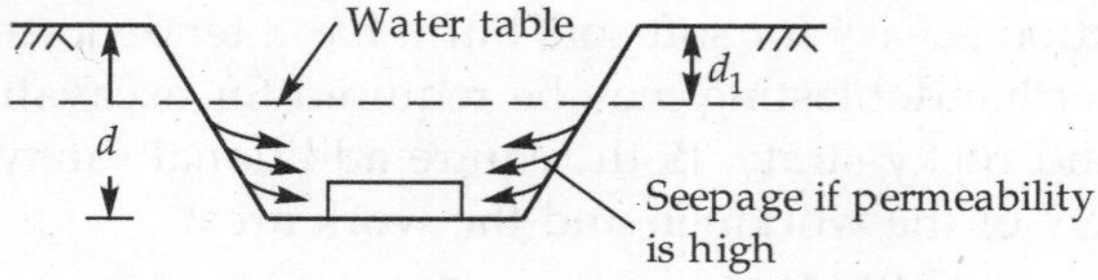

(*b*) Excavation likely to be disturbed by seepage of water and side collapse, unless water tabe is temporarily depressed by dewatering

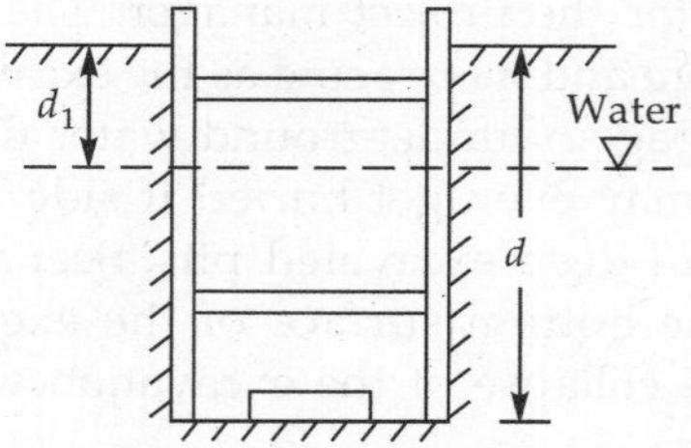

(*c*) Volume of excavation reduced and side collapse prevented by trench protection. But seepage cannot be eliminated completely, for which pumping is necessary ($d > d_1$)

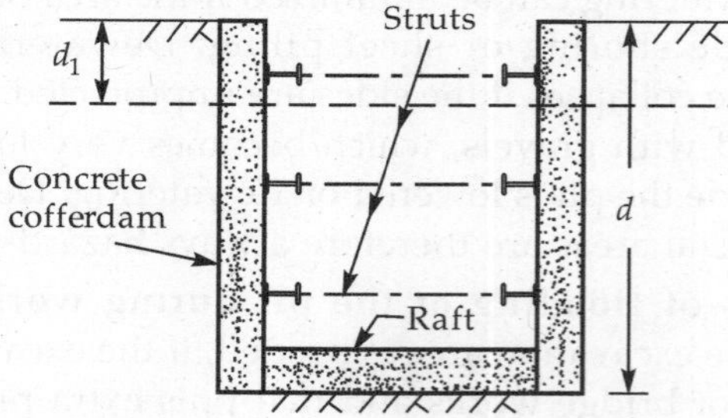

(*d*) Deep excavation ($d > d_1$) with strutted cofferdam

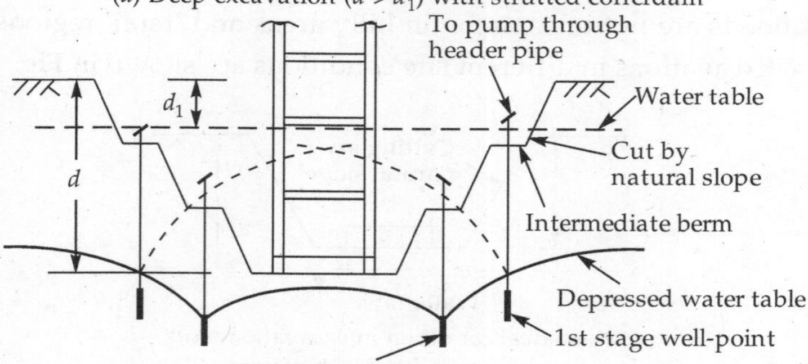

(*e*) Stepped excavation for basement work, well-point system of dewatering adopted when large area is to be excavated

Fig. 15.1 Excavation work in different site condition.

15.2.1 Mechanization in Earthwork

Earth-cutting and earth-moving machines are being used increasingly for speedy completion of the job when large volumes are involved. In this field of earthwork, a lot of improved performance has been observed with the introduction of hydraulic-drive single-bucket excavators, multi-bucket chains and rotor excavators and earth-cutting machines of various capacities. The excavators are normally equipped with interchangeable equipments like forward shovel, back hoe, dragline, grab, grading bucket, plough etc. For example, a dragline of about one cubic metre bucket capacity can be engaged for excavation work, trench cutting, in quarries and may also be used for loading of the excavated earth on haulage vehicles. Similarly bulldozers are used for digging and transportation purposes .with the help of a blade and a cutting tool. Scrapers are most efficient for digging work, if the soil is sandy, clay, mixed with pebbles but free from boulders. These are also used extensively for grading uneven sites.

All the earth-cutting machinery can be advantageously deployed in combination with one another depending on the site conditions and exigency of the work schedule. However when these machines are used, for safety reasons, they must be operated by skilled and properly trained operators and all safety norms as applicable for operating a particular machine must be observed.

15.2.2 Excavation by Blasting

The object of rock blasting is to loosen rock masses so that excavation and removal of debris becomes easy. Blasting is done in places where the rock is too hard or there are huge rock masses that are difficult to remove ordinarily. Various types of explosives are used by contractors for blasting purposes. However charges should preferably be fired electrically using ordinary gunpowder for dry excavations and by using high power gelatin sticks fitted with detonators and fuse wires for wet excavation. Holes for placing charges can be drilled by pneumatic drills. The following are the major safety precautions that should be adopted by the blasting contractor:

- Safe and separate, preferably underground, storage facilities are to be provided for storing blasting materials. The gelatin sticks and the detonators should be kept separated while in storage.
- No explosive should be brought to site near the charge points in excess of what is actually required for a particular

firing. Any surplus left after filling the holes shall be removed at least 500 metres away from the firing point.

- The contractor should have valid blasting license and he should engage a competent licensed blaster to supervise the blasting work.
- An area of 200 metre radius from the blasting point should be marked and encircled by red flags and the inner space should be cleared of all workmen and personnel not related to blasting.
- Firing points, if located very near to existing buildings and equipments, should be covered by M.S. plates with adequate dead weight over it.
- No blasting is permitted within 24 hours of any concreting up to a distance of 100 metres.
- No more than 6 holes should be set off at a time. The charges should be placed firmly with the help of wooden tampers and they should not be rammed or pounded by any metallic object.
- No blasting is usually permitted within 30metres of any existing structure.
- Blasts should tally with the number of charges placed at designated spots. If they do not tally, the misfired charge should be located half an hour after blasting and shall be exploded by drilling a new hole not nearer than 600 mm from the misfired one and exploding there a new charge.
- Sometimes blasting is done under water inside wells during well-sinking work to expedite sinking of wells. Care should be taken in such cases to protect cranes, earth moving equipments and other equipments from ground subsidence due to sand blowing. Workers also should be cautioned against sudden safety hazards in such cases.
- Safety in blasting operations should conform to provisions of IS: 4081-Safety code for blasting and related drilling operations.

15.2.3 Safety Problems in Excavation Work in Specific Circumstances

Artesian flow

Safety problems and difficulties arise in certain specific cases in excavation work where progress of work is often halted. One such example is the sudden appearance of artesian condition of soil when water comes out from the excavated pit continuously without any break on release of overburden earth pressure. It is noticed in many places on the river beds during well sinking work. Such artesian action can be eliminated by bottom plugging of the wells by thick concrete. Spots having the presence of artesian wells should preferably be avoided if they are detected during soil investigations.

Excavation for tunneling work

In tunneling work through solid rocks it may be possible to do excavation work without lining and the lining may be done at a later stage when the excavation work is completed. However, in most cases there is every possibility of subsidence of the tunnel because of soft strata that yields due to overburden pressure. In such cases, it becomes necessary to install the linings immediately after blasting and removing the muck for each round.

Excavation in constrained areas

Sometimes muck needs to be removed from underground sewer pipes and storm water pipes, as they cannot be replaced due to financial constraints. Manual excavation may have to be adopted in such cases because of space constraints to engage machines. All manual activities in such cases should be done, taking all statutary precautions against dangerous poisonous gases and vapour. Gas masks should be used if the presence of such gas is detected. However, now-a-days sophisticated inject machines are also used avoiding direct labour involvement.

15.2.4 Safety Hazards Due to Lack of Supervision in Digging Work

It so happens sometimes that boreholes that are abandoned due to some reasons or other, are not filled up by the contractor before they leave the place. These vacant bore holes become virtual death-traps for small children who accidentally fall in there and are confined at about 40 to 50 feet below the ground in a cramped condition almost without food and water for hours together. Sometimes, it requires the all-out efforts of the army and police personnel, administration and doctors, to rescue the child. This is usually done on an emergency basis by digging a secondary well nearby and a tunnel is dug manually at its bottom to reach the child. This type of serious mishap can only occur due to utter negligence and carelessness of the people involved in the boring work. This type of hazard can only be stopped by strict enforcement of law and safety regulations.

Similar cases are reported in cities and towns where excavations are left without any guard or fencing and pedestrians and motor cyclists have met with serious accidents by falling into the pit. The case becomes still more serious when the entire roadway is inundated after heavy rains and the pits are not at all visible. A little bit of safety awareness on the part of the implementing agencies may help in averting such accidents.

Often an entire stretch of a footpath from one road crossing to other is dug up and all sorts of cables are laid by assorted agencies leaving hardly any space for the pedestrians and injury to pedestrians is common.

It is to be noted that such accidents have one aspect in common. Such mishaps do not generally occur where there is regular supervision. These accidents are reported from places where the work is left to the whims of the digging people and there is nobody to supervise their work.

15.2.5 Safety Measures Needed in Earth-Cutting Operations

The following measures are required to be enforced to avoid safety hazards during earth-cutting operations:

- The area brought under excavation should be fenced off to keep away the general public.
- Earthwork near underground electrical cables and service mains should be carried out only under strict vigilance and instructions of the supervisors.
- Adequate shoring work is to be done around the excavated pit as the excavation work progresses. For deep excavations. Such shoring work may be of timber piles, sheet piles or retaining walls. They should be designed properly so that the stability of these temporary structures are maintained till the foundation work is completed.
- For deep excavations step ladders and/or berms are recommended.
- The excavated spoils should be dumped a safe distance away from the excavated pit so that the sides remain stable.
- No excavator or pump should be placed within areas where the side of the pit is liable to collapse.
- All dewatering equipments should be checked before start of the excavation and stand-by units should be kept ready.

- When an excavator is in operation, no one should be permitted to stand under the bucket or grab. Persons involved in the excavation work should position themselves at least 5metres away from the working radius of the excavator.
- Regular checks should be done to detect cracks or cave-in of side soil and adequate measures should be taken to rectify the safety hazard.
- All safety regulations regarding the operation of the earth-cutting and earth-moving equipments should be strictly observed.

15.3 SAFETY IN CONCRETING WORK

Reinforced concrete work involves mainly three operations, namely, erection of formwork, placing of reinforcements and concreting. Consequently, safety for the installations and workmen have to be ensured at all the above three stages of work in all seasons and in all site conditions. Because of the variations in all these aspects, safety measures are likely to be site-specific.

15.3.1 Formwork

Formwork consists of temporary structures and shutters that support the load of the green concrete, the load of the reinforcements, live loads on the working platform and wind loads, besides the self weight of the forms itself. All forms are to be designed with adequate factor of safety against the above loads for structural stability of the forms. In addition, the following safety measures are needed to be taken depending on the site conditions and nature of the concreting work:

- For formwork in foundation work, precautions are to be taken to prevent burying of the forms due to collapse of soil. In many cases, forms are damaged beyond repair and it is difficult even to extricate the forms after side collapse. Proper planning of dewatering is most needed when working below ground water level with high seepage of water.
- For trestles and other temporary structures that are erected above ground for concreting of superstructures, safety hazards due to strong wind should be prevented. All props are to be tied by bracings at regular intervals along the height both longitudinally and in the transverse directions.

Bracings are all the more important when forms are erected for inclined concrete structures like ramps and concrete approaches of flyovers. Sofit shuttering of slabs at upper stories of multistory constructions may be blown off due to sail effect of wind when there is no load on the shutters. This is to be taken care of by providing adequate ties to the formwork.

- No temporary structure or props or trestles should be erected on soft compressible soil without prior stabilization or compaction of the soil underneath.
- Panel dimensions of prefabricated side shutters should be fixed so that the shutters do not bulge due to side pressure of the green concrete. If the panel dimensions are very large, forms may even burst causing damage to the concrete profile.
- Vibrations produced by needle vibrators may dislodge the props from their support base. It is better to engage separate groups of skilled carpenters to look after exclusively the safety of the props during concreting. It is to be noted that once a particular prop fails, the load carried by this prop is shared by adjacent props and the chances of their yielding also increase.
- Electrical safety against accidental electrocution is to be ensured while operating electric shutter vibrators.
- Adequate lighting the work area should be arranged for night concreting programmes.
- Ladders and staircases should be provided with handrails as per rules.
- All concreting installations should have proper earth connections when the concreting is done very near to live wires, as in the case of road-sover bridges crossing 25 KV railway electrifications. This is very important for the safety of the whole group of the workmen working on top the bridge deck.
- Protective nets should be provided as necessary at site.
- While striking forms of cantilevers, the work of removal of forms should be started from the end of the cantilever, progressing towards the support, so that the cantilever action is maintained throughout the stage of form removal. The reverse process often invites collapse of the concrete, if adequate bottom reinforcement is not provided.

- Fire safety of timber forms is to be ensured at site. Site welding of reinforcement rods should be avoided at site over platforms made of timber shutters.
- All staging work should be protected from flash floods by ring bundhs while working on river beds during pre-monsoon seasons. Ideally, concreting dates should to be so fixed that chances of flash floods are avoided till such time the concrete hardens and the staging is removed from the river bed.

It is to be noted that most of the safety hazards in concreting work originates from the failure of the formwork due to some reason or other. As such, proper design and protection of the forms should be given due attention beforehand.

15.3.2 Reinforcement Work

Reinforcement work comprises cutting, bending to desired shape the reinforcement rods, carrying them to site and placing in position. In all these stages the following safety measures should be taken:

- Workers are often injured, though not always seriously, due to wrong handling of reinforcement rods. Flying rods from the shearing machines and cutting tools are another source of safety hazard. In all such cases proper safety norms should be followed.
- Higher diameter rods are often welded to avoid laps and congestion in reinforcement layout. Usual safety measures as adopted for welding work should be followed to avoid injury to welders.
- In some cases it is required to carry fabricated (welded) full length rods of bridge girders from the fabrication yard to the site and place in position. For pre-stressed bridge girders also, it is required to carry full length pre-stressing wires and tendons to site and place the same as per profile. To avoid excessive sagging of these rods during transit, adequate number of men should be engaged in holding the rods, so that the full length rods are supported at suitable intervals during handling and lifting operations.
- Sometimes road-over bridge girders (both reinforced or pre-stressed concrete) have to be concreted at span locations over high-voltage electrified railway tracks. Placing of full length reinforcements for these girders require extreme care and caution to avoid accidental electrocution. It is advised

to have the whole site installations, including the staging, earth connected as per railway safety norms. In addition it is preferable to do the handling operations after getting shut-down from the concerned authority. While handling reinforcement rods in such cases, sufficient clear distance must be maintained from the live tractions not only during handling the reinforcements but also during all subsequent activities of concreting.

- Another safety hazard is faced by the workers during the actual pre-stressing operation when there is a chance of snapping of the wires. In such cases broken wires fly at terrific speeds and may pierce through any person standing on its flight path. To avoid such serious safety hazard, it is always advisable to erect a stout shield behind the operating pre-stressing jack and nobody should be allowed to come in between the jack and the shield during pulling the wires. Same arrangement should be followed at the opposite end.

Reinforcements are always placed after erecting the staging and the shuttering boards and these give support to the reinforcements. As a result there is always a false complacency that no danger is expected as long as the supports are stable. However usual precautions for fabrication and handling of reinforcements should always be taken even for ordinary stereotype jobs.

15.3.3 Concreting

Although different types of machines are engaged for concreting work now-a-days at major construction works, still some amount of work needs to be done there manually. Machines used for large volume concreting work include the following:

- Batch mixers and portable concrete mixers: for mixing concrete
- Needle vibrators and shutter vibrators and skid vibrators: for vibrating green concrete
- Ready-mix trucks: for transportation of ready-mix controlled concrete from the batching plant to the site of work
- Concrete pumps and cutes: for placing and delivering concrete.
- Cranes and hoists: to unload concrete by buckets for bottom plugging work in well foundations

- Piling rigs: for pile foundation work
- Dewatering pumps: for foundation work in association with other equipments for concreting work
- Other machines as required for any particular site.

For low volume concreting work, however, manual labour is still used predominantly, even though mixing is done with the help of concrete mixers and vibrating job done by needle vibrators. In such cases, manual labour is needed mainly for carrying aggregates and cement into the concrete mixer and carrying the green concrete to sites, spreading and leveling the same, vibrating and finishing. Apart from this, skilled personnel are needed to be deployed to run the machines and do emergency servicing if there are accidental breakdowns when the concreting work is in progress.

Safety has to be ensured therefore for the machines as well as for the persons engaged directly in the concreting work. The following safety measures are generally recommended for concreting work:

- Safety regulations as recommended by the manufacturers are to be strictly observed by all persons handling mechanical equipments.
- All stairs and ladders used by the workmen for carrying green concrete should be at least 1metre wide having handrails
- It is preferable to provide separate stairs for up and down movement of workmen.
- There should be a stable walking platform for moving over slab and beam reinforcements to avoid tripping of the workmen.
- All electrical safety regulations should be maintained for electrical shutter vibrators and night lighting arrangements.
- When green concrete is carried by buckets with the help of cranes, the buckets should be prevented from swinging during lifting and handling.
- Stand-by generators should be kept for concreting work at night.
- For concreting work extending more than 8 hours, adequate number of workmen should be arranged so that they can be deployed on shift basis. This would relieve stresses on workers.

- For bottom plugging work in well foundations of bridges, proper checking of sumps should be done so that the well does not sink abruptly when the concreting work is in progress.
- All regular safety norms are to be maintained while handling and carrying pre-cast slabs, pre-cast poles etc from one place to another.
- All temporary staircases built for concreting work must have intermediate landings at every 3 metre interval.
- Adequate arrangements for night lighting should be made if concreting work has to be done during night time.

15.4 SAFETY MEASURES NEEDED IN FABRICATION AND ERECTION OF STRUCTURAL STEELWORK

The work of structural steelwork can be broadly divided into two distinct stages namely, the fabrication of the structural components and their erection and fixing in position. In both these stages various types of equipments are deployed along with labour, tools and tackles to do the job. Safety in structural steelwork therefore should encompass not only the safe handling of the structural components but also a safe environment for the persons engaged in the job and safety to the equipments, tools and tackles.

Safety measures in the fabrication and erection work should therefore ensure the following:

(*a*) There should be no damage to the structural components at any stage of their fabrication and erection.

(*b*) The workers should not get injured and there must not be fatal accidents.

(*c*) The tools and tackles should have adequate safety margin while in use.

Any item of structural steelwork like construction of multi-storied steel frames or steel bridges can be described to be safely completed only if the above three conditions are satisfied.

15.4.1 Fabrication Work

The fabrication work involves handling of the raw steel, cutting, bending, shearing, drilling, welding, riveting etc to produce erectable steel components before dispatch to site. The fabrication work is usually carried out either at established fabrication shops or at site itself. Large complicated steel structural components needed for bridges and industrial projects are almost always fabricated at established factories that are equipped with heavy-duty sophisticated equipments, cranes and machinery. Miscellaneous small items needed for such projects are often fabricated at temporary fabrication yards established near the site itself, using not so heavy-duty machinery. Such site fabrication yards are also used often as assembly yards to assemble the fabricated components by bolts or rivets before sending them to site for erection. Besides these, there are a large number of small fabrication shops dotted all over the country, where all sorts of light-weight fabrications for grills, doors, rolling shutters and steel windows are being carried out to meet the huge requirements of the housing and real estate construction works. In all such cases a safe work environment is needed covering all types of machine operations and human involvements. Some of the most important safety measures that should be followed to achieve this objective are listed below.

15.4.2 Handling of Raw Steel

The following safety measures should be taken for safe handling of materials:

- The stack yards should have proper road access for heavy vehicles and adequate lighting arrangements should be provided for night work.
- In big stack yards the aisles are to be so planned that the cranes and the lifting tackles can reach all the stacks easily and dragging of raw steel manually is done to the minimum.
- No person should stand below a load when the same is in the process of being lifted or lowered.
- All slings, pulleys and ropes used for handling steel materials should be periodically checked against possible wear and tear or corrosion.
- Workmen should avoid injury from sharp edges of steel material.
- All statutory safety measures should be taken by the workers while operating cranes and other lifting devices.

15.4.3. Welding and Gas-Cutting Work

In all types of fabrication shops, big or small, welding work occupies an important part of the workers' daily activities. Therefore it is imperative to ensure full compliance of safety guidelines recommended in this respect. Some of the most important guidelines are stated here.

Welding work to join steel materials is usually done by several methods depending on the availability of equipment and nature of the job to be done, such as:

- **Metal arc welding:** done manually for welding mild steel materials
- **Submerged arc welding:** this is an automatic welding process to produce high-quality deep-penetration welds of thick mild steel plates and sections.

In arc welding the current is drawn from a generator or a transformer to the work by welding cables. The transformers have an open circuit voltage of about 300 volts and falling to 70 to 90 volts when arcs are formed. The temperature of the arc is approximately 3000 degree centigrade.

- **Gas welding:** done manually for welding sheet metals, non-ferrous metals and for repairing cast iron, aluminium and for brazing work, using a mix of oxygen and acetylene gases supplied from separate cylinders. Here also the flame temperature is about 3100 degree centigrade.
- **Gas-cutting:** done manually for cutting mild steel plates and sections using oxy-acetylene flame as for gas welding work.

All welding and gas-cutting work must be done by qualified welder/gas-cutters who have the requisite certificates and hands-on experience in the art of welding/gas-cutting and they should follow all the safety rules needed for work safety, personal safety, group safety and safety of the equipments and tools. Salient features of these safety rules are given below.

15.4.4 General Safety

Sufficient working space, ventilation and light should be provided at the place of work. The work area should be kept free from any inflammable substances. Fire extinguishers and first-aid box should be kept in the welding section of the fabrication shop.

15.4.5 Personal Safety

Welders and gas-cutters must use shield and goggles during welding or gas-cutting work to protect their eyes. Arc or flames should not be seen by naked eyes. They should not wear loose clothes. He should wear aprons and hand gloves during welding/gas-cutting work to protect his body and hands. He should wash his eyes with salt water after each day's of welding work.

15.4.6 Work Safety During Metal Arc Welding

1. The welding generator should be properly and reliably grounded against electric shock.

2. Correct cable sizes should be used depending on the power supply. Commonly-used cable sizes are 25 mm, 50 mm, 75 mm and 95 mm for max. 200 amp, 300 amp, 450 amp and 450 amp respectively.

3. A protective shield and a helmet made of light-weight vulcanized fibre weighing not more than 600 grams should be used. The shield should be fitted with a welding lens (filter) covered by an ordinary glass shield to protect the eyes from injurious rays and metal splutter. The covering glass should be replaced as it begins to lose transparency.

4. All electric appliances connected to the welding machines should be checked periodically and preventive maintenance is to be planned in advance.

5. When the welding work is done outdoor, all appliances should be protected from rain and storms.

6. Rated currents should not be exceeded.

7. Welding sets should never be dragged by the welding cables to shift the set from one pace to anther.

8. Tools and equipments used for welding work should be checked time to time to keep them in perfect working condition.

9. Welding cables should not be more than 20–30 metres long to avoid loss in voltage.

10. The quality of welds should be checked at regular intervals to ensure safety of the welded joints. A properly welded joint should have 85% to 95% efficiency. This can be achieved by removing all physical deformations, cracks and irregularities in the welds.

15.4.7 Work Safety During Gas-Cutting

As already mentioned gas-cutting and gas-welding of mild steel plates and sections are usually done by oxy-acetylene flame at about 3000 degree centigrade. Oxygen is supplied in different sizes of cylinders varying from 50 lbs to 250 lbs, charged into the cylinders at 120–132 lbs atmospheric pressure (1 atm = 14.7 lbs). Oxygen is colorless, odorless and non-inflammable. Acetylene gas, produced by chemical reaction of water and calcium chloride, is stored in cylinders under pressure with a porous substance. Acetylene cylinders are popularly called D/A cylinders as the gas is stored in dissolved condition under pressure. Acetylene gas forms an explosive mixture when it comes in contact with free air. As such, caution is needed in handling of gas cylinders for welding work. Pertinent safety measures needed in this respect are stated below.

1. Acetylene gas cylinders should be stored separately from oxygen cylinders. No other inflammable material should be kept inside a gas store, particularly paints, kerosene oil etc. The store must have adequate ventilation.

2. Gas cylinders should preferably be carried from store to the place of work using trolleys. It is to be ensured that the cylinders are chained, all valves are shut, regulators are detached and there is no leakage. Gas cylinders must never be lifted by chain pulleys or by magnets. If fork lifts are used, the cylinders should be properly secured. Care is to be taken to ensure that cylinders do not pound against each other and they are not dropped from a height. Cylinders should not be rolled on ground and left on passages of fork lift or crane movements. Cylinders must never be left where molten metal is handled or there are chances of hot blasts and flames coming in contact with cylinders. Cylinders should not be rolled over electric cables or sharp steel edges.

3. Operators should note that all apparatus have their proper distinction marks: red for acetylene and black or green for oxygen.

4. To start the gas-cutting job the acetylene controller should first be opened slightly to light the flame and, then the oxygen supply should be adjusted by opening the oxygen controller to produce the flame desired for the job.

5. Blowpipe valves should be closed promptly to avoid 'backfire'. In case of severe backfire a hissing sound may be heard with black smoke coming out of the nozzle. In such case, the cylinder valves should be turned off promptly and the regulators and the apparatus should be detached from the cylinders. A thorough checking of the whole system should be made before starting work once again. Same precaution is to be taken if any leakage is noticed or if the cylinders become overheated. If there is gas leak, the cylinder should be immediately removed to an open yard and the leak should be promtly attended.

6. Regulators of correct specifications only should be used. Low-pressure regulators must not be used on D/A cylinders.

7. Kinks that may obstruct gas flow in the pipe should be avoided. No vehicle should be allowed to pass over the gas pipe.

8. Only spark lighters are recommended to light a blow-pipe.

9. Personal injury during gas-cutting from contact with hot metal pieces should be avoided.

10. The operator should follow other statutory precautionary measures regarding clothes, fire safety, work environment etc.

Various types of machines and gadgets are used now-a-days in fabrication shops to do shearing, drilling, riveting, bending, straightening etc of steel items. Many fabrication shops have facilities for galvanizing the fabricated items. In all such cases safety measures as per law and manufacturers' guidelines should be followed.

15.4.8 Safety Measures Needed in Transportation of Fabricated Items to Site

The strategy of transporting the fabricated units is dictated by the size, weight and the distance from the fabrication shop to the site. Sometimes the site location may be in remote hilly regions where steel fabricated bridge members are to be sent for construction of bridges. The sharp bends on the way and the rough terrain often create lot of logistical problems. Unless these are visualized correctly beforehand there may be delay, bottlenecks and safety hazards. To overcome these, it is often found to be convenient for the planners to visit the site along with the transport agencies to find out ways and means to deliver the materials safely to site without incurring any damage. Prospective contractors also visit the site before submitting their tenders for the same reason.

The transportation becomes easy and less time-consuming when steel erectable units are fabricated at the site itself. Transportation is also easy if the site located very near to a railway station where materials can be brought from a distant fabrication shop very easily.

The size and fabricated lengths have a lot of influence on the mode of transport. It is convenient to fabricate big-sized long units at the fabrication yard to get good quality fabrication. But the transport becomes difficult and almost impossible in some cases, where access to site is within city limits or hilly areas as stated above. Moreover there may be insurmountable site difficulties in erecting long heavy units. In such cases some trade-off has to be made to arrive at a satisfactory solution.

However, whatever may be the mode of transport, either by railway or road or a combination thereof, manual/mechanical handling of materials cannot be eliminated entirely and the transport agencies have to arrange skilled hands at those places for safe delivery of the materials. The following safety measures are needed for transportation of steel fabricated units:

- Fabricated units are to be supported only at designated support points so that they are not bent or damaged during transit due to bending under its own weight. Particular care is to be taken for long slender units, that may require more than two supports during transit.
- No steel member should project at the back of the transport vehicle more than that stipulated by rules.
- Height of stacks should have adequate clearance at bars erected at railway gates.
- Skilled hands should be deployed for loading and unloading operations at all stages and they should be provided with tools and tackles including derricks and other equipments as necessary.
- For long distance transportation, proper monitoring should be done for a safe journey. It is always pragmatic to adopt a slow but steady approach if safety hazards are anticipated on the way. Accidental overturning or collisions on the way may derail the whole construction schedule and the fabricated units may be damaged beyond repair and may have to be fabricated once again.

Other transportation and handling problems have been enumerated in details in Chapter 14, which may be referred to in this regard.

15.4.9 Safety Measures Needed in Steel Erection

While erecting steel structures and their components, safety management centers around the following aspects:

- **Safety for the erection machinery and equipments.** These include mainly the stationary cranes and derricks, the mobile cranes, winches, wire ropes, lifting jacks, pulley blocks, drilling, welding and gas-cutting sets and various other tools and tackles.

- **Safety for the erectors at site.** They comprise the men engaged for handling, transporting and joining the structural components, the operators and helpers for running the erection machinery and the supervisory staff engaged.
- **Safety for the erectable materials.** The erectable items may vary from heavy fabricated items like plate girders to small items like bolts, rivets, electrodes or very important non-replaceable items like sophisticated bridge bearing sets.

An erection work can be said to have been safely carried out if safety for all the equipments, men and erectable materials, as mentioned above, are assured. In order to achieve this objective the following broad guidelines are suggested.

15.4.10 Safety for the Erection Machinery and Equipments

While the erection work is in progress, care should be taken to ensure that the rated capacity of the lifting mechanisms used on job are not exceeded.

Overturning of cranes and sudden breakage of vital machine components are often found to be the primary causes of accidents while handling loads. These are to be avoided.

Timely maintenance of the cranes and lifting hooks, periodic checking of the wire ropes are very important for their safe operation. Machine parts, wire ropes and tools, tackles should be replaced if they are damaged beyond repair. A good number of cranes and derricks used in fabrication yards and erection sites may be old and it is often found that their main load-carrying structural components are corroded, bent and damaged. There are safety hazards if such equipments are allowed to be used without any rectification.

In many cases the cranes and the lifting machines may have been used long enough to have crossed their fatigue limit. A through inspection is needed in such cases by grounding the lifting devices and all repairs, replacement and renovation work should be carried out as soon as possible immediately after detection of the defects.

Careless handling and over confidence of the operators often invite accidents at site. All crane operators should have adequate experience in running the machines. Often their ill-trained assistants are seen to operate the cranes in absence of the regular operator. This practice should be stopped without fail for the overall safety of the erection process.

Wire rope slings are very often used for outdoor erection purposes and are therefore subjected to wear and tear and environmental corrosion all the time. This reduces ultimately the load carrying capacity and the service life of the wire ropes. Again, a large number of slings are often made up from old used slings by cutting, shaping and joining. The load carrying capacity of such slings are suspect all the time since they are seldom tested except when lifting the actual loads at site. Wire ropes are also damaged due to repeated bending and straightening and consequent fatigue. Chemicals, fumes, dampness during storage and heat also damage wire ropes. Frequent checking and timely maintenance by cleaning and oiling increase the service life of wire ropes and reduce safety hazards during erection.

The following precautionary measures are suggested while using any wire rope sling for erection work:

- Slings should not be subjected to loads beyond their rated capacities.
- Slings should not be shortened by bolts and there should not be kinks or crushing anywhere in its length or any damage by heat.
- Slings are to be removed from service if (*a*) there are 10 randomly distributed wires in one rope or 5 broken wires in one strand in one lay, or, (*b*) one-third of the diameter has been reduced due to wear and tear, or, (*c*) the hooks are opened more than 15% of the standard throat dimensions.
- A test certificate should be asked from the manufacturer while buying ready-made wire rope slings or wire ropes. The certificate should specify the allowable proof load of the wire rope. The minimum breaking force of different varieties of construction wire ropes are specified in **IS: 9282:2002**- Specification for wire ropes and strands. Minimum breaking force for a few standard construction wire ropes used in erection work are given in the table below as reference.

Round strand construction wire rope

Type	*Nominal dia (mm)*	*Mass Kg/100 m*	*Min. breaking force(KN) Rope grade in N/ sq-mm*	
			1420	*1570*
7 × 7(6/1)	12	56.5	73	81
-do-	16	101	130	144
-do-	20	157	204	225
-do-	25	246	318	352
-do-	32	403	522	577
7 × 19M (12/6/1)	25	238	295	326
-do-	32	390	483	534
-do-	38	550	681	752
-do-	42	671	831	919
-do-	48	877	1086	1201
7 × 37M (18/12/6/1)	38	550	653	522
-do-	42	671	798	882
-do-	50	952	1130	1250
-do-	60	1370	1628	1800

In addition, the code also specifies minimum breaking loads for spiral strands of various diameters.

Safety measures as specified by manufacturers are also to be followed when using fibre rope slings, alloy steel chain slings and metal mesh slings, though they are not recommended for erection of heavy steel members.

Safe operation practices suggested for use of wire rope slings

For erection of structural steel components whenever wire rope slings are used the following precautions are to be taken.

- All slings must be securely attached to the load being lifted
- The load must be evenly distributed on the slings used for the lifting operation and there must not be any tilting of the load. Also the included angle between the sling legs should be such that the loads carried by the individual legs do not exceed their rated capacities.
- Slings should be provided with pads of jute or similar materials to protect the slings from rapid wear and tear and attrition with any sharp edges of the load.

- Workmen should stand clear of any suspended load.
- There must not be any obstruction on the path when a load is shifted from one place to another or it is being lifted.
- While lifting any load the slings must not be subjected to shock.
- A sling should not be damaged by pulling when the load is resting on a load.
- Shackles, shackle pins and clamps used for connecting slings should be checked from time to time.
- It should be the duty of the supervisor to inspect all slings and their attachments every day before use and any defect or damage noticed must be rectified and the wire rope should be replaced promptly if necessary.

15.4.11 Human Safety During Erection

Accidents may happen to the erectors handling the load, to the people behind the machines, to the supervisory personnel and even to an outsider, who is not connected to the erection work, but simply having a look at the happenings or passing by. The erection schedule may get seriously disrupted and lot of legal problems may arise in case of any injury or loss of life. Life-threatening situations may arise in any of the following situations.

- Fall from a height
- Falling of an object on the head
- Accidental contact with high voltage live wire
- Caught between load and sling
- Caught unawares in between rotating gears or rollers
- Accident due to failure of false work, scaffolds and gangways during erection.

Workers may also be victims of serious accidents if the safety of the erection machinery is compromised in some way or other, as stated in the earlier sections.

Precautionary measures to be taken to prevent accidents

Accidents may be prevented if the hazards likely to be associated are visualized in advance and proper precautionary measures are taken. A few of such measures that should be usually adopted at all erection sites are stated below:

- The erectors while working at a height must use safety belts and the belt should always be hooked to a permanent structure above the position of the erector.

- All false-work should be constructed to have adequate stability for taking the load of the workmen and the construction tools.
- The erectors and machine operators should take all safety measures as prescribed for handling and operating a particular machinery.
- For site welding work at height the welder and his helper should adopt all necessary precautionary measures like use of goggles, shield etc. All safety measures as adopted for regular welding work at a fabrication shop should be enforced at site also.
- All live electric cables and electrically-operated equipments should be properly earthed.

  Workers should be cautious against accidental slipping from height causing fatal injury and death.
- Workers should be careful against dropping of loose items like bolts, nuts etc accidentally from a height.
- The supervisor should ensure that the planks and supporting members of the working platforms are securely nailed or connected so that the workers can move on the platforms safely. Handrails should also be provided as necessary. Platforms should not be overloaded beyond capacity.
- The erectors should be motivated to use safety devices.

15.5 SAFETY MEASURES NEEDED FOR MASONRY WORK AND OTHER GENERAL BUILDING WORKS

Accidents in masonry works occur in most cases due to fall of the workers from heights and such accidents become almost always fatal when somebody falls from upper storey of a multistory building. The primary causes of such accidents are found to be either failure of the working platform or tipping over a loose plank or tipping over a slippery platform during rainy season. Similar fatal accidents are also reported when workers are engaged in plastering work, painting or even during dismantling of the temporary structures and scaffolds. This can be avoided only by providing a stable working platform for them with handrails and toe guards and they should be motivated to use safety belts when working at heights. It is seen in many cases that worn out and defective members are used in building the scaffolds to cut costs. This should be strictly prohibited for the safety of the workers as well as for the uninterrupted progress of the work. During rainy season the working platforms should be cleaned of mud and the workers' shoes must also be cleaned from time to time.

15.6 SAFETY HAZARDS DUE TO BAD WORKMANSHIP AND FAULTY CONSTRUCTION

Safety hazards are often encountered at site on account of failures due to bad workmanship and faulty construction.

At times proper workmanship is not maintained either due to use of materials of wrong specification or due to engagement of untrained persons for a job. As for example, a ceiling plaster may peel off and fall on the head due to lean mix or due to lack of proper curing. Similarly welded structural components may fail due to inadequate weld or bad clumsy weld produced by an untrained welder. The service life of many structural components like bridge handrails, staircases, ladders and parapets are shortened due to bad workmanship. Catastrophic failures have occurred in many cases when overhead water tanks have failed when they have been subjected to full load immediately after construction, the reason of failure being the use of non-standard materials and bad workmanship. Bad workmanship is manifest in many railway footbridges in India where there is no uniformity in the riser and tread dimensions and the pedestrians are at peril of falling down and get seriously injured.

On the other hand, structures may fail due to faulty construction and such failures are often accompanied by loss of human lives, followed by social unrest, legal problems and disruption in the work schedule. Most common mishaps that may occur due to faulty construction are stated below:

- Sudden collapse of staging during concreting due to absence of proper bracings.
- Excessive deflection under dead load in a pre-stressed concrete girder due to inadequate pre-stressing.
- Subsidence of floor due to inadequate compaction of the soil under the plinth.
- Collapse of cantilever slab on release of soffit shutters due wrong placing of top reinforcements.
- Failure of concrete due to premature striking of shuttering.
- Collapse of newly-erected roof trusses due to strong wind in absence of proper supports.

- Failure of foundation due to construction over soft, compressible or filled-up soil without doing any soil investigation work.
- Failure of existing floors due to stacking of construction materials in excess of its load carrying capacity.

The primary causes of all such failures are very low standard of supervision, when usual safety norms are flouted and workers become careless at the same time. A proper and systematic safety management system is needed to be introduced to avoid all such unwanted mishaps.

15.7 OVERALL STRATEGY FOR SAFETY MANAGEMENT AT CONSTRUCTION SITES

To combat the accidents and related health hazards, a three-fold strategy of safety management should be undertaken at construction sites, namely:

- An efficient accident prevention programme
- Immediate attention in case of an accident
- Comprehensive plan for rehabilitation of the victim.

15.7.1 Accident Prevention Programme

A system approach is needed to achieve success in preventing accidents at construction sites, which includes the following steps:

1. A practical workable erection schedule should be chalked out well in advance before start of the work for effective implementation of any project free from safety hazards. This erection schedule should be prepared considering all incidental loads and construction loads that may act on the erection machinery and the erectable members during the process of erection. Adequate factor of safety should be assured at each stage of erection of the structural components and if necessary the original design should be modified and the members subjected to the most critical combination of forces should be strengthened. This system approach should be adopted for erection of all major steel, RCC and pre-stressed concrete bridges. A work schedule prepared for smaller projects should also ensure a safe construction procedure in a similar way with provisions of on-site inspections.

2. A set of safety guidelines should be circulated in advance for the knowledge of the supervisors and the erectors, following the provisions of codes and conditions of contract.

3. Danger zones at construction sites should be clearly displayed by notice boards for the safety of the passers-by.

4. All safety regulations and instructions given by local authority should be followed, particularly when the construction is being carried out within the city limits.

5. Supervisors and foremen should be posted at all critical points of the erection.

6. All the erection machines should be manned only by trained experienced operators.

7. Timely overhauling and maintenance of the cranes, hoists, tools and tackles, concrete batching plants.

15.7.2 Immediate Attention in Case of an Accident

In-spite of all precautions taken to prevent accidents at site, accidents may happen at site causing injury to the workmen. Such injuries may be of minor nature or they may be serious. Whatever may be the condition of the accident victim, he should be given first aid as quickly as possible, immediately after the occurrence of the accident. For this purpose first aid facilities must be made available all the time at site and at least a few of the staff should have training in this respect.

If the injury is serious the victim must be transferred immediately to the nearest hospital or health center, as approved by rules. In order to shift the patient to the hospital in such an emergency case the site must be provided with the necessary vehicle supported by the driver and fuel. For night shift work also the site must have the transport facility to shift an emergency patient to hospital without delay. A report on the accident should be prepared, clearly stating precisely the nature and cause of the accident, the name of the victim, his designation, the date and time of the accident and other relevant details.

As time is a very crucial factor for any serious accident, the site must have a well-chalked out contingency plan, prepared well in advance with clear cut instructions about what to do in case of a serious accident at site.

15.7.3 Comprehensive Plan for Rehabilitation of the Victim

In case an accident victim is disabled and is not able to perform his normal duties any more or for a long period, he should be adequately compensated both financially, as per rules and by re-employment after his recovery. Safety and health insurance schemes should be drawn in favour of the erection team members in order to provide financial compensation to the victims of accidents.

It is the duty of the project authority to enforce safety codes as stipulated by law and standard engineering practice. In big construction sites it may not be possible to look after all safety related activities by the project manager himself. In that case it is better to set up a suitable safety management cell from among the site staff and they should be given adequate freedom to implement the safety measures at site. Their effort will be successful if regular exchange of views, opinions on safety regulations are done, in which all sections of workers should be involved. A sustained effort in this direction will create safety awareness for working safely at site. In this respect periodic safety meetings should be arranged at site where threadbare discussions should be made for safety measures to be adopted for the work in progress.

QUESTIONS

1. Explain why adequate safety measures are necessary when construction work is dominated by mechanization.
2. How safety in excavation work is affected by high water table and collapse of sides. What are the usual methods of preventing side collapse? When do you think the well-point system of dewatering will be most effective in excavation wok?
3. What safety measures should be adopted during excavation by blasting?
4. What is meant by artesian flow? How does it affect the work of excavation and what is the remedy?
5. What safety measures are needed for excavation work during monsoon, while remodeling city roads and pedestrian walkways, which are likely to be water-logged.?
6. Explain under what conditions temporary structures may be damaged due to wind. How they should be protected?
7. How personal safety of the workers may be ensured during welding and gas-cutting work? What precautions should be taken while handling oxygen and acetylene gas cylinders during gas-cutting work?
8. How accidents may be prevented during transportation of fabricated steel members?

9. Write short notes on thee following:
   (*a*) Safe use of wire rope slings
   (*b*) Round strand construction wire rope
   (*c*) Rehabilitation of accident victims
   (*d*) Safety during excavation in constrained area
   (*e*) Safe disposal of excavated soil
   (*f*) Safety measures needed during handling of raw steel
10. What safety measures should be taken by a worker during welding and gas-cutting work?
11. What facilities should be made available to workers to ensure personal safety at construction sites?
12. What types of management controls are needed to ensure safety of erection machinery and equipments at site?

CHAPTER

16

Post Construction Safety Management

16.1 INTRODUCTION

As and when a structure is built in all respects it is taken over by the owner and the structure is then put into service. It is a common notion among users to take for granted that a structure would be safe for all the times during its service life, just because the structure has been designed properly and the construction has been done following standard engineering practice. Such a conclusion leads to complacency in the minds of the users and they often think that the structure can withstand much more loads than what it has been designed for. However this is not always true, as many structures exhibit serous safety hazards during their service life due to many reasons such as:

- Overloading
- Effect of aggressive environment
- Damages caused by external forces
- Lack of stability due to above

When more than one of the above hazardous conditions appear concurrently during the service period of a structure or occur one after another frequently, the safety and the stability of the structure may be seriously compromised leading to even catastrophic failures. The user authority should anticipate such eventualities and hazard scenario well in advance and take necessary measures.

A few cases related to the above safety hazards that are usually encountered during the service life of important structures are discussed below with suggestions for rectifications.

16.2 OVERLOADING

Many well-built structures fail due to inadvertent overloading beyond their ultimate load-carrying capacity. A glaring example of such failure is the damages caused to mezzanine storage spaces inside a factory, where heavy materials are piled up without considering the allowable load for which the floor was possibly designed. In most such cases it happens that the sections are designed anticipating lesser loads and the matter is forgotten or not known to the workers who pile up materials as per their requirements. To avoid such eventualities it would be appropriate to put up a notice board at a prominent place indicating the live loads allowable on the floor.

A similar situation arises when construction materials like bricks are piled up over a newly-constructed floor slab that has not yet attained full design strength. In many cases it is noticed that materials like bricks, cement and sand are piled on such floors almost immediately after the formwork is removed. It is overlooked that the allowable live load for a residential building floor is only 200 Kg per square metre, whereas the imposed loads from the piled construction materials may far exceed the allowable limit. Often, it so happens that the work is so speeded up that the green concrete load from the upper floor is transferred to the lower floor that is still being cured. Again, such overloading is disastrous for an old existing floor slab, when it is subjected to additional load for construction material piled up for extension work of upper floors. There have been reports of many such cases that have caused damages, cracks and even failure of floor slabs. It is to be clearly understood by all concerned that such practice should be stopped.

Overloading may also occur due to abject misuse of floor slabs, like developing roof gardens over roof by piling earth about 600 to 750 mm high, putting additional loads by laying marble slabs over existing mosaic without removing the same or cutting holes in the floor slab for making internal staircases without caring for the span arrangement of the slab. It is not possible for the designer or the constructor to keep an eye over such misuses, once the building is handed over to the prospective owner. The user should be aware of the likely consequences and he should consult technical experts whenever he wants to make any change to the existing layout.

Overloading of existing facilities is more common in the industrial sector. It has been noticed that in many cases scrap materials and excavated earth have been piled high against the boundary wall exerting lot of additional side pressure not considered in the design. The side pressure eventually increases further during the monsoon period when the earth is fully surcharged with water and the boundary wall may fail in a disastrous manner in such situations. The foremen and the supervisors on shop floor should not encourage such unsafe practice.

An existing old floor slab may be overloaded when it is subjected to additional loads from structural elements like beams rested on the old structure during extension work without checking its load carrying capacity or, when the floor is additionally loaded by way of putting new machines or rearranging existing equipments.

Often loads are lifted by fixing hooks and chain pulleys to the chord members of trusses inside factory premises. If the chord is not strong enough to take that load the chord may bend damaging the roof sheets also. For the safety of the trusses and sheeting this practice should be stopped. If it is found to be absolutely necessary to take the help of truss members to lift loads, they should be designed accordingly and all such loads should be allowed to be lifted only at chord joints to avoid bending.

Damages may also occur if additional floors are constructed without checking the load carrying capacity of the supporting columns and foundations of the existing system. Serious safety hazards like cracks in columns and settlement of foundations may have to be encountered if additional loads are imposed on existing structure, assuming them to be strong enough to withstand such loads. For this reason, for old buildings, it is a common engineering practice to raise independent support column framework right from the ground, with separate foundations to take the loads of the additional floors. Of course this solution is possible only if there is ample side space for erecting the additional framework and the floor layout is conducive for inserting the additional columns.

Overstressing may create safety hazards if design loads are under-estimated or wrongly fixed during the design of structural components. One such case may be cited here is that of the design of small culverts inside factory premises. Such culverts, being small, escape the attention of the designer very often and the construction is done considering loads of light vehicles only. Distresses appear later when heavy vehicles are allowed to pass over such culverts resulting in cracks and eventual collapse of the structure. Such safety hazards can only be eliminated by correct estimation of future moving loads at the design stage. Similarly, allowing heavy vehicles over old suspension bridges designed for lighter ones may be extremely unsafe with snapping of supporting wire ropes, particularly if they are worn out and corroded, leading to disastrous consequences.

16.3 SAFETY HAZARDS DUE TO EFFECT OF AGGRESSIVE ENVIRONMENT

In the post construction stage serious safety hazards are encountered if there is unabated deterioration of structural components due to corrosion and environmental pollution. The following are the main sources of degradation in buildings, industrial structures, bridges and pavements.

Post-construction safety hazards in buildings

Access of rainwater through roof slabs, cracks in walls and continuous absorption of moisture are primary sources that deteriorate building components. Continuous unabated ingress of water inside floor slabs, lintels, chajjas corrodes the reinforcement rods and cracks develop in the concrete because of swelling of the steel reinforcements. Many building roofs are found to have lost their structural strength due to accumulation of rain water over the roof because of faulty slopes and clogged rain water pipes. Rising damp and salt-peter effect damage very rapidly the ground floor and the walls. Blue patches often appear to the underside of roof slabs due to seepage of rain water. If neglected for years, these patches gradually increase in area over the years and eventually droplets of rainwater fall through these patches when the roof slab is fully surcharged during the rainy season. Initially the paint and then the plaster peels off and then cracks appear to the roof slab when it loses its normal strength. This state of affairs in wet environment also generates **fungi and rot** in timber doors and windows.

White ants are another source of rapid decay in timber doors, windows and furniture. Post-construction anti-termite treatment is considered to be the ultimate solution if the termites cannot be killed thoroughly by spraying chemicals. Pre-construction anti-termite treatment should be done in areas largely affected by termites.

Buildings, particularly old buildings, are likely to be un-usable and inhabitable, if proper maintenance is not done periodically every year. Such maintenance programs should include repair of damaged walls, floors and roof, clearing of rain water outlets, redoing plaster of walls and ceilings. Even if no major repair work is found to be necessary, the inside and outside should be provided with new paints at regular intervals for protection against aggressive environment. Regular painting of doors and windows, grill gates and furniture is also necessary to arrest alternate drying and wet expansion of unseasoned timber and corrosion of steelwork Such maintenance strategy is all the more needed for buildings in coastal areas where corrosion effect is very high throughout the year.

Distress in building structures may be linked also to **faulty construction** like leaving plastic sheets between wall and roof slabs. This un-bonded layer may be a great source of seepage of rain water unless they are diligently removed immediately after removal of formwork. A defective porous roof treatment work may damage a roof very rapidly. Similarly a **defective thermal insulation** can render a cold storage non-functional in no time.

Safety is closely linked to the decay of structural components and many old building are found in urban areas in dilapidated condition due to long years of neglect in maintenance and they have been declared as unsafe by the concerned municipal authority.

Post construction distress in industrial structures

Industrial buildings suffer from the same type of distress and deterioration as for general buildings stated above. In addition, industrial structures are often exposed to various types of acid fumes, toxic gases and industrial pollutants that are used in or generated from the production process itself. The major pollutants in this case are:

- Polluted industrial effluents coming in contact with structures
- Toxic suspended particles released in air causing corrosion to structures
- Damage to structures due to hazardous substances stored inside factory and leakage from the containers.
- Chimney dust, soot and fly-ash deposited over sheds and buildings adding to the roof live load substantially.

Though strict guidelines have been formulated to control the ill effects of the above industrial pollutants on permanent structures, property and human being, there are still innumerable industrial concerns in textile, paper and pulp, fertilizers, refineries, sugar, distillery etc where corrosion of buildings and structures is a common phenomenon. The corrosion effect is much more pronounced in factories near the coastal belts and also in port facilities. The safety is seriously compromised in these areas if periodic maintenance supported by repair and rehabilitation work is not undertaken.

Post-construction distresses in bridges

Bridges if properly and regularly maintained can last for more than 100 years. But, in reality, serious damages leading to safety hazards, partial or complete collapse are encountered both in railway and road bridges, be they of reinforced concrete, pre-stressed concrete or steel.

Wearing coat

Wearing coats over road bridges are damaged frequently due to either bad workmanship, accumulation of water in patches or wear and tear under wheel loads, which leads to serious accidents on the bridge, if not attended to and repaired in time. In many such cases damages are so severe that replacement by a new wearing coat becomes necessary for smooth accident-free movement of traffic. Alligator cracks are noticed over wearing coats caused by excessive deck deflection or drying of asphalt overlay. Besides this, there may be edge cracks, cracks at joints, cracks continued from cracks in deck slab, shrinkage cracks and rutting along wheel path. Corrugation and potholes in wearing coats is a common distress phenomenon denoting loss of stability. Wearing coats may be damaged also due to separation of aggregates in overlays due to bad workmanship.

Expansion joints

Alongside the wearing coat the expansion joints are also vulnerable to damages due to poor design, lack of space for expansion, loss of water-tightness in the seals, damage to welds and anchorages, deterioration in joint materials, rusting of steel, broken bolts and components and damage in concrete at joint anchorages.

Handrails

Handrails are damaged mainly due to continuous exposure to aggressive environment and corrosion. Sudden impact of vehicles hitting the handrails may cause irreparable damage and the damaged portion may need immediate replacement for safety of the users. This is often overlooked either due to paucity of fund, indifference of the maintenance staff or complete lack of awareness about the necessity of corrective maintenance. The result is the ushering of fresh accidents and an ugly look of the bridge superstructure. Timely maintenance in such cases often takes a back seat in the mind of the authority concerned because maintenance work does not have the same glamour as the construction of a new bridge.

Bearings

Bearings carry forward all the loads of the bridge superstructure to the foundations and, therefore, any serious unattended damage to the bearing may lead to an unstable superstructure. Many bearings have failed due to faulty installation, poorly concreted seating pedestals and uneven seating. Bearings along with the superstructure have been dislodged at many sites due to earthquake forces in absence of any lateral restraint mechanism. Metallic bearings are prone to damages due to atmospheric corrosion and accumulation of rain water. Replacement of a bearing becomes difficult if there is no space or provision for jacking up the superstructure. Lubricated type bearing are often damaged often due to pilferage of the lubricants (common at bridges in remote areas) or lack of maintenance over a long period of time. The seating grouts are often seen to have cracked and deteriorated. Steel bearing may additionally be damaged due to rusting of metallic parts and bolts, looseness of anchor bolts and missing nuts. Elastomeric bearing pads are vulnerable to excessive deformation, cracking and splitting in extreme cases.

Bridge superstructure

In case of reinforced concrete bridges concrete decks and girders may be damaged due to spalling of concrete, cracking, corrosion of reinforcements, ingress of rain water inside joints and general dampness during continuous rains. Approach slabs are frequently damaged due to flood, settlement of soil underneath and cracks due to heavy vehicular movements. Thin webs of concrete girders are likely to be distressed more rapidly than other members.

In case of pre-stressed concrete bridges, safety during the service life is seriously threatened if there is loss in pre-stress force due to corrosion, spalling of concrete cover and snapping of strands. In case the applied pre-stress is absorbed only at the anchorage region or if the pre-stress is inadequate for taking the full live load, there may be serious cracks in the under-stressed region and failure becomes a distinct safety hazard. In case of critical damages cracks may extend from the bottom flange to the web (which is usually very thin in case of pre-stressed girders) and pre-stressed tendons tend to lose their load carrying capacity very soon. Such a safety hazard is often manifested by excessive deflection and loss of pre-camber.

In case of steel bridges, aggressive environment plays an important part in the distress of steel components. Air and moisture corrodes steel in a great way, particularly when the steel is exposed or is not properly protected by paints. Continued rusting of steel members reduces the effective sectional areas and their load carrying capacities. Cracks may also develop due to fatigue and stress concentration. Fatigue cracks are more damaging to welded structures or welded joints than a riveted or a bolted connection. Thermal cracks, overloads causing buckling of steel compression members and collision with moving vehicles damage steel structures very badly. Cracks in steel structures may be grouped as:

- Fatigue cracks
- Tension cracks
- Brittle-fracture cracks
- Stress-corrosion cracks.

When critically loaded bridge members are severely distressed due any or more of the above causes, catastrophic failures are a distinct possibility if adequate safety measures are not taken to arrest the damage potential.

Bridge foundations

Bridge foundations may lose stability due to:

- Heavy scour around piers
- Settlement of foundations beyond limit
- Failure of the bottom plug of wells
- Fury of flood

The superstructure may also be badly affected and damaged due to above, resulting in cracks and fissures in concrete, tilting and/or dislodgement of superstructure girders, shifting of road/track alignments, damage to bearings etc.

A bridge may be rendered unserviceable also because of complete or partial wash-out of approaches during flood.

In cases of complete wash-out of bridges due to devastating floods or strong earthquakes it may be necessary to dismantle and remove the damaged spans and re-do the part or whole of the bridge damaged. It requires a great effort and additional budgetary support from the authority to remove a damaged span from the river bed, if the flow is perennial. Suitable dismantling programmes are to be adopted in such cases buttressed by workable design supports. On the other hand, when piers and abutments are tilted, shifted or damaged beyond redemption and repair, it may be found to be necessary to change and shift the bridge alignment itself to a new location nearby and build a new bridge with connecting approaches to suit the new alignment. There are cases where a complete bridge has been rendered defunct and useless due to change in the course of the river after a serious flood or an earthquake. Extensive river training works are needed to avoid such an eventuality.

16.4 DAMAGES TO STRUCTURES CAUSED BY EXTERNAL FORCES

A structure or part of it may be rendered unsafe during its service life due to damages caused by various types of external forces like, flood, wind, earthquake, corrosion, impact, vibration etc. The effects of all these external forces have been discussed in details in earlier chapters. However it is to be borne in mind that, even a design based on all the provisions of latest codes of practices cannot guarantee full protection against these forces and some damages are to expected even when forces like wind and earthquake hit a structure well below their design values. Moreover, damages due to these forces may be higher that anticipated, if a structure is ageing and is not well maintained and if the structural components are corroded and lose their full strength. Damages may appear unexpectedly even at earlier stages of the service life if no maintenance is done in time and the structure is allowed to deteriorate under adverse atmospheric conditions.

16.5 INSTABILITY OF FOUNDATIONS

For stability, a foundation must satisfy three basic requirements:

- The foundation must not settle or tilt beyond tolerable limits
- The foundation should be safe against shear failure
- The foundation should be safe with adequate factor of safety against overturning and sliding.

Usually all these are considered at the design stage and foundations are supposed to be safe and useful under design loads and it is taken for granted that there may be some damages due to unexpected external forces and it is also expected that such damages would be repairable and would not cause complete failure of the structure. However in reality the fury of the external forces, like wind, earthquake, cyclonic storm, landslide and flood sometimes becomes so strong that, not only the superstructure but also the foundations lose their structural strength and rigidity. The effect is more pronounced when the structure is subjected to additional deterioration due to corrosion, flood erosion, neglect in maintenance and little or no repair after previous disasters.

Assessment of instability of foundations

It is to be noted that the condition of the superstructure of a building, industrial structure or a bridge can be assessed visually and the effects of distresses can be measured and monitored. However for foundations it is not so easy. Except with the help of sophisticated instruments, it is almost impossible to assess correctly the nature of degradation that has occurred to any foundation system and it is also not possible to record for surety the progression of such distresses over time. For deep foundations like pile systems or well foundations, it is all the more difficult to visualize the extent of damages that have occurred. As a result any likelihood of loss of stability and safety hazard to the superstructure in such cases should be assessed indirectly from observing the following points.

- The type of distress in the foundation: settlement, tilt, shift, cracks etc.
- Measurement of the above distresses.
- The type of foundations provided for the particular structure
- Condition of the soil on which the foundation has been rested
- Present load bearing capacity from fresh soil investigations
- Any visible sign of soil movement around the foundations
- Age of the structure, likely composition of foundation materials and method of construction
- Any overloading allowed to the superstructure during the service life
- Any other pertinent data available from records

An idea about instability of the foundation system can be obtained from analyzing the data obtained from above and rectification should be designed accordingly.

16.6 MAINTENANCE PROGRAMMES

The main objective of maintaining a structure is to retain or restore a part or whole of the structure to an acceptable level of serviceability. The adverse effects of damages and consequent safety hazards can be checked by suitable maintenance programmes, which may be any or more of the following types:

- **Emergency maintenance**

  Any maintenance or repair work that may have to be undertaken within 24 hours to check a system failure may be termed as an emergency maintenance. A sudden leak in a main water line or a gas line will need such emergency maintenance to avert a system failure. Since serviceability is suddenly affected in such cases without notice, an emergency maintenance programme always involves unplanned costs along with disruption of traffic and inconvenience to the users.

- **Corrective maintenance**

  Corrective maintenance is required to bring back a structure or a part of the same to its original shape and serviceability after a failure has occurred. Replacement of a snapped wire rope, correcting a bent chimney shaft, replacement of spring plates of vehicle or repairing a damaged crane boom etc come under this category of maintenance.

- **Preventive maintenance**

  Preventive maintenance is done when a structure or a part of the same is found to have lost its structural strength and load bearing capacity to such an extent that the equilibrium of the structural system is in danger. Replacing of cracked roof sheets (to prevent access of rain water and safety of the men moving over the same), replacement of missing bolts in a structural connection (to retain the joint's strength and equilibrium) or replacing a roof structural system seriously damaged due to fire. A properly executed preventive maintenance programme should prevent unexpected failure and safety hazards.

- **Planned maintenance**

  Planned maintenance is a scheduled maintenance scheme which should be carried out at regular intervals to minimize or offset the need of emergency or corrective maintenance.

Planned maintenance for buildings

In the case of buildings, planned maintenance including repair work includes usually the following:

- Protecting structural components against corrosion and dampness
- Cleaning of gutters, sewer lines, septic tanks etc
- Changing damaged and corroded water pipes and fixtures
- Arranging proper ventilation if there is dampness in closed spaces

- Attending to thermal insulations
- Checking growth of fungus, white ants
- Painting of wood and structural steelwork
- Providing fresh paints to walls and ceilings
- Arranging proper roof insulation
- Checking salt-peter condition in bricks
- Repair of cracks and fissures in concrete and brickworks
- Attending to door and window fixtures
- Attending to electrical fittings

The present condition of the different building components should be inspected and a check list should be prepared for periodic planned maintenance. Usually planning is done on yearly basis and suitable cash flow should be ensured. Planned maintenance enhances the safety and serviceability of a structure and ensures a problem-free service life.

Planned maintenance for industrial structures

In industrial establishments planned maintenance of buildings, machinery, utilities and other services can check breakdowns, interruptions in shop-floor activities, thereby increasing productivity and better working environment. The methodology of planned maintenance in such case should cover the following aspects:

- Necessary shutdown should be allowed to carry out maintenance work in an uninterrupted manner.
- For larger industries planned maintenance should be left to the responsibility of a separate team. In case of difficult cases technical advice of outside experts should be taken. No operational or shop-floor workers should be involved in regular maintenance work.
- All staff and the management should be aware of the need of periodic planned maintenance.
- Suitable provisions should be made in the yearly budget for meeting the expenses of planned maintenance work.
- The progress of maintenance work should be monitored from time to time, even if the work is of a very stereotyped nature.
- Proper record of all maintenance work done should be maintained building-wise for future reference.
- In case of scarcity of resources priorities should be fixed and planning should be done accordingly.

Planned maintenance for bridges

Bridges are likely to be distressed more rapidly than buildings because they are exposed to traffic movements in addition to open weather all the time during the service life. Remoteness of many bridge locations also seriously hinders timely action in many cases. Paucity of fund is also responsible for ill maintenance of scores of bridges. If there is inordinate delay on the part of the authority to take actions, a time may come when it would be noticed that a bridge has become totally unserviceable and unsafe. Such bridges then require not only emergency maintenance but also extensive repair, replacement of seriously-damaged components, additions, alterations, and rehabilitation to the structural system as well.

In view of above it is necessary to inspect the condition of the bridge at regular intervals, preferably every year and take suitable remedial measures so that the maintenance work is limited to preventive maintenance only without having any necessity of resorting to emergency maintenance and rehabilitation work.

In addition, bridges may be damaged due to flood, cyclones and earthquakes and there may be serious safety hazards if such damages are associated with corrosion and fatigue in the structural components due to lack of maintenance. Here also, regular maintenance of the structure will help in limiting the damages within tolerable limits.

Planned maintenance for bridges includes the listing of structural components needing maintenance and repair. The items to be inspected should include the wearing coat or the riding surface, expansion joints, handrails, trolley refuges (for railway bridges), condition of the joints, connecting bolts and welds, bearings, scour level around piers and abutments, condition of the protective aprons, corrosion of structural components, corrosion of steel reinforcements and pre-stressed tendons and assessing the requirement of paints and necessity of crack repairs.

16.7 SAFETY DURING MAINTENANCE WORK

Accidents happen during regular maintenance work primarily due to non-compliance of standard safety rules, over confidence on the part the workers and lack of safety awareness of the supervisory staff. From past records it is revealed that fatal accidents due to fall from a height comprise more than 50% of all fatalities during maintenance work. Other cases reported to be fatal include falling materials/ objects from top, asphyxiation while working inside manholes and underground tanks, collapse of temporary scaffolds and ladders built for maintenance work and electrical shock/fire etc. Even if there are no fatalities, workers suffer from minor injuries, loss of limbs and eyes in innumerable cases that are not properly recorded in absence of reliable statistics.

In almost all cases of maintenance works at a height, temporary scaffolds are to be erected. In absence of a proper bracing system these scaffolds are likely to collapse during high wind. Sometimes the working platforms are not properly fixed to the posts and runners, resulting in fall of workers inadvertently stepping on the wrong plank or a loose plank. Intermediate landings and handrails are often omitted to cut costs and people are seen to be working on a high platform without any safety belt. Suspended scaffolds are often erected from bridge girders to do repair and painting work to the underside of decks and girders. Fatal accidents may occur if any of the suspender mechanisms fail. Such suspended scaffolds should have adequate clearance if the bridge happens to cross an electrified railway track. Scaffolds often lose their lateral stability as they are often not tied to any permanent structure and long scaffolds are seen to have been erected in a serpentine manner alongside a high-rise structure.

In many cases the access to a platform is provided by means of ladders. These ladders are a potential source of fatal accidents if the ladders slip at the base when a worker is climbing up or working by standing on the ladder as in the case of electricians and painters. Workers often fall from the ladders due to abrupt failure of a rung and they are likely to lose balance if they carry loads in one hand while climbing up a ladder.

Workers are often seen to be moving over roofs of industrial sheds covered by asbestos or corrugated iron sheets without verifying their condition and load carrying capacity. There have been many cases of accidents due to fall of the workers below to the shop floor through the roof as the roof coverings are old, cracked and distressed and cannot withstand the load of a man walking over it.

A proper maintenance management scheme should therefore include not only the time-cost aspects but safety factors as well. It should be borne in mind that hardly any maintenance programme can be implemented within the scheduled time frame if the scaffolds, ladders and lifting accessories are not in proper shape and the condition of the existing structure is not thoroughly inspected to look into possible safety hazards. For maintenance work of factories and bridges where maintenance work is often carried out during shut-down only, a safety manual should be prepared specifying in clear terms the safety measures to be adopted in a particular case. The specification for the maintenance work should include references to these safety manual and the workers and the contractor should be compelled to follow the rules through regular monitoring on the part of the supervisors.

From the above it may be noted that the safety of a structure during its service life can be assured to a great extent if maintenance is done regularly and the condition of the structure is monitored periodically. Though no structure is hundred per cent safe for all the time and for all loading conditions and there are lot of unforeseen disasters from external sources that may happen to a structure, still it is imperative to maintain its serviceability and retain its design strength by adopting proper maintenance strategies.

QUESTIONS

1. Explain why post-construction safety management is so important to the users during the service life of a structure.
2. Cite a few examples of inadvertent overloading of existing structures which may lead to collapse of the structure.
3. Explain how free access of rainwater may damage a concrete structure. What types of wooden structural elements are likely to be damaged by white ants and fungi? What are the remedial measures to protect structures in such circumstances?
4. Explain how construction errors are linked to subsequent structural distresses during service life of a structure.
5. Mention how industrial structures are distressed due to exposure to industrial pollutants. How such distresses can be minimized to ensure structural safety?
6. How steel bridges are damaged due to aggressive environmental pollutions? What types of damages are usually noticed in concrete and steel structures, in case periodic maintenance is not done.
7. How foundations may lose their stability during service life? How distresses in foundations may be assessed from site investigations?
8. What are the critical elements of a bridge which should be given priority in maintenance programmes?

9. Write short notes on the adverse effects of the following on the safety of steel and concrete structures:
   (*a*) Spalling of concrete
   (*b*) Development of cracks in concrete structural elements
   (*c*) Corrosion to steelwork, reinforcement rods and pre-stressed tendons
10. Enumerate how structural safety can be assured through emergency and corrective maintenance programmes. Why planned periodic maintenance is necessary?
11. Explain how fatigue cracks are formed in steel structures. How structural safety is endangered when corrosion is associated with fatigue in steel structural systems? What type of remedial measures should be adopted to minimize damages from such cracks?
12. Explain how the following structural elements may be damaged during service life:
   (*a*) Wearing coat over bridge decks
   (*b*) Expansion joints
   (*c*) Handrails
   (*d*) Bridge bearings
13. Write short notes on the following:
   (*a*) Likely causes of instability in bridge foundations
   (*b*) Instability of tall structures due to wind and earthquakes
   (*c*) Emergency maintenance
   (*d*) Planned maintenance
   (*e*) Corrective maintenance

CHAPTER 17

Safety Management in Rehabilitation of Structures

17.1 INTRODUCTION

The rehabilitation of a structure involves the job of bringing back a distressed structure to a serviceable state within an acceptable load-carrying capacity. A structure may be seriously damaged either due to long neglect in regular maintenance or may be suddenly be out of service due to a natural calamity. Some part of the structure may even lose its stability and may verge to the point of a limiting equilibrium. In such a condition the users' safety is seriously compromised, unless the defects are rectified without any delay and the structure is rehabilitated to a serviceable state. If the condition of the structure is such that it has lost its usefulness, then the structure, either a part or whole of it, may have to be dismantled completely or modified with addition of new components and repaired so that the structure retains its functional utility for a greater part of its remaining service life.

The distresses caused to a structure needing rehabilitation of a part or whole of the structure depend on several factors, as under.

17.2 DISTRESSES CAUSED BY NATURAL CALAMITIES

Flood, cyclone, earthquake and landslide are the major natural calamities which damage every year buildings, industrial structures, roads, bridges and many other infrastructure facilities all over the world. All these structures are usually designed to withstand a certain level of unforeseen external forces that are based on previous records and observations. But, even in normal circumstances, low, as well as, serious damages are frequent and the damage is accentuated if an existing structure is denied regular maintenance over a long period of time. In many cases vital installations like bridges are washed away due to unprecedented fury of floods and damages are so severe that major rehabilitation and replacement of damaged spans are necessary to bring the facility back to a serviceable condition. The urgency in such reconstruction works needs not only a systematic, time-bound work schedule, but also a satisfactory safety net for the workers engaged in the rehabilitation work. These types of jobs become all the more difficult and risky when the old damaged span of a bridge or, sometimes, the whole of the superstructure has to be dismantled and removed to the shore before any new work can be started.

17.3 MAN-MADE POST-CONSTRUCTION DAMAGES TO STRUCTURES NEEDING REHABILITATION

Post-construction safety hazards and damages are often encountered due to neglect and wrong use of a structure, a few of which are mentioned below:

- Accidental failure of a part of a structure such as vehicular collision with a building, collision of a ship with a bridge pier, damage to bridge railings due to vehicular accidents occurring on a bridge deck etc.
- Sudden collapse of a cantilever slab due to continuous corrosion of the top reinforcement rods.
- Corrosion inside factories due to adverse effects of industrial effluents, fumes and gases.
- Fatigue failure of structural components in bridges, traveling cranes and steel structures.
- Foundation failure
- Faulty construction like bad welding, wrong placement of rods in cantilever slabs, absence of adequate cover of reinforcements, faulty roof sheeting and roof waterproofing etc.
- Damages to machine foundations due to excessive vibration
- Old historical monuments or buildings losing its structural stability due to long neglect in maintenance or due to prolonged exposure to industrial toxic gases and air pollution.

Rehabilitation jobs in the above cases involve mainly the following items of work:

- **Dismantling** of the structural components that have lost stability
- **Erection of temporary supports** and platforms for rehabilitation work

- **Strengthening** of the structure by addition and modification of selected members
- **Replacement** of badly-damaged structural components
- **Repair** of old structural components that can be restored to its original strength by repair only

A complete rehabilitation package often demands handling of one, two or more of the above items of work. As a result, all rehabilitation jobs need an expert systematic management approach to the problem. These should cover site investigations, data collection including taking photographs of the damaged structure, necessary application of instruments to find out the changes in levels, alignments etc, analyzing all data and finding out the most cost-effective solution, detailed engineering for the rehabilitation work, specifying safety measures to be adopted. In many cases, rehabilitation work has to be carried out at almost inaccessible parts of a structure high above the ground, necessitating additional measures to ensure easy approach to the place of work with all necessary protection to the workers. In all cases, a detailed programme is to be chalked and a meticulous implementation strategy is to be chalked out with field arrangement.

17.4 SAFETY MEASURES IN A REHABILITATION JOB

Safety of the workers and staff engaged for any rehabilitation job needs to be assured in two stages of any rehabilitation process, once during the inspection of a distressed structure and secondly during the actual rehabilitation process at site.

17.4.1 Safety During Inspection of a Distressed Structure

During the course of inspection it may be necessary to install temporarily measuring instruments and men have to reach there to investigate on spot the extent of damage to the structure. There are always chances of fatal accidents if an inadvertent casual approach is made to reach a delapidated building or a historical monument which is heavily damaged. Before the inspection of any part of a damaged structure the approach points should be critically examined and necessary scaffolds or ladders are to be installed. In many cases the approaches are so dangerous that one cannot step on the distressed structural members and, therefore, has to take the help of cranes to reach the damaged locations to have a close look and inspect properly. Similar temporary scaffolds may have to be designed and erected to inspect the condition of the bridge bearings at site. For inspection of the condition of the piers in perennial rivers the inspection team may have no other alternative but to approach the bearings from the superstructure with the help of movable suspended scaffolds, which are to be designed tailor-made to suit a particular site. Such suspended scaffolds are often a must to inspect the soffit of girders in mid-river spans. The major safety hazard for using these scaffolds is the failure of the suspension system, which should be prevented by introducing a reasonable factor of safety in the design.

In case buildings and structures that have lost their stability and equilibrium at several locations, it will be practicable to devise ways and means to first demolish the part of the structure that has become unstable and then a thorough inspection should be done for the rest of the structural components to assess the damages there and find out the means for rehabilitation work. Such an approach is helpful in case of structural damages due to fire, earthquakes and cyclones. When a building is struck by an earthquake or a landslide and is completely covered by debris, there is no way to inspect the condition of the structure but to arrange first the removal of the debris cover. In many such cases only a part of the structure may be salvaged and the structure may have to be built once again from scratch utilizing to the extent possible the salvaged items.

To inspect the inside of a building damaged by fire of earthquake, the power line should be cut off for safety of the inspection team and they should be provided with portable dry-cell torches and lanterns, when visibility is poor inside the building. It is better to deploy self-supported moving ladders for inspection without any necessity of leaning on the damaged structure.

It may be necessary to inspect at night a site of accident outdoor or at a bridge location where there is no regular supply of electricity. There, separate arrangements should be made for lighting up the work area. Preferably, to avoid such inconveniences and for the safety of the inspection team, all inspection work should be carried out during daylight hours, unless an immediate intervention by the inspection team is necessary..

All inspection people working at heights should be advised to use safety belts and wear helmets. If there is continuous flow of traffic where an inspection has to be carried out, the site of work for the inspection team should be cordoned off with fencing and barricades or the place of work should be shielded by CGI sheets and the place should be put under the care of a guard during work and suitable road signs and lanterns should be installed at night when the place is left unattended till the next day's work. Traffic should be controlled if necessary through diversion with the help of the local authority. In case of inspections of railway bridges the safety rules chalked by the railway authority should be strictly adhered to with prior intimation to the local railway authority.

All inspection work should be done keeping safe clearance from any high voltage power line. In case of road over-bridges crossing railway lines having high voltage traction systems, the sides and undersides of the girders should be inspected by obtaining traffic and power block from the authority concerned prior to the commencement of the inspection work. All temporary installations installed for inspection work should be grounded to earth as per electrical safety norms applicable for a high voltage line, maintaining safe distance from the traffic.

17.5 LISTING OF STRUCTURAL DISTRESS

During the inspection of any damaged structure in a rehabilitation job, the job of listing the structural distresses and identifying the causes of distresses are specific for each rehabilitation work. Particular attention should be given in this regard to the following aspects:

- Age of the structure
- Material specifications for the damaged component
- Details of structural layout
- Method of construction adopted earlier
- Present condition of the damaged components and the extent of damage
- Condition of the foundation and soil characteristics
- Environmental conditions now

Depending on the type of structure investigated, the following aspects should also be included in the list of observations:

- Corrosion effect on steel material, concrete and reinforcement rods
- Adverse shop-floor environment for industrial structures

- Seepage of water, dampness to walls, floor and other parts of a building
- Cracks in concrete, brick and steel components and nature of the cracks
- Settlement of foundations if any
- Vibration problem if any
- Present scour level for damaged substructure of bridges

All these aspects should be taken into account and critically observed from site and listed systematically with observation of the inspector about the extent and nature of damage caused by each of these damage factors. Help may be taken from old records as available for getting ideas about ground conditions, flood events, previous cyclones if any.

17.6 PREPARATION OF REHABILITATION SCHEMES

All the data and site information should thereafter be systematically analyzed to arrive at a workable cost-effective solution to the problem. It may be noted that such solutions are not the same for every structure because of their distress levels, structural layout, environment and future functional requirements. Each case should be studied separately and decisions are to be taken on the merit of each case. In many cases, alternative proposals would crop up during the planning stage of a rehabilitation process. In case of rehabilitating a distressed bridge, availability of the right type of cranes and equipments and site conditions may be the guiding factors. Again, one single remedial action may not be sufficient to remove all types of distresses, as a distressed structure is often weakened initially by bad workmanship, compounded layer by other extraneous factors like overloading and atmospheric corrosion. A common example for such cases is that of a damaged RCC cantilever and chajja. Inadequate cover of the top reinforcements due to bad workmanship often quickens the process of water seepage resulting in corrosion of the steel reinforcements. When left unattended for years there may be serious damage to the cantilever and its load carrying capacity. Any rehabilitation plan in such a case should have a two prong strategy, namely, one, to prevent further ingress of water inside and, two, strengthening the cantilever itself.

17.7 SAFETY DURING IMPLEMENTATION OF REHABILITATION WORK

All rehabilitation schemes should take into account the present condition of the structure and should indicate in clear terms the method of rehabilitation keeping intact the structural stability of the whole system. Management of a rehabilitation scheme is all the more difficult because of the compulsion of matching the scheme with the existing structural system. The project manager in charge of such jobs should therefore be experienced and motivated to deal with the difficulties that may arise at site because of the non-standard nature of the job. He should have the initiative and executive power to apply innovative methods in solving site problems, as on-spot changes in methods may be necessary to sort out site problems. To ensure safety during any rehabilitation work the following basic requirements are to be satisfied:

- Safety of the structure being rehabilitated, which means it should never be unstable in any time during the whole process of rehabilitation covering repair, strengthening, replacement of members or dismantling of seriously-damaged items.
- Safety of the people working on the job, at times at considerable heights above the ground in inconvenient spots.
- Safety of the passers-by
- Safe lifting and placement of containers, tools, tackles etc near the place of work.
- Safety and stability of any temporary structure erected for the purpose of rehabilitation

In general rehabilitation jobs cover the following types of works:

- Erection of temporary supports and dismantling of damaged elements
- Repair of cracks
- Strengthening of members
- Replacement of damaged parts of the structure

17.7.1 Temporary Supports

The erection of temporary supports constitutes an important part in any rehabilitation work right from the beginning to the end of the job. The type of supports needed for this purpose vary widely depending on the height required to be reached, the area of coverage and the nature of the job itself. While timber or sal-bally supports may be adequate in ground floor work of residential buildings, bamboo scaffolds are often erected for work on outside of upper stories. However for tall structures, bridges and industrial infrastructure facilities, elaborate pipe or steel scaffolds are designed and erected following the provisions of code and standard engineering practice, in which the locations of landings are clearly specified. Suspended scaffolds, installed for repair of the underside of bridges over perennial rivers also fall under this category of special temporary supports.

Insufficient number of ties and bracings, sudden deposition of materials on the platforms built integrally with the support structures and the inclination of the workers to try to lower dismantled materials with the help of slender horizontal ties are some of the causes of failures of the temporary structures. The temporary support structures are also vulnerable to fire, if timber is used as platform materials and a serious accident may happen if a passing vehicle collides with the temporary structures. A support structure is also liable to be damaged during dismantling. Sometimes the design of the foundations of the temporary structures are not given due attention, as a result of which settlement occurs. In fact, it has been observed that soil conditions are not often properly investigated and heavily-loaded temporary structures have been erected to support bridge girders leading to deformation and collapse.

Considering the above aspects, all the temporary structures should be designed and detailed to satisfy the following basic safety aspects:

- The temporary structures should be so laid as not to trigger further damage or dislodgement of any part the damaged structure for reasons of safety
- They should be stable enough for safe use by the workers and can withstand the loads of equipments, wind forces and are protected from flood, water-logging or fire. If temporary structures are erected for relieving part of the dead load of the damaged structure, they should be designed and proportioned accordingly.

- All temporary structures should be easily demountable on completion of the work
- All temporary supports should be provided with necessary provisions of working platforms at required levels with handrails and toe-guards.
- All temporary structures should be firmly tied to permanent structures near by and they should be provided with adequate bracings and ties.

A few typical temporary support structures are shown in Fig. 17.1 to 17.3.

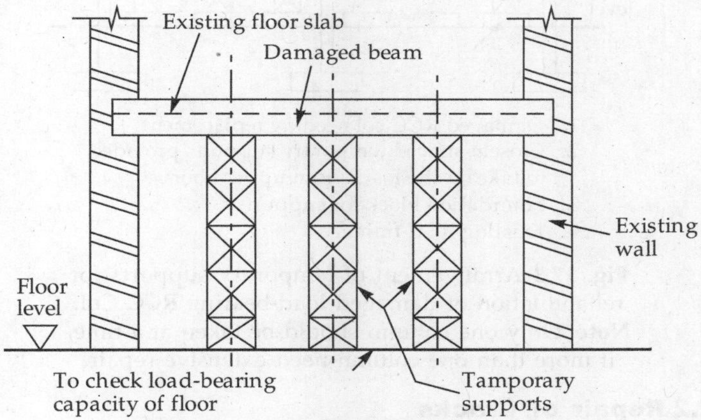

Fig.17.1 Temporary supports provided to damaged beam, before repair in started.

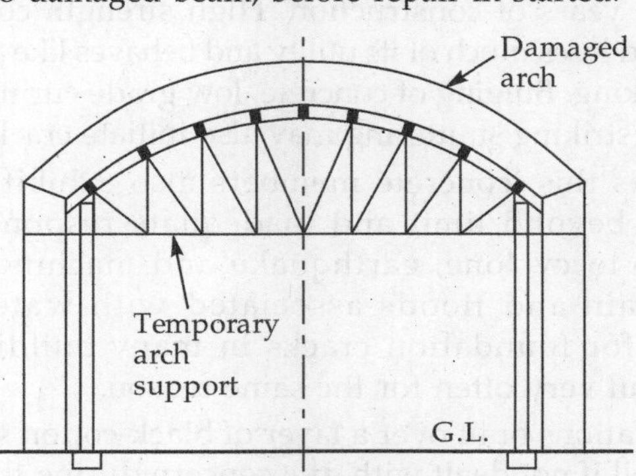

Fig. 17.2 Temporary arch support provided before repair of existing arch is started.

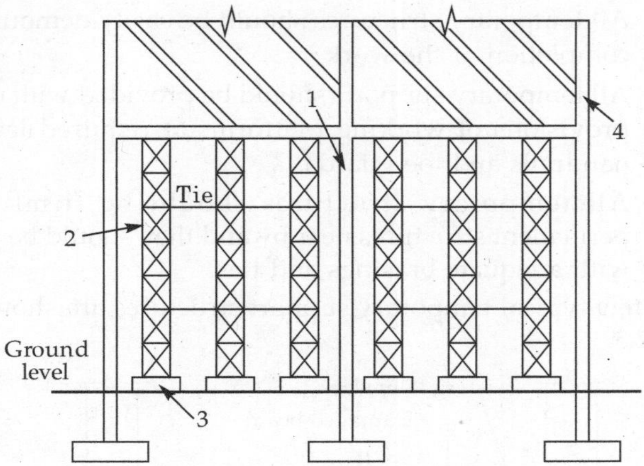

1. Damaged RCC col needing replacement
2. Closely-spaced temporary supports provided to take on the loads from upper floor
3. Foundation block for supports
4. Existing RCC frame

Fig. 17.3 Arrangement of temporary supports for rehabilitation of damaged load-bearing RCC Col.
Note: Only one column should be taken at a time, if more than one column need extensive repair.

17.7.2 Repair of Cracks

The safety and serviceability of a building is often seriously affected within a few years of construction. High strength concrete if is not properly cured loses much of its utility and behaves like a brittle material prone to cracking. Bulging of concrete, low grade curing and excessive deflection on striking shuttering may also initiate cracks in concrete.

Besides this, concrete members also exhibit cracks due to overloading beyond limit and inadequate response to dynamic loading due to cyclone, earthquake and machinery vibrations. Torrential rain and floods associated with water-logging are responsible for foundation cracks in many buildings. Concrete pavements fail very often for the same reason.

Foundations built over a layer of black-cotton soil may exhibit heaving of soil if not dealt with due concern during the design stage, resulting in widespread cracks in floors and tilting, cracking of wall joints.

Lack of proper drainage around a building may also be responsible for cracks in walls and finishes. Welded steel members show cracks in welded joints if the fatigue limit is crossed over the years during the service life. Similarly, anchor bolts may crack due to excessive machine vibration when the dynamic balancing of the machine is seriously disturbed. Cracks in walls, columns and roof are encountered if the structure is not properly braced and is subjected to high-level horizontal forces from wind or earthquake. Lastly, fire may cause irreparable widespread cracks in both steel and concrete structure depending on the intensity and duration of fire. Settlement of bridge foundations may cause tilting and cracks in both substructure and superstructure members. From the above it is to be noted that repair of cracks should be given due priority and importance whenever any building or for that matter any structure is repaired to bring it back to a serviceable condition.

17.7.3 Nature of Cracks

Cracks appear in various forms and dimensions causing safety hazards. The most common types of cracks found in distressed structures and their probable causes are mentioned below:

- Unequal thermal expansion may cause vertical cracks at building junctions, particularly when a very small building is structurally connected to a high-rise rigid structure.
- Settlement of a part of a structure creates diagonal cracks in walls of buildings
- Subsidence of filled up materials may damage the floor concrete and finishes.
- Diagonal cracks near supports in beams are mainly due to shear failure
- Corrosion in reinforcements cause spalling of concrete cover
- Corrosion of structural steel reduces the member thickness and strength of the member.
- Shear failure creates safety hazards in steel beams with development of cracks.
- Welds may fail due to fatigue failure.
- Excessive vibration and loss in dynamic balancing of the machine may damage the anchor bolts.
- Irreparable cracks, and heavy damages and even complete collapse of a part or whole of a structure may occur due to wind, earthquake and flood effects.

17.7.4 Methods of Crack Repairing

Crack repairing is a time-consuming job involving deployment of persons skilled for the work. Repair of cracks in buildings should be taken up along with waterproofing work simultaneously, as seepage of water are in most cases responsible for the cracks. Various types of crack sealants and waterproofing chemicals are available in the market under different brand names. They may be used as per direction of the manufacturers. The most commonly used chemicals are:

- Polysulphate sealants for sealing cracks in walls
- Polyurethene-based compound for roof treatment work
- Epoxy-based compounds for crack sealing of reservoirs
- Cement-based paints for walls and ceiling
- Water-repellant solvent-based coating for waterproofing of basements
- Polysulphide epoxy-based coating for damp-proofing of floor
- Tarfelting for roof waterproofing
- Bitumen joint-fillers for sealing pavement cracks

17.7.5 Repair of Cracks in Steel Members

The basic principle in crack repair of structural steel sections should be to arrest further ingress of moisture, to stop any further propagation of the crack and bringing back the damaged member to its original load carrying capacity. Cracks in steel sections, if small in size and length can arrested by providing cover plates or cover angles with provision of bolts on either side of the crack. Isolated cracks can be sealed easily in such a manner. However, it will be better to replace the structural member itself if there are multiple cracks in a single member. If, however only one portion of the member is damaged with multiple cracks and the rest is good, then only the damaged part may be replaced and additional splices may be provided even if the new member is butt-welded to the old one. In cases where rivets become loose due to corrosion, suitable additional cover plates or splice angles may be inserted and fresh rivets are to be put in place. However, crack repairs should be done keeping in mind the probability and adverse effects of post-rehabilitation corrosion at joints of new members with the old ones.

17.8 STRENGTHENING OF DAMAGED STRUCTURAL COMPONENTS

A few of the most popular methods of strengthening damaged structural elements are explained below.

1. Introducing additional bracings

Knee-braces to trusses increase the resistance against horizontal forces due to wind (Ref. Fig. 17.4). Sub-paneling of chords is often done to enhance the load-carrying capacity of chords of bridge trusses. (Ref. Fig. 17.5). Introduction of link beams to portal bents improves their response to earthquake and dynamic loads. The link beam, if placed near the knee joint reduces the moment of the portal beam. If placed in the middle of the portal leg, the side sway is controlled. Placing the link beam near to the base of the portal leg would substantially reduce footing forces. (Ref. Fig. 17.6).

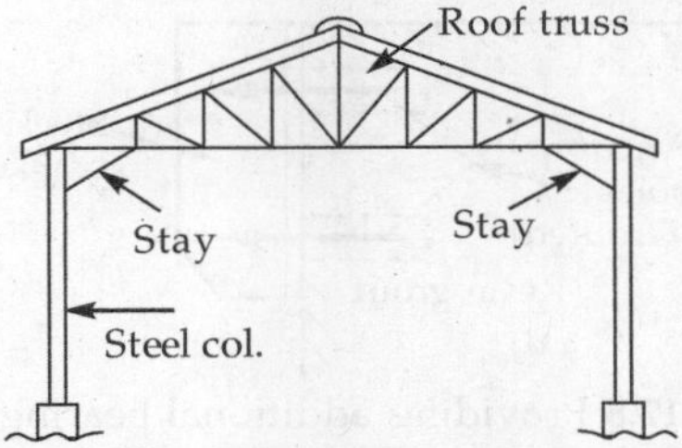

Fig. 17.4 Providing knee braces to truss to enhance rigidity.

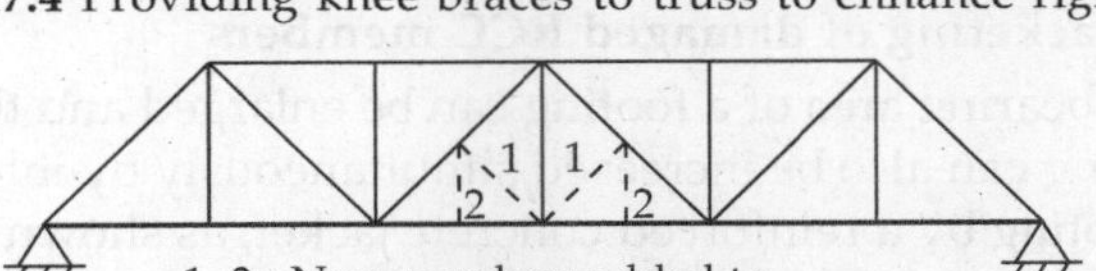

Fig. 17.5 Sub-paneling to increase load-carrying capacity of the bottom chord of a truss.

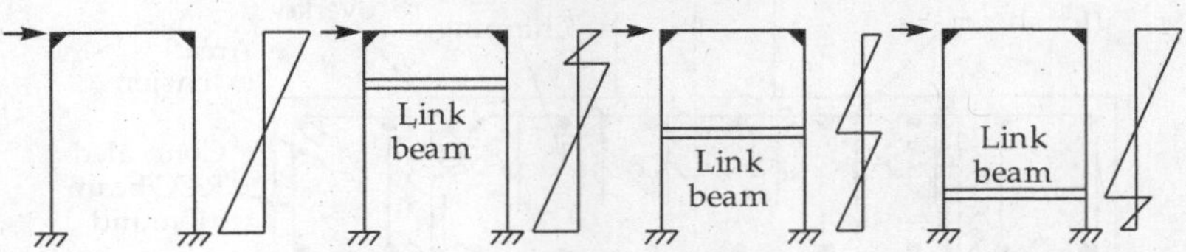

Fig. 17.6 Introducing link beam to portal bents to improve reponse against seismic forces.

2. Providing additional bearing area for beams

At times it is seen that the seat of an existing beam is damaged and needs an increase in its bearing area. This can be done either by a concrete bracket or a steel bracket anchored to the existing seat after repair (Ref. Fig. 17.7 and Fig. 17.8).

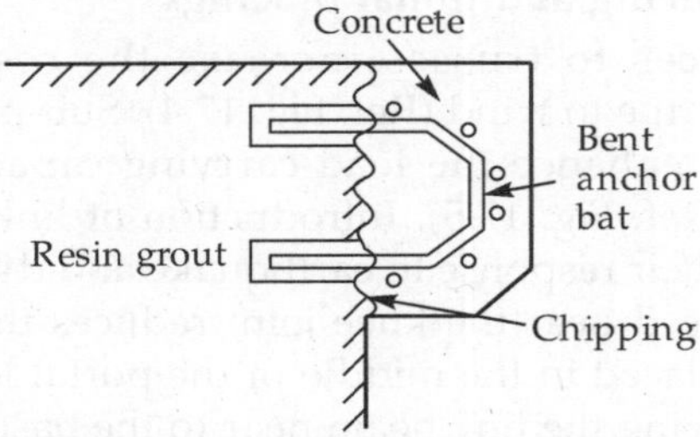

Fig. 17.7 Providing additional bearing area for beam with concrete brackets.

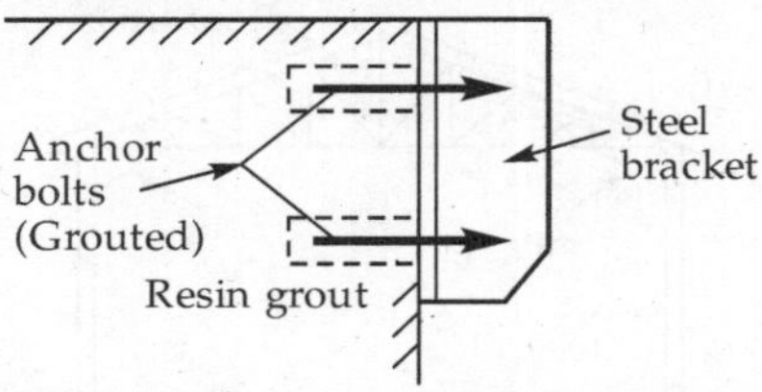

Fig. 17.8 Providing additional bearing area for beam with steel brackets.

3. Jacketing of damaged RCC members

The bearing area of a footing can be enlarged and the thickness of the footing can also be increased simultaneously by integrating the existing footing by a reinforced concrete jacket, as shown in Fig. 17.9. The new concrete is connected to the old one with the introduction

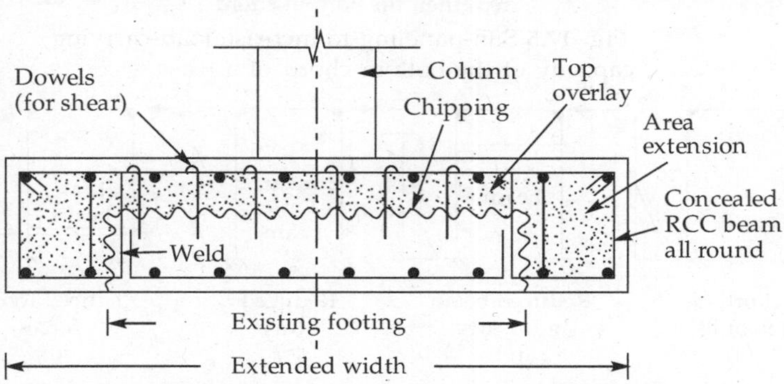

Fig. 17.9 Enlarging bearing area and thickness of footing.

of dowel bars and concealed beams can be effectively used also. This arrangement increases the bearing area as also the shear capacity of the footing.

If, on the other hand, the existing footing needs to have more shear capacity, the concrete jacket may be integrally connected to the top surface of the existing footing, as shown in Fig. 17.10. In both the cases the old concrete surfaces must be properly chipped for better grip.

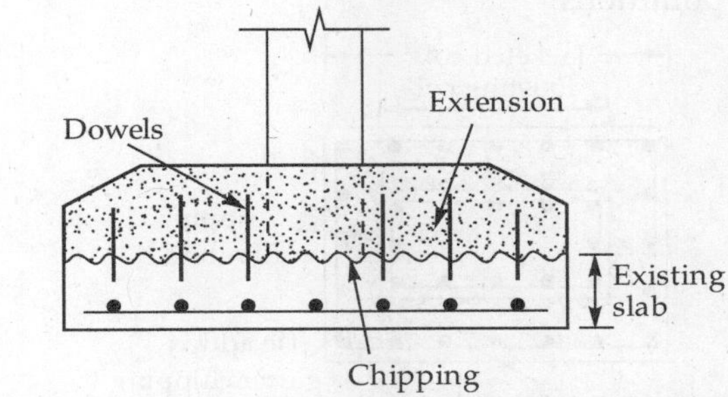

Fig. 17.10 Increasing shear capacity of existing footing.

4. Repair of anchor bolts

If anchor bolts are damaged additional bolts may be inserted by extending the base plate by butt-welding and by providing RCC jacket all round the exiting footing covering the enlarged base plate. This solution is very effective for lightly-loaded columns having small vertical loads only with little or no moments at base. (Ref. Fig. 17.11).

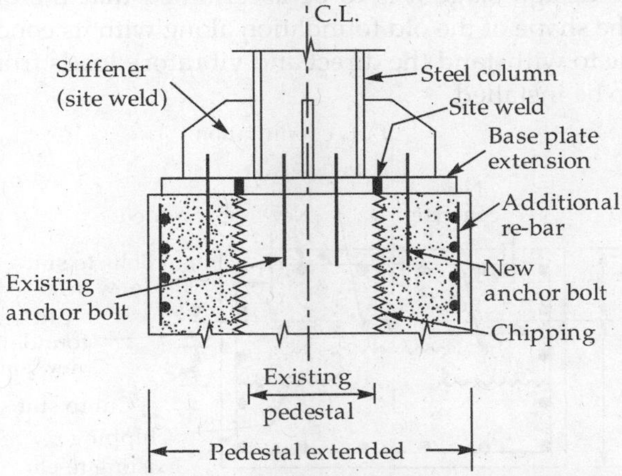

Fig. 17.11 Extending base plate and pedestal for steel column.

5. Rehabilitation by concrete jacketing

In many cases, where existing RCC columns have been damaged due to vehicular collisions or the column has lost much of its original strength, the strength can be substantially restored by concrete jacketing, as shown in Fig. 17.12). In many situations a steel column is encased by reinforced concrete resulting in a substantial increase in its load-bearing capacity. Such encasing work is also done where steel columns are likely to be subjected to harsh environmental or shop-floor pollutions.

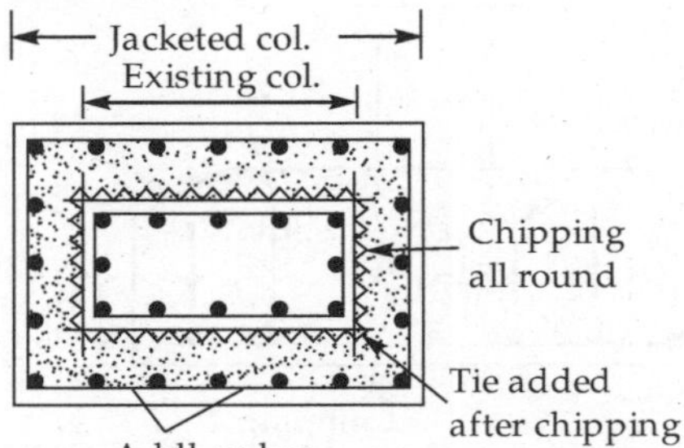

Fig. 17.12 RCC Jacketing for concrete column.

Existing machine foundations can be effectively modified to install new machines over the same by concrete jacketing. In this method the top of the old foundation is chipped off in a stepped manner, leaving a stub of the old foundation and then integrally connecting the new concrete jacket with the old one. (Ref. Fig. 17.13). During the design stage it is to be ascertained that the old bearing area and the shape of the old foundation along with its concrete jacket will be able to withstand the direct and vibratory loads from the new machine to be installed.

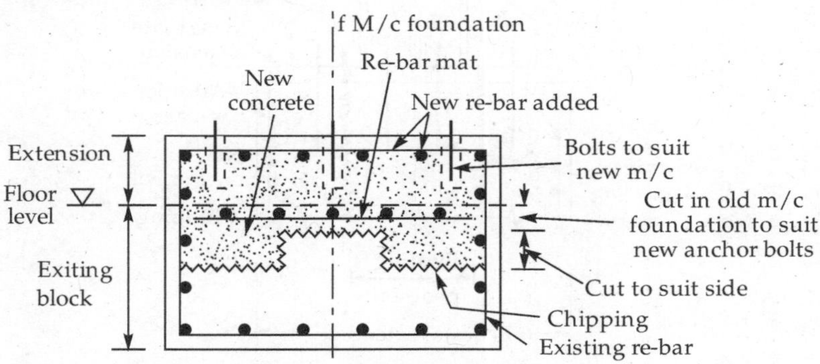

Fig. 17.13 Utilising existing block foundation to install a new machine, by RCC capping.

6. External pre-stressing

Strengthening of structural members of bridge girders may be done by external pre-stressing or by bonding of additional steel plates to the damaged member.

7. Rehabilitation by replacements of members

In many cases the damages may be so severe that a part of the whole structural system may have to be completely dismantled and new members may have to be added in their place having adequate load carrying capacity. In such cases proper temporary supports are to be provided beforehand to the portion of the old structure in such a way that a stable equilibrium is maintained during the replacement work and that, the levels, alignment and dimensions are maintained even after adding the new member to the old one. Steel beams can be used as substitutes for damaged RCC beams in many cases and these steel beams can also be encased by concrete for better strength and look.

17.9 REHABILITATION OF ROAD PAVEMENTS

In India the national and state highways are mostly provided with flexible pavements in the form of bituminous concrete and dense bituminous macadam. Concrete (rigid) pavements have also been introduced in many sectors now-a-days. Many road segments have thin binder course, which shows early signs of distress within a few years of construction.

Rutting is the most common distress observed in bituminous pavements. Heavy tyre pressure and repeated loading accelerates the rutting of pavements. Primary rutting causes only vertical deformation of the road surface. Shear failure occurs when there is secondary and tertiary rutting in two horizontal directions. A bituminous pavement is considered to have failed when the rut depth exceeds 13mm.In addition fatigue failure and formation of big potholes make a pavement unserviceable.

The most common types of distress observed in rigid pavements are: formation of potholes, spalling of concrete, cracking, opening of joints, differential vertical movement of slab panels, pop-outs of stone aggregates from the concrete surface and reinforcement corrosion. In both flexible and rigid pavements, the distress is more acute if there are subsidence and shear failures at the sub-grade or the sub-base level.

The maintenance and rehabilitation of flexible pavements usually involve the following activities:

- Filling up the potholes and patch repair of potholes
- Sealing of cracks
- Laying a thin overlay with small-size aggregates mixed with polymer-modified emulsion binder along with additives

The maintenance and rehabilitation of concrete pavements usually involve the following activities:

- Full or partial depth repair
- Stitching
- Grinding
- Sealing of cracks
- Stabilizing vertical movement of slabs
- Laying a thin overlay of concrete
- Replacement of slabs
- Repair of expansion joints on bridge decks

In any maintenance or rehabilitation work of road pavement, the work activities are stretched horizontally over a long distance along the road in different segments, as decided by the authority, obstructing the smooth flow of traffic in most cases. In many cases traffic jams become a daily affair when a major rehabilitation work is taken in hand on a busy thoroughfare with associated probability of road accidents. As such the safety of the pedestrians and the smooth flow of traffic should be given due importance. To achieve these objectives, it is imperative to adopt the following safety measures during all rehabilitation and maintenance work on important road segments:

1. The road traffic should be diverted from the work area.

2. Firm barricades should be put up to enclose the entire work area. If only one lane of a multi-lane roadway is blocked, there should be barricades not only at the ends but also alongside the stretch taken up for rehabilitation.

3. For work at night, the entire work area should be properly illuminated.

4. Security guards should be posted at night to caution drivers and pedestrians

5. There should be caution signals for vehicles and pedestrians.

6. Usual protective gear as needed for roadwork should be supplied to the workers, particularly when they handle hot bitumen and other chemicals.

7. The machinery deployed for the work, particularly the cranes, fork lifts and hot mixing plants should be so placed on the roadside as not to interfere with the smooth flow of traffic either during the daytime or during night.

8. If possible, service roads may be constructed or existing service roads should be utilized for management of traffic.

9. The work of pavement rehabilitation on bridge decks should be done as quickly as possible without creating undue interference to the traffic flow.

17.10 RISK ASSESSMENT

At the planning and design stage itself, before any site work is started, the risks involved in any scheme of rehabilitation work should be assessed.

This risk assessment should be done without any bias or complacency. If necessary, the scheme of the work and the schedules should be suitably modified to suit the condition of the distressed structure, availability of tools and machines and also to ensure public safety. Local statutory regulations, clearances from permanent structures, particularly railway tracks and roads should be strictly maintained and recorded on the drawings for compliance by the contractor.

Lastly, it is stressed that each rehabilitation work has its distinct characteristics and functional requirements. The roof and walls of a residential building may require only petty repairs, while elaborate security arrangements may have to be made for rehabilitation of outdoor public utility structures like bridges, roads and community buildings. Even traffic management may become part of the rehabilitation process in such cases. As such, any major rehabilitation work should be treated as a separate project and it should be entrusted to the care of experienced persons who have done similar work elsewhere, or at least, some people in the team are familiar with such specialized type of job. All complicated rehabilitation projects should have proper design supports with scheme drawings, working details and sequence of operations, in addition to adequate timely budgetary supports.

QUESTIONS

1. When does a structure need rehabilitation? What are the management functions in a typical rehabilitation scheme?
2. How the inspection of a distressed structure should be done without endangering personal safety?
3. What are the main aspects to be looked into during site investigations to identify the causes of structural distresses?
4. Enumerate the safety provisions to be incorporated while preparing rehabilitation schemes. How such safety provisions should be monitored during implementation of any rehabilitation work?
5. What is the utility of providing temporary supports during rehabilitation work? What should be the basic design considerations for design of temporary supports?
6. Explain how cracks in masonry walls may be repaired during rehabilitation of buildings.
7. What safety measures should be adopted during dismantling of a distressed member during rehabilitation work?
8. Suggest how a structural system may be strengthened against:
   (*a*) Horizontal forces due to wind/earthquake
   (*b*) Inadequate bearing
   (*c*) Cracks in structural steelwork
   (*d*) Corrosion of anchor bolts
9. What should be the strategy of maintaining road pavements avoiding road accidents?
10. Explain how old machine foundations may be strengthened by RCC jacketing to install new machines.

CHAPTER

18

Safety during Demolition and Dismantling of Structures

18.1 INTRODUCTION

In the previous chapters we have discussed safety aspects for different types of construction projects during the planning, design and construction stages. It has also been discussed the various types of safety norms to be observed during the post-construction service life of a structure. In a similar way, even when a structure or a part thereof has to be demolished or dismantled certain safety norms are to be followed for the safety of the adjacent structures and the men engaged in the demolition work

18.2 CIRCUMSTANCES WHEN DEMOLITION IS REQUIRED

A structure needs to be demolished when it loses its static equilibrium and is likely to collapse creating safety hazards or a part of the structure has already collapsed leaving the balance part in a condition of limiting equilibrium. Sometimes a tall structure badly-deflected or twisted due to wind or earthquake cannot be rehabilitated and needs to be demolished. A building may have to be demolished due to foundation failure on account of excessive settlement. Overloading of structures, excessive corrosion, flood-related damages etc may render a structure completely unserviceable needing demolition and replacement. Sometimes, even during the course of construction, a part of the newly-constructed portion may have to be demolished if there is a serious error and deviation from the contract drawings. In many cases, an old structure may have to be demolished to make way for a new establishment, a new factory or a new road. In every year lot of structures are demolished all over the world for many other reasons as well. As such, the art of demolition has also developed with invention of new techniques and processes side by side with new constructions.

18.3 DEMOLITION OF OLD BUILDINGS AND INDUSTRIAL STRUCTURES

Under this category comes old, dilapidated buildings, which have long crossed its service life and is on the verge of collapse. Many such buildings are found in old cities and these buildings often show signs of long neglect for decades with little or no maintenance. Many of these buildings gradually develop wide cracks, the roofs become leaky and the structure is weakened to the extreme due to ingress of rain water. In many cases parts of the building may have already collapsed and the rest of the building is seen to be standing precariously. If on inspection it is found that the building is beyond any repair or rehabilitation and is quite unfit for use, the structure has to be abandoned and demolished for safety reasons.

Similarly, old industrial sheds, warehouses, chimneys and machine foundations are often needed to be demolished to make way for new installations. In some cases old industrial structures become unserviceable and many of them may be on the verge of collapse. Such types of structures are noticed in industrial complexes, that has been closed earlier and there has been no attempt of repair and maintenance, resulting in free ingress of rain water inside, doors and gates either broken or absent, roof coverings damaged beyond salvage and a general look of decay and distress.

18.4 DISMANTLING OF EXISTING SERVICEABLE STRUCTURES

On the other hand, it may so happen that serviceable structures may have to be dismantled under compelling circumstances such as:

- An existing usable industrial structure may have to be dismantled to make way for a new type of structure to meet new functional requirements or when additions and alterations are needed to the existing structure.
- Bridge spans dislodged due to earthquake or ship collision may have to be dismantled and shifted ashore.
- Corroded steel structural components may have to be dismantled and new members are to be refitted.
- Structures hit by moving vehicles may have to be partially or completely dismantled.

- False work erected to support green concrete have to be dismantled after the concrete has hardened. Similarly, temporary structures and platforms raised for erection of structural steel have to be dismantled afterwards.

It is to be noted that though there are striking similarities between the demolition and dismantling work, there are differences also. When a structure is very old and has been rendered unsafe, the structure is demolished for safety reasons, but care is taken to salvage usable items as far as possible. In many cases when old buildings are demolished, usable items like doors, windows, grills etc are dismantled first and then the structure is demolished. Even, while a building is completely demolished and razed to ground, care is taken to salvage old bricks and reinforcement rods that can be used for other structures. There have also been attempts of using even broken pieces of concrete and bricks for road works.

But, when a serviceable structure is dismantled, there is ample scope for using the structural components again to build a similar structure. The structure in that case is never destroyed as a whole, but attempts are always made to dismantle the structural components item by item so that the dismantled units can be salvaged intact and used again without much difficulty.

In view of above, it is to be noted that all demolition and/or dismantling work should have primarily two objectives, namely:

- To ensure safety for the workmen and equipments engaged.
- To salvage usable materials and structural components as much as possible.

18.5 PROGRAMME OF DEMOLITION WORK

All demolition and dismantling work of major and minor structures should be treated as separate projects and all the principal aspects of project management, such as site investigation, planning, designing, implementation and control should be enforced here also. A distinct and specific management team should be selected who will plan, execute and coordinate all activities in this matter with the help of skilled persons and necessary equipments.

18.6 SITE INVESTIGATION

The structure to be demolished should be investigated thoroughly and the present condition of the structure should be assessed. This study should cover the age of the structure, the type of construction, the stability condition of the structural components, the presence of any service facilities and the presence of any hazardous substances (for industrial sheds and warehouses).

While examining the type of construction the following aspects are to be noted:

- The presence of any cantilever element such as projected balcony, parapets, brackets, cantilevered beams etc and their present supporting arrangements. It is to be borne in mind that such cantilever items may have to be dismantled first for safety reasons during the demolition work.
- Many old warehouses built in the pre-independence era in this country had been provided with thick lime terrace roof slab resting on brick arches that were supported by steel joists and connected by tie bars. Special care is to be taken for demolishing such structures as any inadvertent snapping of the tie bars during demolition may render the whole roof unstable and accidents may occur. The demolition work may become doubly difficult where the tie bars and the webs of the steel joists are already corroded and the structure is on the verge of collapse or has collapsed partially. In such cases both the type of construction as well as their present stability condition should be judged objectively.
- If any RCC floor is to be dismantled the direction of its main reinforcements should be assessed. Slabs reinforced one-way should be demolished in strips parallel to the main reinforcements, so that the equilibrium of the un-demolished slab is not disturbed.
- The pre-stressing type for post-tensioned bridge girders often determines the method to be adopted for demolishing such girders. Sometimes it may be necessary to provide elaborate temporary support below the soffit beforehand, as a pre-stressed concrete beam often behaves like a mass concrete without any flexural strength when its pre-stress wires are snapped and if there is not sufficient non-pre-stress reinforcements to take its dead load. Such temporary supports may also be needed for demolishing arches.

18.7 EXAMINING THE STABILITY OF THE STRUCTURE

It is always difficult to quantify the stability and equilibrium condition of an old structure. It is also difficult to find out its residual life when it is subjected to full design load and the residual life if the design load is reduced. The probability of failure of a structure depends on these factors which are associated with probability factors. However attempts should be made to find out how serious is the damage, crack, tilting or corrosion effects. From measurements of reduction in cross sections an idea can be formed about the stability condition of the structure.

In addition, from a visual study of the load path from top to the bottom of a structure, it can be assessed whether there has been any serious damage to any important load carrying member and whether such members need prior strengthening before any attempt is made for the demolition of the main structure itself.

The stability of a structure can also be assessed from the presence of and location of any redundant member that adds to safety during demolition.

18.8 SAFETY PROCEDURES IN DEMOLITION WORK

All demolition jobs are usually carried out in a reverse order to the construction process unless there is an express need to pull down the structure all at a time. The method adopted should be such that the loads coming on each structural component like beams, columns and foundations should be progressively reduced, as the demolition work advances and there is no overloading on the remaining un-demolished components. In no case loads on any element should increase, as for example, the load on lintels may increase substantially if brickwork below lintels are removed without dismantling the bricks above the lintel. Following the same principle debris should not be left accumulating on lower floors when the upper floor of an old building is being demolished.

The entire job of demolition and dismantling a structure may be divided into the following stages:

- Preliminary arrangements
- Deployment of skilled hands and equipments
- Actual demolition work as per sequence
- Shifting of usable items and structural components
- Removal of debris and site clearance

18.8.1 Preliminary Site Arrangements Prior to Demolition Work

Before starting any demolition work all electrical power lines connected with the structure should be disconnected and all stored items (in case or warehouses and buildings) particularly the hazardous materials and all service facilities should be removed. Besides this, the area of demolition should be kept free of all people not connected with the actual demolition process. This is particularly important for old buildings where people may be staying even in an unauthorized manner.

The next step should be to identify the area around the structure that might be affected by debris, vibration or impact during the demolition process and that area should be cordoned off with notice of entry restriction.

The actual demolition process is to be started only when the site engineer is fully satisfied with the above preliminary arrangements.

18.8.2 Deployment of Skilled Hands and Equipments

The deployment of equipments and skilled hands depend on the method of demolition to be followed in a particular case. There is no standard rule for deployment of any particular machinery for this purpose. But generally there are three distinct methods of demolition, such as:

- Demolition manually
- Demolition by mechanical means
- Demolition by inducing complete collapse of the structure.

1. Demolition by hand. Demolition by hand is usually done by using sledge hammers, jack hammers, concrete breakers, hand chisels etc. This is essentially a slow process, but risks are low, if the workers can do their job from a safe distance or from a separate working platform. Broken chunks of debris should not be allowed to pile up on lower tiers of demolition work. They should be removed periodically to the ground. No demolition work should be done when such debris are being removed. All workers engaged in manual demolition work should be properly trained for the job and they should be enforced to use safety belts, helmets and other protective gears as necessary.

2. Demolition by mechanical means. Sometimes a structure or part of it is so distressed and damaged that it becomes extremely risky even for the very skilled workers to handle the demolition work in a safe manner. In that case the next option should be to engage suitable mechanical equipments to do the job from a distance. In the mechanical method, use is made of a steel swinging demolition ball or a pusher arm fitted to a motorized vehicle, which is stationed at a safe distance from the spot of demolition. When swinging balls are used the height of the drop or the angle of swing must not exceed the manufacturer's specifications. A pusher arm is used for demolishing walls. It acts like a battering arm and imparts a large horizontal impact on the wall to be demolished. However the pusher arm should not be placed more than 600mm below the top of the wall.

In many cases both manual and mechanical methods are adopted judiciously as supplements to one another on a particular job to get better results.

3. Demolition by induced collapse. Often a collapse mechanism is introduced deliberately in a structure to expedite the demolition work or when the structure cannot be demolished by either manually or by any mechanical equipment in a safe manner. Such occasions arise in case of jack arched roofs covering a very large area (about 10000 sqm or so) which is on the verge of collapse due to snapping of the tie bars and corrosion of the supporting joists. In such cases it has been found that workers cannot work from the top and machines cannot also be deployed from underneath the damaged roof. Deliberately induced collapse of the whole roof at a time by cutting the roof along the wall supports is often seen to be the alternative way for doing the demolition job. This should be done under strict supervision.

Again it has been seen in industrial plants, particularly in galvanizing sections, the roof trusses and the coverings are damaged and corroded so heavily that no person can stand on the roof sheets for demolition work and machines are ineffective as the lifting mechanisms cannot be fastened to the damaged roof that is inaccessible for safety reasons. In such cases the usual practice is to have a shut down inside the work area and then the roof trusses are gas cut at their bearing supports so that the whole structure collapses all at a time. This method induces a pre-planned weakening of the key supports and therefore it is dangerous though very effective and sometimes very spectacular also. But such operations must be done only after proper planning and consultation with experts.

In some situations, deliberate collapse is initiated by pulling down a wall or an overhead tank structure. This is usually done by fitting wire ropes to the most vulnerable point of the structure and pulling is done by winches. However the winch should be placed away from the line of the pull and workers must be stationed at a safe distance away from the area which may be covered by the debris.

Blasting by putting explosives is another way to induce a deliberate collapse of the structure. This can be done only if it can be assured that no adjoining structure is affected and the whole blasting operation is done under the guidance of experts and all safety regulations regarding blasting work is followed meticulously. Flying debris and dust are also to be controlled properly around the work area. For more details regarding use of blasting materials in construction work the reader may refer to chapter 15 of this book.

18.9 SAFETY PROCEDURES IN DISMANTLING WORK

As in the case of demolition, all dismantling work should be carried out in the reverse order to the construction process. Here there is hardly any opportunity of inducing collapse to the whole structure, as the primary purpose of most dismantling work is to salvage as much of materials and fabricated units as possible for further use. As a result, attempts are made to recover the structural components unit by unit, piece by piece or module by module. The type of joints in the original structure plays an important part in deciding the mode of dismantling. Reinforced concrete beams and lintels embedded in masonry can be dismantled and salvaged piece by piece. But, when the same beam is integrally cast into a reinforced concrete column, it has to be broken and demolished.

Similarly for bolted steel structures, the components can be dismantled by removing the bolts. But in case of welded structures, like portals, the dismantling work should be done unit by unit by removing the splice joints. Small span trusses can however be lowered to the ground almost intact with the help of derricks and cranes after cutting the bolts at the bearing locations.

However in all the above cases proper planning of dismantling is to be done considering the type of structure, their end connections and the load path from top to the foundation. Additional false work or supports may be necessary for dismantling work depending on the site conditions and they are to be erected beforehand as per design and details. Mechanical equipments like steel derricks, mobile cranes, lifting devices and tools that were initially used for erection of the structural components may have to be called once again to do the dismantling job. In fact the dismantling work is typically planned as a reverse of the construction methods adopted earlier.

18.10 DISMANTLING OF BRIDGES

Bridges need to be dismantled sometimes under critical circumstances as mentioned below:

- When a bridge has long past its physical life and has become unstable and unsafe for vehicular movements and public use.
- When the bridge members are damaged due to corrosion and environmental degradation in such a way that repair and rehabilitation work are found to be costlier than a new bridge.
- When a bridge is washed away by flood or swept away inside the river due to extreme wind conditions
- When a bridge is damaged and dislodged beyond repair due to earthquake.
- When a particular span of a bridge is damaged by ship collision, the distressed span may have to be dismantled and a new span is to be erected there.
- When the traffic load increases with the passage of time, the bridge may need replacement after dismantling the old one.
- When the foundation is damaged due to excessive settlement and the bridge superstructure is tilted beyond allowable limit, the foundation may have to be redone after dismantling the old superstructure or the bridge has to be shifted laterally.

In all the above cases the dismantling work should be preceded by a thorough and systematic study of the present condition of the bridge and the preparation of a suitable cost-effective scheme supported by back-up structural design, calculations and detailed engineering. **Such schemes should cover the technological aspects of the demolition work and address to the safety of the workers and equipments deployed there**. Often it is seen that a practical, easy-to-execute method is the best one serving both the above objectives. The most suitable time of execution of the dismantling work again depends on the condition of the river and the availability of the right type of equipments. It is often seen that when railway bridges are to be dismantled the movement of all traffic over the bridge is kept suspended for a long time extending from several months to a few years. Even in the case of a fly-over inside the city limits, the diversion and maintenance of traffic pose lot of safety and operational problems when the fly-over is dismantled.

The adequacy of the structural components of the bridge to be dismantled should be assessed against any possible reversal of stress or overloading during the process of the dismantling work and members should be either strengthened, replaced or its strength supplemented by introducing additional redundant members.

In cases of a fly-over over ground inside city limits, additional trestle supports to the superstructure help in reducing stresses during dismantling work.

When bridges are washed away during floods, the structure remains buried under water and goes down and down inside the river bed on its own self weight and it is doubly difficult to retrieve the bridge members in good condition. In such cases the structural members may have to be cut to pieces and taken out of the water. This type of work needs deployment of suitable river transport system and additional protective gear for the workers to work safely under water.

The dislodgment of a bridge superstructure during earthquake poses lot of safety problems for the traffic movement. When the dislodgement is very small and the superstructure is not damaged much, the superstructure may be repaired and shifted to its original position easily. But for heavily tilted and damaged structures the whole superstructure may need dismantling and replacement by a new superstructure. In some cases it has been seen that the foundation is slightly damaged by earthquake, but the superstructure is more or less intact. Attempts should be made here to try to repair the foundation after jacking up the superstructure over additional supporting trestles and then the superstructure should be finally placed in position. In case of heavily damaged foundations due to excessive settlement due to earthquake, however, the bridge alignment may have to be shifted laterally and a new bridge has to be erected there for safety reasons.

Wind related damages are noticed in the case of slender long span structures like suspension bridges. The damages are mainly due to flutter and wind-induced vortex. Primarily this problem is best addressed during the design stage. Otherwise, once such structures collapse, it is difficult to retrieve the members intact from the river bed, as often suspension bridges are built over deep gorges.

All dismantling and demolition work should be carried out in a neat systematic way. No structure should be demolished or dismantled in a clumsy way, creating chaos in the vicinity of the work site. The equipments that may be necessary for such work should be procured beforehand, they should be placed at site in proper position and workers having proper training and experiences are to be engaged. It is always to be kept in mind that all demolition and dismantling work are risk prone if casually handled and many accidents have occurred in the past due to wrong planning, use of wrong machinery and deployment of unskilled labour for the job.

18.11 SPEED OF DEMOLISHING AND DISMANTLING WORK

The time required for demolishing and dismantling work depends on the condition of the structure and the tools and machinery used for the purpose. Demolishing a wall by using hand chisels is a very slow process, but it is often found to be the safest way to demolish a badly damaged wall or a building floor. Use of jack hammers or concrete breakers accelerates the process of demolition no doubt. But it is to be borne in mind that the effect of its impact and vibration in the neighbour-hood places and also to other parts of the distressed structure may create safety hazards. Considering all these factors, it is always pragmatic to adopt a slow, cautious and steady approach as all demolishing and dismantling work are tricky and very often difficult also.

18.12 HEALTH HAZARDS DURING DEMOLITION AND DISMANTLING WORK

During any demolition or dismantling work, care is to be taken to protect the workers from the following health hazards:

- Any hazardous chemical or toxic substances stored inside the shed or building to be demolished should be removed from site before the start of the demolition work. All live electrical attachments to the structure should also be removed, prior to start of the demolition work.
- Workers should be provided with protective clothing, gloves and gas masks for protection against fumes and floating dust particles during demolition work. Ammonia fumes, asbestos dusts, irritant chemicals etc fall under this category. While demolishing sludge tanks, exposure to toxic sludge and gas must be avoided.

- Usual protections as adopted in gas-cutting work during fabrication of steelwork should also be enforced while flame cutting during demolition work.
- Continuous exposure to high noise level should be avoided. Similarly no individual worker should be exposed continuously to vibrations produced from jack hammers or concrete breakers. Such jobs should be shared between several workers during the day. It is to be borne in mind that continuous exposure to high noise and vibration reduces the mental reflex of the workers and they become prey to accidents.
- Workers should have adequate protection while doing demolition work at sites contaminated by radioactive substances, hazardous chemicals, toxic wastes, methane gas etc.

Workers engaged in demolition or dismantling work should be positioned a safe distance away from the falling debris. Necessary working platforms, ladders are to be designed and erected in advance for movement of the demolition squad during their work. The workers should be trained to use judiciously the safety belts during the demolition work. In short, all demolition and dismantling job should be carried out in a very careful and systematic way so that the job can be completed without any untoward safety hazards to the workers or equipments.

QUESTIONS

1. Under what circumstances a structure may have to be demolished? What is the difference between a demolishing work and a dismantling work?
2. What should the correct sequence for a demolition job? What safety measures should be adopted to ensure safety of men and equipments during a demolition work?
3. What are the risks involved in a manual demolition job? How are these risks different from the risks involved in demolition by mechanical means?
4. What is meant by demolition by induced collapse? When should it be tried?
5. How a dismantling job should be progressed if materials are to be salvaged for further use?

6. Under what circumstances an old bridge may have to be dismantled?
7. How the safety of the men and equipments are to be maintained during any dismantling or demolition work?
8. Explain how the continuous noise generated from jack hammers engaged in demolition of pavements may endanger personal safety.
9. What types of protective gears should be provided to the men engaged in demolition work?
10. Write short notes on the following:
    (*a*) Dismantling of a bridge washed out during a flood
    (*b*) Rehabilitation of a bridge dislodged from the bearings due to earthquake
    (*c*) Need for regular maintenance of structures to avoid rehabilitation or demolition during service life.
    (*d*) Need for examining the stability of a structure before its demolition
    (*e*) Accident from falling debris on workers
11. What additional precautions are to be taken while demolishing a damaged warehouse in which hazardous chemicals are stored? Explain the additional safety hazards created in such circumstances if blasting or gas-cutting is done without proper examination of the stored contents.

CHAPTER 19

Related Important Topics on Safety Management

19.1 SAFETY AUDIT

The term audit means checking by a professional team the accounts prepared by another team of professionals. The aim of such an audit exercise is to ensure that that the accounts have been prepared following all approved norms and also the government rules and regulations. In the case of construction projects a similar audit, called "safety audit" is done, the basic principle of which is to investigate systematically whether the standard safety regulations as formulated by the government and the local authorities and the guidelines given in the design standards and codes of practices have been complied with. The main objective of a safety audit for a construction project is:

- To review the hazard scenarios considered in the design, certify the design from safety point of view and also to recommend additional safety measures as necessary to avert, to the extent possible, the risks and severity of accidents, loss of property during construction and also during the post-construction period of service life.
- To recommend ways and means to reduce, if possible, the cost of repair and maintenances during service life, so that the over-all Life Cycle Cost of the project can be kept to the minimum possible without compromising the safety and reliability at any stage.

The safety audit should be carried out in several stages, namely:

Stage 1: During the planning and preliminary design stage to investigate whether all types of likely safety hazards have been considered. These are usually incorporated in the design in the form of critical combinations of dead load, live load, wind load, earthquake load, vibration effects, water current effect etc. as applicable in the particular project considered.

Stage 2: On completion of detailed engineering and the tendering work to ensure whether all relevant safety rules have been followed in the detailed drawings and whether the terms and conditions in the tender contain all relevant safety clauses.

Stage 3: During construction to ensure the safety of the men, structures and equipments deployed to ensure a trouble-free construction.

Stage 4: To clear the project after completion for safe use of the owners. This is done as a pre-commission safety drill, when, if necessary, load tests are done for the most critical load combinations.

For large construction projects, safety audits in the above stages are usually entrusted to different teams of professional experts. While stage 1 and stage 2 audits may be done by a team of design consultants, the stage 3 audit should preferable be entrusted to persons having requisite site experiences. Again, the stage 4 audit usually includes the representatives of the owners of the project authority, who will be responsible for safe use of the utility constructed. As for example, any completed railway project like a railway bridge or a new permanent way will have to be certified by the railway safety authority before the new system is made operational. Depending on the nature of the construction project, personnel from different disciplines of engineering are often drawn to form a particular audit team.

19.1.1 Safety Audit of Existing Facilities

A safety audit may also be fruitfully done on any exiting infrastructure facility. As for example, a safety audit may be done on a stretch of an existing road to assess any possibility of ribbon development, growth of slums along the road, encroachments or any deterioration that may have occurred to the existing pavement which may invite road accidents in near future.

Safety audits may also help in dealing with crisis management if there is a likelihood of oil spill or hazardous substances stored inside a go-down. Similarly safety hazards due to environmental pollution form other unknown sources can also be identified from safety audits of existing facilities.

19.1.2 Duty of the Safety Audit Teams

The safety auditors will assess the realistic needs of the users at present and also the future needs during the service life of the project. Critical assessment should be made of the likely deficiencies in the functional aspects of the project from safety point of view at all stages of the audit process as mentioned above. At the same time, they will give recommendations to rectify any defects found in the design or the methods of construction.

It is not the duty of the safety auditor to supervise regularly the design process or the construction aspects of any construction project by infringing on the regular activities of the designers, staff and workers engaged on the job. His function will be to suggest low-cost counter measures to overcome the deficiencies and point out if there is any deviation from the standard engineering practice from safety point of view.

Designers often feel that the work of a safety auditor is an infringement on their responsibilities. On the other hand, the persons doing the construction job at site may think that a safety auditor's recommendations only make unnecessary changes in the construction methods thereby delaying the progress of the work. However a strict compliance to the design and construction practices may not always insulate the project from safety hazards coming from unexpected sources which may be anticipated only by a competent safety auditor. As such the recommendations of the safety audit team should always be given due importance and they should be considered a part of the team in the whole construction process.

The project authority also should bestow on the safety auditors the requisite powers to demand proper cooperation from the designers and the site staff.

19.2 ELECTRICAL SAFETY

In any construction project, electricity is consumed for various purposes in fabrication shops, store-yard, stores, site establishments, staff and labour quarters and also for running electrical gadgets and equipments of various dimensions and capacities. Continuous uninterrupted supply of electricity without any safety hazard is an important pre-requisite for timely completion of any project. Sudden power failure or an accident causing electrocution of a person on duty any time during working hours in the day or night may completely upset a time schedule which may render all workers, staff and equipments idle. In fabrication shops where heavy structural steel members are fabricated for use in construction projects, a similar disruption of electrical power or an accident causing severe shock or burn injury to a worker is not uncommon where electrical safety is compromised. Consequently it is necessary to ensure adequate standard safety measures for running safely the electrical gadgets and equipments. There are various acts and rules governing the safe use of electricity formulated by government authority and the Bureau of Standards. It is not possible to mention all of them within the short space of this text. However a few basic safety measures which must be followed for safety reasons are mentioned below.

1. Checking of supply line voltage. The input supply installation should be periodically checked to verify whether proper insulation of wires and cables are maintained. The variation of voltage and frequency in the supply line, if there is any, should be rectified. The size of any bare conductor or a cable conductor should be so selected that the drop in voltage from the consumer's terminal to any point at work spot does not exceed 2.5% of the nominal voltage, when the conductors are carrying full load current, disregarding however the starting condition.

2. Insulation of cable joints. Every switch board installation and joints in cables and electrical wires should be properly taped and insulated. No bare connections should be allowed at the back of any switch board.

3. Switchgears. For a medium to high voltage circuit, suitable switchgears are chosen which includes the necessary protection device that ensures that a particular section of the circuit is automatically turned off and isolated in case of overloads. For medium voltages up to 600 volts, **knife type switches** are still used. The protective device for this generally consists of a fuse which is mounted close to the switch. The knife switches are usually spring-controlled, giving a quick break in the circuit, when the handle is moved. Such switches are so designed that it is not possible to open the case with the switch is in an 'on' position. The normal limit for such a switch is from 300 to 400 amperes. However for high voltage circuits and to avail automatic operation facilities, **oil circuit breakers** are used. This applies to medium voltage, 3-phase systems of 415 volts. While a switch is a device for making or breaking a current not greatly in excess of its rated normal capacity, a circuit breaker is a device which can make or break a circuit under both normal and abnormal conditions. As such oil circuit breakers are considered to be more safe and user-friendly than an ordinary knife switch. A breaker should be selected considering several factors, namely, the circuit voltage, normal current, frequency of the supply, making capacity of instantaneous peak current in amperes and the maximum current it can carry without damage for a specified time, generally 1to 3 seconds. Oil circuit breakers are standardized accordingly and they should be selected under technical advice of a qualified electrician. Similarly fuse wire sizes should be selected considering their normal full load carrying capacity.

4. Earthing of equipments. All electrical equipments particularly the welding generators, electric vibrators, motors, electrically-operated cranes and hoists and similar equipments must be grounded in earth. Similarly, all metal covers to electrical equipments, all steel and other structural units that are erected very near to a power supply line must be adequately grounded in commensurate to the voltage of the power supply line. In case, high or extra high voltage wires and cables are running very near to the work spot, such grounding of the site installations must be completed before start of the erection work using materials of right specifications and by approved methods. Expert advice from qualified electricians should be taken in this regard.

5. Headroom clearance from live wire. Sufficient head room should be allowed from the road level (not less than 20 ft) for any overhead electric supply lines crossing the pathway. The headroom should be increased if necessary in case heavy-duty trailers or cranes are to move along the path. The cranes while moving under an electrical line without load should have its boom down and well secured. Similarly, adequate horizontal clearance as specified in electricity rules should be maintained from existing supply lines to protect the erectable items during the process of erection or after placing it into position.

6. Lightning arresters. All major high rise installations should be provided with lightning arrestors of proper design and specifications.

7. Engaging qualified electricians. Qualified certified electricians should only be engaged for working on high voltage lines. Qualified electricians must be engaged to supervise all day and night shift work. They should be provided with necessary electrical tools, insulated boots, gloves, ladders and other items as necessary. Each electrician should carry a tool box when he is on duty at site and he should be provided with attendants when working at heights. In fact for large construction sites there should be a team of electrical people comprising a supervisor, foremen and electricians with their helpers who will attend to all electrical faults and will maintain the electrical gadgets.

It is to be borne in mind that a good well-maintained electrical circuit and connections save the workers from unwarranted electrical shocks and fatal accidents. The electricity rules and regulations should be followed scrupulously in this regard.

19.3 MANAGEMENT FUNCTIONS IN CASE OF ACCIDENTS

In spite of strict compliance of safety provisions in the design and planning stage and various types of safety measures taken during the construction period, the progress of many projects are sometimes adversely affected by accidents due to unsafe working conditions and unforeseen safety hazards. This eventuality should be taken into consideration and an advance contingency plan should be formulated in advance so that the management is not caught unawares in case there is a serious accident at site. As such, side by side with the regular accident-prevention measures, there should be a well-chalked out plan, prepared in advance about what to do if there is an accident at site. There should be clear-cut instructions for handling situations involving a simple first-aid case or a serious injury. The cause of the accident should be prima-facie detected as quickly as possible at site. A serious fatal accident may be due to a fall from a height (which is very common at construction sites) or the injury may be due some hazardous chemicals, due to collision with moving vehicles, cranes or rotating machine parts. Whatever may be the cause of the accident, first-aid facilities must be made available at site to the victim of an accident as quickly as possible. Simultaneously, a report should be made on a printed form, stating clearly the nature and cause of the accident, the name of the victim, his designation, the date and time of the accident and other relevant details as available. The injured person should be shifted to the nearest hospital without any delay.

In case of serious accidents causing disablement of the worker the employer should arrange for his rehabilitation as per rules, both financially by way of compensation and by re-employment helping him in the process of settling down to earn a fruitful living. In case of fatal accidents, adequate financial compensation along with fruitful rehabilitation to the next of kin to the victim should be arranged as per rules. To meet these eventualities, health insurance schemes help to a great extent to provide financial compensation to the victim of accidents.

In order to develop an effective post-accident rescue or disaster management, all controls should be checked and safety drills should be performed periodically in order to test the preparedness of the team members.

19.4 FORENSIC STUDY

Forensic study is the discipline of investigating and ascertaining the cause of an accident or safety hazard after a disaster has happened at a particular place. While forensic study for disasters due to arson, sabotage etc come mainly under the domain of criminal investigation, structural failures with consequent loss of life and property usually come under the per-view of engineering investigation. Such failures may occur due to design faults, human error, construction error, fire hazards, natural calamities or it may even be due to aggressive environment. The nature and extent of a disaster may affect a structure, an industrial complex or even a big city. An environmental disaster may affect a locality or a region and its people for a long time. Some disasters like erosion of soil and river banks may continue for generations, affecting and displacing people continuously from one place to another.

From the above it is evident that forensic study in many problem situations may require a multi-disciplinary approach to find out the reason behind structural failure. A forensic study in many cases may require physical and chemical examination of metals and other substances like clothes, yarns, containers and construction materials salvaged from the disaster site. However lots of difficulties are usually encountered in finding out the exact reason of a structural failure and the investigator has to apply his good judgment in many cases. A few of them are stated below.

19.4.1 Lack of Concrete Evidence

As any forensic study is conducted after an accident or a structural failure has occurred, it is often the case that much of the evidences are lost. This is particularly true for fire hazards. The forensic team in such cases can approach a disaster site only after the fire is extinguished and the place is made safe for the forensic team to move about safely. Part of the not-so-damaged structural components may have to be dismantled by the fire brigade for the purpose. In such case the forensic team personnel have to apply their own good judgment to locate the **'seat of fire'** and find out the cause of the fire. Once the seat of fire is located, the propagation and advancement of the fire to different directions can be visualized. Moreover the path of destruction should be ascertained as correctly as possible.

19.4.2 Lack of Access

Sometimes the spot of a structural failure does not have easy access. Fatigue failures thus escape the notice of the study team in many cases. Wash-out of a bridge superstructure often obliterates all evidences as the superstructure may be buried under water.

19.4.3.Lack of Visibility

In case of a damage or failure of a superstructure due to settlement of sinking of foundations, the exact reason of failure cannot be seen at all. Failure of bridge foundations due to intense scour poses similar hurdles to any investigating team. In such cases the investigator has to make additional ground investigations to ascertain the integrity of the foundation system before arriving at a conclusion.

The age of a structure at the time of its failure has a very important bearing on the process of the investigation of any forensic team. Sometimes it has been observed that an over-head water tank has collapsed all on a sudden during its filling operation for the first time. Material deficiency or bad workmanship or design fault or a combination of these may be the reason behind such a sudden failure. On the other hand, the fatigue failure of a steel structure or a moving crane would possibly depend on its age, material deficiency if any or the loading pattern.

In all cases of any forensic study, the investigator should always try to **reconstruct the circumstances** leading to the disaster that may have caused a structural failure, loss of life or injury to workmen and others. Only then he will be able to find out correctly the exact cause of the failure and would also be able to recommend any practical remedial solution.

19.5 LEGAL PROBLEMS IN SAFETY MANAGEMENT

A review of the safety management in the construction industry will not be complete, unless the legal problems associated with the numerous cases of accidents happening all over the world causing injury and/or death to the workers, users and even the on-lookers along with the nature of damages, are understood. There are numerous acts and regulations enacted so far in our country to control accidents and assess the financial implications of loss of life and property. Construction engineers and design engineers are usually not conversant with all details and nuances involved in these acts, though they are the people who are entrusted to build tall buildings, bridges, industrial structures and infrastructure projects. Hence, they should at least be aware of the basic aspects of the laws, both in the criminal and civil arenas and their duties and responsibilities.

19.5.1 Criminal Law

The criminal law is applicable when damages are caused to the health of the people and the safety of the structures due to, willful negligence of duties, irresponsible behaviour of the builders refuting all standard norms and regulations, acts of sabotage, arson and conspiratorial actions causing serious safety hazards or accidents. These unlawful acts come under the per-view of the law of the land enforced through legal proceedings presented before a magistrate's court. On conviction, the guilty and his associates may be fined or sentenced to a term of imprisonment as per the prevailing law.

19.5.2. Civil Law

Contrary to the criminal law, the civil law establishes and fixes liabilities in two main aspects, namely:

- The contractual agreement
- Tort

Contractual agreement. Usually, in the case of many construction projects, particularly for big ones where outside agencies are engaged for the work, a contractual document is prepared and signed by the owner and builder based on the agreements and negotiations between them. The civil law of contractual agreement protects both the parties from any financial loss due to any deviation from the conditions laid down in the agreement. This may simply be a fine, compensation or a liquidated damage.

The law of contract is the basis of all commercial agreements, which are usually done in writing on a stamped paper and signed by both the parties with witnesses. For any contractual document the conditions entered in the different clauses must be legal *i.e.* no agreement is legally tenable if any of the conditions violates the statutory rules and regulations framed by the government. The conditions of contract thus entered into the agreement define the conditions of payment, administrative measures and safety measures to be taken by the contractor during the construction period. Any site-specific safety measure to be taken by the contractor is also incorporated in the contract document. Contract agreements are also made between the consultant and owner, between the supplier and the owner also.

So far as the safety provisions are concerned, all such contract agreements should specify the safety requirements and safety factors to be followed in case of design, detailed engineering, fabrication, supply of materials and method of construction and financial involvements in case of deviations. The question of awarding indemnity to the consultant or the constructor at any stage should also be clearly specified in the contract document.

Tort. Tort is the rule of common law which guides everyone to take reasonable care not to hurt or cause injury to others during the construction period. According to this common law, consultants are supposed to take reasonable care to produce a design which is safe, stable and free of faults. By the rule of tort, a contractor is also supposed to take all reasonable care at site to protect the workers and prevent any third-party injury. Negligence to the health of the workers, acts of omissions and commissions which can be foreseen and anticipated also fall under the per-view of common law of tort. In case of violations in the above cases of tort, the liability and consequent redress are fixed by the courts of law. The liability period and the quantum of compensation are also awarded by the courts concerned. Under the rule of tort, an employer may also be held responsible for any of the acts committed by his employees causing safety hazard or injury to a third party.

Structural failures and injury to workers at construction sites are very common and reports of such accidents are reported in the news media very often. These failures can be traced in general to three main factors:

- Design error
- Material deficiency
- Construction error

In addition, there are reports of catastrophic failures of structures followed by huge loss of life due to unprecedented natural calamities like earthquake, wind, flood or landslide. The design responsibility, in this matter, revolves around the following aspects:

- To check the safety factors considered in the basic design
- To check thoroughly the structural details and shopdrawings
- To inspect, verify the safety aspects during construction and to ensure compliance to building codes.
- For very important structures, to get the structural design and erection methods reviewed by a competent

professional person or body and incorporate their suggestions in the final design and details.

The owner's responsibility lies in the preparation of a contract document specifying therein the material specifications, method of construction and the safety measures to be adopted by the contractor. The specifications should cover the material quality, type of equipment to be used and all other special conditions contract related to the safety in construction.

Safety is seriously compromised with legal complications, when the principal contractor entrusted with the work, does not schedule the activities following technological sequences or leaves the job in the hands of inefficient sub-contractors. Safety takes a back seat also when the contractor is forced to deliver a job within a specified period without caring for the minimum days required from technical point of view. In many cases it is noticed that the sub-contractor does not have the technical competence or capability of mobilizing skilled persons required for a particular project. Another arena which invites legal complications involving safety also, is quality control, quality assurance and regular day-to-day supervision of site activities by competent technical persons. The root of many accidents, safety hazards and consequent loss of life can be traced to the absence of proper or nil supervision from the contractor's end. This should be looked into with care and vigilance.

19.6 LEGAL RESPONSIBILITY OF THE OWNER IN THE POST-CONSTRUCTION PERIOD

On completion of a project, the site is handed over to the owner. It is then the owner's responsibility to ensure safety and security to the users during the service life of any structure. It is also the owner's responsibility to see that the structure or any of its components are not overloaded, the structure is periodically maintained, repairs are done and periodic inspections are made by technical experts to check whether there has been any serious deficiency in the structural system due to environmental degradation. It is to be borne in mind that, during the service life of any structure, it is the owner's responsibility to maintain the common law of tort, as mentioned earlier, to avoid safety hazards, legal complications and litigation.

19.7 INSURANCE TO COVER RISKS IN CONSTRUCTION

Construction jobs are always prone to risks of structural damages and injury to workers involving disruption in the work schedule and financial losses. Financial losses are also likely to be incurred by the user of a constructed facility due to damages caused by natural calamities during the service life of a structure. Such damages may be due to fire, theft, accidents etc and they may occur in spite of taking all reasonable safety precautions by the authorities concerned. To cover all these financial risks insurance policies are drawn at different stages of construction and also during the period of use of the structure by the authorities concerned. Such insurance policies may be grouped into the following broad categories:

- Insurances during transit of materials and equipments
- Insurance covering the civil works for the period of construction and erection
- Insurance covering the machines and equipments used in the construction period
- Insurance covering the items stored in warehouses and godowns
- Insurance covering the operating period of machinery
- Insurance covering personal risks of people engaged in construction or during its use

In many cases insurances are grouped together to have unified insurance policy covering all risks in several stages of construction. Usually losses during transit, accidental fire damages, theft, accidental collapse of structures and risks of workers for working at heights are covered by the insurance policies and all these policies are drawn for a specific period of time, after which the policy lapses automatically and new policies are to be drawn if required. The quantum of insurance premiums is decided by the insurance companies considering the risks involved in each case. As such insurance premiums are much higher for storages of hazardous chemicals and low for non-hazardous ordinary storage facilities.

Moreover, insurances are allowed by the insurance companies only after they are satisfied that all statutory safety measures have been adopted as per the prevalent rules and regulations. For this purpose insurance companies conduct inspections and safety audit to have first-hand knowledge about the fire-fighting facilities available, lighting arrangements, electrical safety measures adopted at site, first aid facilities available and security of the plant and machinery. They often suggest additional safety measures, additional security and fencing arrangements and wider passages for movement of fire tenders before agreeing on granting insurance facilities.

Moreover they always insist on construction of structures following provisions of codes and local regulations and sanctioned plans.

There are set rules and procedures to claim for the loss. In case of fire, thefts, accidental cases, it is the rule to file a FIR (First Information Report) to the police mentioning the date of accident, the losses incurred, with information to fire brigade authorities for immediate action in case of a fire. There are set rules for hospitalization of accident victims to claim for injury and loss of lives. After the claim is put up before the insurance authorities, they arrange survey of the site and assess the loss incurred and calculate the claim amount. The settlement of insurance claims often is marred by controversies raised from the claimant and the insurance authorities and the settlement of claims are then delayed.

QUESTIONS

1. What is meant by safety audit? How should it be carried out during the planning, design and construction stages?
2. What is the function of a safety audit team? Who should be included in such a team?
3. List a few important safety requirements for:
   (*a*) Domestic wirings and fittings
   (*b*) Use of domestic cooking appliances
   (*c*) Use of workshop machinery
   (*d*) High voltage equipments used in material handling jobs inside workshops
4. What is the usefulness of a forensic study after a fire hazard? How evidences are collected and what type of hindrances are usually faced by the study team while collecting evidences?
5. Write short on the following:
   (*a*) Earthing of equipments
   (*b*) Lightening arrester
   (*c*) Disaster management in case of accidents at site
   (*d*) Rehabilitation of accident victims
6. Explain how legal complications may arise following an accident in the work place.
7. How accident victims should be compensated as per contractual agreements or by rule of common law?
8. What are the primary reasons of structural failures? How such failures can be prevented?

9. What is the legal responsibility of the owner in ensuring the safety of a structure during its service life?
10. What is the difference between a contractual agreement and the rule of common law? How a contractor can be held responsible if he violates the legal provisions in both these cases?
11. What is the difference between a contractual agreement and the rule of common law ?
12. Explain how the owner is responsible for the safety of a structure during its service life.

CHAPTER 20

Safety and Reliability

20.1 INTRODUCTION

In the previous chapters we have discussed and tried to find out ways and means to have an adequate and acceptable standard of safety right from the planning and design stage to the construction period and also during the post-construction service life of a structure. In all these stages, the design for safety has been done by incorporating safety factors (or, safety margins) in the structural system against various critical combinations of loads.

This is basically a deterministic approach of ensuring safety, in which, the safety margins are fixed beforehand, considering the most likely critical combination of loads. The design considerations, selection of materials, specifications, proportioning of the structural components and, even, the construction methods follow suit to maintain the pre-determined safety margin. As the focus in these exercises is mainly on the likely failures, such an approach often leads to over-designed structures increasing the construction costs. Consequently, it is not uncommon to see that in the case of many important structures, safety factors as high as 5.0 to 6.0 are recommended, as in the design of main cables of suspension bridges. On the other hand, a wrong assessment of loads or material weakness may render a structure unreliable even after the incorporation of all the safety factors in the design giving an illusion that the structure is reliable.

In view of above, it becomes necessary to assess from time to time the reliability of a structure, if there is any change in the loading pattern, a change in the environment or a degradation in the material used.

20.2 RELIABILITY

From the above observations, a few general conclusions may be drawn such as:

- A structure may be safe under a given system of loads, but may become 'unreliable' under a new loading pattern.
- An under-designed structure may be safe under non-critical loads, but may be highly unsafe and unreliable during service life under full loads.
- On the contrary, an apparently 'unsafe' structure can be made 'reliable', if the imposed loads are reduced and/or the members are strengthened.
- Material weaknesses developed in adverse environmental conditions may render a structure unreliable, even though the structure was safe and reliable for some period in the service life.

In all the above cases it is to be noted that 'safety' is a relative term used differently in different circumstances and the question of reliability is closely associated with safety. It is therefore necessary that assessment of reliability should be made from time to time to ensure continuance of safety, in view of the variability in any loading pattern, changes in the environment and the structural response to the same.

20.3 SAFETY VRS RELIABILITY

Safety can be defined as the avoidance of critical conditions which may cause loss to life and property, injury to workers and damages to structures and environment.

Reliability is defined as the probability of a structural system or its components performing the required function over a period of time under a given system of loads.

Obviously, safety and reliability are closely related, but they are not synonymous. While safety measures focus on **'failures'** resulting from safety hazards, the evaluation of reliability relates to the probability of **'non-failure'** over time under variable loading patterns and structural response during the entire useful life of the structure.

Reliability evaluation is based on the concept that a failure can be described as a random event and the probability density function (pdf) of failure takes the shape as shown in Fig. 20.1. The corresponding reliability function is shown in Fig. 20.2.

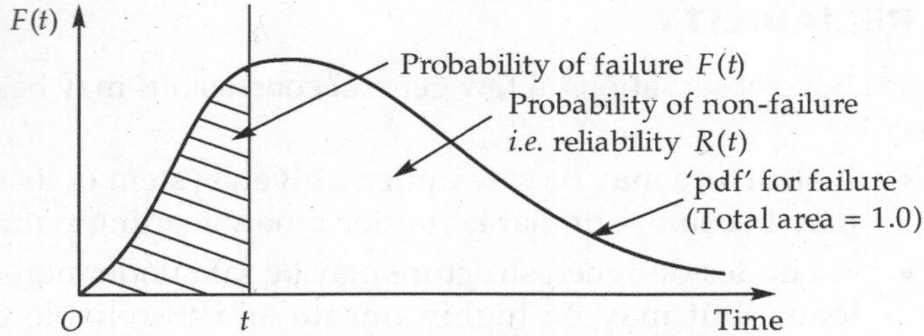

Fig. 20.1 Probability density function.

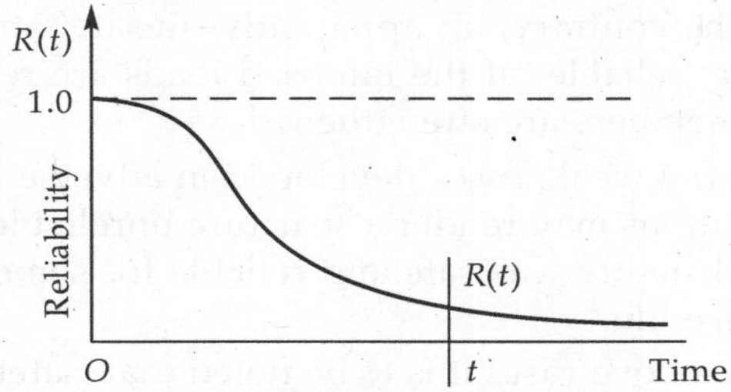

Fig. 20.2 Reliability function.

The curve in Fig. 20.1 shows that the probability of failure is zero when time 't' = 0. Obviously, reliability is 1.0, when 't' = 0. This means that there is hardly any chance of failure of a structure at the very start of its service life, when $t = 0$. On the other hand, when time 't' approaches infinity, the probability of failure is 1.0, *i.e.* no structure can survive an infinite stretch of time. In between these two extremes, at any point of time of its service life, say at time 't' (shown on the above figure, the area of the probability distribution curve for failure from zero to 't' denotes the probability of failure of the structure $F(t)$. The balance area remaining denotes the reliability of the structure $R(t)$. As the total area enclosed by the pdf curve is 1.0, the relation between the probability of failure $F(t)$ before time 't' and the reliability at that time is given by the relation:

$$F(t) = 1.0 - R(t)$$

where $R(t)$ is the reliability of the structure at time 't' and $F(t)$ is the measure of 'unreliability' of the system.

In this respect, it may be noted that, the failure of a structure is considered as a random event. If records of failure of similar structures are available, the frequencies of occurrences of such failures can be obtained. From the frequency of each event, we can find out the relative frequency of occurrence of that event, which is the fraction of the frequency number to the total number of observations. These values of relative frequencies can be approximated to the probability of occurrences of the events, if the number of trials is very large, *i.e.* if records are available of a large number of failures of any particular structural system. If the number of failure data are fairly large (at least 30), and the time intervals are made smaller and smaller, the values of the relative frequencies converge to the probability of occurrence of the failure events. The continuous curve thus obtained is the probability density function (pdf) of the failure pattern of the particular structural system. If however, not many trials (record of failures) are made, a probability distribution curve can still be drawn by joining the apex of the rectangles of class (time) intervals by a smooth curve, as has been shown in the above figure.

As for example, if records are kept of failure modes of a steel gutter made up of a particular thickness of plate and undergoing similar environmental distress and corrosion, a frequency curve and from that a probability distribution curve may be obtained which would give an idea about the probably of failure at any time *'t'* after the gutter system is installed. This would automatically give an idea about the reliability of a similar gutter system installed under a similar environment at any point of time.

Theoretically, failures of structural components can be predicted accurately, if the failure mechanisms (the physics and chemistry involved in the failure process) are known. But, in reality, there are lot of uncertainty and limited data available of many failures, caused by environmental degradation, earthquakes, excessive heat, mechanical vibrations etc. As a result, no deterministic prediction is possible to indicate the exact date on which an earthquake may strike a structure and whether the structure will only be slightly damaged or completely destroyed. This uncertainty of occurrences of future events (failure events) can be tackled statistically, if the failure mechanisms of existing structures are observed and historical records are maintained. This is particularly important for a structural system consisting of different types of components like a steel superstructure, elastomeric bearings, concrete piers, foundations and wearing coats etc. in a bridge, each having their own characteristic structural response to failure modes and each having varied exposure to external loads and environment. From these data, the probability density function (pdf) of the failure mechanism can be developed, which can be analyzed statistically to predict the likely failure modes or the reliability of a structural system.

20.4 CHARACTERISTICS OF PROBABILITY DENSITY FUNCTIONS

To analyze the characteristics of the probability density function (pdf) of any failure process, the standard practice is to find out the measures of central tendency in the following forms depending on the type of the probability density function.

- Mean Time To Failure (MTTF), an useful measure of the working life of the system
- Median , which gives the indication of the time for 50% probability of failure and 50% reliability
- Mode, the most likely observed failure time

Here,

MTTF = $\int_0^{\infty} t \times f(t)\, dt$ which is the moment about origin of the area enclosed, as per statistical methods.

$$R(t)_{\text{madian}} = 0.50$$

$$F(t)_{\text{mode}} = f((t)_{\text{max}}$$

These measures of central tendency are shown in the Fig. 20.3.

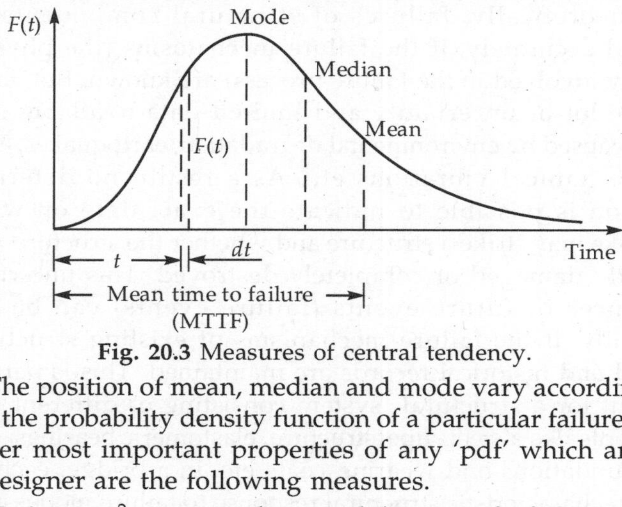

Fig. 20.3 Measures of central tendency.

The position of mean, median and mode vary according to the skew of the probability density function of a particular failure process. The other most important properties of any 'pdf' which are useful to the designer are the following measures.

Variance, σ^2 = averaged squared distance of a failure time from MTTF, which is a measure of dispersion from the mean value.

And, Standard Deviation, σ = root-mean-square of deviation about the mean value.

The reader is advised to refer to standard text books on statistical applications and also the references given at the end of this chapter for further information in this regard.

20.5 RELIABILITY BASED ON HAZARD (FAILURE) RATE FUNCTION

As an alternative to the method of analyzing the probability density functions, described earlier, reliability is often evaluated from the probability of failure at any instantaneous point of time, $T_0 + \Delta t$, assuming that the structural system will survive the warranty period T_0. *i.e.* to find out the answer to the question as to what would be the probability of failure of a structure after say 20 years of useful service or what is the probability of failure of machine after its warranty period of 5 years is over. This is a case of conditional probability of failure and the failure rates are expressed in the form of an Instantaneous Hazard Rate Function or **Failure Rate Function,** which is unique for any particular structural system under a system of loads.

Observations on the failure modes of many structural systems reveal that failures occur in 3 stages of their life cycles in different ways:

(*a*) A decreasing failure rate (DFR) in the early warranty period of life cycle, called also the 'burn-in period'. The failures in this period are characterized by manufacturing or fabrication errors, welding defects, cracks, poor quality of workmanship, selection and use of materials of wrong specifications etc.

(*b*) Thereafter, a Constant Failure Rate (CFR) in which failures are characterized by random overloading, human error in using the structural system and facilities and chance events like accidents, covering almost the full part of the useful life (service life) of the structure.

(*c*) Finally, a steep Increasing Failure Rate (IFR) in which failures occur mainly due to fatigue accompanied by corrosion, aging of the components and fixtures, cyclic loading etc. This is the wear-out period of the structural system.

All the above three stages of failures are shown as a curve in Fig. 20.4, commonly known as the **Bathtub Curve**, because of its shape like a bathtub.

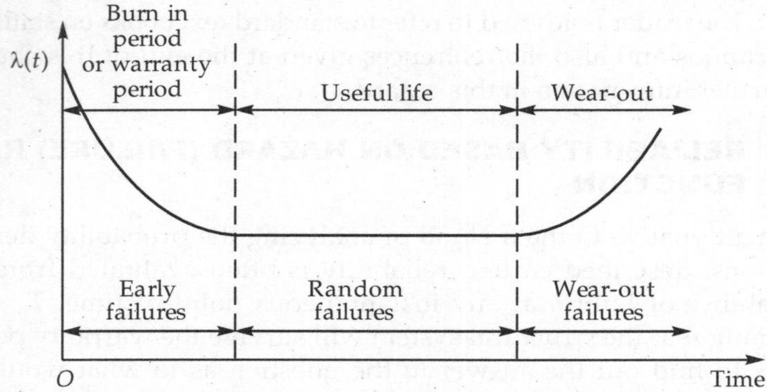

Fig. 20.4 Hazard rate function (The Bathtub Curve).

The ordinate of the curve, $\lambda(t)$ is termed as the instantaneous hazard rate or the failure rate function, which is expressed as:

$$\lambda(t) = \frac{f(t)}{R(t)}$$

Each structural system will have a characteristically unique hazard rate function, depending on its geometry, design, materials, workmanship and age and the unit is the number of failures for a specified period of time. Depending on the nature of the failure process as described above, several mathematical probability models have been developed to depict a particular failure process. Broadly they are divided into 2 categories:

(*a*) Constant Failure Rate Models

(*b*) Time-dependent Failure Models

20.5.1 Constant Failure Rate Model

The constant failure rate model, also known as the exponential probability distribution, is represented by the equation:

$$R(t) = e^{-\lambda t} \quad \text{where } t \geq 0.$$

and,
$$F(t) = 1 - R(t) = 1 - e^{\lambda t}$$

where λ = failure rate (number of failures in a certain period of time)

The corresponding $\text{MTTF} = \frac{1}{\lambda}$

and, $\text{Variance} = \frac{1}{(\lambda)^2}$

Obviously, standard deviation = $(\text{variance})^{1/2} = \frac{1}{\lambda}$ = MTTF

This means that the expected working life of a system with an exponentially-distributed reliability is equal to the reciprocal of its failure rate. Also, the variability of failure time increases as the reliability (MTTF) increases.

Failures due to chance events can be effectively evaluated by this distribution. Apart from the constant failure rate and randomness of occurrence of the failure events, another interesting characteristic of this CFR model is that there is no aging or wear-out effect on the rate of failure. This is based on the consideration that a product or a system may fail anytime, regardless of whether the system is new or old. This characteristic is known as **'memory-less-ness'** of the CFR model.

Example 1. *It is observed that the failure rate of a particular brand of light-bulb, when it is turned on, is 0.001 per operating hour. Calculate its expected working life and reliability if it is operated for 720 hours.*

Solution. Here, $\lambda = 0.001$.

$$\text{Hence, MTTF} = \frac{1}{\lambda} = \frac{1}{0.001} = 1000 \text{ hours}$$

This means that the expected working life of the bulb is 1000 hours.

Reliability for use of 720 hours

$$= R(t) = R(720) = e^{-\lambda t} = e^{-0.001 \times 720} = 0.4868$$

Example 2. *The compressor of an air-conditioner runs on an average of 20 minutes only once in every hour. During operation its failure rate has been reported as 0.005 per operating hour. Calculate the reliability of the compressor for a 24 hours operating period.*

Solution. Here $\lambda = \left(\frac{20}{60}\right) \times 0.005 = 0.00167$

Reliability for operation of 24 hours

$$= R(24 \text{ hrs}) = e^{-0.00167 \times 24} = 0.9607.$$

20.5.2 Time-Dependent Failure Models

In many practical cases, it is observed that the failure rate is not constant over time. This variability in the failure rate has been taken care of with the development of mainly two probability distributions, namely:

- Weibull Distribution
- Normal Distribution

20.5.2.1 Weibull Distribution

The Weibull Distribution is often used to analyze both increasing and decreasing failure rates in the burn-in period and wear-out period of a structural system. Here,

(*a*) $\lambda(t)$, the hazard rate function = $a \times t^b$ When both a and b are greater than zero,the failure rate increases and when '*a*' is greater than zero, but "*b*" is less than zero,the failure rate decreases.

(*b*) Reliability $R(t) = e^{-(t/\theta)^\beta}$

(*c*) Probability of failure $F(t) = \dfrac{\beta}{\theta} \times \left(\dfrac{t}{\theta}\right)^{\beta - 1} \times e^{-(t/\theta)^\beta}$

where, β = shape parameter and, θ = scale parameter.

Properties of β, shape parameter

when,		
	$0 < \beta < 1$	Decreasing failure rate
	$\beta = 1$	Constant failure rate (CFR), exponential distribution
	$1 < \beta < 2$	Increasing failure rate, concave
	$\beta > 2$	Increasing failure rate, convex
	$3 \leq \beta \leq 4$	Increasing failure rate, approaching a normal distribution

The values of β indicate the likely behaviour of the failure process. The scale parameter θ covers both the mean and spread of the distribution. This parameter is also called the characteristic life, having units same as that of the failure rate. The MTTF, median, mode are calculated by applying the usual statistical methods.

20.5.2.2 Normal Distribution

From the reliability point of view, if in a structural system the failure occurs due to cumulative effects of many random factors (variables), each contributing a small amount to the total, then a normal distribution may be effectively used, following the concept of the Central Limit Theorem in statistics. As a result, when structures are affected by fatigue, corrosion and other wear-out aggressive factors, the normal distribution is used to evaluate the reliability of the structural system at any point of time.

The probability density function (pdf) of a normal distribution is a uni-modal, symmetrical, bell-shaped curve decreasing rapidly on both sides of the mode. (Refer Fig. 20.5)

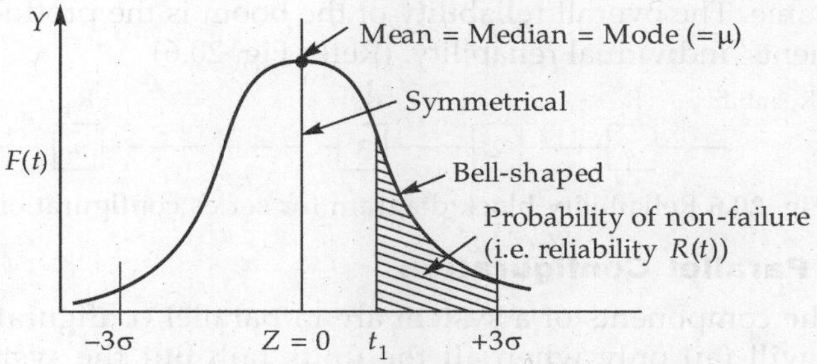

Fig. 20.5 Typical normal distribution curve.

As the curve is symmetrical, its mean, median and mode are the same. The equation of the *'pdf'* is given by:

$$F(t) = \frac{1}{\sqrt{2\pi}\,\sigma} \times \exp.\left[-\frac{1}{2} \times \frac{(t-\mu)^2}{\sigma^2}\right]$$

For most observed values of μ and σ, the normal distribution can be used as a reasonable approximation to a failure process due to the cumulative effects of wear and tear.

20.6 SYSTEM RELIABILITY

The reliability of a structural system is evaluated by identifying a suitable reliability model for failure of each of the components and, then the system reliability is assessed by applying the rules of probability. Two basic configurations are to be considered from reliability point of view.

20.6.1 Series Configuration

When a system is comprised of 2 or more components in series, it is assumed that the components are independent of each other *i.e.* the failure of one component does not alter the reliability of other components. In such cases the system reliability is no greater than the smallest component reliability. Accordingly, if $R_1, R_2, R_3 \ldots\ldots R_n$ are the reliability of components 1, 2, 3 etc in series, then the reliability of the whole system,

$$R(\text{system}) = R_1(t) \times R_2(t) \times R_3(t) \ldots\ldots \times R_n(t)$$

In a series configuration all the components must have a high reliability, if the system comprises of a large number of components in series. A common example of series configuration is the boom of an erection crane made up of 3-4 pieces joined together. For a failure-free operation of the crane, each component of the boom should carry the load safely, though the stresses in the components may or may not be the same. The overall reliability of the boom is the product of the components' individual reliability. (Refer Fig. 20.6)

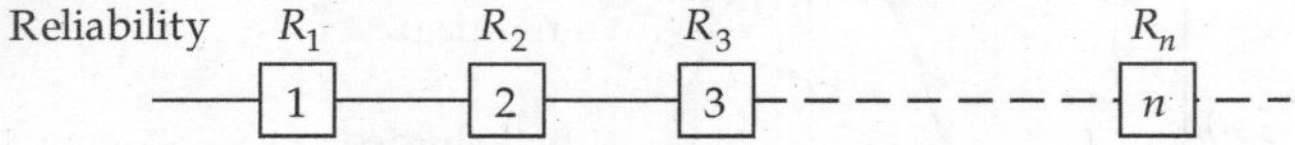

Fig. 20.6 Reliaibility block diagram for series configuration.

20.6.2 Parallel Configuration

When the components of a system are in parallel configuration, the system will fail only when all the units fail. But the system will continue to function, if at least one or more of the redundant members function properly.

The system reliability, comprising '*n*' parallel components, is given by:

$$R_s = 1 - (1 - R_1) \times (1 - R_2) \times \ldots\ldots \times (1 - R_n)$$

If a 2 component system in parallel exhibits a constant failure rate (CFR), then the reliability of the whole system will be:

$$R_s = 1 - (1 - e^{-\lambda 1t}) \times (1 - e^{-\lambda 2t})$$

$$\text{And, its MTTF will be} = \frac{1}{\lambda_1} + \frac{1}{\lambda_2} - \left\{\frac{1}{(\lambda_1 + \lambda_2)}\right\}$$

Redundant diagonals in a bridge truss are good examples of parallel configuration in system reliability. (Refer Fig. 20.7)

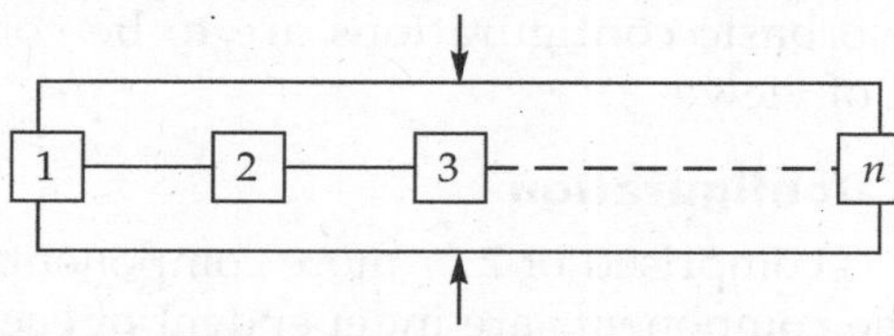

Fig. 20.7 Reliability block diagram for parallel configuration.

In a similar way, complex structural systems may have components in both series and parallel configuration combined together. These configurations are almost similar to the series and parallel configurations of resistances in an electric circuit.

Example 3. *Examine the reliability of a system when a concrete mixer and a vibrator are put in series, as shown in Fig. 20.8, the reliability of the concrete mixer being 0.90 and that of the vibrator is 0.60.*

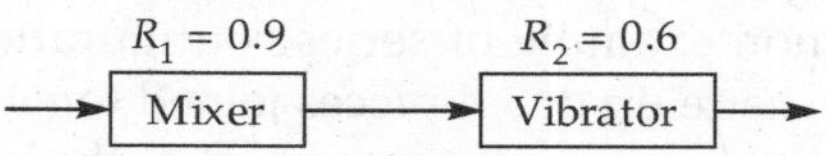

Fig. 20.8 1-Mixer and 1-Vibrator.

Solution. Since the units are in series,

$$R(\text{system}) = R_1 \times R_2 = 0.90 \times 0.60 = 0.54.$$

Example 4. *Compute the reliability of the following system when one additional concrete mixer and one vibrator are added and operated in the following configuration, as shown in Fig. 20.9.*

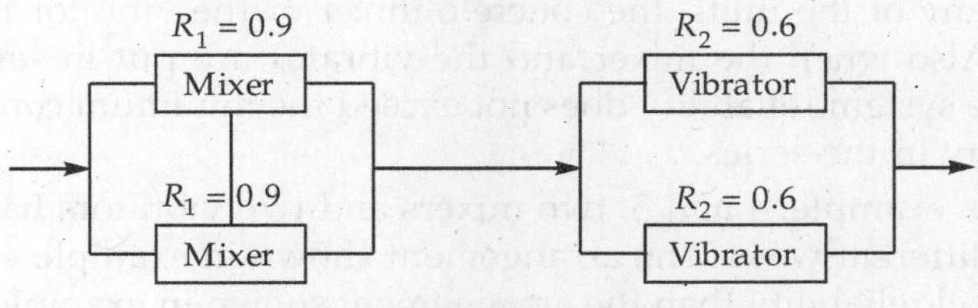

Fig. 20.9 2-Mixers + 2-Vibrators.

Solution. Combined reliability of 2 mixers put in parallel (say R_3)

$$= 1 - (1 - 0.9) \times (1 - 0.9) = 0.99$$

Combined reliability of 2 vibrators put in parallel (say R_4)

$$= 1 - (1 - 0.6) \times (1 - 0.6) = 0.84$$

Reliability of the whole system (R_3 and R_4 will be in series)

$$= R(\text{system}) = R_3 \times R_4 = 0.99 \times 0.84 = 0.8316. \textbf{ Ans.}$$

Example 5. *Examine the reliability of the system, if the mixers and vibrators of example 4 are re-arranged as shown in Fig. 20.10, their individual reliabilities remaining unchanged.*

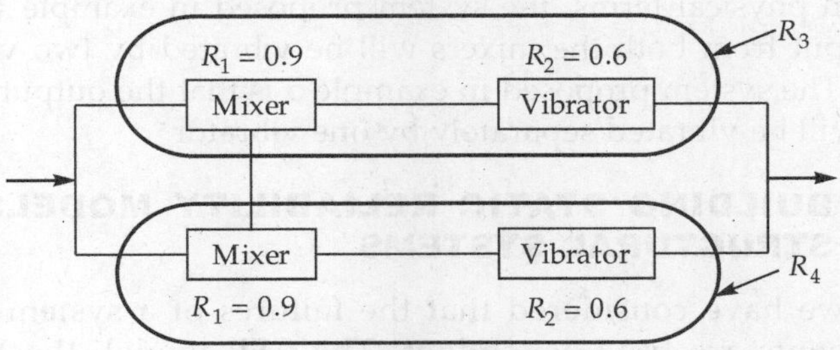

Fig. 20.10

Solution. Combined reliability of 1 mixer and 1ibrator put in series

Say, $R_3 = R_1 \times R_2 = 0.9 \times 0.6 = 0.54$

Combined reliability of the other 1 mixer and 1 vibrator put in series

Say, $R_4 = R_1 \times R_2 = 0.9 \times 0.6 = 0.54$

Reliability of the whole system (R_3 and R_4 will now be in parallel configuration

$$R(\text{system}) = 1 - (1 - R_3) \times (1 - R_4)$$
$$= 1 - (1 - 0.54) \times (1 - 0.54) = 0.7884 \textbf{ Ans.}$$

Observations. From example 3, it is apparent that the system fails if any of the units, the concrete mixer or the vibrator is out of order. Also when the mixer and the vibrator are put in series, the ultimate system reliability does not exceed the minimum component reliability in the series.

In example, 4 and 5, two mixers and two vibrators have been put in different ways. The arrangement shown in example 4 gives a high-level reliability than the arrangement shown in example 5. This is because of the following reasons.

Both the systems will fail if either, both the mixers are out of order or, both the vibrators are out of order. In that respect, both the arrangements are on the same footing.

The arrangement shown in example 5 exhibits an additional failure mode, if one mixer and one vibrator fail on separate paths. Because of this additional failure mode, the reliability of the system proposed in example 5 is less than that in example 4, though the total number of mixers and vibrators are the same in both the cases. Here lies the usefulness of evaluating reliability of systems, before they are put to use.

In physical terms, the system proposed in example 4 is that the output from both the mixers will be vibrated by two vibrators jointly. The system proposed in example 5 is that the output of each mixer will be vibrated separately by one vibrator.

20.7 BUILDING STATIC RELIABILITY MODELS FOR STRUCTURAL SYSTEMS

So far we have considered that the failures of a system and its components are time-dependent. The CFR model, the Weibull Distribution and the Normal distribution-all are time-dependent failure models based on observation of failures of many mechanical, electrical and electronic equipments and even many structural systems and these observations have been extended right from their burn-in stage to wear-out. However, it has also been observed that in the construction field, structures have also failed suddenly without exhibiting any time-dependent failure mode. Very often it is observed that structural failures have occurred abruptly when a load of magnitude greater than its ultimate strength is imposed on the structural system. These loads may be static loads, impact loads, thermal, electrical or chemical loads of varying magnitudes and these loads have to be measured in different units like, tons, degrees centigrade (in case of fire loads), cycles per second (for vibration loads) etc. In all such cases the reliability is considered as a static factor, not as a function of time.

The system reliability in such cases is the probability that stresses will not exceed strength. (Refer Fig. 20.11)

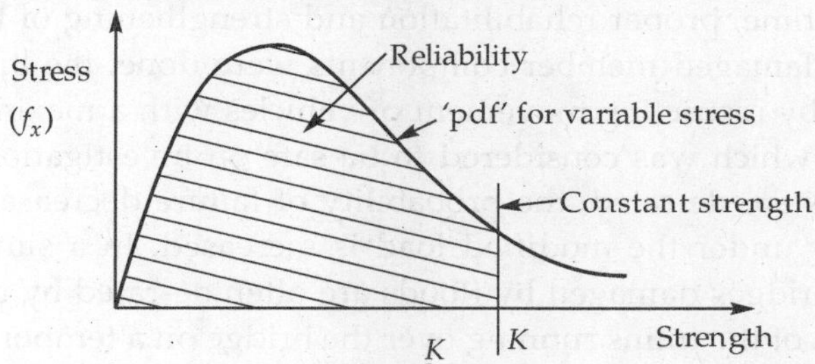

$$\text{Reliability } R = \int_0^K f_x \, dx$$

Fig. 20.11 Reliability when stress does not exceed strength.

The safety margin as evaluated in conventional design of structures is the difference between the system capacity (strength) and the imposed loads (stresses). Failure will occur on occasions when the safety margin will be less than 1.0 *i.e.* the ultimate strength is less than the stresses imposed on the structure.

20.8 DESIGN FOR RELIABILITY

As already stated, whenever a structure is designed for a pre-determined set of imposed and incidental loads and is built following certain safety norms, reliability, to a large degree, is inherently built in the system. **This reliability however does not remain static all the time.** The reliability reduces with time as additional unknown environmental stresses, accidental force, high-intensity wind and earthquake forces strike the structural components. The reliability is further reduced, if there is lack of maintenance or if it is subjected to additional loads not considered in the original design. To retain the safety and serviceability in such circumstances, it is necessary to check the reliability of the structural system occasionally and devise ways and means to augment the system reliability. The methods and procedures which are usually adopted to improve reliability in a system are described in the following paragraphs without going through complex mathematical expositions.

20.8.1 De-rating

De-rating means using a structure much below its rated capacity considered in the original design. In this respect, an example may be cited of an old suspension bridge, which could not be negotiated safely with a 12 ton loaded lorry after 50 years of its construction. Till such time, proper rehabilitation and strengthening of the worn-out and damaged member components were done, the bridge was de-rated by restricting movement of vehicles with a maximum load of 5tons, which was considered to be safe on investigations. When structures are de-rated, the probability of failure decreases and the reliability under the modified load is increased. In a similar way, railway bridges damaged by floods are often de-rated by restricting the speed of the trains running over the bridge on a temporary basis. Reliability is thus temporarily increased and safety is ensured.

20.8.2. Reducing the Dead Load of the Structural System

Reliability is often increased in the case of worn-out old structures by off-loading a part of its superfluous dead load and superimposed loads to the extent possible. Removing an existing concrete deck and replacing the same by an orthotropic steel deck reduces considerably the dead load of a suspension bridge and its safety is increased. Removing surplus materials, un-used machines from existing floors increase the reliability of an existing floor system and the floor can then be used safely under reduced superimposed dead loads for a considerable period of time.

20.8.3 Adding Redundancy to the Structural System

In case of determinate structural systems, redundant members are often added to increase the reliability. When failure modes become un-controllable as result of external environmental stresses during the service period of a structure, the structural reliability can be restored by adding redundant members in the structural system. This is required particularly for thin structural sections, whose safety margins are low. For example, redundant diagonals are often introduced in bridge trusses (Refer Fig. 20.12).

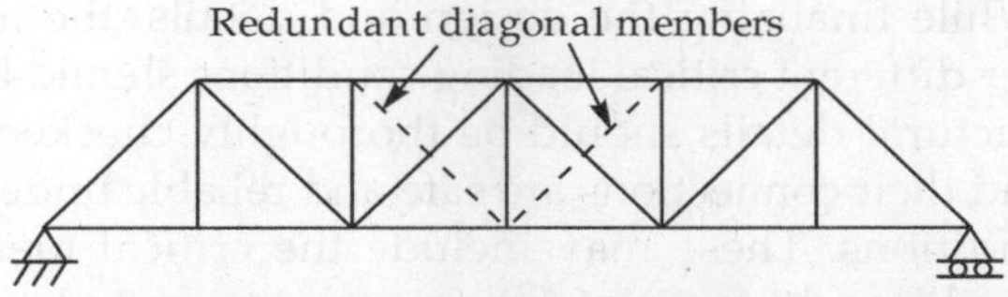

Fig. 20.12 Redundant diagonals in a truss.

Redundancy may be introduced in both the active and stand-by components of structural system. Redundancy may also be introduced by way of providing extra supports to a simply-supported member. Repairing of failed components becomes easy if there are redundant members in the structural system. However, indiscriminate use of redundant members does not add to its reliability in a proportionate way, since many of such redundant members remain inactive during most of its service life. (Refer Fig. 20.13). The dead load and the unit costs are inordinately increased in such cases. Hence the designer should optimize the use of redundant members with a view to make the design cost-effective.

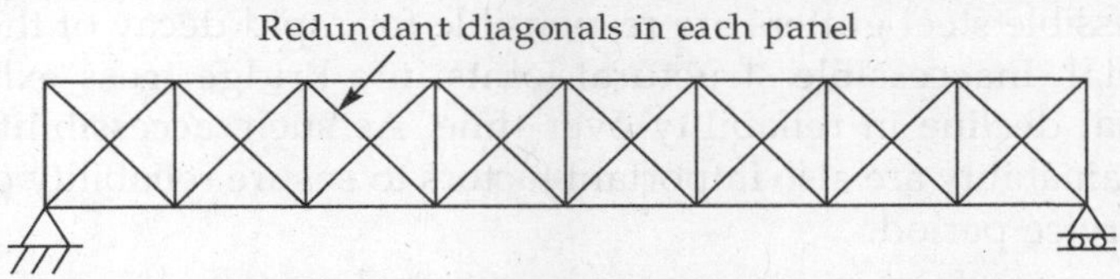

Fig. 20.13 Too many redundant members in a truss system (not a cost-effective solution, if stresses are low).

20.9 DESIGN CONSIDERATION TO AUGMENT RELIABILITY

A few simple design principles are mentioned below, which should be given due considerations in the design stage to introduce adequate inherent reliability in the system.

1. Complexity should be avoided in the structural configuration, unless it is needed for the sake of functional requirements. It is to be noted in this connection that a simple solution is often the best solution both from the safety point of view and reliability.

2. Alternate possible solutions should be chalked out and a reliable safe structural system should be adopted keeping in view their ranking in reliability as well as cost-effectiveness.

3. If an alternative design using a new technology is safe and reliable, the scheme may be adopted if costs permit to do so.

4. While finalizing the design and details, the likely failure modes under different critical loading conditions should be identified and the structural details should be thoroughly checked so that the members and their connections are safe and reliable under the critical loading conditions. These may include the critical member joints, welding details, anchorages of reinforcements, support connections of thin box sections subjected to twist etc.

5. If redundant members are introduced proper stress-strain analysis should be done to ascertain correctly the load-sharing of the members.

6. The specification of materials should conform to the reliability requirements.

7. System reliability during the service period can be retained, if all critical joints in the structural system have easy access for maintenance. Reliability becomes doubtful if such accesses are denied. Stair roofs and inaccessible monitors are often damaged due to seepage of rain water and corrosion effects. Clogging of outlets of inaccessible steel gutters are responsible for rapid decay of the steel material. Inaccessible structural joints in a bridge truss exhibit a gradual decline in reliability over time. As such, accessibility and maintainability are also important factors to ensure reliability during the service period.

20.10 SAFETY, RELIABILITY AND QUALITY CONTROL

The principal objective of ascertaining reliability in construction of different types of structures is to find out a design solution and construct a structure which will be both **'economically viable' and 'reliably safe'.** The term 'economically viable' means that reliability has been established in the design and construction of a structure with due consideration to its life-cycle costs, which includes the cost of construction and the yearly maintenance costs during the whole service life of the structure. The term 'reliably safe' demands a design solution which would provide an adequate in-built reliability to ensure that damages from all kinds of safety hazards are within an acceptable limit. To meet these twin goals, the following aspects are to be considered in the design and construction of structures.

- **In the design process:** Specifications, stress-strain analysis, identification of the failure modes and their likely effects, criticality analysis and review of design

- **During construction:** Quality control and quality assurance for materials and workmanship, testing of materials, as necessary for the purpose.
- **During service period:** Assessing reliability of the structural system periodically and take proper maintenance, repair and rehabilitation programmes.

In this connection, it may be noted that, the reliability of a product (or a structure) can be assured from the failure rate of a similar product. Example may be drawn in this regard of concrete cubes prepared at site and later tested for 7-day and 28-day strength to assess the reliability of the concrete poured, from which the cubes were drawn. Similarly, reliability of the steel material may be assessed from the results of the testing of samples for various properties and analyzing statistically the results for acceptance of the material. The entire quality control and quality assurance measures have strong bearings on the issue of assessing the reliability of the product.

In fact, reliability is closely related to the quality of a product and is often considered a sub-set of quality. Quality is achieved through a comprehensive quality control and quality assurance programme. On the other hand, reliability is related to the time period a product or a structure continues to function and remain operational as per functional requirements.

If a structural system exhibits continued degradation (due to adverse environmental stresses), wear and tear (due to continued vibration or reversal of stresses) or if there is lack of maintenance and repair, the number of failures of such structures increase with the age of the structures. For this reason, the system reliability should be assessed periodically and a scheme of minimum repair should be arranged to prevent un-called-for safety hazards. On the other hand, a faulty design may render a structure extremely unreliable right from the beginning of its use and may fail abruptly causing serious injury to the users with damages to property. Again, due to wrong handling, a structure may become unsafe and unreliable. Site splicing of steel derrick members using wrong bolts, improper maintenance, and operational error of a traveling crane etc may be cited as examples in this regard.

20.11 PERFORMANCE EVALUATION OF STRUCTURES

Two basic aspects of any structural system which is of interest to the designer and constructor are the nature of the structure itself and its behaviour under load. These general concepts are sometimes not understood properly in their proper perspective and are often confused with each other. A structure may be defined as a system consisting of several components (members) and the description of the structure merely defines their material specifications, sizes and connection details with no functional information. Only when a structure is subjected to external loads (including its own weight), we may observe its behaviour. In the design process the members of a structure are proportioned assessing the likely behaviour of the structural system under different load combinations, some of which may be critical from the safety point of view and some may be not so critical. However, in actual practice, the behaviour of the overall structural system may deviate from the anticipated desired behaviour, resulting in erratic performance under certain combinations of loads during its service life. In order to verify this, a **'performance evaluation'** should be carried out periodically during its service life, which would give important feedback data for determining the maintenance strategy and/or replacement or rehabilitation partly or wholly.

Reliability of a structural system falls below the desired level, when faults (which may be only in one component or more) are detected during the course of performance evaluation. Faults may be evaluated analytically if sufficient data is obtained to build a deterministic mathematical model. On the other hand, for structures subjected to external loads of stochastic nature, the performance evaluation is sometimes done through simulation techniques, which is a difficult and time-consuming process. Because of these hindrances a probabilistic subjective approach is adopted in many ill-structured problem situations to assess reliability, residual life and future safety hazards.

20.12 AVAILABILITY OF A STRUCTURE FOR USE IN SERVICE LIFE

Periodic maintenance, repair, rehabilitation and even the answer to the often-raised question as to whether a structure should be dismantled or not depend on the outcome of the performance evaluation process, whatever method may be adopted to for the purpose. In a dynamic system, like a rotating machine or a moving crane used for construction, the system is subjected to repair immediately after it stops working and the equipment is allowed to run when the faults are rectified. In such cases the working life of the system consists of a chain of fault-free service, a sudden break-down, then an inspection, again some time is spent for repairs. The system's actual availability for fault-free safe use can then be expressed as:

$$\text{Availability} = \frac{[\text{Uptime}]}{[\text{Uptime} + \text{Downtime}]}$$

where Uptime = average working life of the unit and

Downtime = expected time between the system failure and completion of repair.

It is obvious that a system's availability in service life is increased either by increasing its inherent reliability or, by reducing the time needed for repair. Availability can therefore be defined as the percentage of the time a component or a system would remain operational over a specific time interval. As there is uncertainty of any system remaining operational over a period of time, availability can also be expressed as the **probability** that a structural system or any of its components would be performing their required functions at any given point of time when used under specified working conditions.

To augment the availability of a system in running condition, it is often suggested to use a stand-by (say a batch mixer or a vibrator or an additional mobile crane). The result may be beneficial in some cases. But the hidden problem in installing a stand-by is that failures of stand-by units are not detected until the unit is required to operate. These are called **dormant or undetected' failure modes.** Addition of redundancy in the structural system may also be mentioned here. Dormant failures may create safety hazards if the redundant components are corroded over the years un-noticed or, if there is a fracture un-noticed in a stand-by machine or, if there is a manufacturing defect in the redundant or stand-by components. This is one of the reasons why the whole system sometimes fails with catastrophic safety hazards in-spite of having stand-by components in the system.

20.13 MAINTAINABILITY

The primary criterion for deciding to repair or replace by a new one is an economical one. For important projects like bridges, marine structures, irrigation projects and industrial structures, it becomes almost impossible to replace a whole structure by a new one without seriously disturbing the present available facilities. But replacement by components may be rather easy from practical point of view. Again in many cases, particularly for building components like roof, gutter, walls etc it is the standard practice to carry on with repair and periodic maintenance for as long as it is possible in a cost–effective way. In many cases preventive maintenance may reduce the frequency of failures, but repeated preventive maintenance (as in the case of roof) restricts the availability of the facility for regular use.

The alternative may be a **predictive or diagnostic maintenance programme**, in which the performance behaviour of the structure is evaluated from time to time, monitored and, at an opportune time, a proper corrective maintenance/repair measure is adopted to prevent failure. Safety hazards due to fatigue failure, wear and tear of materials can be averted, if such predictive maintenance is applied to machines and equipments also, for which the operating conditions can be monitored and distressed components may be replaced in time.

In order to adopt predictive maintenance measures, a **bottom-up analysis** is usually done. This comprises estimating the maintenance/repair needs, urgency of repairs and assessing whether there is any immediate chance of failures. This assessment is done component-wise with proper records. The same assessment is done for higher-level assemblies and ultimately to the whole structural system. As for example, in case of bridges, the individual components may be the expansion joints, handrails, pavement/track, bearings etc. Higher level s may constitute the girder assemblies, the pier caps and the piers. Lastly, the whole system is covered. Individual tasks for repair/maintenance can be decided directly from site observations and the detailed engineering of the repair and maintenance work may be carried out following the provisions of codes, past experience and their results. Simple spreadsheets are often adequate for evaluating the costs aand the time likely to be spent in such maintenance efforts. Alternatives may also be explored with comparative cost figures for taking management decisions. In many cases, however, cost-benefit trade-offs are done heuristically to achieve an optimum acceptable level of reliability and safety.

20.14 LIABILITY, WARRANTY AND SERVICE CONTRACTS

Liabilities in construction projects are generally fixed from anticipation of the likely failures and their effects. The records of previous failure modes and the analysis of their effect on life and property form an important data base in the estimation of the probability of recurrence of such failures. In the absence of sufficient data for quantifying the probability of recurrence, the following qualitative ranking is usually done which forms the basis for fixing liability and corrective actions:

- **Catastrophic failure:** loss of life and major damage to property.
- **Critical failure:** system failure with performance reduced to an unaccepted level
- **Marginal:** structure is degraded
- **Negligible:** minor failure of components.

The failure mechanisms may be overloading, environmental distress, natural calamity, vibration, accidents, human faults in operation etc. While some of these failures are beyond the control of the contractor or user, a great number of failures can be prevented by effective monitoring and quality control. Liabilities are fixed in this regard by including suitable clauses in the contract documents. The question of fixing liability in the contract relates to the events when failures occur due to negligence, non-application of mind, or wrong specifications adopted in materials used on job and adopting wrong unsafe methods of construction. Liability in all such cases shifts the responsibility of repair and maintenance from the user (consumer) to the contractor (manufacturer).

Liabilities are fixed for failure modes which may damage newly-built structures reducing their reliability and level of safety with likely injury or death to the users. It is always taken for granted that the contractor will assess the failure modes and would build the structure accordingly taking necessary precautions. But, in reality, there is always anticipation of structural deficiencies resulting to unsafe conditions. In order to cover this, clauses for warrantees are often introduced in the conditions of contract.

A **warranty** is a contractual guarantee binding a manufacturer for satisfactory performance of the product produced by him. Similar warrantees are often demanded for work done by a contractor in the construction field. In case if a structure fails, or is rendered unsafe due to wrong doings by the constructor or if a structure does not perform satisfactorily (as in the case of a leaky roof), costs of all rehabilitation work or repairs are allocated to the constructor. In such cases, the contractor is supposed to do all repair work including supply of all materials and labour during the warranty period. Usually this warranty period extends to 6 months, one year, one or two rainy seasons (for water-proofing work) or in special cases for several years. Replacing an entire unit, repairing, replacing defective components and/or reimbursing a fixed amount as penalty to the owner are some of clauses included in a warranty. However, misuse, or wrong use or uncontrolled damages to structures are not covered by warranty clauses.

In some cases, particularly when the operation of sophisticated machinery is involved in a project or when the entire construction is a very large conglomeration of different types of structures and the contract includes the supply of machinery also, a **service contract** is executed between the owner and the contractor. This service contract is in fact an extended warranty. They may be for a 5-year period, a 7-year period or even more for big construction projects like power plants and river-valley projects. During this period, the contractor is responsible for successful commissioning of all units and machinery, their repair and maintenance, training to owner's representatives so that the whole unit may be run by them in a safe condition without any safety hazards after the project is finally handed over by the contractor to the owner.

QUESTIONS

1. Define the term reliability. How the reliability of a structural system alters at different times during service life of a structure, depending on its response to imposed loads and environment.
2. Define the term safety. In what respect is it different from the term reliability?

   What is the relationship between the reliability and the probability of failure of any structural system?
3. Explain how the reliability of any structural system can be assessed from the probability density function (pdf) of failures of similar structures.
4. What are the measures of central tendency in a typical probability density function of failures?
5. What is meant by MTTF, variance and standard deviation of a failure distribution?
6. Describe the characteristics of a typical Bathtub Curve. Draw a typical Bathtub Curve showing the range of early failures, random failures and wear-out failures of a structural system.
7. Write short notes on the following:

   (*a*) Constant failure rate model

   (*b*) Time-dependent Weibull distribution

   (*c*) Normal distribution
8. What is meant by system reliability? How reliability is assessed

from a series configuration or a parallel configuration?

9. "Reliability does not remain static all the time": What is the significance of this statement? Cite examples from real-life structural systems to justify the statement.
10. What are the usual methods adopted at site to augment the reliability of a structural system? How reliability is altered if redundant elements are added to a structural system. What is the limitation to adding such redundant members to a structural system?
11. How the terms quality, safety and reliability are related to each other? What is meant by a design solution which is 'reliably safe'?
12. Explain how the reliability of concrete products is ascertained from cube tests. What is the function of quality control to have a reliable product during the construction period?
13. "Reliability is a sub-set of quality." Elaborate the statement.
14. Write short notes on the following:
    (*a*) Availability
    (*b*) Maintainability
    (*c*) Uptime and down-time of equipments
    (*d*) Predictive maintenance to retain the desired reliability of a structural system
15. Elaborate the terms liability, warranty and service contracts. How are these features related to the reliability of a product? In what manner these are binding on an equipment manufacturer?

CHAPTER 21

Controlling Safety Hazards in Industrial and General Building Construction Work

21.1 INTRODUCTION

It is common experience that safety hazards cannot altogether be avoided during any construction work involving buildings, particularly tall buildings and industrial structures. The chances of accidents are more where more and more hazardous working conditions exist. Generally accidents at construction sites occur mainly due to two factors, namely:

- unsafe working condition
- and/or unsafe acts of operation.

The probability of accidents are great when these deficiencies are compounded with ignorance, complacency or laxity in supervision or due to employment of unskilled, unfit or ill-trained labour for any hazardous job. Under these circumstances, it is incumbent on the project manager to see and ensure that the construction work is carried out in the field with utmost precautionary measures and control.

21.2 HOW TO CONTROL UNSAFE WORKING CONDITIONS

The most common cases of unsafe working conditions are listed below with suggestions of controlling them to avoid accidents.

- **Unsafe approach** to the work spot: The approach to the spot where the men on duty would have to reach or the place where they have to stay and work for the duration of their work in a day should not be slippery, slushy or made up by loose compressible filling material. The pathways should be rough, preferably made by brick-flat soling or plain cement concrete or made up by compacted brickbats or similar materials as available. This is particularly important when the ground becomes slushy when the excavation work is in progress in the rainy season.

- All machinery should be well-guarded with **cages or partitions** and unwanted entry of outsiders should be prevented at worksite by proper fencing.
- There should be proper house-keeping for storing of innumerable small items, particularly if they are hazardous.
- All hazardous and **inflammable materials** like petrol, diesel oil, lubricants and paints should be segregated and stores in a proper fashion complying with the rules and guidelines.
- Whenever there are programmes of **night work** for concreting, shuttering or piling work, the work site should be adequately illuminated to avoid accidents. All electrical safety norms should be followed in such cases. Even otherwise, the work site should have adequate lighting arrangement for reasons of safety.
- **Improper ventilation** often causes major accidents, as in the case of working inside underground sewers or inside covered water tanks or inside covered oil tanks. If the work involves welding work inside a confined space, the chances of suffocation from fumes are all the more great, which is to be avoided at all costs.
- Workers should be provided with **protective gears** when they have to work in excessive heat or in extreme cold climates. The efficiency of the people on job deteriorates rapidly if they are exposed to hot humid weather or if they have to do their duty at night under severe cold climate. Their dress materials, caps and shoes should conform to the prevailing climate and they should be advised to wear helmets whenever they are on duty at site.

21.3 HOW TO PREVENT UNSAFE ACTS OF OPERATION AT SITE

Violation of the standard engineering practice and lack of coordination at site are the primary reasons of unsafe operations inviting accidents. In a big industrial construction work they may be hundreds of workers engaged and they have to perform their assigned duties without infringing on the work of others. They also have to operate various types of machinery like pile driving rigs, compressors, pumps and motors, pavement breakers, mobile cranes, dumpers, concrete mixers etc. The placement and operation of all these machinery should be done in a planned manner with deployment of skilled workers on job. While operating machines the following general guidelines are to be followed:

- No machine should be allowed to be run by any **unauthorized person**.
- The **speed limits** for mobile cranes, dumpers etc., should be assigned within the work site.
- Transferring or **shifting materials** from a height by throwing down should be banned.
- **No machine, particularly the crane booms should be left untied** or uncared-for at site after the day's work.
- **Safety latches,** hooks and clamps etc., are to be used as per norms.
- **No person should stand under a load** when it is being lifted off the ground.
- **All mobile equipments should be properly shut down after work,** shifted to their respective garages and the machines should be locked. They should not be left here and there at site.
- **All machines should be regularly oiled, cleaned** and their moving parts should be checked before starting at the start of the day.
- The supervisor on duty at site should see that all site **activities are well coordinated** with no friction among workers and the running of the machines and the transport vehicles are synchronized.
- Machine operators should have **adequate experience** to run the particular machine on which they have been deputed. In case of welders it is to be ensured that they have the requisite welder's certificate. Similarly, all vehicle operators should have the proper license for the type of the vehicle they would be handling.
- The **slings** used for erection work should be flexible, light and without any knots or worn-out parts. The clamps used on job should not be slide over the wire ropes.
- In specific site conditions, where there are chances of accidents from falling of men and material, **nylon nets** should be used for protection.

21.4 SAFETY WHILE WORKING AT HEIGHTS

A major part of the total number of worksite accidents are caused due to workers falling from a height or due to impact on persons from objects falling on them. In all cases of such accidents, except but a few, there are chances of spinal injuries, head injuries, broken limbs and injury to the nervous system of the person injured. Fatal or near-fatal injuries are most commonly experienced in such cases, resulting in loss of valuable human lives, disruption in the work schedule and chaos at site. With a little care and precaution this unacceptable state of affairs can be avoided. With this end in view, the following guidelines are suggested for compliance at site.

- When any work is being carried out **overhead**, the area below the work spot should be cordoned off with necessary caution board on the ground, mentioning that people are at work.
- Necessary **ladders, scaffolds and working platforms** should be provided for the safety of the workers working at heights. All temporary structures built for this purpose should be strong enough to take the load of the working people and live loads. When the height is more than 3 metres, the ladders should have landings and side rails. All working platforms should be provided with toe guards for the protection of the workers.
- Workers working at heights should wear **shoes with clean non-slippery soles,** free from mud or slush.
- All **temporary structures** built for working at heights should be certified by the supervising authority before they are put to use. All defects in the temporary structures should be rectified to the satisfaction of the engineer-in-charge.
- All **ladders** should be at least 1 metre wide and securely tied with any permanent structural member to prevent sliding or sudden displacement.
- No worker should be allowed to **climb ladders with unusually heavy weights.** These weights should be lifted separately by separate lifting devices.
- **All access to the work spot at heights must be kept free from loose materials.** No erectable material beyond the load-carrying capacity of a working platform should be placed over the same.

- The **lifting arrangements** should be made ready and certified by the supervisor before start of the lifting operation. The wire ropes, tools, tackles and pulleys should be checked for this purpose. Any worn-out wire rope must be replaced by new ones.
- No **loose planks** should remain projected from the end of any working platform and these planks should be properly tied to their supports.
- All **tools** required by the workers at their elevated platforms must be kept at a safe distance away from the edge of the platform.
- **Walking under any overhead traveling crane** is strictly prohibited.
- All people working inside a shed where cranes travel frequently overhead, must wear **helmets** for their personal safety.
- All **suspended scaffolds** must be built strong enough to take the design load. Design of these suspended scaffolds should have adequate factor of safety on the conservative side and their suspension mechanisms should also be properly designed and certified by the engineer-in-charge.
- When erection work is carried out over any existing workplace where people are engaged for other work daily, as in a running workshop, it is practicable to schedule the **erection work in off-duty hours.**
- **Fire prevention systems** should be kept ready in case of any emergency.
- Whenever workers do erection or maintenance work inside any shed, in which there are **open tanks containing water or inflammable liquids,** these tanks should either be properly covered or they should be emptied when people will work overhead.
- People should be discouraged from **gossiping** when ascending or descending a ladder.

21.5 SAFETY RULES FOR HANDLING AND OPERATING LIFTING MACHINERY

Intelligence, care, common sense and training are required for handling overhead cranes and other lifting devices like derricks, mobile cranes, winches with lifting blocks and various other machine devices used in construction work. In tall buildings, it is a common practice to deploy hoists or tower cranes. The workers handling these devices should be selected on the basis of their level of training, previous work experience and physical fitness. No compromise should be made in these matters. As the management is ultimately responsible for any untoward incident or accidents, involving loss of life and property, the selection of the right personnel for crane operators and erectors should be given due importance right at the stage when the organizational set-up is built up.

In addition, the following precautionary measures are to taken at site for safety reasons:

- The operator should know the **safe working** load of the crane and hoisting devices being operated by him.
- The **weight of the erectable item** to be lifted should be determined. The snatch exerted on any material to be lifted is more than the static load of the item. The operator should see that this snatch load does not exceed the load carrying capacity of the lifting equipment.
- The **tools, tackles, winches, pulleys** and all other lifting gadgets used are to be checked before use.
- The cranes fitted with jibs have different load carrying capacities according to variations in the **inclination of the boom.** These restrictions should not be violated.
- For outdoor cranes, the erection work should be done under favourable **wind conditions** only.
- **All loads should be properly secured** and the load is to be tested by wire ropes in taut condition and then lifted above.
- The men on ground should keep a **safe distance** of 1 metre when a load is being lifted.
- The **loads to be lifted must be controlled** all the times and they should be attached to hooks in such a way that the centre of gravity of the load coincides with that of the lifting mechanism . Make sure that all wire ropes carry equal loads and there is no slack rope while the lifting operation is on.
- Undue **jerk during lifting** is to be avoided and the loads are to be gently landed on their temporary supports at heights and anchored there before releasing the hook.
- Whenever a wire rope sling is tightened by operating the lifting mechanism, the workers should avoid their **hands**

being trapped by the rope. All workers handling wire ropes should preferably wear **gloves**. They should never be allowed to ride over the load being lifted.

- No **swinging** is permitted while a load is being lifted.
- Lift loads only after making their seats ready at height. Never keep **loads suspended in air** for an unnecessary long time.
- **Protect the wire ropes from the sharp corners** of loads by introducing packs or timber wedges.
- All wire ropes and other lifting tools and tackles are to be properly **stored and maintained** by regular oiling.
- While lifting operation is in progress, established standard **signals** are to be used by the workers for communication purposes.
- When a load is being carried from the one end of the fabrication shop to the other end by an EOT crane, **the load must be carried high enough to clear all obstacles** on the floor.
- When a mobile crane is deployed for lifting operation, the crane must be stabilized and rested on sleeper cribs at the rear end so that the crane **does not topple** while lifting a load.
- All personnel engaged in operation and maintenance of cranes and erection work must be selected considering their **experience, efficiency and level of training** and physical fitness.

21.6 PERSONAL SAFETY DURING WORK AT HEIGHTS

There are innumerable items of work which require persons to be engaged to work at considerable heights. Notable among these are brickwork, plaster and painting jobs to outside walls of multi-storied buildings, structural erection work of sheds, buildings lifts of chimneys, ESP structures, overhead tanks etc. In all these cases people are exposed to all types of risks associated with work at heights. To avoid accidents from falling down, they must be trained and motivated to take certain basic precautionary measures, which are stated below, which are in addition to those already listed earlier

- **Good quality helmets, safety belts, gloves and jackets** should be provided for those people who have to work at heights.

- For welding work at heights, the welders are to be provided **gloves, goggles and boots,** in addition to additional **helping hands**, both on the ground and at heights where the welding work would have to be carried out.
- Warning signs to be put on ground and the area of welding work should be **cordoned of.**
- No **inflammable material** should be kept on ground where welding work would have to be done at a height. The temporary cables and the welding sets are to be properly grounded (earthed).
- The workers working at heights in structural erection work should have adequate **supply of bolts, nuts, drifts in bolt baskets** and the connecting gussets and cleats should also be kept ready. The erection work should not be halted and the workers should not be kept waiting at heights, because of **wrong supply or non-supply of the above items.** The workers should also have their tools ready at hand in tool boxes.
- **Welding generators and gas cylinders** should not be installed over temporary working platforms. They should be placed at suitable places on ground and the cables should be long enough to reach the work spot.
- All statutory and **standard safety precautions** are to be taken in welding and gas-cutting jobs at site.
- **Good house-keeping** is always preferred to untidy work at site. Some extra time spent in this respect help in the long run avoid many unacceptable incidents.

21.7 CONTROLLING SAFETY OF STRUCTURES

Any construction work, be it structural steelwork, RCC or masonry, high or low, having shallow or deep foundations can be said to have been carried out satisfactorily and safely, only when safety is assured, not only for the personnel or equipments, but also for the structures already erected or structures already existing by the side of the new ones. A few instances are cited below to lay emphasis on how to assure structural safety during construction jobs.

General

All construction work should so carried out that no adjacent existing structure is damaged. Sometimes elaborate safety arrangements are needed, as in the case of piling jobs, to control transfer of vibration from pile driving operations to adjacent buildings. Contractors very often have to face litigations from the owners of adjacent buildings, if they are not mindful of the structural condition of those structures and their distances from the spot of pile driving work.

Foundation work

1. The **depth of foundation** of any structure should not preferably be less that that of any adjacent one, if that foundation is quite in the vicinity of the new one. Ideally, all foundations, old and new should have the same depth, in order to transfer the superstructure load uniformly over the ground.

2. There should not be any **overlapping of new foundations** with existing ones. No foundation should be constructed by the side of any existing piling work or retaining wall, without investigating their capacity for resisting lateral thrusts.

3. Construction of new foundations over any **filled-up ground** is always prone to foundation-settlements in future. In such cases, the ground soil should be first compacted or stabilized if, at all any new construction has to be built there. Alternative designs with pile foundations should be thought in such cases instead of shallow footings or raft.

4. A **minimum depth of foundation** in firm soil is to be provided to all structures, following standard engineering practice and provided in the code.

5. For **machine foundations,** no machine or equipment load should be put over it, until the foundation concrete attains its full strength after 28 days.

6. All **block machine foundations** should be cast in one go without any vertical or horizontal joint in the concrete. In case of very heavy turbo-generator foundations suitable dowel rods or shear keys are to be given if concreting has to be interrupted.

7. For **pile foundations,** the piles are to be arranged in such a way that the distance between any two piles is not less than three times the diameter of the piles. Outer piles should be driven first, then, the inner piles are to be driven.

8. All **reinforcement rods** in foundations should have adequate cover for protection against corrosion.

9. In case of heavy seepage from underground water during foundation work, proper and adequate **dewatering arrangements** are to be made to keep the water table low and keep the excavated

foundation pit dry during shuttering, placement of rods and concreting. Well-point dewatering systems may have to be adopted, where the water table and the seepage is exceptionally high due to soil characteristics.

10. **Collapse of sides** of deep excavated pits is to be prevented for the safety of plant machinery, equipments and workers. The foundation work may become highly unsafe if proper attention is not given in this respect.

11. **Pre-cast RCC piles** should not be driven very close to old existing structures to avoid damage due to vibrations.

12. All **foundation pits** should be provided with **adequate enclosures** for reasons of safety. This is particularly important for pits dug where vehicular traffic and pedestrians are present. Such pits should be provided with danger signals and caution lights at night also.

Superstructure

Industrial superstructure mainly comprises of structural steelwork, reinforced concrete as well as masonry constructions depending on the functional requirements for operational reasons. While masonry structures are common for ordinary buildings like time office, security corners etc., reinforced concrete is used for tall framed structures, chimneys, water tanks, administrative buildings and machine supports. Similarly, structural steelwork has its usage in process buildings, chimneys, tall *ESP structures*, power hose and many other important installations. For uninterrupted work and future operational safety, it is necessary to maintain and ensure safety while erecting all superstructure components. To this end in view there are certain general safety guidelines, stated below, which must be followed meticulously by the constructors.

Reinforced Concrete Structures

The **formwork** for all reinforced concrete structures are to be designed to withstand the loads from the green concrete, as well as the imposed loads from the equipment and men working during the concreting work.

The **staging** supporting the forms are to be adequately braced to withstand wind loads. Staging built for inclined slabs should be strong enough to withstand horizontal thrust of the superimposed loads due to the inclination of the slab.

Old **unserviceable formwork** should not be used and all formwork should be cleaned and oiled after stripping.

The **stripping time and method of stripping** should be strictly maintained for safety. Advancing the stripping time may cause cracks or even failure to the green concrete. On the other hand, too much delay in stripping a formwork creates hindrance to usual curing of the green concrete. Only skilled men should be engaged for stripping of formwork.

The **reinforcements** are to be evenly placed so that there are enough gaps between rods for the green concrete to pass through. Reinforcements should be welded to avoid congestion if necessary. In important connections of column to beams, where there are lot of reinforcement rods, welding of rods is the best option. Welding of reinforcements should be done in accordance with the recommendations and guidelines given in **IS: 2751** and **IS: 9417**.

Head-carrying of rods from fabrication yard to site should be done with care so as not to hurt others. Rods should have **safe distance** from bare electric wires.

Rough **handling,** shock loading and dropping of reinforcement rods from a height should be avoided.

Temporary planks should be suitably placed over reinforcement mesh for slabs so that people walking over the same are not caught in the gaps.

Staging should not be unequally loaded during concreting to avoid failure. This point is often overlooked during heavy concreting work. Dumping of green concrete should not create shock waves or the green concrete should not be heaved at one place beyond the carrying capacity of the staging supports of formwork. It is to be remembered that, once a prop fails, the load carried by it is shifted to the adjacent props making them vulnerable to failure. Many a structure has failed in this manner while the concrete is in progress.

Safety of Steel Structures

Steel structural members, being lighter than similar concrete members, pose safety problems from wind loads if not properly addressed to during erection work.

Steel columns should be fixed with their holding down bolts and cross ties should be provided as soon as possible after alignment of the columns.

Cross beams should be provided with seating cleats and rested there before being fixed to the columns.

The **steel trusses** are vulnerable to wind forces which may destabilize them if not properly braced or tied after erection or during off-duty hours.

Roofing sheets to be properly fixed to the purlins to avoid dislodgement during storms. Special attention should be given while fixing corner sheets.

Crane girders, being top-heavy, should never be left on top in an un-tied condition.

All lifting mechanisms should be so arranged that **slender members** are not laterally bent during erection.

Protruding **corners of gussets** and cleats should not be allowed to be bent on being hit with other structural components during erection.

The **erection scheme** should be so scheduled that no structural member is overloaded beyond its carrying capacity during erection. To this end in view, it is imperative to think twice before putting erectable materials on light floors or walkways made of light angles and chequered plates.

Impact from erectable items during erection is to be avoided.

The erectable items should be lifted according to their **sequence of erection,** to avoid accumulation of unused erectable members on top.

21.8 EFFECT OF ACCIDENTAL MISHAPS ON HUMANS

The human body is a very complex mechanical system, which readily reacts to any external forces bringing about various types of changes. Though it is difficult to predict exactly the magnitude and nature of the forces to break the resistance in a human being, the application of any strong mechanical force brings about several immediate effects, which can be summarized as under:

- The external applied forces may interfere directly with the physical activity of the accident victim.
- There may be mechanical damage.
- There may be secondary or immediate biological effects on the immune system.

It is to be noted that, the above-mentioned externally applied forces acting on a human being, when he or she meets an accident at a construction site may be in the form of (*a*) impact from falling from a height, (*b*) resultant shock (*c*) transfer of mechanical vibration, when struck by a vibrating machine (*d*) exposure to hazardous chemicals or, (*e*) exposure to extreme heat, fire, inclement weather condition etc. The ultimate result may be a minor injury, a near-fatal accident or a fatal one.

21.9 INJURY TO HUMAN BEING ON TRANSFER OF MECHANICAL VIBRATIONS

When an accelerative force acting on a human being is large, the body and its internal mechanisms are affected. Excessive vibration transferred to the body through regular operation of jack hammers, riveting machines or pavement breakers may cause vascular, neurological and muscular distresses. Again, low-frequency, large amplitude motions out of repetitive movements of hands or repetitive wrist rotations may cause long-term fatigue problems and numbness of hands. In such cases common therapeutic treatment is necessary to bring back the limbs to its proper ability. Usual therapeutic treatment results in an enhancement of limb functions through the use of rehabilitation medicine.

Sometimes, vibration from running machinery creates a feeling of discomfort and apprehension, once the stimulus is felt. The extent of discomfort depends on the direction, magnitude and frequency of the applied vibratory force and also on the posture of the body receiving the vibration. The discomfort is acute when a whole floor vibrates under the feet of the workers during runnings of various types of machinery installed over suspended floors. This type of vibration has to be minimized at all costs through proper design modifications or rehabilitation processes. However, in some cases like joy rides a person may feel exhilarating feelings. In general, unpleasant subjective responses to vibrations arise from three basic causes, threshold of perception, complexity of motions and limit of tolerance of any particular person.

21.10 INJURY FROM MECHANICAL SHOCK

Mechanical shocks which may incapacitate a person include shock and injury due to fall from height (most common in construction sites), impact from a strong object, blasts of hazardous chemicals and gases and explosive compression or de-compression. Impacts often cause a rapid change in the body velocity and shock forces of large magnitude. The impact experienced in falls from a height may cause bruises, crushing of tender tissues, fracture of bones, rupture of vital organs and concussion.

A person is reported as suffering from bruises, when there is a superficial small area of slight tissue damage with little or no blood-shed. In some cases, bruises caused from impacts may result in blood clotting in the injured region.

A crushing injury causes a compression of tissues, usually between the impinging solid causing the impact and the underlying bones in that place. Sometimes the tissues are irreparably damaged due to crushing effects.

Bone fractures are caused often due to twisting of the human body, sustained forces causing displacement of the bones or due to effect of impact from blunt objects. Sudden fall from heights are very often found to be the primary cause of bone fracture.

Internal injuries with hemorrhages are caused when soft tissues are displaced or snapped due to impact. Such injuries are often found to be fatal.

Sometimes persons are thrown up during an explosion or **failure of mechanical running systems.** In such cases, feet or ankles may be injured due to tissue destruction or bone fracture in an area close to the application of the force. If the upward velocity reaches 5 to 10 ft/sec. the person may be thrown up causing such damages. However, the energy absorbed by the fractured portion of the body often protects other body structures higher up. Sudden impacts from high-velocity flying objects may cause irreparable tissue disruption associated with bone fracture, causing trauma to the victim.

Impacts may also cause longitudinal displacements which may topple a person from a high platform on which he is standing to the ground level. Such accidents happen, when the slings of a crane with or without load swings very dangerously and hit a person working at a height.

21.11 HEAD INJURY

Injury of the head is possibly the most dreaded effect of any impact either from fall from heights or due to other causes. Any injury to head due to impact or otherwise may result in superficial bruises, which are easily curable, or fracture of the skull with concussion of the brain. This may create pain, dizziness through disorientation, depression and even unconsciousness and loss of memory. In a very critical situation there may be almost instant fatality from a head injury. Since the head is held by the neck muscles, any impact on the head gives the neck a 'flying' sensation, resulting in a strong possibility of dislocation of vertebral joints. Dislocation of a few upper joints of the vertibra may not be critical, but any injury or crushing of the spinal chord may turn out to be most critical.

21.12 RESPONSE OF THE HEAD AGAINST IMPACT

The head response can be somewhat sustained, if the person hit by an impact is conscious of the coming missile and if the impact is not so severe or if it is padded, as in the case of a football player hitting a ball by his head. However, in a construction site, workers may be hit by a falling bolt, nut, bunch of washers, a hammer or other implements falling on his head from above. Since the impact in all such cases is sudden, the person is wholly unaware of the impending danger and often succumbs to the blow.

The ill-effect of a **head impact** is directly proportional to the velocity of the missile, the area of impact and the transfer of momentum. Immediately after a person is hit by a falling substance, compression waves flow to the brain. As the brain material is mostly incompressible, even a small impact can cause substantial damage to brain tissues. **Concussion** results from a blow to an unsupported head. When the head is supported there is concussion due to compression of the skull and increase in the celebro-spinal fluid pressure. Investigations reveal that, when the impact velocity is about 30 ft/sec. about 200 pound-inch of energy is absorbed in 0.002 seconds resulting in acceleration to the head to the order of 47 g. Brain concussions are a distinct possibility in such cases.

Skull fracture occurs when the deformation is high, though skin and hair of the skull may reduce the impact effects slightly. Impact from a high-velocity blunt object may create localized skull fractures. On the other hand, a low-velocity blunt blow, insufficient to cause any initial depression to the skull, happens when a person falls or crashes on another object. However, if the energy of such blows is large, cracks will appear on the skull radiating from the point of impact. The skull has both weak and strong areas and the effect of a blow depends on which area of the skull has been hit.

From investigations, it is known that a skull can be fractured at an average energy of 600 pound-inch from the impact. This is the critical energy situation when the head hits a flat surface due to fall from a height of only about 5 feet. It is therefore easily understood why a free fall even from a small height can be critical for a victim under the most unfavourable circumstances. On the other hand, an **impact on a sharp corner** requires only a tenth of the above energy to facture a skull.

21.13 EFFECT OF SHOCK AND VIBRATION ON WORKERS' PERFORMANCE AT SITE

When workers are subjected to **repeated shocks** at short intervals, their performance level comes down even if the shock is of low magnitude. On the other hand, exposure to continuous vibration may cause degradation of mental faculties. Moreover, vibration is often associated with noise, which makes a worker unmindful to his immediate tasks, leading to accidents. The whole body of a driver vibrates when he drives a transport vehicle and the effect is more severe when the vehicle is old and the springs are ineffective. At construction sites, performance level is low when machines are manually operated. A 'stiff' control over a vibrating mechanism hurts more with lesser and lesser performance levels. Hands can feel a vibration at frequencies between 2 to 6 Hz. However, the performance level can be temporarily maintained if the workers adapts to the low frequency vibrations.

21.14 PROTECTION AGAINST HEAD INJURY

From the above it is obvious that a head injury is the most formidable danger likely to be faced by a construction worker in various work situations mentioned earlier in this text. To avoid fatal accidents against impact, **protective helmets** should be used compulsorily by all site staff, site workers, irrespective of whether they are working at height or not, by vehicle and machine operators and even by the outsiders visiting the site. In order to achieve this objective, helmets of different designs are available in the market. All these protective helmets should have two basic impact-reducing properties, namely, proper distribution of the impact load over as large area of skull as possible and the interposition of the energy-absorbing facilities.

The first condition is served by helmets with a stiff hard shell and the second requirement is met by providing proper support pads over the whole side of the skull to avoid any injury from a relatively shell object. A better way to distribute loads would be in those helmets which are provided with web suspensions. But a helmet with contact padding would permit lesser slippage during impact. Consequently, better quality helmets are now provided with a combination of contact padding and web suspension. These pads are usually made up from rubber, felt, foam-plastics like polystyrene resulting in lower transmitted accelerations. However most helmets, as available in the market make a compromise of the above necessities, but provide protection against impact to a great extent.

Injury Due to Crash

Another major safety hazard to workers engaged at construction site is due to crash or frontal accidental exposure to shock with vibration. These crashes occur when there is a collision with a running vehicle, an impact from a vehicle during its backward movement or running over under a vehicle. The crash injury is fatal when there is head-on collision of two vehicles with a force having acceleration between 40 g and 50 g for durations of less than 0.1 second. When there is no **lap belt** or any other type of lateral restraint to the driver, the above limit of tolerance is estimated to be between 10 g and 20 g. Consequently, all drivers of commercial vehicles engaged in transportation of construction materials and other fabricated items should be compelled to use lap belts for their body protection in case of a crash with another running vehicle. For automobile head-on collisions there are recorded typical deceleration pattern for the car structure under the driver's seat which are given below.

Impact velocity (MPH)	Underbody peak deceleration (in multiple of gravity)
20	22 g
30	35 g
40	55 g

From the above it is apparent that any collision with impact velocity greater than 40 miles per hour will have a very serous and fatal consequence on the driver and other persons travelling in the vehicle. In view of this it is imperative on the part of the management to select a properly-trained driver with valid commercial license to ply in a construction site or on the highway for transportation of materials and fabricated items.

21.15 PROTECTION FROM HAND-TRANSMITTED VIBRATION EXPOSURE

Workers engaged in operating vibrating tools like pavement breakers and hand-held drill machines are subjected to serous injury to their nerves if they are continuously exposed to such vibrations. To mitigate this effect, it is necessary to isolate the hand and arm from the vibration of the hand-held vibrating power tools. This can be done in two ways:

- The most common method is to **isolate** the handles of the power tool using springs or dampers.

- The other method is to **modify** the power tools itself so that the primary vibration created by the tool is counter balanced by an equal and opposite vibrating mechanism. To get this relief, the power tools are to be specially designed.

Gloves are usually provided to the workers to handle power tools. While conventional gloves may not help much to give relief to the worker from vibrations, the so-called anti-vibration gloves are most effective in such cases. It will be worthwhile to mention in this respect that there are numerable types of specially-designed gloves to withstand not only vibrations, but also attack from chemicals and other corrosive substances. Though these gloves are costly, they are most effective in specific cases.

Other preventive measures to tackle with hand-arm vibration problems can be accomplished by **minimizing the duration of exposure** to vibration, wearing proper sufficient clothes to keep warm in cold climate and maintaining the power tools in good running condition. However regular medical check-up would be required, if workers who are handling power tools develop vascular deficiencies or nerve disorders.

Among other physiological responses to vibration-related forces, mention may be made of cardio-vascular, respiratory, skeletal and metabolic disorders. **Chronic illness** in the nervous system may be produced when the hand is exposed to intense vibration, such as power tools, hammers, grinders and riveting guns. Numbness of fingers are a very common symptomatic result of such exposures. In addition, the tendons, muscles, ligaments and nerves of the hand and arms are likely to be damaged due to repeated movement of the hand relative to other parts of the body. Repeated keyboard operation may cause flexure to the wrist for white-collared employees.

21.16 SUBJECTIVE RESPONSES TO ADVERSE WORK SITUATIONS

Workers sometimes feel extreme discomfort due to sitting or working in an **awkward position** for a long time during the working hours. Mention may be made here of insufficient space for moving about a running machine, long wait at a height for the erectable materials from the ground, improper driver's cushion for tractors etc. The extent of discomfort depends on the posture of the person and the duration of the exposure in such a condition. People become edgy and irritant, even quarrelsome in these circumstances. The authority in charge of the construction activity should investigate and find out the root cause of the worker's odd behaviours in such cases and do the needful to ameliorate the grievances. A little effort in such cases may avert major mishaps at site.

21.17 EFFECT OF BLASTS AND SHOCK WAVES ON THE HUMAN BODY

When hazardous chemicals, blasting material or LPG etc., are handled at site there are always risk of **inadvertent blasts** caused from these inflammable materials. Even if there is a cylinder blast at a distance from the worker's duty spot, he may be hurt due to the rapid changes in the environmental pressure and sudden increase in the noise level beyond the tolerable limit. The air-filled cavities inside a human's body is affected by such blasts and his ears, lungs and the gastrointestinal tract are likely to be damaged, even if he is not directly hit by the blast. The internal mismatch of the organs may also displace tissues inside a body following a strong blast.

The ear is very sensitive to blast waves. **Ruptures of the ear drums** are common manifestations of such injuries. The ear is vulnerable to short-duration blast waves. Peak pressures of only a few psi may damage the human ears. However, individuals show marked variations in response to sudden noise and blasts, even if they are not injured. There are cases of workers falling from heights when there is a sudden blast very near to the person. In case of blast injury, compared to the dynamic mechanical effect, the static pressure is the most injurious part of the blast waves.

Induced blasts below water (as in the case of bridge wells) are diffused in water. But blasts in open air (as in road works) may be fatal. These blast waves move instantaneously through the thoracic walls producing injurious effects to the tissues. On the other hand, high-explosive blasts may cause lung hemorrhage causing an almost instant fatal injury to the victim.

Intermittent exposure to even **low category blasts** (originating from road work) may cause psychological disturbances like loss of memory, abnormal emotions, irritant behaviour and loss of attention to the work. All these after effects may invite greater trouble to the worker and to others working with him at site.

Considering all the above ill effects of blasts at worksites, there should be stringent rules for controlling blast-related injuries. Some such regulations as observed usually at sites are stated below:

1. All blasting material should be in charge of a responsible person and blasting items are to be issued at site strictly as per requirements following written order from the site-in-charge. The supervisors should see that the blasting materials are fully utilized on job without leaving behind any unexploded blasting material. The blasts should be carried out at site as per standard safety norms for using such materials.

2. All LPG cylinders, gas containers and other inflammable store materials should be kept segregated from blasting materials and proper precautionary measures are to be taken for storing all these inflammable materials as per norms.

3. There should a well-drawn contingency plan for rescuing blast victims. They should be given immediate first-aid and removed to the nearest hospital where there are facilities of treating burn injuries and treatment of trauma cases.

21.18 SAFETY HAZARDS DUE TO HUMAN FATIGUE AT WORK PLACE

Fatigue is primarily a psychological state of mind when a person's performance capacity is diminished with loss of mental alertness and efficiency. Monotonous work with no respite, regular overtime work without rest, no worthwhile holidays, long hours of duty schedule, pressure of meeting datelines of production—all these factors contribute to the development of fatigue stresses in the mind of workers. Such fatigue stresses are also present in vehicle drivers who are engaged in transportation of construction materials and finished products over a long distance covering several days and nights to reach the designated site. Inordinate delay on the way at octeroi gates also contributes to the fatigue of the transport men.

Accidents at work places due to fatigue happen as the worker concerned becomes inattentive, careless and mentally sluggish. Environment factors like a sultry weather also contribute to generating fatigue stresses in workers, particularly who have to work under the sun. In addition, poor lighting arrangement, excessive noise and vibration cause fatigue. Even if there is no fatal accident in a work site fatigue-related misbehaviour, carelessness and irresponsible acts on the part of the workers cause numerous accidents, which are often not reported, but the work is interrupted no doubt.

A site may be free from accidents if all the above causes which create fatigue are eliminated by closely watching the production process and analyzing to find out the root **cause of human fatigue.**

It is to be investigated why a person is unable to deliver his job and why he is unable to adjust to the work schedule and follow the regular safety procedures at site, in spite of his being an efficient skilled worker. If necessary the schedule of activities should be modified and suitable incentives should be given along with a regular duty hour with compulsory rest days and leave in times of urgency.

21.19 GUIDELINES FOR SAFETY AND OCCUPATIONAL HEALTH

The Willium-Steiger Act of 1970 formulated the Occupational Safety and Health Administration (OSHA) in USA to control and oversee industrial and agricultural activities. Later, British Standards Institution have formulated a detailed guideline called OHSAS (Occupational Health and Safety Assessment Series: 18001–1999, revised in 2007) dealing with the problems of occupational health and safety. Though the OSHA was prepared to meet the requirements of the activities in the process industries mainly, the guidelines are equally applicable for building and industrial construction projects as well. The following are the principal features of this assessment series:

- Participation of the employees
- Assessment of hazard scenarios
- Analysis of the probable hazard situations
- Operating procedures to combat hazards
- In-house training of personnel
- Selection of implementing agencies
- Safety review in different stages
- Assessing equipment integrity
- Controlling non-routine activities
- Review of all changes and their effects
- Investigation of any incident of accident
- Contingency planning and response to disaster situations
- Safety audit

The reader will note that all the above aspects brought fore in the OSHA guidelines have been discussed in detail in various chapters of this book with special reference to safety in construction, both during the period of project implementation and also in the service period. The OSHA guidelines also formulate system safety programmes and lay stress on risk assessment also. The risk assessment should cover the legal problems, threat and danger assessment with emphasis on continual improvement.

Among the health hazards mentioned in OSHA guidelines are the following cases which are very much applicable to construction workers.

- Hazards from smoke, fumes, gases vapours and dust particles.
- Hazards from noise, vibration and thermal stresses
- Biological problems and occupational diseases
- Hazards from running machines
- Psychological problems of the workers

The OSHA also gives excellent guidelines about how to evaluate hazards, their threshold limits, method of rating different hazards and their control. The OSHA series as mentioned above is a very well documented standard, which is compatible with **ISO 9001:2000** and **ISO: 14001-2004** series and should be consulted by the contracting agencies and owners alike for achieving a satisfactory solution to the safety hazards at construction work sites.

According to OSHA, the rate of incidents of safety hazards may be expressed in terms of incidence rate, expressed as:

$$= \frac{[(\text{No. of recordable injuries}) \times 200000]}{(\text{No. of employee hours worked})}$$

which is based on the standard of 100 full time workers at 40 hours per week for 50 weeks = a factor of 100 × 40 × 50 = 200000. In this calculation, any incidence of accident may be a minor injury, a fatal one and even the period of absence of workers due to illness.

QUESTIONS

1. Explain how the frequency of accidents is related to the unsafe working conditions at a construction site.
2. How unsafe acts of workers bring about fatal accidents?
3. What precautions should be taken by a person working at a height?
4. How movements of people should be restricted and regulated at site to prevent accidents?
5. What are the basic safety rules for operating machines at site?
6. What are the precautions to be taken by erection crew while lifting erectable fabricated items?

7. Explain the utility of safety belts, hand gloves and goggles in a work site mentioning the area of uses.
8. What safety precautions should be taken by a contractor to avoid litigation from damages to adjoining buildings when he is carrying out excavation work for foundation?
9. What are the ill effects of noise and vibration on the workers at construction sites?
10. How a human body reacts to an impact or impulsive force? What are the possible ill effects of a hit by an object falling on him?
11. Under what work environment fatigue stresses are developed in workers? What is the remedy of removing the ill effects of fatigue?
12. Write short notes on the following:
    - Head injury due to fall from a height.
    - Effect of blasts on human beings
    - Subjective response of workers to adverse environmental conditions
    - Bone fracture and internal injury for accident victims
    - OSHA guidelines for safety
13. Explain how the probabilities of fatal accidents can be minimized at a construction site where the movements of mobiles cranes, transport lorries and dumpers are too frequent.

CHAPTER

22 Disaster Management at Construction Sites

22.1 INTRODUCTION

When a community or a region is struck by a sudden calamity in which the normal life is totally destroyed with serious loss in life and property we call it a disaster. Such a situation is frequently encountered in India during floods, earthquakes and wind related hazards. When the environment is polluted to the extreme we call it an environmental disaster, as happened in the Bhopal gas tragedy killing and maiming thousands of people in the vicinity of the factory. Sometimes it takes generations for a community to recover from the ill effects of such a disastrous situation.

There are other kinds of disasters which happen at construction sites paralyzing all activities of the site, sometimes killing people and damaging irreparably the machines, equipments and structures. Though such incidences are localized at a particular site, they also cast a long spell over the future of the project on many occasions. The following are a few examples of such disasters:

- At construction sites in hilly areas, flash floods often destroy and wash out all assets lying on the river bed, paralyzing the work.
- A complete road network is often disrupted due to failure of a road bridge due to flood, earthquake or due to many other extraneous reasons. Similarly railway bridges are also damaged disrupting rail traffic.
- Disasters often strike a particular facility like a boiler or a chimney disrupting the output of a whole power plant.
- Failure of a newly-erected structure may bring about complete halt to the work schedule, attracting penalty as well as loss in revenue to the constructor.

- A wrong design or a wrong handling may cause an irrepairable damage to critical structural components which may take a long time to replace.

Disasters occur at a particular site very often suddenly without any notice and people are caught unawares, thereby they get little time to take any immediate remedial measure and the loss of life and property happens too often very conspicuously before the eyes of everybody present at site. Disasters at construction sites are of different kinds, namely:

- Man-made disasters due to design or construction fault or an outbreak of fire.
- Disasters due natural calamities, like cyclone, earthquake, flood, landslide etc.

In the previous chapters, detailed discussions have been made to explain the different types of safety hazards which are likely to be encountered at a construction project due to above reasons with suggestions about the ways and means to avoid or minimize the ill effects of such disasters. It is also to be noted that there may be complete disaster even during the service life of the structure causing immense damage to life and property with disruption in basic amenities. The impact of a disaster in a construction project is felt in manifold ways, namely:

- Loss of life
- Injury to workers deployed at the time of a disaster
- Damage to structures
- Disruptions in the usual communication network and power lines
- Disruption in the transport system
- Loss in productive activities
- Delay in work schedule
- Loss of business for the contractor engaged in construction
- Idle labour
- A general panic in case of a serious disastrous situation

Some of the above consequences of a disaster are felt immediately after the accident or disaster, as in the case of loss of lives, injury, structural failures and idle labour. The ill effect of a major disaster is also felt for a long period after the incident in the form of disruption in communications, loss in business, delay in the work schedule etc. The activities of the site come to a standstill causing immense dismay and helplessness on the part of the management in case the secondary effects disrupt the site activities for an inordinately long period.

Consequently, in the interest of both the workers and the management, as also for achieving the scheduled date of completion of the project, it is absolutely necessary to control and monitor all site activities in such a way that disasters are avoided. On the other hand, if disasters fall on a site inevitably, as in the case of natural calamities, the management should be mentally and physically prepared in advance for all the eventualities and manage the after effects of disasters in a systematic way so that the damages to life, property, machines, equipments and the structures are the least possible. Thus the disaster management has become now-a-days as important apart of overall management activity along with the management of the day-to-day work at site.

22.2 ELEMENTS OF A DISASTER MANAGEMENT PLAN

The following are the principal aspects of any fruitful disaster management programme at a construction site:

Planning to avoid disasters at site

- **Planning** for prevention of disasters to save construction machinery and infrastructure elements.
- **Zone-mapping** of site according to degree of safety hazards
- Preparation of a **contingency plan** to combat a disaster.

Actions at site

- Deployment of the **rescue teams** with necessary tools and implements to rescue disaster victims.
- Providing medical attention and immediate **relief** to the victims of disasters
- **Rehabilitation** plan for the victims
- **Removing all debris** from the site of a disaster so that work may be resumed once again

Post-disaster action plan

- **Re-scheduling** the work packages for the balance items of work and deploy men and material accordingly
- **Estimating the losses** and arranging further budgetary support for restoring loss due to a disaster

From the above, it may be observed that losses due to disasters can be mitigated to a great extent at the design and planning stages, if a practical pragmatic approach is taken to evaluate the likely safety hazards in case of a disaster at site. This can be done only if all necessary safety features are incorporated in the design as per standard engineering practice and guidelines of the national codes as applicable for any particular construction project. The concept of value engineering and its proper application help tremendously to examine and evaluate all future safety hazards in a systematic way.

Zone Mapping

The zone mapping of any construction site is done by classifying and dividing the construction site as per their threat perception against any likely disaster. This includes a prohibitive zone, a restricted zone, a warning zone and a safe zone. The threat perception is altered from time to time in conditions of flood, a landslide or a wind-related disaster. Some part of the ground area or the upper working platforms may be put under the restricted zone or a warning zone to ward off and caution outsiders against likely hazards from work activities. Similarly, though storage spaces housing ordinary hardware items may be open to all, the store area for hazardous chemicals should be kept out of bounds for people not concerned with the use of such chemicals. Such segregation of the site area reduces to a great extent the chances of unauthorized entry inside prohibited areas.

Contingency Plan

Contingency plans include the organizational preparedness, rescue and relief operations along with the supporting action plans. Several contingency plans may have to be thought of depending on the likelihood of a worker's accident due to fall from a height, wash-out due to flood, a serious mechanical failure, sudden disruption in electricity supply at night or the outbreak of a sudden fire at the work site. The organization should be prepared to meet all such eventualities with proper mobilization of men and equipment, tools and tackles for rescue or relief in case of an emergency. A contingency evacuation plan should also be thought of in case of a disaster involving the whole site, when all workers have to be evacuated within a short notice.

While preparing the organizational set-up for meeting emergency situations in times of disasters, the following operational structure has to be developed:

1. A central level command should be fixed who can take decisions.

2. The middle level management people should be selected for carrying out contingency plans.

3. The workers should be motivated in the rescue operations.

4. Necessary first-aid facility should be kept ready at site at all hours.

5. Necessary vehicles should be kept ready for shifting a victim to the nearest hospital if necessary.

6. To control disruptions due to mob violence, for which help may be necessary from the local administration.

7. To arrange for sending communications to local administration and the relatives of the victim.

8. The area affected by a disaster should be cordoned off.

9. The damaged structural components should be provided with temporary supports to avoid further damage.

10. It is to be ensured that further damages do not occur to the existing structures through chain reactions. This is particularly important where structures are likely to be damaged by erosion after a flood.

The professional persons involved in the contingency operations at site may include the management personnel, the engineers, the physicians, the workers of the rescue team, people manning the vehicles or directly involved in rescue operations and also the contractor himself to supervise the rescue operations. A good effective co-operation and team spirit are needed to execute any contingency plan immediately after a major disaster, as time becomes an important factor in the rescue operations and first-aid. Any inordinate delay in these aspects may aggravate the miseries of the victims, creating more chaos at site. It is to be borne in mind that an immediate post-disaster rescue operation enhances the confidence level of the victims and lot of trouble may be avoided. As for example, if the people trapped in a fire can be rescued promptly without any loss of life, the rescue team always gets the accolade for their actions. On the other hand, an inordinate delay may lead to loss of lives inviting public protests and outcry over the inefficiency and lack of contingency of the organization.

22.3 EXTREME DISASTROUS SITUATIONS AT CONSTRUCTION SITES

In a construction site, an accident may be a localized one involving only a few people or a part of the work area. For example, it is a common occurrence at site that a person gets injured while working with various tools and machines or a person may even be seriously hurt due to fall from a height. This may prove to be a serious consequence to the worker himself and the work section may be temporarily paralyzed due to such accidents. However, such incidents, though localized, should not be taken in a casual manner and all efforts should be taken for the rescue and treatment of the victim without any delay.

However, a construction site often is engulfed by a much bigger catastrophe like a fire hazard, a complete wash-out during flood or damages during strong cyclones or tornado. Such natural calamities take the toll of life and property covering a large area surrounding the work site and therefore the damages become part of the whole deluge of the region. In such cases the management must have good co-ordination with the local administration to get immediate relief as necessary for tiding over the ill effects of the disaster.

22.4 POST-DISASTER ASSESSMENT OF DAMAGES

The post-disaster response must be quick and efficient not only for the rescue of the victims, but there must be a quick assessment of the damages incurred by the organization due to a disaster. The future activity schedules can be framed properly, if the damages can be assessed and recovery mechanisms are initiated at site without any delay. In this respect the following aspects should be given utmost importance:

The debris created by any disaster must be removed from the site as quickly as possible. Sometimes, machines are immobilized, mobile cranes are bogged down in mud, construction materials are buried under such immediately after a flash flood. Again, plant, machinery and timber formwork may be irreparably lost in fires. Sometimes an important structural component or a part of the constructed facility may be damaged. A completed structure may also collapse during loading. In all such cases, it is necessary first to remove from the site all damaged and unusable materials as quickly as possible and a realistic estimate should be prepared to ascertain the quantum of losses in monetary terms and assess the extent of damages.

Necessary budgetary support is to be provided to repair or replace the items damaged in a disaster.

A fresh plan and work schedule is to be prepared considering the extent of damages to the structural components. It so happens that, in many cases, the previous work schedule gets so disturbed that a lot of preliminary rehabilitation and replacement work are needed to be completed before starting the regular work schedule. After a major disaster, some of the machines and equipments may be damaged and may become out of service. All such machines and equipments are to be repaired immediately after a disaster so that all these machines can again be utilized on job. Some machines, if badly damaged, may be out of use for a considerable period. They may have to be replaced.

22.5 ANTICIPATING ON-COMING DISASTERS AND CONTROLLING SITE ACTIVITIES

At many sites the environment and geological conditions are such that flash floods, landslides or wind-related hazards are anticipated during a particular season or at a particular time of a year. Mention may be made here of the following disaster situations:

- Damage to plant, machines and construction materials on the river bed, where there are instances of flash floods every year during monsoon.
- Landslides occur frequently after monsoons in hilly regions
- Construction sites along the coastal belt of India are prone to cyclonic storms, heavy rains and corrosion.
- Industrial construction sites are often likely to be affected by environmental pollution from fumes and gases of the industry itself

The safety hazards likely to be encountered in the above situations can be effectively avoided and controlled or the damages can be minimized if the project authority takes timely measures to protect the plant, machinery and other materials. This can be done by keeping a regular contact with the nearest meteorological departments to get advance warning for the natural calamities. Such contacts are all the more necessary where the site is situated at such a place that it is likely to be inundated from water released from a nearby reservoir or dam. In fact, many construction sites near the Himalayan region are winded up before the monsoon to avoid disasters due to sudden flash floods.

Safety engineering at construction sites has developed to a considerable extent and workers are vigilant so that the impending hazards are controlled by effective application of known accident-prevention or disaster-prevention procedures. There are elaborate basic safety norms which are incorporated in the safety codes which should be followed in this respect. Controlling an impending disaster at a construction site requires vigilance, presence of mind, coordination and advance planning to meet the dangers. Sometimes crisis situations may crop up suddenly without any prior notice and leave little time to think about the correcting steps. A contingency plan is absolutely necessary to meet such situations to achieve satisfactory results.

22.6 MITIGATION OF FLOOD DISASTERS

For sustainable development and safety of completed construction infrastructure and all other facilities it is necessary to mitigate the ill effects of flood disasters in India, as the Gangetic flood plain comes under devastating floods every year. Vast areas are submerged under flood water due to melting of the glaciers in the Himalayan region and the flood condition further worsens when extra water from the reservoirs and barrages are released simultaneously. So far as the disaster management in our country is concerned, the vicious after-effects of floods are felt by the general public at the cost of their life and property. As durable solutions are often eluded, the flood victims get themselves entangled in indebtedness year after year. The construction projects, whether those under construction or the completed ones are equally affected by floods causing tremendous loss of the owners of such installations. Sometimes the on-going projects are halted and delayed for years together because of the recurrence of floods and disruption in the transport and communications.

It is noteworthy that the Government of India has recently woken up to the problem and have enacted **The Disaster**

Management Act in 2005, for preventing and mitigating the disastrous effects of recurrent floods by initiating a coordinated response mechanism to meet any disaster situation. As a follow-up of the enactment of this act, the following disaster management authorities have been set up:

- A **National Disaster Management Authority** under the Chairmanship of the Prime Minister
- State Disaster Management Authorities under the Chairmanship of the respective Chief Ministers
- Constitution of a National Disaster Management Force
- Setting up of a **National Institute of Disaster Management**

The act also provides for constitution of a **National Fund** for Disaster Response and National Fund for Disaster Mitigation. The act also provides rules and guidelines for the states, local bodies and Panchayats in disaster management. The National Institute of Disaster Management formulates and organizes the training modules for disaster management, undertake research and implement the human resource development schemes for this purpose. **A National Disaster Response Force** has also been constituted for the purpose of building up a specialist trained force to tackle effectively a disaster situation. In addition there is a **Calamity Relief Fund (CRF)** to provide long-term assistance to the flood victims. All these measures would help in maintaining the human resources and their output levels, which are most essential for setting up and develop any worthwhile industry or infrastructure in a region.

The people affected by flood and erosion face hunger, malnutrition, shortage of clothes, particularly warm clothes in winter and they are compelled to live under make-shift hutments with acute health problems. Most of these flood victims suffer from long indebtedness. A long exposure to such wretched condition takes out from them the vital energy needed for any productive output in the industrial, agricultural and construction sectors. To keep the local economy in proper shape, it is therefore absolutely necessary to look after the flood victims, which would also help indirectly the construction industry which are likely to come up in a flood-prone region.

QUESTIONS

1. How would you differentiate between a man-made disaster and a natural calamity?
2. State what preventive measures should be taken to protect timber items from the onslaught of fire at a construction site?
3. What may be the immediate effect of a construction site inundated by flood water?
4. State how a rescue operation should be initiated at site after a major accident at site?
5. What is meant by a contingency plan? What is the utility of drawing a contingency plan?
6. Write short notes on the following:
   (*a*) Zone mapping for disaster prevention
   (*b*) Post-disaster assessment of damages
   (*c*) The Disaster Management Act
   (*d*) Calamity Relief Fund
   (*e*) National Institute of Disaster Management
7. What are the management functions to be carried out immediately after a major disaster at a construction site?

APPENDIX A-1

List of Important Safety Codes in Construction Work

List of important Indian Standards related to safety in construction published by Bureau of Indian Standards, Manak Bhavan, 9, Bahadur Shah Zafar Marg, New Delhi 110002.

IS: 1641-1988	Code of practice for fire safety of buildings (general): General principles of fire grading and classification
IS: 1642- 1989	Code of practice for fire safety of buildings (general): Details of construction
IS: 1643-1988	Code of practice for fire safety of buildings (general): Exposure hazard
IS: 1644-1988	Code of practice for fire safety of buildings (general): Exit requirements and personal hazard
IS: 1645-1960	Code of practice for fire safety of chimneys, flues and flue pipes
IS: 1646-1982	Code of practice for fire safety of buildings (general): Electrical installations
IS: 1904-1978	Code of practice for structural safety of buildings: Shallow foundations
IS: 1905-1980	Code of practice for structural safety of buildings: Masonry walls
IS: 3594-1991	Code of practice for fire safety of industrial buildings: General storage and warehousing including cold storage
IS: 3696 (Part 1)-1987	Safety code of scaffolds and ladders (Part 1): Scaffolds
IS: 3696 (Part 2)-1991	Safety code for scaffolds and ladders:

IS: 3764-1992	Code of safety for excavation work
IS: 4014 (Part 2)-1967	Code of practice for steel tubular scaffolding: Safety regulations for scaffolding
IS: 4081-1986	Safety code for blasting and related drilling operation
IS: 4082-1996	Recommendations on stacking and storage of construction materials at site
IS: 4130-1993	Safety code for demolition of buildings (second revision)
IS: 4912-1978	Safety requirements for floor and wall openings, railings and toe boards (first revision)
IS: 5121-1969	Safety code for piling and other deep foundations
IS: 5916-1970	Safety code for construction involving use of hot bitumen materials
IS: 7205-1974	Safety code for erection of structural steelwork
IS: 7293-1974	Safety code for working with construction machinery
IS: 7969-1975	Safety code for handling and storage of building materials
IS: 8989-1978	Safety code for erection of concrete frame structures
IS: 13415-1992	Code of safety for protective barriers in and around buildings
IS: 13416-(Pt1)-1992	Recommendations for preventive measures against hazards at work places (Part 1): Falling material hazard prevention
IS: 13416-(Pt2)-1992	Recommendations for preventive measures against hazards at work places (Part 2): Fall prevention
IS: 13416-(Pt3)-1994	Recommendations for preventive measures against hazards at work places (Part 3): Disposal of debris
IS: 13416-(Pt4)-1994	Recommendations for preventive measures against hazards at work places (Part 4): Timber structure

IS: 13416-(Pt5)-1994	Recommendations for preventive measures against hazards at work places (Part 5): Fire protection
IS: 13430-1992	Code of practice for safety during additional construction and alteration to existing buildings
SP-7	National building Code of India
SP-70	Handbook on construction safety practices

Important safety guidelines published by Indian Roads Congress, New Delhi

IRC: SP-44-1994	Highway safety code
IRC: SP-55-2001	Guidelines for safety in construction zones

Important design standards to meet safety and functional requirements in construction

1. Standards published by Bureau of Indian Standards, New Delhi.

IS: 456-2000	Code of practice-plain and reinforced concrete
IS: 800-2007	Code of practice for general construction in steel (Third revision)
IS: 875-1987	Code of practice for design loads (other than earthquake) for buildings and structures Part-1: Dead loads Part-2: Imposed loads Part-3: Wind loads Part-4: Snow loads Part-5: Special loads and load combinations
IS: 1893 (Part 1)-2002	Criteria for earthquake resistant design of structures: General provisions and buildings

2. Standards published by Indian Railways.

Steel Bridge code	Published by Directorate of bridge and structures: Indian Railways, Second revision-2004

3. Standards published by Indian Roads Congress

IRC: 5-1998	Standard specifications & code of practice for road bridges **Section-1:** General features of design

IRC: 6-2000	Standard specifications & code of practice for road bridges **Section-II:** Loads and stresses (Fourth revision)
IRC: 21-2000	Standard specifications & code of practice for road bridges **Section-III:** Cement concrete (plain and reinforced)
IRC: 40-2002	Standard specifications & code of practice for road bridges **Section-IV:** Brick, stone and block masonry
IRC: 24-2001	Standard specifications & code of practice for road bridges **Section V:** Steel road bridges
IRC: 22-2008	Standard specifications & code of practice for road bridges **Section VI:** Composite construction (Limit state design)
IRC: 78-2000	Standard specifications & code of practice for road bridges **Section VII:** Foundations and substructure
IRC: 18-2000	Design criteria of pre-stressed concrete road bridges (Post-tensioned concrete), third revision.
IRC: 83-1999 (Part 1)	Standard specifications & code of practice for road bridges **Section IX:** Metallic bearings.
IRC: 83-1987 (Part 2)	Standard specifications & code of practice for road bridges **Section IX:** Elastomeric bearings
IRC: 83-2002 (Part 3)	Standard specifications & code of practice for road bridges **Section IX:** POT, POT-cum-PTFE, PIN and Metallic Guide bearings.
IRC: 89-1997	Guidelines for design and construction of river-training and control works of road bridges (First revision)

The above gives a list of only the important guidelines and standards usually needed for general construction work of buildings and bridges. There are many other specific guidelines for design and construction of special structures and there are also separate safety guidelines for repair and rehabilitation of bridges and buildings. For marine structures and irrigation structures additional important safety features have been provided by the concerned regulating authority. The reader should consult them as and when needed before introducing safety and reliability features in the design and construction contracts.

APPENDIX A-2

List of Important Acts and Legislation Concerning Safety in Construction

List of important acts and legislations concerning safety in construction

1. Industrial Disputes Act, 1947
2. Factories Act, 1948
3. Workmen's Compensation Act
4. Employees State Insurance Act
5. Environment Protection Act (1986), including environment protection rules.
6. Revised EIA Notification (2006)
7. Noise Pollution (Regulation and control) Rules (2000)
8. Hazardous Waste (management and handling) Rules (2002)
9. Manufacture, Storage and Import of Hazardous Chemical Rules (2000)
10. Circular for utilization of fly-ash from Thermal Power Plants, issued by MORTH
11. Coastal Regulation Zone (1991)
12. Air (Prevention and control of pollution) Act (1981)
13. Water (Prevention and control of pollution) Act (1974) with rules
14. Forest Conservation Act (1980)
15. The Wildlife Protection Act (1972)
16. Ancient Monuments and Archaeological sites and Remains Act (1958)
17. Land Acquisition Act (1894), revised in 1989
18. National Policy on Resettlement and Rehabilitation (2004)
19. Petroleum Act with Rules (2000)

20. Groundwater Use Regulations issued by different states in India
21. Public Liability Insurance Act (1991).
22. Guidelines for Rail, Road and Highway Projects, Ministry of Environment and Forests (1988)
23. Environmental Impact Assessment Guidelines for Highway Projects (IRC-104-1989), Indian Roads Congress, New Delhi
24. Chemical Accidents Rules, 1996
25. Gas Cylinder Rules, 2004
26. Explosives Act, 1984
27. The Electricity Act, 2003
28. India Electricity Rules, 1956

APPENDIX A-3

Typical Case Reports of Safety Hazards

Typical case reports of safety hazards

In a big country like India, accidents, major or minor, occur almost everyday involving infrastructure facilities causing injury to human beings. Only a few of these are reported in the news dailies and draw the attention of the general public. Many minor cases are never reported though they involve loss and/or damage to life and property. In this section an attempt has been made to draw the notice of the readers to a few typical cases of safety hazards caused by natural calamities, errors and mistakes, non-compliance of statutory safety regulations and wrong judgment or ignorance on the part of the constructors and users. The case reports have been chosen at random from several news-dailies during the last few years, when this text was being prepared and no aspersion is meant to any organization, institution or individual for this. The main object of bringing fore the following case reports is to focus on the fact that many of the mishaps recorded below could be averted by application of adequate safety measures and caution and by avoiding complacency and negligence. The sources of the following case reports are acknowledged by the author with due gratitude.

Case Report No. 1 (Bore-hole tragedy)

Agra: "The lifeless body of two-year old Sonu was today pulled out by rescue workers, four days after he fell into a 150 ft deep bore-well that was carelessly left uncovered."

Source: The Statesman, Kolkata, Oct' 14, 2008.

Kanauj: In a tragic repeat of bore-well accidents, a nine-year old boy died after falling into a 32ft deep bore well He could not be rescued alive despite being provided with oxygen from outside and efforts by local administration and army personnel.

Source: The Statesman, Kolkata, 10 November, 2008.

Case Report No. 2 (Cylinder Blast)

Chennai: Three persons of a family were killed in a LPG cylinder blast at Porur, near Chennai. According to police, a possible leak could have led to the explosion after one of them switched on an electrical appliance.

Source: The Statesman, Kolkata, 21 Aug. 2007.

Case Report No. 3 (Coal mine flooded due to roof collapse)

Fourteen coal miners were trapped inside a mine after the roof of an adjacent mine caved in. The incident happened in Bhurkhunda mine with disastrous consequences for 14 families. On enquiry it revealed that a 27 metre thick layer of rock separated two coal seams, one of which was abandoned. Generally abandoned seams are kept dry by regularly pumping out water through bore holes. It was learnt that this simple precaution was not taken and the old mine was not completely dry when the roof collapsed. As a result, cracks developed in the rocks separating the seams and water rushed in taking the miners by surprise.

Source: The Telegraph, Calcutta, 16 June, 2005.

Case Report No. 4 (Peru earthquake)

A strong earthquake of magnitude 8.0 hit Peru on 16 August, 2007, killing hundreds of people with thousands injured. In the city of Ica, near the epicenter, a fourth of the buildings collapsed and several churches were damaged. Thick stone and masonry walls collapsed and the quake knocked out telephone and mobile phone network. Electricity also was cut with power lines hanging dangerously over the streets. Traffic was paralyzed on the Pan-American Highways south of Lima. At least 15 after-shocks followed the main quake, some as strong as of magnitude 6.3.

Source: The Statesman, Kolkata, 17 August, 2007.

Case Report No. 5 (major earthquakes 2003-2007)

- 2003: Southeastern Iran hit by an earthquake of magnitude 6.6 killing 31000 people
- 2004: Sumatra hit by an earthquake of magnitude 9.1 claiming 2,83,000 lives.
- 2005: Pakistan hit by an earthquake of magnitude 7.6 in which 80,360 people died
- 2006: Java, Indonesia hit by an earthquake of magnitude 6.3 when a total of 5,749 lives were lost.

- 2007: Solomon Islands hit by an earthquake of magnitude of 8.1 claiming 54 lives.

Source: The Statesman, Kolkata, 17 August, 2007.

Case Report No: 6 (Landslide disaster)

At least 37 persons were killed and scores injured in landslides triggered by heavy rains near Islamabad, Pakistan on 21 March, 2007. A huge landslide hit a village in the Jhelum valley and a house in Bagh district was swept away. Incidentally, all those killed were survivors of the devastating earthquake in Pakistan (mentioned in case report no. 5) living in temporary shelters. According to the government relief department, some 79 people had died in house collapses since February to March in 2007.

Source: The Statesman, Kolkata, 22 March, 2007.

Case Report No. 7 (Coal mine flooded due to breach in river embankment)

Xintai, China: August, 20: Torrential rains had swept the area around Xintai continuously for two days dropping 232 mm of rains which triggered a flash flood and a 50 metre breach in an embankment of the Wenhe river. The flooding took place at Huayuan mine in Xintai city and later at Minggong Coal Mine. A total of 181 miners were trapped in these two mines. The Huayuan mine was estimated to be filled with 12 million cubic metre of water. The breach in the embankment was initially blocked by more than 2000 troops, armed police and others. Four pumps were initially engaged to expel 660 cubic metre of water from the Huayuan mine and the water level had fallen by 8.9 metres in 12 hours. Two more pumps, each drawing 1000 cubic metre per hour, were subsequently engaged. Meanwhile, four well drilling sets were also called from a mine in the east of the province and were engaged to drill wells from the ground to the flooded shaft to speed up the pumping process. It is also reported that the rescuers promptly mobilized all equipment and personnel resources and had taken all necessary measures to rescue the trapped miners.

Source: The Statesman, Kolkata, 21 August, 2007.

Case Report No. 8 (Cylinder blast inside hospital premises)

Kolkata, July 13, 2007: Two persons were killed and two injured after a fire broke out in a canteen inside the premises of a premier hospital in Kolkata. Preliminary investigations revealed that careless handling of gas cylinders led to an explosion when the LPG came in contact with an electric oven that was on. The incident triggered panic among patients and their relatives in different wards close to the canteen, though health services remained functional. Three fire tenders took 40 minutes to douse the flames. Subsequently eight cylinders were seized by the police from the place. On enquiry it revealed that there was no fire fighting equipment in the canteen and the canteen itself was too narrow. The canteen employed 32 people and at least 40 people were taking lunch when the fire broke out. The canteen was subsequently closed for an indefinite period. Later, the following fire safety guidelines were prepared by the fire and emergency department and sent to the hospital.

- A hydrant network in the hospital compound with riser in every floor of all the buildings for easy access to water source in case of emergency.
- An independent pump house inside the hospital that would be used only by the fire brigade. The pump should be automatically switched into action in case a fire breaks out.
- A centralized fire detection system that would locate the exact seat of fire inside the hospital premises.
- Installation of improvised ramps to facilitate evacuation of patients from one ward to another without using the stairs.
- Adequate fire extinguishers be placed in every floor of all the buildings of the hospital and the hospital staff should be given training to handle these equipments.
- Separate and adequately demarcated entry and exit points in all wards and floors of the hospital

Source: The Statesman, July 14, 2007.

Case Report No. 9 (Safety hazard in an industrial establishment)

Liquid steel at 1300 degrees Celsius from the blast furnace of a steel plant spilled out of the laddle from a height of 40 feet, causing very serious burn injury to the workers present there. The accident took place as the laddle carrying more than 90 metric tons of liquid steel tilted after the steel rope gave in. The effect was so severe that several vehicles parked nearby were also charred.

Source: The Telegraph, Calcutta, 16 February, 2005.

Case Report No. 10 (Highway subsidence)

Asansol: An area of one square km area including a stretch of 600 metre of National Highway No: 6 subsided on 16 January, 2007 following explosion of methane gas inside an abandoned mine on the outskirts of Asansol town, creating panic among the residents and disruption of traffic on the highway. On enquiry it revealed that an abandoned mine was not filled up properly creating a vaccum and methane gas accumulated there. The concrete seal of an air tunnel, which was sealed by the municipal authority two years back following the death of a two year old boy who fell into it, was blown off. Huge multiple cracks appeared on the highway and industrial cargo movement was stalled. Subsequently, 171 spots have been located in the coal belt, which are vulnerable to such disasters and need immediate attention.

Source: The Statesman, 17 January, 2007.

Ranigunj, 29 March, 2007: About 1500 square metre of metalled road caved in due to ground subsidence causing complete halt of traffic on the highway and disruption in water supply lines to ten villages. Rampant illegal extraction of coal was blamed for the disaster. Subsequent investigations revealed about 150 locations where holes were left after coal was taken out. The damaged road was repaired by filling up the subsided portion and the water supply lines were restored afterwards.

Source: The Statesman, 30 March, 2007.

Case Report No. 11 (Likely cause of Titanic sinking)

In a recently-published research work, Timothy Foecke and co-author Hooper McCarty, both metallurgists, claimed that low-strength rivets were probably used in the fabrication of the hull section of the iconic passenger liner Titanic, which sank with a loss of 1500 lives after its collision with a huge iceberg about 100 years ago. Although most shipyards switched to all-steel rivets at that time, the shipyard responsible for the fabrication of this liner might have settled for low strength iron rivets (made of No. 3 Bar) for the central section of the hull, as they could not procure the right quality material (made of No-4 bar) and they were also in a hurry to complete the job, so that they could take up the fabrication of two other passenger liners, the Olympic and the Britannic.

In their book, the authors claim that 48 rivets collected from the seabed show they contained slag. Most of the cracks that appeared after the collision with the iceberg were in the forward portion of the hull where these low strength rivets were used. The researchers engaged a blacksmith to make rivets as per 1912 specifications and found that rivets of 4-bar quality withstood 9000Kg, whereas the rivets of 3-bar quality popped at 4000 Kg only.

Source: The Independent, as reported in The Statesman, Calcutta, 17 April, 2008.

Case Report No. 12 (ship collision causing dislodgement of a bridge)

A bridge over river Tapti was completely destroyed, when four shipping vessels struck against the bridge one after the other after their anchors snapped in the port nearby during high wind. No person was injured, but two spans of the bridge were dislodged and fell into the river.

Source: TV coverage, 10 January, 2009.

Case report No: 13 (Safety hazard due to sudden release of water from a dam)

Bhopal, April 12: As many as 150 pilgrims died and many were missing while they were caught unawares after water was released from one of the multiple dams of the Narmada Valley Project for power generation without realizing that thousands of pilgrims had gathered downstream. The sudden release of water swept away even those who were sleeping on the banks. Almost all the bodies recovered showed multiple fractures due to dashing against the boulders and the rocky beds.

Source: The Telegraph, 13 April, 2005.

Case report No: 14 (landslide)

Itanagar, 14 June: Landslides triggered by incessant rains killed 14 persons around the capital, including four members of a family killed when a large chunk of earth fell on their hut.

Source: The Statesman, 15 June, 2008.

Case report No: 15 (Ship collision with Howrah Bridge, renamed 'Rabindra Setu')

Kolkata, 24 June, 2005: The mast of a 600 ton almost-empty barge got stuck to the underside trolley track of the landmark bridge and was jammed between two girders, while negotiating during high tide along a wrong channel at the Howrah end where the headroom was low. An official of the Inland Water Authority said that it was clearly the fault of the crew who could not assess the gravity of the situation. They should have pumped water into the barge to make it heavy to dip it further into the water and clear the mast. Instead, in panic the crew tried to extricate the vessel by tugging it out of the mess with the help of another vessel, thereby inflicting further damage to the underside structural system of the bridge. Finally they had no other alternative but to cut off the mast and a part of the deck to clear the vessel after a long three and a half hours ordeal. Two of the six longitudinal girders, a few of the cross girders and the trolley guides, used for movement of the maintenance trolleys were damaged and were subsequently repaired.

Source: The Telegraph, 25 June, 2005.

Case Report No. 16 (Safety hazards due to water-logging)

Mumbai 27 July, 2005: Satra-Cruz recorded a 944mm rainfall in 21 hours, equivalent to three feet of water in that locality at any point of time. This is comparable only to the heaviest single-day shower of 370mm in Kolkata in 1978, when most of the districts in West Bengal were flooded. Life was completely paralyzed in the financial capital due to torrential rain followed by water-logging.

The financial capital turned into a veritable black hole, which seemed to engulf all activities of normal life. All ATM counters were closed, the banks and RBI stopped transactions, the currency and trading markets in the Bombay Stock Exchange were abandoned and many companies postponed their board meetings. Communication links were snapped and there was no power supply. Without power the cell-phones could not be recharged. Thousands were forced to sleep over in offices and school children were stranded in their school premises. Some brave people reached home in 14 hours wading through chest-deep water and walking on rail tracks. The incessant rain triggered landslides in Jui, a village 150 Km south of Mumbai. Thirty housed collapsed and more than 150 people lost their home in mud-slides. It looked like a river outside railway stations. In Mumbai alone, the death toll reached 80, with over 200 casualties all over Maharastra. Immense damages were caused to roads, railway tracks, communication networks, buildings and other infrastructure facilities during this period.

Source: The Telegraph, 28 July, 2005.

Case Report No. 17 (Mithi overflow: follow-up of Mumbai deluge)

Mumbai, 1 August, 2005: It is believed that the Mithi river overflow is the root cause of the great Mumbai flood. The Mithi river is formed from the overflow of water from the Vihar and Powai lakes. After flowing by about 18 Km through the suburbs of Mumbai it meets the Arabian Sea at Maheem Creek. As it stands now, untreated sewage is dumped at 43 places along its length. Besides that, the flow is choked with plastics, domestic wastes and industrial wastes. The newly-built Bandra-Worli sea link has choked the river at Maheem Creek. The land reclamation schemes also claimed 730 acres from the Mithi river estuary. Again, in Kurla, big walls built for airfield infrastructure has put obstacles to the free flow of the river, which has turned about 90 degrees at this place. Here the water had risen about 12 to 15 feet during the rains, killing 40 people. Again the extension projects of the airport and the construction of innumerable buildings for different airlines blocked the river. The water in these parts rose by about 30 feet killing many people. The river Mithi has been further channelised, when new-age corporate hubs were developed under the garb of city development. All these created a serious backflow of the sea water through the sewer mains during high tides when the river was choked by itself and Mumbai was flooded. It is no wonder therefore that it took a long time to drain out the water accumulated on the streets of Mumbai after the rains and the loss of life and property was very high.

Source: The Telegraph, 1 August, 2005.

Case Report No. 18 (Collapse of an under-construction structure)

Hyderabad: Nine construction workers were killed when the roof of an under-construction building collapsed on them. These workers were resting under the roof when the accident occurred.

Source: The Telegraph, 5 November, 2006.

Case Report No. 19 (Tsunami disaster)

On Sunday, 26 December, 2004, a deadly Earthquake hit the Asian continents with its epicenter near the Sumatra islands, releasing huge tidal waves that spread to seven countries in South Asia inflicting a staggering death toll of more than 125000 people. The earthquake was caused due to slip of the India plate beneath the Burma plate causing a huge displacement of the ocean floor, forcing the sea water upwards. The swelling water sent very strong tidal waves to the shore lines of several countries in the region, creating what is now known as the "Tsunami". This was a merciless unpredictable natural calamity which brought untold disaster to the people of several continents with destruction of roads, buildings, industrial establishments and various other infrastructure facilities. Even many of the navy infrastructure facilities in the Andaman Islands were destroyed by the Tsunami waves.

The Andaman and Nicober Islands were battered with reports of more than 3000 deaths with destruction of property. The effect of Tsunami was also destructive in Indonesia and Thailand., Sri Lanka and the Maldives. About 60% of Car Nicober islands were lost with all huts and men washed away. The entire island of Sumatra close to the epicenter was bodily shifted by about 100 feet, so great was the impact of the earthquake. The tsunami waves took 45 to 60 minutes to reach the Andaman Islands from the fault line of the Burma plate and three hours to Tamil Nadu, where more than 3000 people died. Coast lines have sunk by a metre or two in many places and at the Indira Point, the lighthouse over the southern-most tip of India was lost under the sea waves. On the mainland, the inner harbour off Chennai was down by a metre and its entry point had sunk by two metres.

As a Tsunami hits a particular place, every minute counts for the safety of the people. Life-saving Tsunami early warning systems have since been installed for the benefit of the people along the coastal line of India. It has been suggested that three basic safety measures should be followed by the people immediately after getting a Tsunami warning:

- The people should move away from the beaches for higher ground
- They should stay away from rivers near their confluence with the sea.
- Even if there is no sight of an immediate Tsunami wave, people should wait for the all-clear signal, as there may be several giant tidal waves hitting the coastline in rapid succession.

Source: The Telegraph, 28-31 December, 2004, 3 January, 2005.

Case report No. 20 (Tornado disaster)

On 14 April, 2010 at 11.32 AM, A thunderstorm with a wind speed more than 120mph swept over seven districts of Bihar, West Bengal, thereafter crossing over to Bangladesh and finally striking Assam, leaving a trail of disaster with:

- 120 people dead
- 20000 buildings razed to ground
- 25000 buildings damaged
- trees and electric poles uprooted
- Communication and power supply cut off

- Vehicular movement on NH 34 suspended throughout the day
- Extensive damage to crop

According to Indian Meteorological Department, the storm was the result of a Nor'wester which developed rapidly to a tornado with a vertical extent of 18 Km and wind moving at a terrific speed. Many villagers and cattle were buried alive under the rubble of collapsed mud hutments and buildings and thousands were rendered homeless within a few minutes.

Source: The Statesman, 15 April, 2010.

Case Report No. 21 (Earthquake at China)

A series of strong earthquakes of magnitude 7.1, struck a remote north-western province of China on 14 April, 2010, killing 589 people and leaving 10000 injured. Hundreds of houses were completely destroyed. The quake had its epicenter at Rima village, about 800 Km from Xining, a provincial capital. Some people could save their lives by fleeing from their homes, as their houses of mud and wood crumbled under the shock. Racing against time, the rescue workers could save 900 people from the debris of collapsed buildings. But communications, power lines and access roads were all cut off including the airport nearby. The main quake was followed by a series of aftershocks which was felt even in the Tibetan plateau.

Source: The Statesman, 15 April, 2010.

Case Report No. 22 (Land subsidence due to indiscriminate extraction of ground water)

Land subsidence with cracks and fissures in land surface has been noticed recently in a few villages of Khejuri and Nandigram blocks in the district of Midnapur East, West Bengal. This is posing a threat to the residents of the area which falls under the coastal Zone. A team of hydrologists visiting the area have confirmed that the area does not fall under any zone of strong earthquakes and there is no mining activity in the area. They are of the opinion that excessive extraction of ground water for irrigation purposes from shallow aquifers through cavity wells from a more or less uniform depth of 30 to 40 metres has led to ground subsidence and cracking. It is also reported that thousands of farmers rely on ground water in this region for irrigation of their fields.

Source: The Statesman, 25th May, 2010.

Case Report No. 23 (Typical bridge failure due to natural calamity)

The bridge over river Jhajjar on NH-22 at Km 53 on Ambala-Kalka section (built in 1956 with 11 spans of 14 m with RCC decks resting on masonry piers with its two spans washed away and the pier no 4 settled causing rotation in the vertical plane.

The same bridge suffered damages during a flash flood in 1976 causing scour to a depth of 3 metres from the river bed. Protective measures were taken by way of toe walls both on the upstream and downstream sides for the full waterway of 160 metres and aprons of crate boulders downstream. This proved to remain effective till 1982 when the bridge was again subjected to heavy flood and this time the scour depth increased to 4.5 metres. Again the earlier protective measures were strengthened and the bridge continued to remain functional till 1988, when there was a heavy flood discharge causing damages to two spans and a pier as stated above.

It revealed during site investigations that the river is of quasi-alluvial type with rigid erosion-resistant banks and erodable bed consisting of loose granular materials. As a result, the bed was increasingly scoured without any chance of flattening of the channel during successive floods to reach a regime condition and the bridge completely failed in 1988 with two spans dislodged.

After this mishap, the following protective measure were taken:

- Wire crate boulders were placed upstream for a length of 100 metres.
- Pier nos 3, 5 and 7 subjected to heavy scour were protected by wire crates.
- Stepped concrete walls and pitching provided on the downstream side.
- Pier no 4 constructed and the spans dislodged were re-laid.
- The bed was re-graded on the upstream side to distribute the flood discharge uniformly over the entire waterway.

Source: M.K. Aggarwal: Case history of failure of bridge due to natural calamity, Indian Highways, March, 2001.

Case Report No. 24 (Post-Tsunami geological observations)

The Tsunami in 2004 has brought about significant geological changes.

- The earthquakes generated through Tsunami was a "mega-thrust", which is equivalent to detonating a million atom bombs.

- The Indian plate has dived below the Burma plate, as a result of which the Sumatra Island may have shifted laterally by 100 feet southwest. There has been vertical motion (uplift) to the islands also due to the earthquake following the Tsunami.
- It is apprehended by the scientists that the earthquake generated by Tsunami may have changed the rate of earth's rotation by less than three microseconds *i.e.* the earth is possibly rotating a bit faster, meaning a shorter day. The scientists also believe that a 9+ earthquake in Chile in 1960 also changed the earth's rotation.

Source: The Telegraph, 29th December, 2004.

Case Report No. 25 (Major fire hazards in a single metropolitan city during the last decade)

Reported cases of major fire hazards in Kolkata during the last decade:

- Fire at Dasgupta & Co, booksellers and publishers: The building was severely gutted by fire and valuable stocks of books were lost.
- There was a fire in the Kolkata Book Fair, gutting the majority of the book stalls to ashes. With extraordinary efforts from the authorities, the fair was however started again within a couple of days.
- There had been fire damages to Everest House, Mehta's building, Firpo's, a garment factory at Topsia, Nandaram Market at Burrabazar, Stephen Court on Park street and even once inside the metro tunnel and many other places.

The Kolkata High Court has since asked the department of fire and emergency to set fresh safety norms for new buildings and apartments in the city. Delivering the directive Hon'ble justice Sri Amitava Lala said: "The city is rapidly turning into a concrete jungle. The existing norms of building construction need to be revised to ensure safety and security of the people...... Moreover, special measures have to be taken for safety of the children in educational institutions.

Source: The Telegraph: 4th August, 2004.

References

Chapter 1

1. E.O. Pfrang: Building Structural Failures, Their Causes and Prevention: IABSE Surveys S-35/86.
2. Special Issue on Construction Management: Journal of the Institution of Engineers (India), September, 1988.
3. V.J. Davies, C. Eng. FICE & K.Tomasin, DIC (London): Construction Safety Handbook, 2nd ed, 1996, Thomas Telford, London.
4. S.K. Bhattacharjee: Fundamentals of PERT/CPM and Project Management, 3rd ed, 2008, Khanna Publishers, Delhi.

Chapter 2

1. P. Hughes: Limit State Theory for Reinforced Concrete Design: Pitman Publishing Limited, London.
2. J. Schneider: Hazard Scenario and Structural Design: IABSE Surveys, S-33-85.
3. P. Dayaratnam: Analysis of Statically Determinate Structures: Affiliated East-West Press Private Limited.
4. Swami Saran: Analysis and Design of Substructures: Oxford & IBH Publishing Co. Pvt Ltd, New Delhi, 1996.
5. IS: 456-2000: Code of Practice for Plain and Reinforced Concrete.
6. IS: 800-1984: Code of Practice for General Construction in Steel.
7. IS: 1080-1980: Code of Practice for Design and Construction of Simple Spread foundations.
8. IS: 1904-1978: Code of Practice for Structural Safety of Buildings: Shallow Foundations.

9. IS: 6403-1981: Code of Practice for Determination of Bearing Capacity of Shallow Foundations.
10. IRC: 78-1983: Standard Specifications and Code of Practice for Road Bridges: Section VII-Foundations and Substructure.

Chapter 3

1. Howard D. Curtis: Fundamentals of Aircraft Structural Analysis: Irwin, 1997.
2. S. Timoshenko & D.H. Young: Elements of Strength of Materials: Fifth edition:
3. Utpal K. Ghosh, 2006: Design and Construction of Steel Bridges: Taylor & Francis, London/New York.
4. IABSE Surveys, S-42/89: Structural Properties of Semi-rigid Joints in Steel Frames, May 1989.
5. IABSE Surveys, S-29/84: Fatigue Design Concepts: November 1984

Chapter 4

1. H.P. Huges: Limit State Theory for Reinforced Concrete Design: Pitman, 1976.
2. G. Winter & A.H. Nilson: Design of Concrete Structures: McGraw Hill International Book Company, 1983.
3. V. Baikov & E. Sigalov: Reinforced Concrete Structures: Mir Publishers, Moscow, 1983.
4. M.L. Gambhir: Concrete Technology: Tata McGraw Hill Publishing Company Limited, New Delhi, 1986.
5. S.N. Manohar: Tall Chimneys, Design and Construction: Tata McGraw Hill Publishing Company Limited, New Delhi, 1985.
6. IS; 456-2000: Code of Practice for Reinforced Concrete, 4th Revision, Bureau of Indian Standards, New Delhi.

Chapter 5

1. M. V. Joshi: Process Equipment Design, 2nd ed: Macmillan India Limited, Delhi.
2. M.L. Gambhir: Concrete Technology: Tata McGraw-Hill Publishing Co Limited, New Delhi.
3. R.B. Leighou: Chemistry of Engineering Materials, 4th ed: McGraw-Hill Book Co. Inc., New York, 1942.

4. Howard D. Curtis: Fundamentals of Aircraft Structural Analysis: Irwin, Chicago.

Chapter 6

1. J.P. Baker, M.P. Horne and J. Heyman: The Steel Skeleton, Vol 2: Cambridge University Press.
2. B.P. Hughes: Limit State Theory of Reinforced Concrete Design: Pitman
3. G. Winter & A.H. Nilson: Design of Concrete Structures, 9th edition : McGraw Hills International Book Co. Ltd.
4. Indian Railways Steel Bridge Code.
5. N. Krishna Raju: Pre-stressed Concrete : Tata McGraw Hill Publishing Co. Ltd, New Delhi.
6. IS: 456-2000: Code of Practice for Plain and Reinforced Concrete.
7. IS: 1343-1960: Code of Practice for Pre-stressed Concrete.
8. IS: 800-1984: Code of Practice for General Construction in Steel.
10. Sulata Kayal: Nonlinear Behaviour of RCC T-Beam Bridges and Cross Diaphragms: Highway Research Board, IRC, November 2004.

Chapter 7

1. J. Brozzetti, M. Law, O. Pettersson, J. Witteveen: Fire Protection of Steel Structures, Examples and Applications: IABSE Proceedings P-61/83, May 1983.
2. IS: 3594-1967: Code of Practice for Fire Safety of Industrial Buildings: Indian Standards Institution, New Delhi, 1967.
3. IS: 3614 (Part 1): 1966: Specification for Fire Check Doors, Indian Standards Institution.
4. R.B. Leighou: Chemistry of Engineering Materials, 4th ed: McGraw Hill Book Co, N.Y.
5. Steel Designers' Manual, 3rd Ed: ELBS & Crosby Lockwood & Sons Ltd.
6. E.W. Steel: Water Supply and Sewerage, 5th ed: McGraw Hill International Book Co. London.

Chapter 8

1. The Penguin Dictionary of Physics: Edited by Valeric H. Pit.
2. D.P. Ray Chaudhuri & J. K. Mukherjee: Sound: Chayan, Kolkata.

3. Robert Resnick & David Halliday: Physics, Part 1: Wiley Eastern Limited, New Delhi.
4. G.N. Pandey: Environmental Management: Vikas Publishing House Pvt Ltd, New Delhi.
5. Surindar Mohan, Nabonita Dutta & Dr. S.M. Sarin: Need for Construction of Noise Barriers in India: Indian Highways, December 2002.
6. Noise and Vibration in Railway Operation: Inst of Civil Engrs. Proc. 1976.
7. Surinder Mohan & Nabonita Dutta: Noise Pollution in Work Environment and Its Health Impact in Indian Conditions: IRC Journal.

Chapter 9

1. Advances in Structural Dynamics and Design: Proceedings of the National Symposium: Structural Engineering Research Center, Madras in 2001.
2. Design of Marine Facilities: John W. Gaithwaite, P.E.: Van Rostrand Reinhold.
3. On the Theory of Ship Collision against Bridge Piers: R. Saul & H. Stevensson: IABSE Proceedings, P-51/82.
4. Shock and Vibration Handbook, 4th edition: Edited by Cyrill M. Harris: McGraw Hill, New York.
5. Response of Ground During Pile Driving: C.K. Madheswaran & Others: IE(I) Journal, May, 2005.
6. Ground and Structural Vibrations During Driving of Concrete and Steel Piles: C.K. Madheswaran & Others: IE(I) Journal, May, 2005.

Chapter 10

1. Dr. K.S. Rao: The Bhuj Earthquake, IGS News, January-March, 2001.
2. Dr. K. S. Rao: The Bhuj Earthquake and Lessons from Damages, IGS News, April-June, 2001.
3. Dr. K.S. Rao: Magnitude Scales and Related Issues of Eearthquakes, IGS News, July-December, 2001.
4. Dr. K.S. Rao: History of October, 2005 earthquake, IGS News, January- March, 2006.
5. E. Kuribayashi: Earthquake Engineering for Practicing Engineers, IABSE Surveys, S-38/87, April, 1987.

6. M.J.N. Priestley, F. Seible, G.M. Kalvi: Seismic Design and Retrofitting of Bridges, John Wiley and Sons, Inc, New York.
7. The Concrete Association of India: Earthquake Resistant Design of Buildings.
8. Prof. Mahesh Tandon: Earthquake resistant design of bridges, Indian Roads Congress Journal, Vol. 62-3, December, 2001.
9. Journal of the Institution of Engineers (India): Special Issue on Earthquake Resistant Buildings, Vol. 83, August, 2003.
10. IS: 1893 (Part I)-2002: Criteria for Earthquake Resistant Design of Structures, General Provisions for Buildings.
11. SP: 22-1982: Explanatory Handbook on Codes for Earthquake Engineering.

Chapter 11

1. E.J. Monkhouse: Principles of Physical Geography (3rd edition), University of London Press.
2. J.H. Stembridge: The World, 2nd edition: Oxford University Press.
3. CP-3 (Chapter V): Part 2: Sept, 1972: Basic Data for the Design of Buildings: Wind Loads.
4. IS: 875(Part 3)-1987: Wind Loads
5. S.N. Monohar: Tall Chimneys: Tata Mc Graw Hill Publishing Co. New Delhi, 1985.
6. Advances in Structural Dynamics, Proceedings 2001: Structural Engineering Research Centre, Madras.

Chapter 12

1. Geology: A.J. Smith, PhD, FGS: Hamlyn, London.
2. A Text Book of Geology: P.K. Mukherjee; The world Press Private Limited, Calcutta.
3. Mountanous Highways-Problems and Control Measures: V.K. Sarda & Ashoke Kumar: Indian Highways, May 1993.
4. Landslide at KM 213.00 on National Highway 21-Analysis and Correction: Indian Highways, May 2001.
5. Landslide Hazard Zonation around Bhuntar (Kullu Town), Himachal Pradesh-Indian Highways, May 2007.
6. Kishore Kumar & Others: Design of Corrective Measures for Stability of a Critical Slope near Koldam, H.P. - A Case Study: Indin Highways, January, 2008.

Chapter 13

1. E.J. Monkhouse: Principles off Physical Geography, 3rd ed, University of London Press.
2. Ministry of Road Transport and Highways: Specification for Road and Bridge Works: IRC, New Delhi, 2001.
3. Dr. P.K. Parua: Fluvial Geo-morphology of the River Ganga around Farakka: IE(I) Journal, CV Vol 82, February 2002.
4. R.K. Dhiman: Damages to Bridges due to Floods in Hilly Areas - A Case Study: Indian Highways, October, 2004.
5. M. Zoghi, Joel Sprague & Sam Allen: Emerging Geo-materials for Ground Improvement: Emerging Materials for Civil Infrastructure (State of the Art), ASCE, 2000.
6. Dr. Ing. Reiffteck Philippe: Erosion Assessment and Control of Earthwork: Journal of the Indian Roads Congress, April-June 2006.
7. Guidelines for the Design of Small Bridges and Culverts: Indian Roads Congress, Special Publication No: SP-13.
8. S.K. Mazumdar: Determining of Waterway under a Bridge in Himalayan Region-Some Case Studies: Journal of the Indian Roads Congress, July-September, 2009.

Chapter 14

1. Theodore H. Allegri, Sr: Material Handling, Principles and Practices: CBS Publishers & Distributors, Delhi, 1987.
2. S.S. Atev: Construction Technology: Mir Publishers, Moscow.
3. R.L. Peurifoy: Construction, Planning, Equipments and Methods, 2nd ed, Mc-GrawHill Kogakusha Limited, Tokyo.
4. S.C. Sharma: Construction Equipment and its Management: Khanna Publishers: Delhi, 2009.

Chapter 15

1. S.S. Atev: Construction Technology: MIR Publishers Moscow.
2. T.R. Ranga & S.C. Sharma: Industrial Organization & Engineering Economics: 21st Ed, 1995: Khanna Publishers, Delhi.
3. A. Banerjee: Welding, Procedures and Practices: New Central Book Agency Pvt Ltd, Kolkata.
4. Utpal K.Ghosh: Design & Construction of Steel Bridges: Taylor & Francis, London, 1999.

5. IS: 9282-2002: Indian Standard Specification for Wire ropes and Strands for Suspension Bridges, 2002.
6. S.K. Bhattacharjee: Fundamentals of PERT/CPM & Project Management, 3rd Ed, 2008: Khanna Publishers, Delhi.

Chapter 16

1. V.J. Davis & K. Tomasin: Construction Safety Handbook: Thomas Telford, 1996
2. Dr. V.K. Raina: Bridge Inspection (Why and What To Look For): Journal Of IRC, Vol: 63-3, December, 2002.

Chapter 17

1. M.J.N. Priestley, F. Seible & G.M. Calvi: Seismic Design and Retrofit of Bridges: John Wiley & Sons, New York.
2. V.J. Davies & K. Tomasin: Construction Safety Handbook: Thomas Telford, 1996.
3. Utpal K. Ghosh: Repair and Rehabilitation of Steel bridges: Oxford & IBH Publishing Co. Pvt. Ltd., 2000.
4. Rajib B. Mallick & Tahar El-Korchi: Pavement Engineering: CRC Press, Taylor & Francis Group, 2009.
5. Dr. Baffour Kwaku Akoto & Eufemio E. Nilles: Repair and Restoration of Concrete Pavements: Jounal of the Indian Roads Congress, April-June, 2007.
6. S.K. Bhattacharjee: Construction Management of Industrial Projects: Khanna Publishers, New Delhi, 2004.

Chapter 18

1. V.I. Davies & K. Tomasin: Construction Safety Handbook, Second Edition, Thomas Telford, New York.

Chapter 19

1. R.R. Sheoran: Road Safety Audit: Indian Highways, January, 2004.
2. Dr. S.M. Sarina & Dr. Nishi Mittal: Need for Safety Audit on Indian Roads, IRC Journal. November, 1999.
3. V.J. Davies & K. Tomlinson: Construction Safety Handbook: 2nd edition: Thomas Telford.
4. S. Rao & Prof. H.L. Saluja: Electrical Safety, Fire Safety Engineering and Safety Management.

Chapter 20

1. Charles E. Ebeling: An Introduction to Reliability and Maintainability Engineering: The McGraw Hill Companies Inc.: International edition, 1997.
2. L.S. Srinath: Reliability Engineering, 4th edition: East West Private Limited, New Delhi, 2005.

Chapter 21

1. Theodore H. Allegri, Sr: Material Handling, Principle and Practices: CBS Publishers & Distributors, Delhi 1987.
2. V.J. Davies, C.Eng. FICE & K.Tomasin DIC (London): Construction Safety Handbook, 2nd ed, 1996, Thomas Telford.
3. S.K. Bhattcharjee: Construction Management of Industrial Projects: Khanna Publishers, Delhi.

Chapter 22

1. R.L. Peurifoy: Construction Planning, Equipment and Methods, 2nd edition, International Students Edition, McGraw Hill Kogakusha Ltd, London.
2. R.K. Jain & Sunil Rao: Industrial Safety, Health and Environment Management System, 3rd edition, Khanna Publishers, Delhi.

Index

T

U

V

W

Y

Z